To the memory of net 10 and our
connections: 10.0.0.37 and 10.2.0.37

Internetworking With TCP/IP

Vol II:

Design, Implementation, and Internals

DOUGLAS E. COMER

and

DAVID L. STEVENS

Department of Computer Sciences
Purdue University
West Lafayette, IN 47907

Prentice-Hall International, Inc.

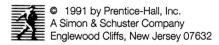 © 1991 by Prentice-Hall, Inc.
A Simon & Schuster Company
Englewood Cliffs, New Jersey 07632

The author and publisher of this book have used their best efforts in preparing this book.
These efforts include the development, research, and testing of the theories and programs to
determine their effectiveness. The author and publisher make no warranty of any kind,
expressed or implied, with regard to these programs or the documentation contained in this
book. The author and publisher shall not be liable in any event for incidental or consequential
damages in connection with, or arising out of, the furnishing, performance, or use of these
programs.

UNIX is a registered trademark of AT&T Bell
Laboratories.
proNET-10 is a trademark of Proteon Corporation.
VAX, Microvax, and DECstation are trademarks
of Digital Equipment Corporation.

Printed in the United States of America

10 9 8 7 6 5 4 3

ISBN 0-13-465378-5

Prentice-Hall International (UK) Limited, *London*
Prentice-Hall of Australia Pty. Limited, *Sydney*
Prentice-Hall Canada Inc., *Toronto*
Prentice-Hall Hispanoamericana, S.A., *Mexico*
Prentice-Hall of India Private Limited, *New Delhi*
Prentice-Hall of Japan, Inc., *Tokyo*
Simon & Schuster Asia Pte. Ltd., *Singapore*
Editora Prentice-Hall do Brasil, Ltda., *Rio de Janeiro*
Prentice-Hall, Inc., *Englewood Cliffs, New Jersey*

Contents

Foreword

This second volume of work from Douglas Comer and David Stevens represents a very important contribution to the TCP/IP protocol suite literature. While the first volume concentrated on the specifications of the protocols and their functionality, this second volume considers in detail how one implementation has been made to work. Such an examination is extremely valuable because a study only of the specifications for a set of protocols can barely scratch the surface of the detailed issues and choices which must be addressed when implementing them.

At the same time, it is equally important to distinguish between specification and implementation. Indeed, it is important that, for many specifications, there is great latitude available in implementing software which can meet the specified behavior. Thus, in reading this book, one should keep in mind that the interpretation of the specifications articulated in the book's implementation may be only one possible choice. The implementation is *not* the specification.

Another reason to study implementations of protocols is to understand something about the performance one can achieve for any particular protocol specification. Experience with the TCP/IP protocol suite over the last 15 years has taught us that there are dramatic performance gains to be had as a consequence of careful implementation choices. By the same token, the operating system environment may influence implementation choices and performance potential in significant ways.

The author's mention that the Xinu implementation offered in the text "does not have cost accounting or other administrative overhead, [so] the TCP/IP code in Xinu is free from unnecessary details..." From a purely pedagogical standpoint, one may take this view (that accounting is unnecessary), but it seems fair to observe that as the Internet system grows, many of its components will need to operate in commercial environments in which accounting is a principal pre-requisite. The reader should bear in mind that in some circumstances, accounting for use of TCP/IP services may prove necessary.

It has often been observed that every book contains the seeds of its next edition and this important new volume is no different. In particular, the Internet Engineering Task Force, which is responsible for recommending protocol extensions to the Internet Activities Board for standardization, is about to introduce new features for TCP which will enable it to function in gigabit speed networks where latency (network round-trip time) is significant (i.e. more than microseconds).

An extremely important point for readers to bear in mind about this volume is that it is intended to explore the panoply of software which one must implement to construct an Internet *gateway* or *router*. This is very important if readers are to apply what they learn from this text to the construction of *Internet hosts*. Since most implementors are likely to construct host-based systems and applications, it is imperative that they become familiar with two Request for Comment (RFC) documents: RFC 1122 and RFC 1123 which speak to the way in which the TCP/IP protocols apply in the implementation of an Internet host. For example, one would *not* implement the active RIP (routing) protocol in a host, nor would one fragment Internet packets prior to transmission. One might implement SNMP, but the Management Information Base (MIB) associated with a host would differ from that in a gateway or router.

With regard to routing, the present volume offers details for the Routing Information Protocol (RIP). As has become very apparent in the recent past, this protocol is inadequate to deal with the complexity and scale of Internet components one sees regularly today. One might reasonably expect successive editions to address other intra- and inter-domain routing protocols such as the Border Gateway Protocol, Dual IS-IS, Open Shortest Path First and the Inter-Domain Policy Routing protocol.

Readers should take away from scrutiny of the RIP section an appreciation for the fact that routers and gateways must deal with a great deal other than simply routing. Congestion detection and management is another significant area of concern. Resource allocation and policy conformance are equally important. The general construction of gateways and their configuration into autonomous systems, intra- and inter-domain routing and the potential need for accounting are all part and parcel of the universe of function surrounding the basic packet relay functions of a gateway. The text covers the more basic of these functions but interested readers are urged to obtain and read copies of the Router Requirements RFC when it becomes available to gain perspective on the full functionality needed.

In addition to obvious extensions to existing content, one hopes that the author's might have the energy to deal with higher level protocol implementations above the TCP and UDP level in, perhaps, a third volume in the series.

There is a rich and growing literature on the TCP/IP protocol suite and readers are encouraged to take advantage of it. The Internet system comprises some 5,000 networks of over 300,000 hosts in approximately 35 countries. A great deal has been learned about how these protocols operate in extremely varied environments and large scale and there is still much more to learn. Out of all this experience one hopes that fundamental concepts can be distilled which will be of value in developing new protocols within the TCP/IP protocol suite and in parallel systems such as the Open Systems Interconnection protocols which, recently, have been introduced into the Internet to support multi-protocol operation.

Serious students of protocol design will find this book very helpful for its concreteness and focus on implementation choices and issues.

Vint Cerf
Annandale, Virginia
January 1991

Preface

Since the publication of *Internetworking With TCP/IP* in 1988, many readers have asked for a second volume that provides more information on how the TCP/IP protocols operate. This text attempts to satisfy the need for additional information. It places TCP/IP under a magnifying glass, and examines the details of individual protocols. It discusses their implementation, and focuses on the internals of protocol software.

Of course, the official specifications for individual protocols, as well as discussions of their implementation and use, appear in Request For Comments documents (RFCs). Although some RFCs can be difficult for beginners to understand, they remain the authoritative source of detailed information; no author can hope to reproduce all that information in a textbook. More important, while the RFCs cover individual protocols, they leave many unanswered questions about the interactions among protocols. For example, the Routing Information Protocol (RIP) specifies how a gateway installs routes in its IP routing table, and how the gateway advertises routes in its table to other gateways. RIP also specifies that routes must be timed out and removed. But the interaction between RIP and other protocols may not be apparent from the RFC. The question arises, "how does route timeout affect routes in the table that were not installed by RIP?" One must also consider the question, "should RIP updates override routes that the manager installs manually?"

To help explain the interaction among protocols and to insure that our solutions fit together, we designed and built a working system that serves as a central example throughout the text. The system provides most of the protocols in the TCP/IP suite, including: TCP, IP, ICMP, UDP, ARP, RIP, and SNMP. In addition, it has an example client and server for the finger service. Because the text contains the code for each protocol, the reader can study the implementation and understand its internal structure. Most important, because the example system integrates the protocol software into a working whole, the reader can clearly understand the interaction among protocols.

The example code attempts to conform to the protocol standards and to include the latest ideas. For example, our TCP code includes silly window avoidance and the Jacobson-Karels slow-start and congestion avoidance optimizations, features often missing from commercial implementations. However, we are realistic enough to realize that the commercial world does not always follow the published standards, and have tried to adapt the system for use in a practical environment. For example, the code includes a configuration parameter that allows it to use either the Internet standard or BSD UNIX interpretation of TCP's urgent data pointer.

We do not claim that the code presented here is bug-free, or even that it is better than other implementations. Indeed, after many months of testing, we continue to find ways to improve the software, and hope that readers will look for them as well. To help, the publisher has agreed to make machine-readable copies of all the code available, so readers can use computer tools to examine, modify, and test it. We are interested in learning of improvements, and will start an electronic mail list or newsgroup if sufficient readers are interested.

The text can be used in an upper-division course on networking or in a graduate course. Undergraduate courses should focus on the earlier chapters, omitting the chapters on *SNMP* and *RIP*. Graduate students will find the most interesting and challenging concepts in the chapters on TCP. Adaptive retransmission and the related heuristics for high performance are especially important and deserve careful attention. Throughout the text, exercises suggest alternative implementations and generalizations; they rarely call for rote repetition of the information presented. Thus, students may need to venture beyond the text to solve many of the exercises.

As in any effort this size, many people share the credit; we thank them. David Stevens, one of the authors, implemented most of the software, including a complete version of TCP. Victor Norman built the SNMP software, and revised it several times. Shawn Ostermann integrated the TCP/IP code into Xinu version 8, and ported it from the original Sun 3 platform to a DECstation 3100. In the process, he uncovered and helped solve several problems, including byte-ordering and memory allocation bugs. Andy Muckelbauer and Steve Chapin built a UNIX compatibility library, and, along with Shawn Ostermann and Scott Mark, used the TCP code to run an X window server. Their testing exercised TCP extensively, and pointed out several performance problems. Scott M. Ballew participated in some of the software development, and provided an extensive review of all the text and code. Various other members of the Internetworking Research Group at Purdue contributed to earlier versions of the code. Charlotte Tubis proofread the text. Christine Comer reviewed the manuscript several times, made many suggestions, and helped incorporate the editing changes. Finally, we thank the Department of Computer Sciences and the Computing Center at Purdue University for their support.

Douglas E. Comer
David L. Stevens

January, 1991

1

Introduction And Overview

1.1 TCP/IP Protocols

The TCP/IP Internet Protocol Suite has become, de facto, the standard for open system interconnection in the computer industry. Computer systems worldwide use TCP/IP Internet protocols to communicate because TCP/IP provides the highest degree of interoperability, encompasses the widest set of vendors' systems, and runs over more network technologies than any other protocol suite. Research and education institutions use TCP/IP as their primary platform for data communication. In addition, industries that use TCP/IP include aerospace, automotive, electronics, hotel, petroleum, printing, pharmaceutical, and many others.

Besides conventional use on private industrial networks, many academic, government, and military sites use TCP/IP protocols to communicate over the connected Internet. Schools with Internet access via TCP/IP exchange information and research results more quickly than those that are not connected, giving researchers at such institutions a competitive advantage.

1.2 The Need To Understand Details

Despite its popularity and widespread use, the details of TCP/IP protocols and the structure of software that implements them remain a mystery to most computer professionals. While it may seem that understanding the internal details is not important, programmers who use TCP/IP learn that they can produce more robust code if they understand how the protocols operate. For example, programmers who understand TCP *urgent data* processing can add functionality to their applications that is impossible otherwise.

1

Understanding even simple ideas such as how TCP buffers data can help programmers design, implement, and debug applications. For example, some programs that use TCP fail because programmers misunderstand the relationships between output buffering, segment transmission, input buffering, and the *push* operation. Studying the details of TCP input and output allows programmers to form a conceptual model that explains how the pieces interact, and helps them understand how to use the underlying mechanisms.

1.3 Complexity Of Interactions Among Protocols

The main reason the TCP/IP technology remains so elusive is that documentation often discusses each protocol independently, without considering how multiple protocols operate together. A protocol standard document, for example, usually describes how a single protocol should operate; it discusses the action of the protocol and its response to messages in isolation from the rest of the system. The most difficult aspect of protocols to understand, however, lies in their interaction. When one considers the operation of all protocols together, the interactions produce complicated, and sometimes unexpected, effects. Minor details that may seem unimportant suddenly become essential. Heuristics to handle problems and nuances in protocol design can make important differences in overall operation or performance.

As many programmers have found, the interactions among protocols often dictate how they must be implemented. Data structures must be chosen with all protocols in mind. For example, IP uses a routing table to make decisions about how to forward datagrams. However, the routing table data structures cannot be chosen without considering protocols such as the Routing Information Protocol, the Internet Control Message Protocol, and the Exterior Gateway Protocol, because all may need to update routes in the table. More important, the routing table update policies must be chosen carefully to accommodate all protocols or the interaction among them can lead to unexpected results. We can summarize:

> *The TCP/IP technology comprises many protocols that all interact. To fully understand the details and implementation of a protocol, one must consider its interaction with other protocols in the suite.*

1.4 The Approach In This Text

This book explores TCP/IP protocols in great detail. It reviews concepts and explains nuances in each protocol. It discusses abstractions that underlie TCP/IP software, and describes the data structures and procedures that implement the protocols. Finally, it reviews design choices, and discusses the consequence of design alternatives.

To provide a concrete example of protocol implementation, and to help the reader understand the relationships among protocols, the text takes an integrated view – it focuses on a complete working system. It shows data structures and source code, and explains the principles underlying each.

Code from the example system helps answer many questions and explain many subtleties that could not be understood otherwise. It fills in details and provides the reader with an understanding of the relative difficulty of implementing each part. It shows how the judicious choice of data representation can make some protocols easier to implement (and conversely how a poor choice of representation can make the implementation tedious and difficult). The example code allows the reader to understand ideas like urgent data processing and network management that spread across many parts of the code. More to the point, the example system clearly shows the reader how protocols interact and how the implementation of individual protocols can be integrated. To summarize:

> To explain the details, internal organization, and implementation of TCP/IP protocols, this text focuses on an example working system. Source code for the example system allows the reader to understand how the protocols interact and how the software can be integrated into a simple and efficient system.

1.5 The Importance Of Studying Code

The example TCP/IP system is the centerpiece of the text. To understand the data structures, the interaction among procedures, and the subtleties of the protocol internals, it is necessary to read and study the source code.† Thus,

> The example programs should be considered part of the text, and not merely a supplement to it.

1.6 The Xinu Operating System

On most machines, TCP/IP protocol software resides in the operating system kernel. A single copy of the TCP/IP software is shared by all application programs. The software presented in this text is part of the Xinu operating system.‡ We have chosen to use Xinu for several reasons. First, Xinu has been documented in two textbooks, so source code for the entire system is completely available for study. Second, because Xinu does not have cost accounting or other administrative overhead, the TCP/IP code in Xinu is free from unnecessary details and, therefore, much easier to understand. Third, because the text concentrates on explaining abstractions underlying the code, most of the ideas presented apply directly to other implementations. Fourth, using Xinu and TCP/IP software designed by the authors completely avoids the problem of com-

---

†To make it easy to use computer tools to explore parts of the system, the publisher has made machine readable copies of the code from the text available.

‡Xinu is a small, elegant operating system that has many features similar to UNIX. Several vendors have used versions of Xinu as an embedded system in commercial products.

mercial licensing, and allows us to sell the text freely. While the Xinu system and the TCP/IP code presented have resulted from a research project, readers will find that they are surprisingly complete and, in many cases, provide more functionality than their commercial counterparts. Finally, because we have attempted to follow the RFC specifications rigorously, readers may be surprised to learn that the Xinu implementation of TCP/IP obeys the protocols standards more strictly than many popular implementations.

1.7 Organization Of The Remainder Of The Book

This text is organized around the TCP/IP protocol stack in approximately the same order as Volume I. It begins with a review of the operating system functions that TCP uses, followed by a brief description of the device interface layer. Remaining chapters describe the TCP/IP protocols, and show example code to illustrate the implementation of each.

Some chapters describe entire protocols, while others concentrate on specific aspects of the design. For example, Chapter 15 discusses heuristics for round trip estimation, retransmission, and exponential backoff. The code appears in the chapter that is most pertinent; references appear in other chapters.

Appendix *1* contains a cross reference of the procedures that comprise the TCP/IP protocol software discussed throughout the text. For each procedure, function, or in-line macro, the cross reference tells the file in which it is defined, the page on which that file appears in the text, the list of procedures called in that file, and the list of procedures that call it. The cross reference is especially helpful in finding the context in which a given procedure is called, something that is not immediately obvious from the code.

Appendix *2* provides a list of those functions and procedures used in the code that are not contained in the text. Most of the procedures listed come from the C run-time support libraries or the underlying operating system, including the Xinu system calls that appear in the TCP/IP code. For each procedure or function, Appendix *2* lists the name and arguments, and gives a brief description of the operation it performs.

1.8 Summary

This text explores the subtleties of TCP/IP protocols, details of their implementation, and the internal structure of software that implements them. It focuses on an example implementation from the Xinu operating system, including the source code that forms a working system. Although the Xinu implementation was not designed as a commercial product, it obeys the protocol standards. To fully understand the protocols, the reader must study the example programs. The appendices help the reader understand the code. They provide a cross reference of the TCP/IP routines and a list of the operating system routines used.

FOR FURTHER STUDY

Volume I [Comer 1988] presents the concepts underlying the TCP/IP Internet Protocol Suite, a synopsis of each protocol, and a summary of Internet architecture. We assume the reader is already familiar with most of this material. Comer [1984] and Comer [1987] describe the structure of the Xinu operating system, including an early version of ARP, UDP, and IP code. Leffler, McKusick, Karels, and Quarterman [1989] describes the Berkeley UNIX system. Stevens [1990] provides examples of using the TCP/IP interface in various operating systems.

2

The Structure Of TCP/IP Software In An Operating System

2.1 Introduction

Most TCP/IP software runs on computers that use an *operating system* to manage resources, like peripheral devices. Operating systems provide support for concurrent processing. Even on machines with a single processor, they give the illusion that multiple programs can execute simultaneously by switching the CPU among them rapidly. In addition, operating systems manage main memory that contains executing programs, as well as secondary (nonvolatile) storage, where file systems reside.

TCP/IP software usually resides in the operating system, where it can be shared by all application programs running on the machine. That is, the operating system contains a single copy of the code for a protocol like TCP, even though multiple programs can invoke that code. As we will see, code that can be used by multiple, concurrently executing programs is significantly more complex than code that is part of a single program.

This chapter provides a brief overview of operating system concepts that we will use throughout the text. It shows the general structure of protocol software and explains in general terms how the software fits into the operating system. Later chapters review individual pieces of protocol software and present extensive detail.

The examples in this chapter come from Xinu, the operating system used throughout the text. Although the examples refer to system calls and arguments that are only available in Xinu, the concepts apply across a wide variety of operating systems, including the popular UNIX timesharing system.

2.2 The Process Concept

Operating systems provide several abstractions that are needed for understanding the implementation of TCP/IP protocols. Perhaps the most important is that of a *process* (sometimes called a *task* or *thread of control*). Conceptually, a process is a computation that proceeds independent of other computations. An operating system provides mechanisms to create new processes and to terminate existing processes. In the example system we will use, a program calls function *create* to form a new process. *Create* returns an integer *process identifier* used to reference the process when performing operations on it.

```
procid = create(arguments);    /* create a new process */
```

Once created, a process proceeds independent of its creator. To terminate an existing process, a program calls *kill*, passing as an argument the process identifier that *create* returned.

```
kill(procid);                  /* terminate a process */
```

Unlike conventional (sequential) programs in which a single thread of control steps through the code belonging to a *program*, processes are not bound to any particular code or data. The operating system can allow two or more processes to execute a single piece of code. For example, two processes can execute operating system code concurrently, even though only one copy of the operating system exists. In fact, it is possible for two or more processes to execute code in a single procedure concurrently.

Because processes execute independently, they can proceed at different rates. In particular, processes sometimes perform operations that cause them to be *blocked* or *suspended*. For example, if a process attempts to read a character from a keyboard, it may need to wait for the user to press a key. To avoid having the process use the CPU while waiting, the operating system blocks the process but allows others to continue executing. Later, when the operating system receives a keystroke event, it will allow the process waiting for that keystroke to *resume* execution.

The implementation of TCP/IP software we will examine uses multiple, concurrently executing processes. Instead of trying to write a single program that handles all possible sequences of events, the code uses processes to help partition the software into smaller, more manageable pieces. As we will see, using processes simplifies the design and keeps the code easy to understand and modify.

Processes are especially useful in handling the timeout and retransmission algorithms found in many protocols. Using a single program to implement timeout for multiple protocols makes the program complex because the timeouts can overlap. For example, consider trying to write a single program to manage timers for all TCP/IP protocols. A high-level protocol like TCP may create a segment, encapsulate it in a datagram, send the datagram, and start a timer. Meanwhile, IP must route the datagram and pass it to the network interface. Eventually a low-level protocol like ARP may be invoked and it may go through several cycles of transmitting a request, setting a timer, having the timer expire, and retransmitting the request independent of the TCP timer. In a single program, it can be difficult to handle events when a timer for one protocol expires while the program is executing code for another protocol. If the system uses a separate process to implement each protocol that requires a timeout, the process only needs to handle timeout events related to its protocol. Thus, the code in each process is easier to understand and less prone to errors.

2.3 Process Priority

We said that all processes execute concurrently, but that is an oversimplification. In fact, each process is assigned a *priority* by the programmer who designs the software. The operating system honors priorities when granting processes the use of the CPU. The priority scheme we will use is simple and easy to understand: the CPU is granted to the highest priority process that is not blocked; if multiple processes share the same high priority, the system will switch the CPU among them rapidly.

The priority scheme is valuable in protocol software because it allows a programmer to give one process precedence over another. For example, compare an ordinary application program to the protocol software that must accept packets from the hardware as they arrive. The designer can assign higher priority to the process that implements protocol software, forcing it to take precedence over application processes. Because the operating system handles all the details of process scheduling, the processes themselves need not contain any code to handle scheduling.

2.4 Communicating Processes

If each process is an independent computation, how can data flow from one to another? The answer is that the operating system must provide mechanisms that permit processes to communicate. We will use three such mechanisms: *counting semaphores*, *ports*, and *message passing*.

A counting semaphore is a general purpose process synchronization mechanism. The operating system provides a function, *screate*, that can be called to create semaphores as needed. *Screate* returns a semaphore identifier that must be used in subsequent operations on the semaphore.

```
semid = screate(initcount);   /* create semaphore, specifying count */
```

Each semaphore contains an integer used for counting; the caller gives an initial value for the integer when creating a semaphore. Once a semaphore has been created, processes can use the operating system functions *wait* and *signal* to manipulate the count. When a process calls *wait*, the operating system decrements the semaphore's count by *1*, and blocks the process if the count becomes negative. When a process calls *signal*, the operating system increments the semaphore count, and unblocks one process if any process happens to be blocked on that semaphore.

Although the semantics of *wait* and *signal* may seem confusing, they can be used to solve several important process synchronization problems. Of most importance, they can be used to provide *mutual exclusion*. Mutual exclusion means allowing only one process to execute a given piece of code at a given time; it is important because multiple processes can execute the same piece of code. To understand why mutual exclusion is essential, consider what might happen if two processes concurrently execute code that adds a new item to a linked list. If the two processes execute concurrently, they might each start at the same point in the list and try to insert their new item. Depending on how much CPU time the processes receive, one of them could execute for a short time, then the other, then the first, and so on. As a result, one could override the other (leaving one of the new items out altogether), or they could produce a malformed list that contained incorrect pointers.

To prevent processes from interfering with one another, all the protocol software that can be executed by multiple processes must use semaphores to implement mutual exclusion. To do so, the programmer creates a semaphore with initial count of *1* for every piece of code that must be protected.

```
s = screate(1);              /* create mutual exclusion semaphore */
```

Then, the programmer places calls to *wait* and *signal* around the critical piece of code as the following illustrates.

```
wait(s);                     /* before code to be protected */
...critical code...
signal(s);                   /* after code to be protected */
```

The first process that executes *wait(s)* decrements the count of semaphore *s* to zero and continues execution (because the count remains nonnegative). If that process finishes and executes *signal(s)*, the count of *s* returns to *1*. However, if the first process is still using the critical code when a second process calls *wait(s)*, the count becomes negative and the second process will be blocked. Similarly, if a third happens to execute *wait(s)* during this time, the count remains negative and the third process will also be blocked. When the first process finally finishes using the critical code, it will execute *signal(s)*, incrementing the count and unblocking the second process. The second process will begin executing the critical code while the third waits. When the second process finishes and executes *signal(s)*, the third can begin using the critical code. The point is that at any time only one process can execute the critical code; all others that try will be blocked by the semaphore.

In addition to providing mutual exclusion, we will use semaphores to provide synchronization for queue access. Synchronization is needed because we will implement queues of finite capacity. Assume that a queue contains space for N items, and that some set of concurrent processes is generating items to be placed in the queue. Also assume that some other set of processes is extracting items and processing them (typically many processes insert items and one process extracts them). A process that inserts items in the queue is called a *producer*, and a process that extracts items is called a *consumer*. For example, the items might be IP datagrams generated by a set of user applications, and a single IP process might extract the datagrams and route each to its destination. If the application programs producing datagrams generate them faster than the IP process can consume and route them, the queue eventually becomes full. Any producer that attempts to insert an item when the queue is full must be blocked until the consumer removes an item and makes space available. Similarly, if the consumer executes quickly, it may extract all the items from the queue and must be blocked until another item arrives. Two semaphores are required for coordination of producers and consumers as they access a queue of N items. The semaphores are initialized as follows.

```
s1 = screate(N);            /* counts space in queue */
s2 = screate(0);            /* counts items in queue */
```

After the semaphores have been initialized, producers and consumers use them to synchronize. A producer executes the following

```
wait(s1);                   /* wait for space */
...insert item in next available slot...
signal(s2);                 /* signal item available */
```

And the consumer executes

```
wait(s2);                   /* wait for item in queue */
...extract oldest item from queue...
signal(s1);                 /* signal space available */
```

The semaphores guarantee that a producer process will be blocked if the queue is full, and a consumer will be blocked if the queue is empty. At all other times both producers and consumers can proceed.

2.5 Interprocess Communication

2.5.1 Ports

The *port* abstraction provides a rendezvous point through which processes can pass data. We think of a port as a finite queue of messages plus two semaphores that control access. A program creates a port by calling function *pcreate* and specifying the size of the queue as an argument. *Pcreate* returns an identifier used to reference the port.

```
portid = pcreate(size);      /* create a port specifying size */
```

Once a port has been created, processes call procedures *psend* and *preceive* to deposit or remove items. *Psend* sends a message to a port.

```
psend(portid, message);      /* send a message to a port */
```

It takes two arguments: a port identifier and a one-word message to send (in the TCP/IP code, the message will usually consist of a pointer to a packet).

Preceive extracts a message from a port.

```
message = preceive(port);    /* extract next message from port */
```

As we suggested, the implementation uses semaphores so that *psend* will block the calling process if the port is full, and *preceive* will block the calling process if the port is empty. Once a process blocks on *psend* it remains blocked until another process calls *preceive*, and vice versa. Thus, when designing systems of processes that use ports, the programmer must be careful to guarantee that the system will not block processes forever (this is the equivalent of warning programmers to avoid endless loops in sequential programs).

In addition to prohibiting interactions that block processes indefinitely, some designs add even more stringent requirements. They specify that a select group of processes may not block under any circumstances, even for short times. If the processes do block, the system may not operate correctly. For example, a network design may require that the network input process never block to avoid having the entire system halt if an application program stops accepting incoming packets. In such cases, the process needs to check whether a call to *psend* will block and, if so, take alternative action (e.g., discard a packet).

To allow processes to determine whether *psend* will block, the system provides a function, *pcount*, that allows a process to find out whether a port is full.

```
n = pcount(portid);          /* find out whether a port is full */
```

The process calls *pcount*, supplying the identifier of a port to check; *pcount* returns the current count of items in the port. If the count is zero no items remain in the port. If the count equals the size of the port, the port is full.

2.5.2 Message Passing

We said that processes also communicate and synchronize through message passing. Message passing allows one process to send a message directly to another. A process calls *send* to send a message to another process. *Send* takes a process identifier and a message as arguments; it sends the specified message to the specified process.

```
send(msg, pid);              /* send integer msg to process pid */
```

A process calls *receive* to wait for a message to arrive.

```
message = receive();         /* wait for msg and return it */
```

In our system, *receive* blocks the caller until a message arrives, but *send* always proceeds. If the receiving process does not execute *receive* between two successive calls of *send*, the second call to *send* will return *SYSERR*, and the message will not be sent. It is the programmer's responsibility to construct the system in such a way that messages are not lost. To help synchronize messages, the programmer can use *recvclr*, a function that removes any waiting message but does not block.

```
message = recvclr();         /* clear message buffer */
```

Because protocols often specify a maximum time to wait for acknowledgements, they often use the message passing function *recvtim*, a version of *receive* that allows the caller to specify a maximum time to wait. If a message arrives within the specified time, *recvtim* returns it to the caller. Otherwise, *recvtim* returns a special value, *TIMEOUT*.

```
message = recvtim(50);       /* wait 5 secs. for msg and return it */
```

2.6 Device Drivers, Input, And Output

Network interface hardware transfers incoming packets from the network to the computer's memory and informs the operating system that a packet has arrived. Usually, the network interface uses the *interrupt* mechanism to do so. An interrupt causes the CPU to temporarily suspend normal processing and jump to code called a *device driver*. The device driver software takes care of minor details. For example, it resets the hardware interrupt mechanism and (possibly) restarts the network interface hardware so it can accept another packet. The device driver also informs protocol software that a packet has arrived and must be processed. Once the device driver completes its chores, it returns from the interrupt to the place where the CPU was executing when the interrupt occurred. Thus, we can think of an interrupt as temporarily "borrowing" the CPU to handle an I/O activity.

Like most operating systems, the Xinu system arranges to have network interface devices interrupt the processor when a packet arrives. The device driver code handles the interrupt and restarts the device so it can accept the next packet.

The device driver also provides a convenient interface for programs that send or receive packets. In particular, it allows a process to block (wait) for an incoming packet. From the process' point of view, the device driver is hidden beneath a general-purpose I/O interface, making it easy to capture incoming packets. For example, to send a packet (frame) on an Ethernet interface, a program invokes the following:

```
    write(device, buff, len);              /* write one Ethernet packet */
```

where *device* is a device descriptor that identifies a particular Ethernet interface device, *buff* gives the address of a buffer that contains the packet to be sent, and *len* is the length of the packet measured in bytes (octets).

2.7 Network Input and Interrupts

Now that we understand the facilities the operating system supplies, we can examine the general structure of example TCP/IP software. Recall that the operating system contains device driver software that communicates with hardware I/O devices and handles interrupts. The code is hidden in an abstraction called a *device*; the system contains one such device for each network to which it attaches (most hosts have only one network interface but gateways have multiple network interfaces).

To accommodate random packet arrivals, the system needs the ability to read packets from any network interface. It is possible to solve the problem of waiting for a random interface in several ways. Some operating systems use the computer's *software interrupt* mechanism. When a packet arrives, a hardware interrupt occurs and the device driver performs its usual duties of accepting the packet and restarting the device. Before returning from the interrupt, the device driver tells the hardware to schedule a

second, lower priority interrupt. As soon as the hardware interrupt completes, the low
priority interrupt occurs *exactly as if another hardware device had interrupted*. This
"software interrupt" suspends processing and causes the CPU to jump to code that will
handle it. Thus, in some systems, all input processing occurs as a series of interrupts.
This idea has been formalized in a UNIX System V mechanism known as *STREAMS*.

Software interrupts are efficient, but require hardware not available on all computers. To make the protocol software portable, we chose to avoid software interrupts and
design code that relies only on a conventional interrupt mechanism.

Even operating systems that use conventional hardware interrupts have a variety of
ways to handle multiple interfaces. Some have mechanisms that allow a single process
to block on a set of input devices and be informed as soon as a packet arrives on one of
them. Others use a process per interface, allowing that process to block until a packet
arrives on its interface. To make the design efficient, we use the organization that Figure 2.1 illustrates.

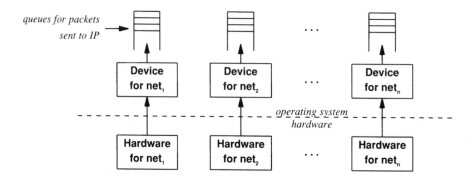

Figure 2.1 The flow of packets from the network interface hardware through
the device driver in the operating system to an input queue associated with the device.

The Ethernet interrupt routine uses the packet type field of arriving packets to
determine which protocol was used in the packet. For example, if the packet type of an
Ethernet packet is 0800_{16}, the packet carries an IP datagram. On networks that do not
have self-identifying frames, the system designer must either choose to use a link-level
protocol that identifies the packet contents, or choose the packet type *a priori*.

2.8 Passing Packets To Higher Level Protocols

Because input occurs at interrupt time, the device driver code cannot call arbitrary procedures to process the packet; it must return from the interrupt quickly. Therefore, the interrupt procedure does not call IP directly. Furthermore, because the system uses a separate process to implement IP, the device driver cannot call IP directly. Instead, the system uses a queue along with the message passing primitives described earlier in this chapter to synchronize communication. When a packet that carries an IP datagram arrives, the interrupt software must enqueue the packet and invoke *send* to notify the IP process that a datagram has arrived. When the IP process has no packets to handle, it calls *receive* to wait for the arrival of another datagram. There is an input queue associated with each network device; a single IP process extracts datagrams from all queues and processes them. Figure 2.2 illustrates the concept.

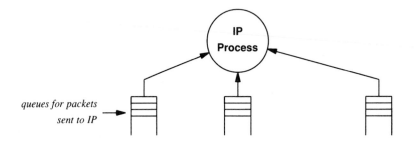

Figure 2.2 Communication between the network device drivers and the process that implements IP uses a set of queues. When a datagram arrives, the network input process enqueues it and sends IP a message.

2.9 Passing Datagrams From IP To Transport Protocols

Once the IP process accepts an incoming datagram, it must decide where to send it for further processing. If the datagram carries a TCP segment, it must go to the TCP module; it if carries a UDP datagram, it must go to the UDP module, and so on. We will examine the internals of each module later; at this point, only the process structure is important.

2.9.1 Passing Incoming Datagrams to TCP

Because TCP is complex, most designs use a separate process to handle incoming TCP segments. Because they execute as separate processes, IP and TCP must use an interprocess communication mechanism to communicate. They use the port mechanism described earlier. IP calls *psend* to deposit segments in the port, and TCP calls *preceive* to retrieve them. As we will see later, other processes send messages to TCP using this port as well.

Once TCP receives a segment, it uses the TCP protocol port numbers to find the connection to which the segment belongs. If the segment contains data, TCP will add the data to a buffer associated with the connection and return an acknowledgement to the sender. If the incoming segment carries an acknowledgement for outbound data, the TCP input process must also communicate with the TCP timer process to cancel the pending retransmission.

2.9.2 Passing Incoming Datagrams to UDP

The process structure for incoming UDP datagrams is quite different from TCP. Because UDP is much simpler than TCP, the UDP software module does not execute as a separate process. Instead, it consists of conventional procedures that the IP process executes to handle an incoming UDP datagram. These procedures examine the destination UDP protocol port number and use it to select an operating system queue (port) for the user datagram. The IP process deposits the UDP datagram on the appropriate port, where an application program can extract it. Figure 2.3 illustrates the difference.

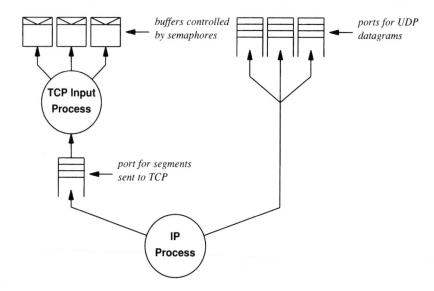

Figure 2.3 The flow of datagrams through higher layers of software. The IP
process sends incoming segments to the TCP process, but places
incoming UDP datagrams directly in separate ports where they
can be accessed by application programs.

2.10 Delivery To Application Programs

As Figure 2.3 shows, UDP demultiplexes incoming user datagrams based on protocol port number and places them in operating system queues. Meanwhile, TCP
separates incoming data streams and places the data in buffers. When application programs want to receive either UDP datagrams or data from a TCP stream, they must access the UDP ports or TCP buffers. While the details are complex, the reader should
understand a simple idea at this point:

> *Because each application program executes as a separate process, it
> must use system communication primitives to coordinate with the
> processes that implement protocols.*

For example, an application program calls the operating system function *preceive*
to retrieve a UDP datagram. Of course, the interaction is much more complex when an
application program interacts with a process in the operating system than when two
processes inside the operating system interact.

For incoming TCP data, application programs do not use *preceive*. Instead, the system uses semaphores to control access to the data in a TCP buffer. An application program that wishes to read incoming data from the stream calls *wait* on the semaphore that controls the buffer; the TCP process calls *signal* when it adds data to the buffer.

2.11 Information Flow On Output

Outgoing packets originate for one of two reasons. Either (1) application programs pass data to high-level protocols which, in turn, send messages (or datagrams) to low-level protocols and eventually cause transmission on a network, or (2) protocol software in the operating system needs to transmit information (e.g., an acknowledgement or a response to an echo request). In either case, a hardware frame must be sent out over a particular network interface.

To help isolate the transmission of packets from the execution of processes that implement application programs and protocols, the system has a separate output queue for each network interface. Figure 2.4 illustrates the design.

The queues associated with output devices provide an important piece of the design. They allow processes to generate a packet, enqueue it for output, and continue execution without waiting for the packet to be sent. Meanwhile, the hardware can continue transmitting packets simultaneously. If the hardware is idle when a packet arrives (i.e., there are no packets in the queue), the process performing output enqueues its packet and calls a device driver routine to start the hardware. When the output operation completes, the hardware interrupts the CPU. The interrupt handler, which is part of the device driver, dequeues the packet that was just sent, and restarts the hardware to send the next packet if any additional packets remain in the queue. The interrupt handler then returns from the interrupt, allowing normal processing to continue.

Thus, from the point of view of the IP process, transmission of packets occurs automatically in the background. As long as packets remain on a queue, the hardware continues to transmit them. The hardware only needs to be started when IP deposits a packet on an empty queue.

Of course, each output queue has finite capacity and can become full if the system generates packets faster than the network hardware can transmit them. We assume that such cases are rare, but if they do occur, processes that generate packets must make a choice: discard the packet or block until the hardware finishes transmitting a packet and makes more space available.

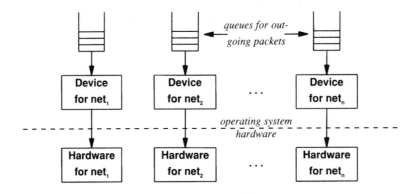

Figure 2.4 Network output and the queues that buffer output packets. Using queues isolates processing from network transmission.

2.12 From TCP Through IP To Network Output

Like TCP input, TCP output is complex. Connections must be established, data must be placed in segments, and the segments must be retransmitted until acknowledgements arrive. Once the segments have been placed in a datagram, they can be passed to IP for routing and delivery. The software uses two TCP processes to handle the complexity. The first, called *tcpout*, handles most of the segmentation and data transmission details. The second, called *tcptimer*, manages a timer, schedules retransmission timeouts, and prompts *tcpout* when a segment must be retransmitted.

The *tcpout* process uses a port to synchronize input from multiple processes. Because TCP is stream oriented, allowing application programs to send a few bytes of data at a time, items in the port do not correspond to individual packets or segments. Instead, a process that emits data places the data in an output buffer and places a single message in the port informing TCP that more data has been written. The timer process deposits a message in the port whenever a timer expires and TCP needs to retransmit a segment. Thus, we can think of the port as a queue of events for TCP to process – each event can cause transmission or retransmission of a segment. Alternatively, an event may not cause an action (e.g., if data arrives while the receiver's window is closed). We will review the exact details of events and TCP's responses in a later chapter.

Once TCP produces a datagram, it passes the datagram to IP for delivery. Usually, the destination lies on a remote machine, so IP chooses a network interface over which the datagram must be sent and passes it to the corresponding network output process. Figure 2.5 illustrates the path of outgoing TCP data.

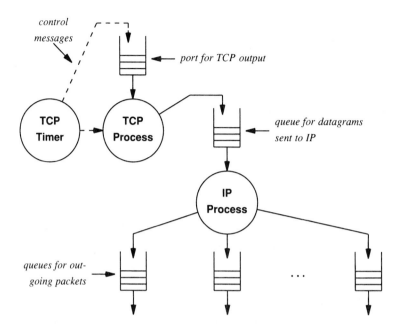

Figure 2.5 The TCP output and timer processes use the IP process to send
data.

2.13 UDP Output

The path for outgoing UDP traffic is much simpler. Because UDP does not
guarantee reliable delivery, the sending machine does not keep a copy of the datagram
nor does it need to time retransmissions. Once the datagram has been formatted, it can
be transmitted.

Any process that sends a UDP datagram must execute the UDP procedures needed
to format it, as well as the procedures needed to encapsulate it and pass the resulting datagram to the IP process.

2.14 Summary

TCP/IP protocol software is part of the computer operating system. It uses the
process abstraction to isolate pieces of protocol software, making each easier to design,
understand, and modify. Each process executes independently, providing apparent
parallelism. The system has a process for IP, TCP input, TCP output, and TCP timer
management, as well as a process for each application program.

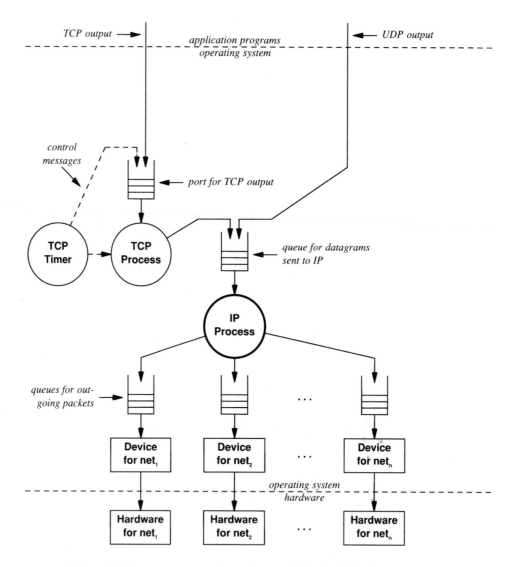

Figure 2.6 Output process structure showing the path of data between an application program and the network hardware. Output from the device queues is started at interrupt time. IP is a central part of the design – the software for input and output both share a single IP process.

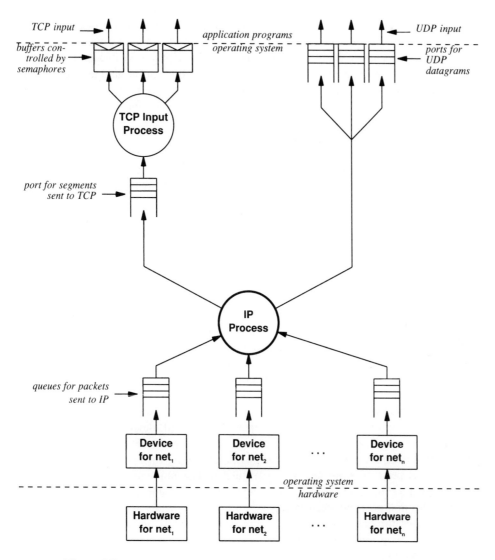

Figure 2.7 Input process structure showing the path of data between the network hardware and an application program. Input to the device queues occurs asynchronously with processing. IP is a central part of the design – the software for input and output share a single IP process.

The operating system provides a semaphore mechanism that processes used to synchronize their execution. We will use semaphores for mutual exclusion (i.e., to guarantee that only one process accesses a piece of code at a given time), and for producer-consumer relationships (i.e., when a set of processes produces data items that another set of processes consumes). The operating system also provides a port mechanism that allows processes to send messages to one another through a finite queue. The port mechanism uses semaphores to coordinate the processes that use the queue. If a process attempts to send a message to a port that is full, it will be blocked until another process extracts a message. Similarly, if a process attempts to extract a message from an empty port, it will be blocked until some other process deposits a message in the port.

We saw that processes implementing protocols use both conventional queues and ports to pass packets among themselves. For example, the IP input process sends TCP segments to a port from which the TCP process extracts them, while the network input processes place arriving datagrams in a queue from which IP extracts them. When data is passed through conventional queues, the system must use message passing or semaphores to synchronize the actions of independent processes.

Figure 2.6 summarizes the flow of information between an application program and the network hardware during output. An application program, executing as a separate process, calls system routines to pass stream data to TCP or datagrams to UDP. For UDP output, the process executing the application program transfers into the operating system (through a system call), where it executes UDP procedures that allocate an IP datagram, fill in the appropriate destination address, encapsulate the UDP datagram in it, and send the IP datagram to the IP process for delivery.

For TCP output, the process executing an application program calls a system routine to transfer data across the operating system boundary and place it in a buffer. The application process then informs the TCP output process that new data is waiting to be sent. When the TCP output process executes, it divides the data stream into segments and encapsulates each segment in an IP datagram for delivery. Finally, the TCP output process enqueues the IP datagram on the port where IP will extract and send it.

Figure 2.7 summarizes the flow on input. The network device drivers enqueue all incoming packets that carry IP datagrams on queues for the IP process. IP extracts packets from the queues and demultiplexes them, delivering each packet to the appropriate high-level protocol software. When IP finds a datagram carrying UDP, it invokes UDP procedures that deposit the incoming datagram on the appropriate port, from which application programs read them. When IP finds a datagram carrying a TCP segment, it passes the datagram to a port from which the TCP input process extracts it. Note that the IP process is a central part of the design – a single IP process handles both input and output.

FOR FURTHER STUDY

Our examples use the Xinu operating system. Comer [1984] provides a detailed description of the system, including the process and port abstractions. Comer [1987] shows how processes and ports can be used for simple protocols like UDP.

EXERCISES

2.1 Why do protocol implementations try to minimize the number of processes they use?

2.2 If the system described in this chapter executes on a computer in which the CPU is slow compared to the speed at which the network hardware can deliver packets, what will happen?

2.3 Read more about software interrupts and sketch the design of a protocol implementation that uses software interrupts instead of processes.

2.4 Read about the UNIX *STREAMS* facility and compare it to the process-oriented implementation described in this chapter. What are the advantages and disadvantages of each?

2.5 Compare two designs: one in which each application program that sends a UDP datagram executes all the UDP and IP code directly, and an alternative in which a separate UDP process accepts outgoing datagrams from all application programs. What are the two main advantages and disadvantages of each?

3

Network Interface Layer

3.1 Introduction

TCP/IP Internet Protocol software is organized into five conceptual layers as Figure 3.1 shows.

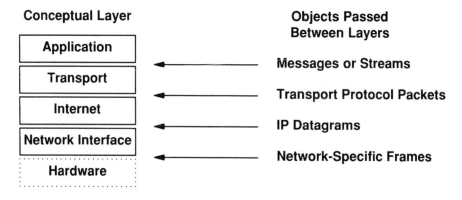

Figure 3.1 The conceptual organization of TCP/IP protocol software into layers.

This chapter examines the lowest layer, known as the *network interface layer*. Conceptually, the network interface layer controls the network hardware, performs mappings from IP addresses to hardware addresses, encapsulates and transmits outgoing packets, and accepts and demultiplexes incoming packets. This chapter shows how device driver and interface software can be organized to allow higher layers of protocol software to recognize and control multiple network hardware interfaces attached to a single machine. It also considers buffer management and packet demultiplexing. Chapter 4 discusses address resolution and encapsulation.

We have chosen to omit the network device driver code because it contains many low-level details that can only be understood completely by someone intimately familiar with the particular network hardware devices. Instead, this chapter concentrates on the elements of the network interface layer that are fundamental to an understanding of high-level protocol software.

3.2 The Network Interface Abstraction

Software in the network interface layer provides a *network interface abstraction* that is used throughout the rest of the system. The idea is simple:

> *The network interface abstraction defines the interface between proto-col software in the operating system and the underlying hardware. It hides hardware details and allows protocol software to interact with a variety of network hardware using the same data structures.*

3.2.1 Interface Structure

To achieve hardware independence, we define a data structure that holds all hardware-independent information about an interface (e.g., whether the hardware is *up* or *down*), and arrange protocol software to interact with the hardware primarily through this data structure. In our example code, the network interface consists of an array, *nif*, with one element for each hardware interface attached to the machine. Items in the in-terface array are known throughout the system by their index in the array. Thus, we can talk about "network interface number zero" or "the first network interface." File *netif.h* contains the pertinent declarations.

```
/* netif.h - NIGET */

#define NI_MAXHWA 14              /* max size of any hardware      */
                                 /*   (physical) net address      */
struct  hwa     {                /* a hardware address            */
        int     ha_len;          /* length of this address        */
        char    ha_addr[NI_MAXHWA];  /* actual bytes of the address   */
};

#define NI_INQSZ        30       /* interface input queue size    */
#define NETNLEN         30       /* length of network name        */

#define NI_LOCAL        0        /* index of local interface      */
#define NI_PRIMARY      1        /* index of primary interface    */
```

```
/* interface states */

#define NIS_UP          0x1
#define NIS_DOWN        0x2
#define NIS_TESTING     0x3


/* Definitions of network interface structure (one per interface)     */

struct  netif {                         /* info about one net interface */
        char    ni_name[NETNLEN];       /* domain name of this interface*/
        char    ni_state;               /* interface states: NIS_ above */
        IPaddr  ni_ip;                  /* IP address for this interface*/
        IPaddr  ni_net;                 /* network IP address           */
        IPaddr  ni_subnet;              /* subnetwork IP address        */
        IPaddr  ni_mask;                /* IP subnet mask for interface */
        IPaddr  ni_brc;                 /* IP broadcast address         */
        IPaddr  ni_nbrc;                /* IP net broadcast address     */
        int     ni_mtu;                 /* max transfer unit (bytes)    */
        int     ni_hwtype;              /* hardware type (for ARP)      */
        struct  hwa     ni_hwa;         /* hardware address of interface*/
        struct  hwa     ni_hwb;         /* hardware broadcast address   */
        Bool    ni_ivalid;              /* is ni_ip valid?              */
        Bool    ni_nvalid;              /* is ni_name valid?            */
        Bool    ni_svalid;              /* is ni_subnet valid?          */
        int     ni_dev;                 /* the Xinu device descriptor   */
        int     ni_ipinq;               /* IP input queue               */
        int     ni_outq;                /* (device) output queue        */
        /* Interface MIB */
        char    *ni_descr;              /* text description of hardware */
        int     ni_mtype;               /* MIB interface type           */
        long    ni_speed;               /* bits per second              */
        char    ni_admstate;            /* administrative status (NIS_*)*/
        long    ni_lastchange;          /* last state change (1/100 sec)*/
        long    ni_ioctets;             /* # of octets received         */
        long    ni_iucast;              /* # of unicast received        */
        long    ni_inucast;             /* # of non-unicast received    */
        long    ni_idiscard;            /* # dropped - output queue full*/
        long    ni_ierrors;             /* # input packet errors        */
        long    ni_iunkproto;           /* # in packets for unk. protos */
        long    ni_ooctets;             /* # of octets sent             */
        long    ni_oucast;              /* # of unicast sent            */
        long    ni_onucast;             /* # of non-unicast sent        */
        long    ni_odiscard;            /* # output packets discarded   */
        long    ni_oerrors;             /* # output packet errors       */
        long    ni_oqlen;               /* output queue length          */
};
```

```
#define NIGET(ifn)        ((struct ep *)deq(nif[ifn].ni_ipinq))

#define NIF       Neth+Noth+1                  /* # of interfaces, +1 for local*/

extern struct netif       nif[];
```

Structure *netif* defines the contents of each element in *nif*. Fields in *netif* define all the data items that protocol software needs as well as variables used to collect statistics. For example, field *ni_ip* contains the IP address assigned to the interface, and field *ni_mtu* contains the *maximum transfer unit*, the maximum size in octets of the data that can be sent in one packet on the network. Fields with names that end in *valid* contain Boolean variables that tell whether other fields are valid; initialization software sets them to *TRUE* once the fields have been assigned values. For example, *ni_ivalid* is *TRUE* when *ni_ip* contains a valid IP address.

The device driver software places arriving datagrams for the IP process in a queue. Field *ni_ipinq* contains a pointer to that queue. To extract the next datagram, programs use the macro *NIGET*, which takes an interface number as an argument, dequeues the next packet from the interface queue, and returns a pointer to it.

3.2.2 Statistics About Use

Keeping statistics about an interface is important for debugging and for network management. For example, field *ni_ucast* holds a count of incoming unicast (nonbroadcast) packets, while fields *ni_idiscard* and *ni_odiscard* count input and output packets that must be discarded due to errors.

The interface structure holds the physical (hardware) address in field *ni_hwa* and the physical (hardware) broadcast address in field *ni_hwb*. Because the length of a physical address depends on the underlying hardware, the software uses structure *hwa* to represent such addresses. Each hardware address begins with an integer length field followed by the address. Thus, high-level software can manipulate hardware addresses without understanding the hardware details.

3.3 Logical State Of An Interface

When debugging, managers often need to disable one or more of the interfaces on a given machine. Field *ni_state* provides a mechanism to control the logical state of an interface, independent of the underlying hardware. For example, a network manager can assign *ni_state* the value *NIS_DOWN* to stop input and output completely. Later, the manager can assign *ni_state* the value *NIS_UP* to restart I/O.

It is important to separate the logical state of an interface from the status of the physical hardware because it allows a manager freedom to control its operation. Of course, a manager can declare an interface *down* if the hardware fails. However, declar-

ing an interface down does not disconnect the physical hardware, nor does it mean the
hardware cannot work correctly. Instead, the declaration merely causes software to stop
accepting incoming packets and to block outgoing packets. For example, a manager can
declare an interface down when the network to which it attaches is overloaded.

3.4 Local Host Interface

In addition to routing datagrams among network interfaces, IP must also route datagrams to and from higher-level protocol software on the local computer. The interaction between IP and the local machine can either be implemented as:

- Explicit tests in the IP code, or

- An additional network interface for the local machine.

Our design uses a *pseudo-network interface*. The pseudo-network interface does
not have associated device driver routines, nor does it correspond to real hardware, as
Figure 3.2 shows. Instead, a datagram sent to the pseudo-network will be delivered to
protocol software on the local machine. Similarly, when protocol software generates an
outgoing datagram, it sends the datagram to IP through the pseudo-network interface.

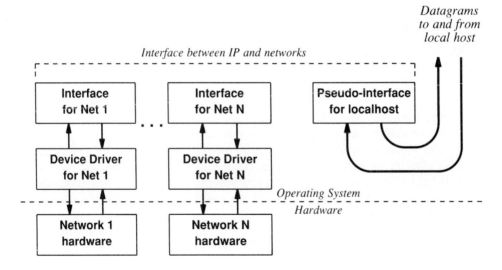

Figure 3.2 The pseudo-network interface used for communication with the local host.

Using a pseudo-network for the local machine has several advantages. First, it eliminates special cases, simplifying the IP code. Second, it allows the local machine to be represented in the routing table exactly like other destinations. Third, it allows a network manager to interrogate the local interface as easily as other interfaces (e.g., to obtain a count of packets generated by local applications).

3.5 Buffer Management

Incoming packets must be placed in memory and passed to the appropriate protocol software for processing. Meanwhile, when an application program generates output, it must be stored in packets in memory and passed to a network hardware device for transmission. Thus, the network interface layer accepts outgoing data in memory and passes incoming data to higher-level protocol software in memory. The ultimate efficiency of protocol software depends on how it manages the memory used to hold packets. A good design allocates space quickly and avoids copying data as packets move between layers of protocol software.

Ideally, a system could make memory allocation efficient by dividing memory into fixed-size buffers, where each buffer is sufficient to hold a packet. In practice, however, choosing an optimum buffer size is complex for several reasons. First, a computer may connect to several networks, each of which has its own notion of maximum packet size. Furthermore, it should be possible to add connections to new types of networks without changing the system's buffer size. Second, IP may need to store datagrams larger than the underlying network packet sizes (e.g., to reassemble a large datagram). Third, an application program may choose to send or receive arbitrary size messages.

3.5.1 Large Buffer Solution

It may seem that the ideal solution is to allocate buffers that are capable of storing the largest possible message or packet. However, because an IP datagram can be 64K octets long, allocating buffers large enough for arbitrary datagrams quickly expends all available memory on only a few buffers. Furthermore, small packets are the norm; large datagrams are rare. Thus, using large buffers can result in a situation where memory utilization remains low even though the system does not have sufficient buffers to accommodate traffic.

In practice, designers who use the large buffer approach usually choose an upper bound on the size of datagrams the system will handle, D, and make buffers large enough to hold a datagram of size D plus the physical network frame header. The choice of D is a tradeoff between allowing large datagrams and having sufficient buffers for the expected traffic. Thus, D depends on the expected size of buffer memory as well as the expected use of the system. Typically, timesharing systems choose values of D between 4K and 8K bytes.

3.5.2 Linked List Solutions (mbufs)

The chief alternative to large buffers uses linked lists of smaller buffers to handle arbitrary datagram sizes. In linked list designs, the individual buffers on the list can be fixed or variable size. Most systems allocate fixed size buffers because doing so prevents fragmentation and guarantees high memory utilization. Usually, each buffer is small (e.g., between 128 and 1K bytes), so many buffers must be linked together to represent a complete datagram. For example, Berkeley UNIX uses a linked structure known as the *mbuf*, where each mbuf is 128 bytes long. Individual mbufs need not be completely full; a short header specifies where data starts in the mbuf and how many bytes are present.

Permitting buffers on the linked list to contain partial data has another advantage: it allows quick encapsulation without copying. When a layer of software receives a message from a higher layer, it allocates a new buffer, fills in its header information, and prepends the new buffer to the linked list that represents the message. Thus, additional bytes can be inserted at the front of a message without moving the existing data.

3.5.3 Our Example Solution

Our example system chooses a compromise between having large buffers sufficient to store arbitrary datagrams and linked lists of small buffers: it allocates many network buffers large enough to hold a single packet and allocates a few buffers large enough to hold large datagrams. The system performs packet-level I/O using the small buffers, and only resorts to using large buffers when generating or reassembling large datagrams. This design was chosen because we expect most datagrams to be smaller than a conventional network MTU, but want to be able to reassemble larger datagrams as well. Thus, in most instances, it will be possible to pass an entire buffer to IP after reading a packet into it; the system will only need to copy data when reassembling a large datagram.

To make buffer processing uniform, our system uses a self-identifying buffer scheme provided by the operating system. To allocate a buffer, the system calls function *getbuf* and specifies whether it needs a large buffer or a small one. However, once the buffer has been allocated, only the pointer to it need be saved. To return the buffer to the free list, the system calls *freebuf*, passing it a pointer to the buffer being released; *freebuf* deduces the size of the buffer automatically. The advantage of having the buffer be self-identifying is that protocol software can pass along a pointer to the buffer without having to remember whether it was allocated from the large or small group. Thus, outgoing packets can be kept in a simple list that identifies them by address. Once a device has transmitted a packet, the driver software can call *freebuf* to dispose of the buffer without having to know the buffer type.

3.5.4 Other Buffer Issues

DMA Memory. Hardware requirements often complicate buffer management. For example, some devices can only perform I/O in an area of memory reserved for *direct memory access* (DMA). In such systems, the operating system may choose to allocate two sets of buffers: those used by protocol software and those used for device transfer. The system must copy outgoing data from conventional buffers to the DMA area before transmission, and must copy incoming data from the DMA area to conventional buffers.

Gather-write, scatter-read. Some devices can transmit or receive packets in non-contiguous memory locations. On output, such devices accept a list of buffer addresses and lengths. They gather pieces of the packet from buffers on the list, and transmit the resulting sequence of bytes without requiring the system to assemble the packet in contiguous memory locations. The technique is known as *gather-write.* Similarly, the hardware may also support *scatter-read* in which the hardware deposits the packet in noncontiguous memory locations according to a list of buffer addresses specified by the device driver. Obviously, gather-write and scatter-read make linked buffer allocation easy and efficient because they allow the hardware to pick up pieces of the packet from the buffers on the linked list without requiring the processor to assemble a complete packet in memory. These techniques can also be used with fixed-size buffers because they allow the driver to encapsulate a datagram without copying it. To do so, the driver places the frame header in one part of memory and passes to the hardware the address of the header along with the address of the datagram, which becomes the data portion of the physical packet.

Page alignment. In a computer system that supports paged virtual memory, protocol software can attempt to allocate buffers on page boundaries, making it possible to pass the buffer to other processes by exchanging page table entries instead of copying. The technique is especially useful on machines with small page sizes (e.g., a Digital Equipment Corporation VAX architecture, which has 512 byte pages), but it does not work well on computers with large page sizes (e.g., Sun Microsystems Sun 3 architecture, which has 8K byte pages). Furthermore, swapping page table entries improves efficiency most when moving data between the operating system and an application program. However, incoming packets contain a set of headers that make the exact offset of user data difficult or impossible to determine before a packet has been read. Therefore, few implementations try to align data on page boundaries.

3.6 Demultiplexing Incoming Packets

When a packet arrives, the device driver software in the network interface layer examines the packet type field to determine which protocol software will handle the packet. In general, designers take one of two basic approaches when building interface software: either they encode the demultiplexing in a procedure or use a table that maps the packet type to an appropriate procedure. Using code is often more efficient, but it means the software must be recompiled when new protocols are added. Using a table makes experimentation easier. In our implementation, we have chosen to demultiplex packets in a procedure. Procedure *ni_in* contains the demultiplexing code.

```c
/* ni_in.c - ni_in */

#include <conf.h>
#include <kernel.h>
#include <network.h>


/*------------------------------------------------------------------------
 *  ni_in - network interface input function
 *------------------------------------------------------------------------
 */
int ni_in(pni, pep, len)
struct  netif   *pni;           /* the interface         */
struct  ep      *pep;           /* the packet            */
int             len;            /* length, in octets     */
{
        int     rv;

        switch (pep->ep_type) {
        case EPT_ARP:   rv = arp_in(pni, pep);  break;
        case EPT_RARP:  rv = rarp_in(pni, pep); break;
        case EPT_IP:    rv = ip_in(pni, pep);   break;
        default:
                pni->ni_iunkproto++;
                freebuf(pep);
                return OK;
        }
        pni->ni_ioctets += len;
        if (blkequ(pni->ni_hwa.ha_addr, pep->ep_dst, EP_ALEN))
                pni->ni_iucast++;
        else
                pni->ni_inucast++;
        return rv;
}
```

In our implementation, the device driver calls *ni_in* whenever an interrupt occurs to signal that a new packet has arrived. *Ni_in* handles four cases. If the packet carries an ARP message, RARP message, or IP datagram, *ni_in* passes the packet to the appropriate protocol routine and returns the result. Otherwise, it discards the packet by returning the buffer to the buffer pool. If the packet is accepted, *ni_in* increments appropriate counters to record the arrival of either a broadcast packet or a unicast packet. We will examine the procedures that *ni_in* calls in later chapters.

3.7 Summary

The network interface layer contains software that communicates between other protocol software and the network hardware devices. It includes buffer management routines, low-level device driver code, and contains many hardware-dependent details. Most important, it provides an abstraction known as the *network interface* that isolates higher-level protocols from the details of the hardware.

The *netif* structure defines the information kept for each network interface. It contains all information pertinent to the interface, making it possible for higher-level protocols to access the information without understanding the details of the specific hardware interface. Among the fields in *netif*, some contain information about the hardware (e.g., the hardware address), while others contain information used by protocol software (e.g., the subnet mask).

FOR FURTHER STUDY

Comer [1984] presents more details on the buffer pool scheme used in the example code. Comer [1987] explains the details of an Ethernet device driver and shows how the code fits into an operating system. Leffler, McKusick, Karels, and Quarterman [1989] describes the use of mbufs in 4BSD UNIX.

EXERCISES

3.1 Examine the MIB used with SNMP (RFC 1066). What statistics does it specify keeping for each network interface? Does the interface structure contain a field for each of them?

3.2 Read the BSD UNIX source code to see how mbufs are structured. Why does the header contain two pointers to other mbuf nodes?

3.3 Experiment with the 4BSD UNIX *ping* program (i.e., ICMP echo request/reply) to determine the largest datagram size that machines in your local environment can send and receive. How does it compare to the network MTU?

3.4 Find a hardware description of the Lance Ethernet interface device. Is it possible to enqueue *multiple* packets for transmission? If so, does this provide any advantages for the software designer?

3.5 Find a hardware architecture manual that describes DMA memory. How does a device driver use DMA memory for buffers?

4

Address Discovery And Binding (ARP)

4.1 Introduction

The previous chapter showed the organization of a network interface layer that contains device drivers for network hardware, as well as the associated software that sends outgoing packets and accepts incoming packets. Device drivers communicate directly with the network hardware and use only physical network addresses when transmitting and receiving packets.

This chapter examines ARP software that also resides in the network interface layer. ARP binds high-level, IP addresses to low-level, physical addresses. Address binding software forms a boundary between higher layers of protocol software, which use only IP addresses, and the lower layers of device driver software, which use only hardware addresses. Later chapters that discuss higher-layer protocols illustrate clearly how ARP insulates those layers from hardware addresses.

We said that address binding is part of the network interface layer, and our implementation reflects this idea. Although the ARP software maintains an address mapping that binds IP addresses to hardware addresses, we do not intend higher layers of protocol software to access the table directly. Instead, the ARP software encapsulates the mapping table and handles both table lookup as well as table update.

4.2 Conceptual Organization Of ARP Software

Conceptually, the ARP software can be divided into three parts: an *output side*, an *input side*, and a *cache manager*. When sending a datagram, the network interface software calls the output side to bind a high-level protocol address (e.g., an IP address) to its corresponding hardware address. The output side procedures return the binding, which the network interface routines use to encapsulate and transmit the packet. The input side handles ARP packets that arrive from the network. The input side procedures update the ARP cache by adding new bindings. The cache manager implements the cache replacement policy. It examines entries in the cache and removes them when they reach a specified age.

Before reviewing the procedures that implement ARP, we need to understand the basic design and the data structures used for the ARP address binding cache. The next sections discuss the design and the data structures used to implement it.

4.3 Example ARP Design

Although the ARP protocol seems simple, details can complicate the software. Many implementations fail to interpret the protocol specification correctly. Other implementations supply incorrect bindings because they eliminate cache timeout in an attempt to improve efficiency. It is important to consider the design of ARP software carefully and to include all aspects of the protocol.

Our example ARP software follows a few simple design rules:

- **Single Cache.** A single physical cache holds entries for all networks, and each entry contains a field that specifies the network from which the binding was obtained. The alternative is to have a separate ARP cache for each network interface. The choice between using a single cache and multiple caches only makes a difference for gateways or multi-homed hosts that have multiple network connections.

- **Global Replacement Policy.** Our cache policy specifies that if a new binding must be added to the cache after it is already full, an existing item in the cache can be removed, independent of whether the new binding comes from the same network. The alternative is a local replacement policy in which a new binding can only replace a binding from the same network. In essence, a local replacement policy requires preallocation of cache space to each network interface and achieves the same effect as using separate caches.

- **Cache Timeout and Removal.** We have said it is important to revalidate entries after they remain in the ARP cache for a fixed time. In our design, each cache entry has a time-to-live field associated with it. When an entry is added to the cache (or whenever an entry is validated), ARP software initializes the time-to-live field on the entry. As time proceeds, the cache manager decrements the value in the time-to-live field, and discards the entry when the value reaches zero. Removal from the cache is independent of the frequency with which the entry is used. Discarding an entry forces the ARP software to use the network to obtain a new binding from the destination machine. ARP does not automatically revalidate entries removed from the cache – the software waits until an outgoing packet needs the binding before obtaining it again.

- **Multiple Queues of Waiting Packets.** Our design allows multiple outstanding packets to be enqueued waiting for an address to be resolved. Each entry in the ARP cache has a queue of outgoing packets destined for the address in that entry. When an ARP reply arrives that contains the needed hardware address, the software removes packets from the queue and transmits them.

- **Exclusive Access.** Our software disables interrupts and avoids context switching to guarantee that only one process accesses the ARP cache at any time. Procedures that operate on the cache (e.g., search it) specify in their comments that exclusive access is required; it is the caller's responsibility to insure mutual exclusion.

In general, using a separate physical cache for each interface or using a local replacement policy provides some isolation between network interfaces. In the worst case, if the traffic on one network interface involves substantially more destinations than the traffic on others, bindings from the heavily-used interface may dominate the cache by replacing bindings from other networks. The symptom is the same as for any poorly-tuned cache: the cache remains 100% full at all times, but the probability of finding an entry in the cache is low. Our design assumes that the manager will monitor performance problems and allocate additional cache space when they occur.

While our design can behave poorly in the worst case, it provides more flexibility in the usual case because it allows cache allocation to vary dynamically with network load. If most of the traffic at a given time involves only a few networks, those networks will dominate the cache. If the traffic later shifts to a different set of networks, entries for the new networks will eventually dominate the cache.

4.4 Data Structures For The ARP Cache

File *arp.h* contains the declaration of the data structures for the ARP packet format, the internal data structures for the ARP cache, and the definitions for symbolic constants used throughout the ARP code.

```
/* arp.h - SHA, SPA, THA, TPA */

/* Internet Address Resolution Protocol  (see RFCs 826, 920)              */

#define AR_HARDWARE       1          /* Ethernet hardware type code         */

/* Definitions of codes used in operation field of ARP packet */

#define AR_REQUEST        1          /* ARP request to resolve address      */
#define AR_REPLY          2          /* reply to a resolve request          */

#define RA_REQUEST        3          /* reverse ARP request (RARP packets)  */
#define RA_REPLY          4          /* reply to a reverse request (RARP ") */

struct  arp    {
        short   ar_hwtype;           /* hardware type                       */
        short   ar_prtype;           /* protocol type                       */
        char    ar_hwlen;            /* hardware address length             */
        char    ar_prlen;            /* protocol address length             */
        short   ar_op;               /* ARP operation (see list above)      */
        char    ar_addrs[1];         /* sender and target hw & proto addrs  */
/*      char    ar_sha[???];         /* sender's physical hardware address  */
/*      char    ar_spa[???];         /* sender's protocol address (IP addr.) */
/*      char    ar_tha[???];         /* target's physical hardware address  */
/*      char    ar_tpa[???];         /* target's protocol address (IP)      */
};

#define SHA(p)   (&p->ar_addrs[0])
#define SPA(p)   (&p->ar_addrs[p->ar_hwlen])
#define THA(p)   (&p->ar_addrs[p->ar_hwlen + p->ar_prlen])
#define TPA(p)   (&p->ar_addrs[(p->ar_hwlen*2) + p->ar_prlen])


#define MAXHWALEN         EP_ALEN /* Ethernet                               */
#define MAXPRALEN         IP_ALEN /* IP                                     */

#define ARP_TSIZE         50         /* ARP cache size                      */
#define ARP_QSIZE         10         /* ARP port queue size                 */

/* cache timeouts */

#define ARP_TIMEOUT       600        /* 10 minutes                          */
#define ARP_RESEND        1          /* resend if no reply in 1 sec         */
#define ARP_MAXRETRY      4          /* give up after a ~30 seconds         */
```

```
struct   arpentry {                   /* format of entry in ARP cache      */
         short   ae_state;            /* state of this entry (see below)   */
         short   ae_hwtype;           /* hardware type                     */
         short   ae_prtype;           /* protocol type                     */
         char    ae_hwlen;            /* hardware address length           */
         char    ae_prlen;            /* protocol address length           */
         struct netif *ae_pni;        /* pointer to interface structure    */
         int     ae_queue;            /* queue of packets for this address */
         int     ae_attempts;         /* number of retries so far          */
         int     ae_ttl;              /* time to live                      */
         char    ae_hwa[MAXHWALEN];      /* Hardware address               */
         char    ae_pra[MAXPRALEN];      /* Protocol address               */
};

#define AS_FREE        0      /* Entry is unused (initial value)   */
#define AS_PENDING     1      /* Entry is used but incomplete       */
#define AS_RESOLVED    2      /* Entry has been resolved            */

/* RARP variables */

extern int      rarppid;      /* id of process waiting for RARP reply */
extern int      rarpsem;      /* semaphore for access to RARP service */

/* ARP variables */

extern struct   arpentry       arptable[ARP_TSIZE];
```

Array *arptable* forms the global ARP cache. Each entry in the array corresponds to a single binding between a protocol (IP) address (field *ae_pra*), and a hardware address (*ae_hwa*). Field *ae_state* gives the state of the entry, which must be one of *AS_FREE* (unused), *AS_PENDING* (entry is being used but binding has not yet been found), or *AS_RESOLVED* (entry is used and the binding is correct). Each entry also contains fields that give the hardware and protocol types (*ae_hwtype* and *ae_prtype*), and the hardware and protocol address lengths (*ae_hwlen* and *ae_prlen*). Field *ae_pni* points to the network interface structure corresponding to the network from which the binding was obtained. For entries that have not yet been resolved, field *ae_queue* points to a queue of packets that can be sent when an answer arrives. For entries in state *AS_PENDING*, field *ae_attempts* specifies the number of times a request for this entry has been broadcast. Finally, field *ae_ttl* specifies the time (in seconds) an entry can remain in the cache before the timer expires and it must be removed.

Structure *arp* defines the format of an ARP packet. Fields *ar_hwtype* and *ar_prtype* specify the hardware and protocol types, and fields *ar_hwlen* and *ar_prlen* contain integers that specify the sizes of the hardware address and the protocol address, respectively. Field *ar_op* specifies whether the packet contains a request or a reply.

Because the size of addresses carried in an ARP packet depends on the type of hardware and type of protocol address being mapped, the *arp* structure cannot specify the size of all fields in a packet. Instead, the structure only specifies the fixed-size fields at the beginning of the packet, and uses field name *ar_addrs* to mark the remainder of the packet. Conceptually, the bytes starting at field *ar_addrs* comprise four fields: the hardware and protocol address pairs for the sender and target, as the comments in the declaration illustrate. Because the size of each address field can be determined from information in the fixed fields of the header, the location of each address field can be computed efficiently. In-line functions *SHA*, *SPA*, *THA*, and *TPA* perform the computations. Each function takes a single argument that gives the address of an ARP packet, and returns the location of one of the address fields in that packet.

4.5 ARP Output Processing

4.5.1 Searching The ARP Cache

As we have seen, the network interface code that handles output uses ARP to resolve IP addresses into the corresponding hardware addresses. In particular, the network output process calls procedure *arpfind* to search the ARP cache and find an entry that matches a given protocol address.

```
/* arpfind.c - sendarp */

#include <conf.h>
#include <kernel.h>
#include <network.h>


/*------------------------------------------------------------------
 * arpfind - find an ARP entry given a protocol address and interface
 *------------------------------------------------------------------
 */
struct arpentry *arpfind(pra, prtype, pni)
char            *pra;
int             prtype;
struct netif    *pni;
{
        struct arpentry *pae;
        int             i;

        for (i=0; i<ARP_TSIZE; ++i) {
                pae = &arptable[i];
                if (pae->ae_state == AS_FREE)
                        continue;
```

```
                    if (pae->ae_prtype == prtype &&
                        pae->ae_pni == pni &&
                        blkequ(pae->ae_pra, pra, pae->ae_prlen))
                            return pae;
        }
        return 0;
}
```

Argument *pra* points to a high-level (protocol) address that must be resolved, argument *prtype* gives the type of the address (using the standard ARP values for protocol types), and argument *pni* points to a network interface structure. *Arpfind* searches the ARP cache sequentially until it finds an entry that matches the specified address. It returns a pointer to the entry.

Recall that our design places all ARP bindings in a single table. For technologies like Ethernet, where hardware addresses are globally unique, a single table does not present a problem. However, some technologies allow reuse of hardware addresses on separate physical networks. Thus, a gateway might have multiple occurrences of a given hardware address (e.g., address 5) in its cache. Argument *pni* insures that *arpfind* will select bindings that correspond to the correct network interface. Conceptually, our implementation uses the combination of a network interface number and hardware address to uniquely identify an entry in the table.

4.5.2 Broadcasting An ARP Request

Once an ARP cache entry has been allocated for a given IP address, the network interface software calls procedure *arpsend* to format and broadcast an ARP request for the corresponding hardware address.

```
/* arpsend.c - arpsend */

#include <conf.h>
#include <kernel.h>
#include <network.h>


/*------------------------------------------------------------------------
 * arpsend - broadcast an ARP request
 *        N.B. Assumes interrupts disabled
 *------------------------------------------------------------------------
 */
int arpsend(pae)
struct  arpentry        *pae;
{
        struct  netif   *pni = pae->ae_pni;
        struct  ep      *pep;
        struct  arp     *parp;
        int     arplen;

        pep = (struct ep *) getbuf(Net.netpool);
        if (pep == SYSERR)
                return SYSERR;
        blkcopy(pep->ep_dst, pni->ni_hwb.ha_addr, pae->ae_hwlen);
        pep->ep_type = EPT_ARP;
        parp = (struct arp *) pep->ep_data;
        parp->ar_hwtype = hs2net(pae->ae_hwtype);
        parp->ar_prtype = hs2net(pae->ae_prtype);
        parp->ar_hwlen = pae->ae_hwlen;
        parp->ar_prlen = pae->ae_prlen;
        parp->ar_op = hs2net(AR_REQUEST);
        blkcopy(SHA(parp), pni->ni_hwa.ha_addr, pae->ae_hwlen);
        blkcopy(SPA(parp), pni->ni_ip, pae->ae_prlen);
        bzero(THA(parp), pae->ae_hwlen);
        blkcopy(TPA(parp), pae->ae_pra, pae->ae_prlen);
        arplen = sizeof(struct arp) + 2*(parp->ar_hwlen + parp->ar_prlen);
        write(pni->ni_dev, pep, arplen);
        return OK;
}
```

Arpsend takes a pointer to an entry in the cache as an argument, forms an ARP request for the IP address in that entry, and transmits the request. The code is much simpler than it appears. After allocating a buffer to hold the packet, *arpsend* fills in each field, obtaining most of the needed information from the arp cache entry given by argument *pae*. It uses the hardware broadcast for the packet destination address and specifies that the packet is an ARP request (*AR_REQUEST*). After the hardware and protocol address length fields have been assigned, *arpsend* can use in-line procedures *SHA*, *SPA*, *THA*, and *TPA* to compute the locations in the ARP packet of the variable-length address fields.

After *arpsend* creates the ARP request packet, it invokes system call *write* to send it.

4.5.3 Output Procedure

Procedure *netwrite* accepts packets for transmission on a given network interface.

```
/* netwrite.c - netwrite */

#include <conf.h>
#include <kernel.h>
#include <network.h>
#include <q.h>

struct   arpentry         *arpalloc(), *arpfind();

/*------------------------------------------------------------------------
 * netwrite - write a packet on an interface, using ARP if needed
 *------------------------------------------------------------------------
 */
int netwrite(pni, pep, len)
struct   netif    *pni;
struct   ep       *pep;
int               len;
{
        struct   arpentry         *pae;
        STATWORD                  ps;
        int                       i;

        if (pni->ni_state != NIS_UP) {
                freebuf(pep);
                return SYSERR;
        }
        pep->ep_len = len;
        if (pni == &nif[NI_LOCAL])
                return local_out(pep);
        else if (isbrc(pep->ep_nexthop)) {
                blkcopy(pep->ep_dst, pni->ni_hwb.ha_addr, EP_ALEN);
                write(pni->ni_dev, pep, len);
                return OK;
        }
```

```
        /* else, look up the protocol address... */

        disable(ps);
        pae = arpfind(pep->ep_nexthop, pep->ep_type, pni);
        if (pae && pae->ae_state == AS_RESOLVED) {
                blkcopy(pep->ep_dst, pae->ae_hwa, pae->ae_hwlen);
                restore(ps);
                write(pni->ni_dev, pep, len);
                return OK;
        }
        if (pae == 0) {
                pae = arpalloc();
                pae->ae_hwtype = AR_HARDWARE;
                pae->ae_prtype = EPT_IP;
                pae->ae_hwlen = EP_ALEN;
                pae->ae_prlen = IP_ALEN;
                pae->ae_pni = pni;
                pae->ae_queue = EMPTY;
                blkcopy(pae->ae_pra, pep->ep_nexthop, pae->ae_prlen);
                pae->ae_attempts = 0;
                pae->ae_ttl = ARP_RESEND;
                arpsend(pae);
        }
        if (pae->ae_queue < 1)
                pae->ae_queue = newq(ARP_QSIZE, QF_NOWAIT);
        if (enq(pae->ae_queue, pep, 0) < 0)
                freebuf(pep);
        restore(ps);
        return OK;
}
```

Netwrite calls *arpfind* to look up an entry in the cache for the destination address. If
the entry has been resolved, *netwrite* copies the hardware address into the packet and
calls *write* to transmit the packet. If the entry has not been resolved and is not pending,
netwrite calls *arpalloc* to allocate an ARP request. It then fills in fields in the ARP entry, and calls *arpsend* to broadcast the request.

   Because *netwrite* must return to its caller without delay, it leaves packets awaiting
address resolution on the queue of packets associated with the ARP cache entry for that
address. It checks to see if a queue exists. If one is needed, it calls *newq* to create a
queue. Finally, *netwrite* calls *enq* to enqueue the packet for transmission later, after the
address has been resolved. If the queue is full, *netwrite* discards the packet.

4.6 ARP Input Processing

4.6.1 Adding Resolved Entries To The Table

ARP input processing uses two utility procedures, *arpadd* and *arpqsend*. *Arpadd* takes information from an ARP packet that has arrived over the network, allocates an entry in the cache, and fills the entry with information from the packet. Because it fills in both the hardware and protocol address fields, *arpadd* assigns *AS_RESOLVED* to the entry's state field. It also assigns the entry's time-to-live field and the maximum timeout value, *ARP_TIMEOUT*.

```
/* arpadd.c - arpadd */

#include <conf.h>
#include <kernel.h>
#include <network.h>

struct   arpentry        *arpalloc();

/*-------------------------------------------------------------------
 * arpadd - Add a RESOLVED entry to the ARP cache
 *       N.B. Assumes interrupts disabled
 *-------------------------------------------------------------------
 */
struct  arpentry *arpadd(pni, parp)
struct  netif    *pni;
struct  arp      *parp;
{
        struct   arpentry         *pae;

        pae = arpalloc();

        pae->ae_hwtype = parp->ar_hwtype;
        pae->ae_prtype = parp->ar_prtype;
        pae->ae_hwlen = parp->ar_hwlen;
        pae->ae_prlen = parp->ar_prlen;
        pae->ae_pni = pni;
        pae->ae_queue = EMPTY;
        blkcopy(pae->ae_hwa, SHA(parp), parp->ar_hwlen);
        blkcopy(pae->ae_pra, SPA(parp), parp->ar_prlen);
        pae->ae_ttl = ARP_TIMEOUT;
        pae->ae_state = AS_RESOLVED;
        return pae;
}
```

4.6.2 Sending Waiting Packets

We have seen that the ARP output procedures enqueue packets that are waiting for address resolution. When an ARP packet arrives that contains information needed to resolve an entry, the ARP input procedure calls *arpqsend* to transmit the waiting packets.

```
/* arpqsend.c - arpqsend */

#include <conf.h>
#include <kernel.h>
#include <network.h>

/*------------------------------------------------------------------------
 * arpqsend - write packets queued waiting for an ARP resolution
 *------------------------------------------------------------------------
 */
void arpqsend(pae)
struct   arpentry       *pae;
{
        struct   ep       *pep;
        struct   netif    *pni;

        if (pae->ae_queue == EMPTY)
                return;

        pni = pae->ae_pni;
        while (pep = (struct ep *)deq(pae->ae_queue))
                netwrite(pni, pep, pep->ep_len);
        freeq(pae->ae_queue);
        pae->ae_queue = EMPTY;
}
```

Arpqsend does not transmit waiting packets directly. Instead, it iterates through the queue extracting packets and calling *netwrite* to place each packet on the network output queue (where the network device will extract and transmit it). Once it has removed all packets, *arpqsend* calls *freeq* to deallocate the queue itself.

4.6.3 ARP Input Procedure

As we have seen, when an ARP packet arrives, the network device driver passes it to procedure *arp_in* for processing.

```
/* arp_in.c - arp_in */

#include <conf.h>
#include <kernel.h>
#include <network.h>

struct  arpentry         *arpfind(), *arpadd();

/*------------------------------------------------------------------------
 *  arp_in  -  handle ARP packet coming in from Ethernet network
 *      N.B. - Called by ni_in-- SHOULD NOT BLOCK
 *------------------------------------------------------------------------
 */
int arp_in(pni, pep)
struct  netif   *pni;
struct  ep      *pep;
{
        struct  arp             *parp = (struct arp *)pep->ep_data;
        struct  arpentry        *pae;
        int                     arplen;

        parp->ar_hwtype = net2hs(parp->ar_hwtype);
        parp->ar_prtype = net2hs(parp->ar_prtype);
        parp->ar_op = net2hs(parp->ar_op);

        if (parp->ar_hwtype != pni->ni_hwtype ||
            parp->ar_prtype != EPT_IP) {
                freebuf(pep);
                return OK;
        }

        if (pae = arpfind(SPA(parp), parp->ar_prtype, pni)) {
                blkcopy(pae->ae_hwa, SHA(parp), pae->ae_hwlen);
                pae->ae_ttl = ARP_TIMEOUT;
        }
        if (!blkequ(TPA(parp), pni->ni_ip, IP_ALEN)) {
                freebuf(pep);
                return OK;
        }
        if (pae == 0)
                pae = arpadd(pni, parp);
        if (pae->ae_state == AS_PENDING) {
                pae->ae_state = AS_RESOLVED;
                arpqsend(pae);
        }
```

```
    if (parp->ar_op == AR_REQUEST) {
            parp->ar_op = AR_REPLY;
            blkcopy(TPA(parp), SPA(parp), parp->ar_prlen);
            blkcopy(THA(parp), SHA(parp), parp->ar_hwlen);
            blkcopy(pep->ep_dst, THA(parp), EP_ALEN);
            blkcopy(SHA(parp), pni->ni_hwa.ha_addr,
                    pni->ni_hwa.ha_len);
            blkcopy(SPA(parp), pni->ni_ip, IP_ALEN);

            parp->ar_hwtype = hs2net(parp->ar_hwtype);
            parp->ar_prtype = hs2net(parp->ar_prtype);
            parp->ar_op = hs2net(parp->ar_op);

            arplen = sizeof(struct arp) +
                    2*(parp->ar_prlen + parp->ar_hwlen);

            write(pni->ni_dev, pep, arplen);
    } else
            freebuf(pep);
    return OK;
}
```

The protocol standard specifies that ARP should discard any messages that specify a high-level protocol the machine does not recognize. Thus, our implementation of *arp_in* only recognizes ARP packets that specify a protocol address type *IP* and a hardware address type that matches the hardware type of the network interface over which the packet arrives. If packets arrive containing other address types, ARP discards them.

When processing a valid packet, *arp_in* calls *arpfind* to search the ARP cache for an entry that matches the sender's IP address. The protocol specifies that a receiver should first use incoming requests to satisfy pending entries (i.e., it should use the sender's addresses to update its cache). Thus, if a matching entry is found, *arp_in* updates the hardware address from the sender's hardware address field in the packet and sets the timeout field of the entry to *ARP_TIMEOUT*.

The protocol also specifies that if the incoming packet contains a request directed at the receiver, the receiver *must* add the sender's address to its cache (even if the receiver did not have an entry pending for that address). Thus, *arp_in* checks to see if the target IP address matches the local machine's IP address. If it does, *arp_in* calls *arpadd* to insert it. After inserting an entry in the cache, *arp_in* checks to see whether the address was pending resolution. If so, it calls *arpqsend* to transmit the queue of waiting packets.

Finally, *arp_in* checks to see if the packet contained a request. If it does, *arp_in* forms a reply by interchanging the target and sender address fields, supplying the requested hardware address, and changing the operation from *AR_REQUEST* to *AR_REPLY*. It transmits the reply directly.

4.7 ARP Cache Management

So far, we have focused on input and output processing. However, management of the ARP cache requires coordination between the input and output software. It also requires periodic computation independent of either input or output. The next sections explain the cache policy and show how the software enforces it.

4.7.1 Allocating A Cache Entry

If a process (e.g., the IP process) needs to send a datagram but no entry is present in the ARP cache for the destination IP address, IP must create a new cache entry, broadcast a request, and enqueue the packet awaiting transmission. Procedure *arpalloc* chooses an entry in the ARP cache that will be used for a new binding.

```
/* arpalloc.c - arpalloc */

#include <conf.h>
#include <kernel.h>
#include <proc.h>
#include <network.h>

void arpdq();

/*-------------------------------------------------------------------
 * arpalloc - allocate an entry in the ARP table
 *        N.B. Assumes interrupts DISABLED
 *-------------------------------------------------------------------
 */
struct arpentry *arpalloc()
{
        static  int      aenext = 0;
        struct  arpentry *pae;
        int      i;

        for (i=0; i<ARP_TSIZE; ++i) {
                if (arptable[aenext].ae_state == AS_FREE)
                        break;
                aenext = (aenext + 1) % ARP_TSIZE;
        }
        pae = & arptable[aenext];
        aenext = (aenext + 1) % ARP_TSIZE;

        if (pae->ae_state == AS_PENDING && pae->ae_queue >= 0)
                arpdq(pae);
        pae->ae_state = AS_PENDING;
        return pae;
}
```

Arpalloc implements the cache replacement policy because it must decide which existing entry to eliminate from a full cache when finding space for a new entry. We have chosen a simple replacement policy.

> *When allocating space for a new addition to the ARP cache, choose an unused entry in the table if one exists. Otherwise, delete entries in a round-robin fashion.*

That is, each time it selects an entry to delete, the cache manager moves to the next entry. It cycles around the table completely before returning to the new entry. Thus, once it deletes an entry and reuses it for a new binding, the cache manager will leave that entry in place until it has been forced to delete and replace all other bindings.

In considering an ARP cache policy, it is important to remember that a full cache is always undesirable because it means the system is operating at saturation. If a datagram transmission causes the system to insert a new binding in the cache, the system must delete an existing binding. When the old, deleted binding is needed again, ARP will delete yet another binding and broadcast a request. In the worst case, ARP will broadcast a request each time it needs to deliver a datagram. We assume that a system manager will detect such situations and reconfigure the system with a larger cache. Thus, preemption of existing entries will seldom occur, so our simple policy works well in practice.

To implement the policy, *arpalloc* maintains a static integer, *aenext*. The for-loop in *arpalloc* searches the entire table, starting at the entry with index *aenext*, wrapping around to the beginning of the table, and finishing back at position *aenext*. The search stops immediately if an unused entry is found. If no unused space remains in the cache, *arpalloc* removes the old entry with index *aenext*. Finally, *arpalloc* increments *aenext* so the next search will start beyond the newly allocated entry.

4.7.2 Periodic Cache Maintenance

Our design arranges to have an independent timer process execute procedure *arptimer* periodically.

```
/* arptimer.c - arptimer */

#include <conf.h>
#include <kernel.h>
#include <network.h>

/*------------------------------------------------------------------------
 * arptimer - Iterate through ARP cache, aging (possibly removing) entries
 *------------------------------------------------------------------------
 */
void arptimer(gran)
int     gran;                                /* time since last iteration    */
{
        struct arpentry *pae;
        STATWORD        ps;
        int             i;

        disable(ps);    /* mutex */

        for (i=0; i<ARP_TSIZE; ++i) {
                if ((pae = &arptable[i])->ae_state == AS_FREE)
                        continue;
                if ((pae->ae_ttl -= gran) <= 0)
                        if (pae->ae_state == AS_RESOLVED)
                                pae->ae_state = AS_FREE;
                        else if (++pae->ae_attempts > ARP_MAXRETRY) {
                                pae->ae_state = AS_FREE;
                                arpdq(pae);
                        } else {
                                pae->ae_ttl = ARP_RESEND;
                                arpsend(pae);
                        }
        }
        restore(ps);
}
```

When it calls *arptimer*, the timer process passes an argument that specifies the time elapsed since the previous call. *Arptimer* uses the elapsed time to "age" entries in the cache. It iterates through each entry and decrements the time-to-live field in the entry by *gran*, where *gran* is the number of seconds since the last iteration. If the time-to-live becomes zero or negative, *arptimer* removes the entry from the cache. Removing a resolved entry merely means changing the state to *AS_FREE*, which allows *arpalloc* to use the entry the next time it needs one. If the time-to-live expires on an entry that is pending resolution, *arptimer* examines field *ae_attempts* to see whether the request has been rebroadcast *ARP_MAXRETRY* times. If not, *arptimer* calls *arpsend* to broadcast the request again. If the request has already been rebroadcast *ARP_MAXRETRY* times, *arptimer* deallocates the queue of waiting packets and removes the entry.

4.7.3 Deallocating Queued Packets

If the ARP cache is full, the existing entry *arpalloc* selects to remove may have a queue of outgoing packets associated with it. If so, *arpalloc* calls *arpdq* to remove packets from the list and discard them.

```
/* arpdq.c - arpdq */

#include <conf.h>
#include <kernel.h>
#include <network.h>

/*------------------------------------------------------------------------
 * arpdq - destroy an arp queue that has expired
 *------------------------------------------------------------------------
 */
void arpdq(pae)
struct   arpentry *pae;
{
        struct   ep        *pep;
        struct   ip        *pip;

        if (pae->ae_queue < 0)              /* nothing to do */
                return;

        while (pep = (struct ep *)deq(pae->ae_queue)) {
                if (gateway && pae->ae_prtype == EPT_IP) {
                        pip = (struct ip *)pep->ep_data;
                        icmp(ICT_DESTUR, ICC_HOSTUR, pip->ip_src, pep);
                } else
                        freebuf(pep);
        }
        freeq(pae->ae_queue);
        pae->ae_queue = EMPTY;
}
```

Arpdq iterates through the queue of packets associated with an ARP cache entry and discards them. If the packet is an IP datagram and the machine is a gateway, *arpdq* calls procedure *icmp* to generate an ICMP *destination unreachable* message for the datagram it discards. Finally, *arpdq* calls *freeq* to release the queue itself.

4.8 ARP Initialization

The system calls procedure *arpinit* once, at system startup. *Arpinit* creates *rarpsem*, the mutual exclusion semaphore used with RARP, and assigns state *AS_FREE* to all entries in the ARP cache. In addition, *arpinit* initializes a few data items for the related RARP protocol; these are irrelevant to the code in this chapter. Note that *arpinit* does not initialize the timer process or set up calls to *arptimer*. These details are handled separately because our design uses a single timer process for many protocols.

```
/* arpinit.c - arpinit */

#include <conf.h>
#include <kernel.h>
#include <proc.h>
#include <network.h>

/*------------------------------------------------------------------------
 * arpinit  -  initialize data structures for ARP processing
 *------------------------------------------------------------------------
 */
void arpinit()
{
        struct  arpent  *atabptr;
        int     i, j;

        rarpsem = screate(1);
        rarppid = BADPID;

        for (i=0; i<ARP_TSIZE; ++i)
                arptable[i].ae_state = AS_FREE;
}

int     rarpsem;
int     rarppid;

struct  arpentry        arptable[ARP_TSIZE];
```

4.9 ARP Configuration Parameters

When building ARP software, the programmer configures the system by choosing values for parameters such as:

- Size of the ARP cache
- Timeout interval the client waits for an ARP response
- Number of times a client retries a request
- Time interval between retries
- Timeout (time-to-live) for a cache entry
- Size of packet retransmission queue

Typical designs use symbolic constants for parameters such as cache size, allowing the system manager to change the configuration for specific installations. For installations in which managers need more control, utility programs can be written that allow a manager to make changes at run time. For example, in some software it is possible for a manager to examine the ARP cache, delete an entry, or change values (e.g., the time-to-live field). However, some parameters cannot be changed easily. For example, many programmers choose between fixed retransmission delays or exponential backoff and embed their choice in the code itself, as in our example.

4.10 Summary

Our implementation of ARP uses a single, global cache to hold bindings obtained from all networks. It permits multiple packets to be enqueued waiting for an address to be resolved, and uses an independent timer to age cache entries. Eventually, entries timeout. If the cache is completely full when a new entry must be inserted, an old entry must be discarded. Our design uses a round-robin replacement policy, implemented with a global pointer that moves to the next cache entry each time one is taken. We reviewed the declarations of data structures that comprise the cache and the procedures that operate on them.

FOR FURTHER STUDY

Plummer [RFC 826] defines the ARP standard, while Clark [RFC 814] discusses addresses and bindings in general. Parr [RFC 1029] considers fault tolerant address resolution.

EXERCISES

4.1   What network hardware uses ARP?

4.2   Sketch the design of address binding software for a network interface that does not use ARP.

4.3   What is the chief disadvantage of using a single table to hold the ARP cache in a gateway? What is the chief advantage?

4.4   Suppose a site decided to use ARP on its proNET-10 ring networks (even though it is possible to bind proNET-10 addresses without ARP). Would our implementation operate correctly on a gateway that connected multiple rings? Hint: proNET-10 addresses are only unique within a given network.

4.5   The Ethernet hardware specification enforces a minimum packet size of *60* octets. Examine the Ethernet device driver software in an operating system. How does the driver send an ARP packet, which is shorter than *60* octets?

4.6   Would users perceive any difference in performance if the ARP software did not allow multiple packets to be enqueued for a pending ARP binding?

4.7   How does one choose reasonable values for *ARP_MAXRETRY*, *ARP_TIMEOUT*, and the granularity of aging?

4.8   ARP is especially susceptible to ''spoofing'' because an arbitrary machine can answer an ARP broadcast. Revise the example software by adding checks that detect when (a) two or more machines answer a request for a given IP address, (b) a machine receives an ARP binding for its own IP address, and (c) a single machine answers requests for multiple IP addresses.

5

IP: Global Software Organization

5.1 Introduction

This chapter considers the organization of software that implements the Internet Protocol (IP). While the functionality IP provides may seem simple, intricacies make implementing the software complicated and subtleties make it difficult to insure correctness. To help explain IP without becoming overwhelmed with all the parts at once, we will consider the implementation in three chapters. This chapter presents data structures and describes the overall software organization. It discusses the conceptual operation of IP software and the flow of datagrams through the IP layer. Later chapters, which provide details on routing and error handling, show how various pieces of IP software use these data structures.

5.2 The Central Switch

Conceptually, IP is a central switching point in the protocol software. It accepts incoming datagrams from the network interface software as well as outgoing datagrams that higher-level protocols generate. After routing a datagram, IP either sends it to one of the network interfaces or to a higher-level protocol on the local machine.

In a host, it seems natural to think of IP software in two distinct parts: one that handles input and one that handles output. The input part uses the *PROTO* field of the IP header to decide which higher-level protocol module should receive an incoming datagram. The output part uses the local routing table to choose a next hop for outgoing datagrams.

Despite its intuitive appeal, separating IP input and output makes the interaction between IP and the higher-level protocol software awkward. In addition, IP software must work in gateways, where routing is more complex than in hosts. In particular, gateway software cannot easily be partitioned into input and output parts because a gateway must route an arriving datagram on to its next hop. Thus, IP may generate output while handling an incoming datagram. A gateway must also generate ICMP error messages when arriving datagrams cause errors, which further blurs the distinction between input and output. In the discussion that follows, we will concentrate on gateways and treat hosts as a special case.

5.3 IP Software Design

To keep the IP software simple and uniform, our implementation uses three main organizational techniques:

- **Uniform Input Queue and Uniform Routing.** The IP process uses the same input queue style for all datagrams it must handle, independent of whether they arrive from the network or are generated by the local machine. IP extracts each datagram from a queue and routes it without regard to the datagram's source. A uniform input structure results in simplicity: IP does not need a special case in the code for locally generated datagrams. Furthermore, because IP uses a single routing algorithm to route all datagrams, humans can easily understand the route a datagram will take.
- **Independent IP Process.** The IP software executes as a single, self-contained process. Using a process for IP keeps the software easy to understand and modify. It allows us to create IP software that does not depend on hardware interrupts or procedure calls by application programs.
- **Local Host Interface.** To avoid making delivery to the local machine a special case, our implementation creates a pseudo-network interface for local delivery. Recall that the local interface has the same structure as other network interfaces, but corresponds to the local protocol software instead of a physical network. The IP algorithm routes each datagram and passes it to a network interface, including datagrams destined for the local machine. When a conventional network interface receives a datagram, it sends the datagram over a physical network. When the local interface receives a datagram, it uses the *PROTO* field to determine which protocol software module on the local machine should receive the datagram. Thus, IP views all routing as uniform and symmetric: it accepts a datagram from any interface and routes it to some other interface; no exceptions need to be made for datagrams generated by (or sent to) the local machine.

Although our desire to build gateways motivates many of the design decisions, a gateway design works equally well for hosts, and allows us to use the same code for both hosts and gateways. Obviously, combining a uniform routing algorithm with a local machine interface eliminates several special cases in the code. More important, because the local machine is a valid destination controlled by entries in the routing table, it is possible to add access protections that permit managers to enforce policies on delivery. For example, managers can allow or disallow exchange of information between two applications on a given machine as easily as they can allow or disallow communication between applications on separate machines.

5.4 IP Software Organization And Datagram Flow

Chapter 2 described the conceptual organization of IP software, and showed datagram flow for both input and output; this section expands the description and fills in details. Recall that IP consists of a single process and a set of network interface queues through which datagrams must be sent to that process. IP repeatedly extracts a datagram from one of the queues, uses a routing table to choose a next hop for the datagram, and sends the datagram to the appropriate network output process for transmission.

5.4.1 A Policy For Selecting Incoming Datagrams

Chapter 3 stated that each network interface, including the pseudo-network interface had its own queue of datagrams sent to IP. Figure 5.1 illustrates the flow.

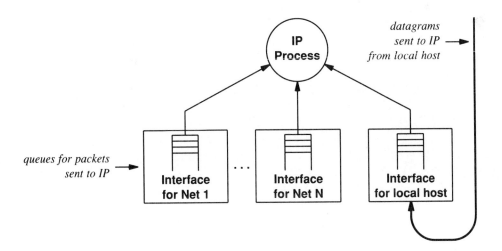

Figure 5.1 IP must select the next datagram for processing from the queues associated with network interfaces. The pseudo-network interface provides a queue used for datagrams generated locally.

If multiple datagrams are waiting in the input queues, the IP process must select one of them to route. The choice of which datagram IP will route determines the behavior of the system:

> *The IP code that chooses a datagram to route implements an impor-*
> *tant policy – it decides the relative priorities of datagram sources.*

For example, if IP always selects from the pseudo-network interface queue first, it gives highest priority to outgoing datagrams generated by the local machine. If it only chooses the pseudo-network queue when all others are empty, it gives highest priority to datagrams that arrive from the network and lowest priority to datagrams generated locally.

It should be obvious that neither extreme is desirable. On one hand, assigning high priority to arriving datagrams means that local software can be blocked arbitrarily long while waiting for IP to route datagrams. For a gateway attached to busy networks, the delay can prevent the local system from communicating. On the other hand, giving priority to datagrams generated locally means that any application program running on the local machine takes precedent over IP traffic that arrives from the network. If an error causes an application program to emit datagrams continuously, the outgoing datagrams will prevent arriving datagrams from reaching the network management software. Thus, the manager will not be able to use network management tools to correct the problem.

A correct policy assigns priority fairly and allows both incoming and outgoing traffic to be routed with equal priority. Our implementation achieves fairness by selecting datagrams in a *round-robin* manner. That is, it selects and routes one datagram from a queue, and then moves on to check the next queue. If K queues contain datagrams waiting to be routed, IP will process one datagram from each of the K queues before processing a second datagram from any of them.

Procedure *ipgetp* implements the round-robin selection policy.

```
/* ipgetp.c - ipgetp */

#include <conf.h>
#include <kernel.h>
#include <network.h>

static  int     ifnext = NI_LOCAL;

/*------------------------------------------------------------------------
 * ipgetp  --  choose next IP input queue and extract a packet
 *------------------------------------------------------------------------
 */
struct ep *ipgetp(pifnum)
int     *pifnum;
```

```
{
        struct   ep        *pep;
        int                i;

        recvclr();        /* make sure no old messages are waiting */
        while (TRUE) {
                for (i=0; i < Net.nif; ++i, ++ifnext) {
                        if (ifnext >= Net.nif)
                                ifnext = 0;
                        if (nif[ifnext].ni_state == NIS_DOWN)
                                continue;
                        if (pep = NIGET(ifnext)) {
                                *pifnum = ifnext;
                                return pep;
                        }
                }
                ifnext = receive();
        }
        /* can't reach here */
}
```

As the code shows, the static variable *ifnext* serves as an index into the array of interfaces. It iterates through the entire set of network interface structures. At each interface, it checks the state variable *ni_state* to make sure the interface is enabled. As soon as *ipgetp* finds an enabled interface with datagrams waiting, it uses macro *NIGET* to extract and return the first datagram. The next call to *ipgetp* will continue searching where the previous one left off.

5.4.2 Allowing The IP Process To Block

Procedure *ipgetp* contains a subtle optimization:

> *When all input queues are empty, the IP process blocks in procedure* ipgetp. *Once a datagram arrives, the IP process resumes execution and immediately examines the interface on which the datagram arrived.*

To understand the optimization, it is necessary to understand two facts. First, the device driver associated with a particular interface sends the IP process a message whenever it deposits a datagram on its input queue. Second, the loop in *ipgetp* ends with a call to *receive*. After *ipgetp* iterates through all network interfaces without finding any datagrams, it calls *receive*, which blocks until a message arrives. The message contains the index of an interface on which a datagram has arrived. *Ipgetp* assigns the interface index to *ifnext* and begins the iteration again.

Now that we understand the IP selection policy, we can examine the structure of the IP process. The basic algorithm is straightforward. IP repeatedly calls *ipgetp* to select a datagram, calls a procedure to compute the next-hop address, and deposits the datagram on a queue associated with the network interface over which the datagram must be sent.

Despite its conceptual simplicity, many details complicate the code. For example, if the datagram has arrived from a network, IP must verify that the datagram checksum is correct. If the gateway does not have a route to the specified destination, it must generate an ICMP *destination unreachable* message. If the routing table specifies that the datagram should be sent to a destination on the network over which it arrived, IP must generate an ICMP *redirect* message. Finally, IP must handle the special case of a directed broadcast by sending a copy of the datagram on the specified network and delivering a copy to higher-level protocol software on the gateway itself. The IP process begins execution at procedure *ipproc*.

```
/* ipproc.c - ipproc */

#include <conf.h>
#include <kernel.h>
#include <network.h>

struct  ep      *ipgetp();
struct  route   *rtget();

/*------------------------------------------------------------------------
 *  ipproc  -  handle an IP datagram coming in from the network
 *------------------------------------------------------------------------
 */
PROCESS ipproc()
{
        struct  ep      *pep;
        struct  ip      *pip;
        struct  route   *prt;
        Bool            nonlocal;
        int             ifnum, rdtype;

        ippid = getpid();       /* so others can find us      */

        signal(Net.sema);       /* signal initialization done  */

        while (TRUE) {
                pep = ipgetp(&ifnum);
                pip = (struct ip *)pep->ep_data;
```

```
if ((pip->ip_verlen>>4) != IP_VERSION) {
        IpInHdrErrors++;
        freebuf(pep);
        continue;
}
if (IP_CLASSD(pip->ip_dst) || IP_CLASSE(pip->ip_dst)) {
        IpInAddrErrors++;
        freebuf(pep);
        continue;
}
if (ifnum != NI_LOCAL) {
        if (cksum(pip, IP_HLEN(pip)>>1)) {
                IpInHdrErrors++;
                freebuf(pep);
                continue;
        }
        ipnet2h(pip);
}
prt = rtget(pip->ip_dst, (ifnum == NI_LOCAL));

if (prt == NULL) {
        if (gateway)
                icmp(ICT_DESTUR, ICC_NETUR,
                                pip->ip_src, pep);
        else {
                IpOutNoRoutes++;
                freebuf(pep);
        }
        continue;
}
nonlocal = ifnum != NI_LOCAL && prt->rt_ifnum != NI_LOCAL;
if (!gateway && nonlocal) {
        IpInAddrErrors++;
        freebuf(pep);
        rtfree(prt);
        continue;
}
if (nonlocal)
        IpForwDatagrams++;
/* fill in src IP, if we're the sender */

if (ifnum == NI_LOCAL)
        if (blkequ(pip->ip_src, ip_anyaddr, IP_ALEN))
                if (prt->rt_ifnum == NI_LOCAL)
```

```
                                        blkcopy(pip->ip_src, pip->ip_dst,
                                                IP_ALEN);
                        else
                                        blkcopy(pip->ip_src,
                                                nif[prt->rt_ifnum].ni_ip,
                                                IP_ALEN);
                if (--(pip->ip_ttl) == 0 && prt->rt_ifnum != NI_LOCAL) {
                        IpInHdrErrors++;
                        icmp(ICT_TIMEX, ICC_TIMEX, pip->ip_src, pep);
                        rtfree(prt);
                        continue;
                }
                pip->ip_cksum = 0;
                pip->ip_cksum = cksum(pip, IP_HLEN(pip)>>1);

                ipdbc(ifnum, pep, prt);  /* handle directed broadcasts  */
                ipredirect(pep, ifnum, prt); /* do redirect, if needed  */
                if (prt->rt_metric != 0)
                        ipputp(prt->rt_ifnum, prt->rt_gw, pep);
                else
                        ipputp(prt->rt_ifnum, pip->ip_dst, pep);
                rtfree(prt);
        }
}

int     ippid, gateway, bsdbrc;
```

After storing its process id in global variable *ippid* and signaling the network initialization semaphore, *ipproc* enters an infinite loop. During each iteration of the loop, *ipproc* processes one datagram. It calls *ipgetp* to select a datagram and set *ifnum* to the index of the interface from which the datagram was obtained. After checking the datagram version, and verifying that the datagram does not contain a class *D* or *E* address, *ipproc* calls *cksum* to verify the checksum (unless the datagram was generated on the local machine).

Once it has obtained a valid datagram, *ipproc* calls procedure *rtget* to route the datagram. The next chapter reviews the details of *rtget*; for now, it is only important to understand that *rtget* computes a route and returns a pointer to a structure that describes the route. If no route exists, *ipproc* calls procedure *icmp*† to form and send an ICMP *destination unreachable* message.

---

†Chapter 7 describes the implementation of *icmp*.

Ipproc must fill in a correct source address for datagrams that originate on the local machine. To do so, it examines the datagram to see if higher-level protocol software has specified a fixed source address. If not, *ipproc* fills in the source address field. Following the standard, *ipproc* assigns the datagram source the IP address of the network interface over which the datagram will be sent. If the route refers to the local host interface (i.e., the datagram is being routed from the local machine back to the local machine), *ipproc* copies the datagram destination address into the source address field.

Once routing is complete, *ipproc* decrements the time-to-live counter (*ip_ttl*) and recomputes the datagram checksum. If the time-to-live field reaches zero, *ipproc* generates an ICMP *time exceeded* message.

Ipproc calls procedure *ipdbc* to handle directed broadcasts. *Ipdbc*, shown in section 5.4.5, creates a copy of those directed broadcast datagrams destined for the local machine, and sends a copy to the local software. *Ipproc* transmits the original copy to the specified network.

Ipproc also generates ICMP *redirect* messages. To determine if such a message is needed, *ipproc* compares the interface from which the datagram was obtained to the interface to which it was routed. If they are the same, a redirect is needed. *Ipproc* examines the network's subnet to determine whether it should send a *network redirect* or a *host redirect*.

Finally, *ipproc* examines the routing metric to determine whether it should deliver the datagram to its destination or send it to the next-hop address. A routing metric of zero means the gateway can deliver the datagram directly; any larger value means the gateway should send the datagram to the next-hop address. After selecting either the next-hop address or the destination address, *ipproc* calls *ipputp* to insert the datagram on one of the network output queues.

5.4.3 Definitions Of Constants Used By IP

File *ip.h* contains definitions of symbolic constants used in the IP software. It also defines the format of an IP datagram with structure *ip*.

```
/* ip.h - IP_HLEN */

/* Internet Protocol (IP)  Constants and Datagram Format                 */

#define IP_ALEN 4                     /* IP address length in bytes (octets)  */
typedef char IPaddr[IP_ALEN];   /*   internet address                    */

#define IP_CLASSA(x)     ((x[0] & 0x80) == 0x00) /* IP Class A address    */
#define IP_CLASSB(x)     ((x[0] & 0xc0) == 0x80) /* IP Class B address    */
#define IP_CLASSC(x)     ((x[0] & 0xd0) == 0xc0) /* IP Class C address    */
#define IP_CLASSD(x)     ((x[0] & 0xf0) == 0xd0) /* IP Class D address    */
#define IP_CLASSE(x)     ((x[0] & 0xf0) == 0xf0) /* IP Class E address    */

/* Some Assigned Protocol Numbers */

#define IPT_ICMP         1        /* protocol type for ICMP packets       */
#define IPT_TCP          6        /* protocol type for TCP packets        */
#define IPT_EGP          8        /* protocol type for EGP packets        */
#define IPT_UDP          17       /* protocol type for UDP packets        */

struct  ip      {
        char    ip_verlen;      /* IP version & header length (in longs)*/
        char    ip_tos;         /* type of service                      */
        short   ip_len;         /* total packet length (in octets)      */
        short   ip_id;          /* datagram id                          */
        short   ip_fragoff;     /* fragment offset (in 8-octet's)       */
        char    ip_ttl;         /* time to live, in gateway hops        */
        char    ip_proto;       /* IP protocol (see IPT_* above)        */
        short   ip_cksum;       /* header checksum                      */
        IPaddr  ip_src;         /* IP address of source                 */
        IPaddr  ip_dst;         /* IP address of destination            */
        char    ip_data[1];     /* variable length data                 */
};

#define IP_VERSION       4        /* current version value                */
#define IP_MINHLEN       5        /* minimum IP header length (in longs)  */
#define IP_TTL           16       /* Initial time-to-live value           */

#define IP_MF            0x2000  /* more fragments bit                    */
#define IP_DF            0x4000  /* don't fragment bit                    */
#define IP_FRAGOFF       0x1fff  /* fragment offset mask                  */
#define IP_PREC          0xe0    /* precedence portion of TOS             */

/* macro to compute a datagram's header length (in bytes)                */
```

```
#define IP_HLEN(pip)       ((pip->ip_verlen & 0xf)<<2)
#define IPMHLEN            20        /* minimum IP header length (in bytes)  */


/* IP options */
#define IPO_COPY           0x80     /* copy on fragment mask                */
#define IPO_CLASS          0x60     /* option class                         */
#define IPO_NUM            0x17     /* option number                        */


#define IPO_EOOP           0x00     /* end of options                       */
#define IPO_NOP            0x01     /* no operation                         */
#define IPO_SEC            0x82     /* DoD security/compartmentalization    */
#define IPO_LSRCRT         0x83     /* loose source routing                 */
#define IPO_SSRCRT         0x89     /* strict source routing                */
#define IPO_RECRT          0x07     /* record route                         */
#define IPO_STRID          0x88     /* stream ID                            */
#define IPO_TIME           0x44     /* internet timestamp                   */


#define IP_MAXLEN         BPMAXB-EP_HLEN  /* Maximum IP datagram length     */


/* IP process info */

extern  int               ipproc();
#define IPSTK             1000     /* stack size for IP process             */
#define IPPRI             100      /* IP runs at high priority              */
#define IPNAM             "ip"     /* name of IP process                    */
#define IPARGC            0        /* count of args to IP                   */


extern IPaddr   ip_maskall;       /* = 255.255.255.255                      */
extern IPaddr   ip_anyaddr;       /* = 0.0.0.0                              */
extern IPaddr   ip_loopback;      /* = 127.0.0.1                            */


extern  int     ippid, gateway;
```

5.4.4 Checksum Computation

Ipproc uses procedure *cksum* to compute or verify the header checksum. The header checksum treats the header as a sequence of 16-bit integers, and defines the checksum to be the ones complement of the sum of all 16-bit integers in the header. Also, the sum and complement are defined to use ones complement arithmetic.

Most machines compute in twos-complement arithmetic, so accumulating a 16-bit cksum will not produce the desired result. To make it portable and avoid coding in assembler language, procedure *cksum* has been written in C. The implementation uses 32-bit (long) arithmetic to accumulate a sum, and then adds any carry bits into the sum explicitly. Finally, it returns the ones complement of the result.

```
/* cksum.c - cksum */


/*-------------------------------------------------------------------------
 * cksum  -  Return 16-bit ones complement of 16-bit ones complement sum
 *-------------------------------------------------------------------------
 */
short cksum(buf, nwords)
unsigned short  *buf;
int             nwords;
{
        unsigned long   sum;

        for (sum=0; nwords>0; nwords--)
                sum += *buf++;
        sum = (sum >> 16) + (sum & 0xffff);     /* add in carry   */
        sum += (sum >> 16);                      /* maybe one more */
        return ~sum;
}
```

5.4.5 Handling Directed Broadcasts

Whenever a datagram is sent to a directed broadcast address, all machines on the specified destination network must receive a copy. The subtle point to remember is that:

> *Directed broadcast includes both gateways and hosts on the destination network, even if one of those gateways is responsible for forwarding the datagram onto the network.*

However, most network hardware does not deliver a copy of a broadcast packet back to the machine that transmits the broadcast. If a gateway needs a copy of a broadcast datagram, software must take explicit action to keep one. Thus, if a gateway receives a datagram with destination address equal to the directed broadcast address for one of its directly connected networks, the gateway must do two things: (1) make a copy of the datagram for protocol software on the local machine, and (2) broadcast the datagram on the specified network. Procedure *ipdbc* contains the code to handle such broadcasts.

```
/* ipdbc.c - ipdbc */

#include <conf.h>
#include <kernel.h>
#include <network.h>
```

```
struct   route *rtget();

/*-------------------------------------------------------------------------
 * ipdbc - handle IP directed broadcast copying
 *-------------------------------------------------------------------------
 */
void ipdbc(ifnum, pep, prt)
int             ifnum;
struct   ep       *pep;
struct   route    *prt;
{
        struct   ip      *pip = (struct ip *)pep->ep_data;
        struct   ep      *pep2;
        struct   route   *prt2;
        int              len;

        if (prt->rt_ifnum != NI_LOCAL)
                return;                        /* not ours            */
        if (!isbrc(pip->ip_dst))
                return;                        /* not broadcast       */

        prt2 = rtget(pip->ip_dst, RTF_LOCAL);
        if (prt2 == NULL)
                return;
        if (prt2->rt_ifnum == ifnum) {   /* not directed          */
                rtfree(prt2);
                return;
        }

        /* directed broadcast; make a copy */

        /* len = ether header + IP packet */

        len = EP_HLEN + pip->ip_len;
        if (len > EP_MAXLEN)
                pep2 = (struct ep *)getbuf(Net.lrgpool);
        else
                pep2 = (struct ep *)getbuf(Net.netpool);
        if (pep2 == (struct ep *)SYSERR) {
                rtfree(prt2);
                return;
        }
        blkcopy(pep2, pep, len);
        /* send a copy to the net */
```

```
        ipputp(prt2->rt_ifnum, pip->ip_dst, pep2);
        rtfree(prt2);


        return;          /* continue; "pep" goes locally in IP    */
}
```

Ipproc calls *ipdbc* for all datagrams, most of which do not specify directed broadcast. *Ipdbc* begins by checking the source of the datagram because datagrams that originate on the local machine do not need copies. *Ipdbc* then calls *isbrc* to compare the destination address to the directed broadcast addresses for all directly connected networks, because nonbroadcasts do not need copies. For cases that do not need copies, *ipdbc* returns without taking any action; *ipproc* will choose a route and forward the datagram as usual.

Datagrams sent to the directed broadcast address for one of the directly connected networks must be duplicated. One copy must be sent to the local host software, while the other copy is forwarded as usual. To make a copy, *ipdbc* allocates a buffer, choosing from the standard network buffer pool or the pool for large buffers, depending on the datagram size. If the buffer allocation is successful, *ipdbc* copies the datagram into the new buffer and deposits the new buffer on the output port associated with the network interface over which it must be sent. After *ipdbc* returns, *ipproc* passes the original copy to the local machine through the pseudo-network interface.

5.4.6 Recognizing A Broadcast Address

The IP protocol standard specifies three types of broadcast addresses: a local network broadcast address (all 1's), a directed network broadcast address (a class A, B, or C IP address with host portion of all 1's), and a subnet broadcast address (subnetted IP address with host portion all 1's). Unfortunately, when Berkeley incorporated TCP/IP into the BSD UNIX distribution, they decided to use nonstandard broadcast addresses. Sometimes called *Berkeley broadcast*, these forms of broadcast use all 0's in place of all 1's.

While the Berkeley form of broadcast address is definitely nonstandard, many commercial systems derived from the Berkeley code have adopted it. To accommodate the widespread Berkeley convention, our example code accepts broadcasts using either all 0's or all 1's. Procedure *isbrc* contains the code.

```
/* isbrc.c - isbrc */

#include <conf.h>
#include <kernel.h>
#include <sleep.h>
#include <network.h>
```

```
/*-------------------------------------------------------------------
 *  isbrc   -   Is "dest" a broadcast address?
 *-------------------------------------------------------------------
 */
Bool isbrc(dest)
IPaddr  dest;
{
        int     inum;

        /* all 0's and all 1's are broadcast */

        if (blkequ(dest, ip_anyaddr, IP_ALEN) ||
            blkequ(dest, ip_maskall, IP_ALEN))
                return TRUE;

        /* check real broadcast address and BSD-style for net & subnet  */

        for (inum=0; inum < Net.nif; ++inum)
                if (blkequ(dest, nif[inum].ni_brc, IP_ALEN) ||
                    blkequ(dest, nif[inum].ni_nbrc, IP_ALEN) ||
                    blkequ(dest, nif[inum].ni_subnet, IP_ALEN) ||
                    blkequ(dest, nif[inum].ni_net, IP_ALEN))
                        return TRUE;

        return FALSE;
}
```

5.5 Byte-Ordering In The IP Header

To keep the Internet Protocol independent of the machines on which it runs, the protocol standard specifies *network byte ordering* for all integer quantities in the header:

> *Before sending a datagram, the host must convert all integers from the local machine byte order to standard network byte order; upon receiving a datagram, the host must convert integers from standard network byte order to the local machine byte order.*

Procedures *ipnet2h* and *iph2net* perform the conversions; *ipnet2h* is called from *ipproc*, and *iph2net* is called from *ipfsend* and *ipputp*. To convert individual fields, the utility routines use functions *net2hs* (network-to-host-short) and *h2nets* (host-to-network-short). The terminology is derived from the C programming language, where *short* generally refers to a 16-bit integer and *long* generally refers to a 32-bit integer.

To optimize processing time, our code stores all IP addresses in network byte order and does not convert address fields in protocol headers. Thus, the code only converts integer fields that do not contain IP addresses.

```
/* iph2net.c - iph2net */

#include <conf.h>
#include <kernel.h>
#include <network.h>

/*------------------------------------------------------------------------
 *  iph2net - convert an IP packet header from host to net byte order
 *------------------------------------------------------------------------
 */
struct ip *iph2net(pip)
struct   ip      *pip;
{
        /* NOTE: does not include IP options    */

        pip->ip_len = hs2net(pip->ip_len);
        pip->ip_id = hs2net(pip->ip_id);
        pip->ip_fragoff = hs2net(pip->ip_fragoff);
        return pip;
}


/* ipnet2h.c - ipnet2h */

#include <conf.h>
#include <kernel.h>
#include <network.h>

/*------------------------------------------------------------------------
 *  ipnet2h - convert an IP packet header from net to host byte order
 *------------------------------------------------------------------------
 */
struct ip *ipnet2h(pip)
struct   ip      *pip;
{
        /* NOTE: does not include IP options    */

        pip->ip_len = net2hs(pip->ip_len);
        pip->ip_id = net2hs(pip->ip_id);
        pip->ip_fragoff = net2hs(pip->ip_fragoff);
        return pip;
}
```

5.6 Sending A Datagram To IP

5.6.1 Sending Locally-Generated Datagrams

Given a locally-generated datagram and an IP destination address, procedure *ipsend* fills in the IP header and enqueues the datagram on the local host interface, where the IP process will extract and send it.

```
/* ipsend.c - ipsend */

#include <conf.h>
#include <kernel.h>
#include <network.h>

static ipackid = 1;

/*------------------------------------------------------------------------
 *  ipsend  -  fill in IP header and send datagram to specified address
 *------------------------------------------------------------------------
 */
int ipsend(faddr, pep, datalen)
IPaddr          faddr;
struct   ep     *pep;
int             datalen;
{
        struct  ip *pip = (struct ip *) pep->ep_data;

        pep->ep_type = EPT_IP;
        pip->ip_verlen = (IP_VERSION<<4) | IP_MINHLEN;
        pip->ip_tos = 0;
        pip->ip_len = datalen+IP_HLEN(pip);
        pip->ip_id = ipackid++;
        pip->ip_fragoff = 0;
        pip->ip_ttl = IP_TTL;
        blkcopy(pip->ip_dst, faddr, IP_ALEN);

        /*
         * special case for ICMP, so source matches destination
         * with multiple interfaces.
         */
        if (pip->ip_proto != IPT_ICMP)
                blkcopy(pip->ip_src, ip_anyaddr, IP_ALEN);
```

```
        if (enq(nif[NI_LOCAL].ni_ipinq, pep, 0) < 0) {
                freebuf(pep);
                IpOutDiscards++;
        }
        send(ippid, NI_LOCAL);
        IpOutRequests++;
        return OK;
}
/* special IP addresses */

IPaddr  ip_anyaddr = { 0, 0, 0, 0 };
IPaddr  ip_loopback = { 127, 0, 0, 1 };
```

Most of the code is self-explanatory. *Ipsend* fills in each of the header fields, including the specified destination address. It then calls *enq* to enqueue the datagram on the queue located in the local host (pseudo-network) interface. Observe that although the *ni_ipinq* queues in network interfaces normally contain incoming datagrams (i.e., datagrams arriving from other sites), the queue in the pseudo-network interface contains datagrams that are "outgoing" from the point of view of application software. Finally, *ipsend* calls *send* to send a message to the IP process in case it was blocked waiting for datagrams to arrive.

5.6.2 Sending Incoming Datagrams

When an IP datagram arrives over a network, device driver code in the network interface layer must deposit it on the appropriate queue for IP.

```
/* ip_in.c - ip_in */

#include <conf.h>
#include <kernel.h>
#include <network.h>


/*-------------------------------------------------------------------
 *  ip_in - IP input function
 *-------------------------------------------------------------------
 */
int ip_in(pni, pep)
struct  netif   *pni;
struct  ep      *pep;
{
        struct  ip      *pip = (struct ip *)pep->ep_data;
```

```
IpInReceives++;
if (enq(pni->ni_ipinq, pep, pip->ip_tos & IP_PREC) < 0) {
        IpInDiscards++;
        freebuf(pep);
}
send(ippid, (pni-&nif[0]));
return OK;
}
```

Given a pointer to a buffer that contains a packet, *ip_in* calls *enq* to enqueue the packet on the queue in the interface. If the queue is full, *ip_in* increments variable *IpInDiscards* to record the queue overflow error and discards the packet. Finally, *ip_in* sends a message to the IP process in case it is blocked waiting for a datagram.

5.7 Table Maintenance

IP software needs a timing mechanism for maintenance of network data structures, including the IP routing table and fragment reassembly table. Our example implements such periodic tasks with a timer process. In fact, the timer is not limited to IP tasks – it also triggers ARP cache timeouts, and can be used for any other long-term periodic tasks that do not have stringent delay requirements. The code, in procedure *slowtimer*, shows how easily new tasks can be added to the list.

```
/* slowtimer.c - slowtimer */

#include <conf.h>
#include <kernel.h>
#include <proc.h>
#include <network.h>

#define STGRAN  1                      /* Timer granularity (delay) in seconds */

/*------------------------------------------------------------------------
 * slowtimer - handle long-term periodic maintenance of network tables
 *------------------------------------------------------------------------
 */
PROCESS slowtimer()
{
        long    lasttime, now;   /* previous and current times in seconds*/
        int     delay;           /* actual delay in seconds              */

        signal(Net.sema);

        gettime(&lasttime);
        while (1) {
                sleep(STGRAN);
                gettime(&now);
                delay = now - lasttime;
                lasttime = now;
                arptimer(delay);
                ipftimer(delay);
                rttimer(delay);
        }
}
```

As the code shows, *slowtimer* consists of an infinite loop that repeatedly invokes a set of maintenance procedures. A given maintenance procedure may take arbitrarily long to complete its chore, and the execution time may vary between one invocation and the next. Thus, *slowtimer* computes the actual delay between executions and reports it to the maintenance procedures as an argument.

5.8 Summary

To simplify the code, our implementation of IP executes as a single, independent process, and interaction with higher-level protocol software on the local machine occurs through a pseudo-network interface. When no datagrams are available, the IP process blocks. As soon as one or more datagrams are available from any source, the IP process awakens and processes them until they have all been routed. To make processing fair and avoid starvation, our implementation uses a round-robin policy among input sources, including the pseudo-interface that corresponds to the local machine. Thus, neither locally generated traffic nor incoming traffic from the network connections has priority.

Directed broadcasting means delivery to all hosts and gateways on the specified network. The protocol standard allows designers to decide whether to forward directed broadcasts that originate on foreign networks. If the gateway chooses to allow directed broadcasts, it routes them as usual. If the destination address specifies a directly connected network, IP must be sure that higher-level protocol software on the local machine receives a copy of the datagram. To increase its utility, our example implementation allows either the TCP/IP standard (all 1's) or 4.2 BSD UNIX (all 0's) forms of broadcast address. It creates a copy of a broadcast datagram and arranges for the network interface to broadcast the copy, while it routes the original to protocol software on the local machine.

The IP checksum consists of a 16-bit 1's complement value that can be computed using 32-bit 2's complement arithmetic and carry propagation.

FOR FURTHER STUDY

The standard for IP is found in Postel [RFC 791]. Braden and Postel [RFC 1009] summarizes requirements for Internet gateways. Mallory [RFC 1141] discusses incremental update of IP checksums. Braden, Borman, and Partridge [RFC 1071] gives an earlier discussion. Mogul and Postel [RFC 950] gives the standard for subnet addressing. Padlipsky [RFC 875], and Hinden and Sheltzer [RFC 823] describe early ideas about gateways.

EXERCISES

5.1   One's complement arithmetic has two values for zero. Which will *cksum* return?

5.2   Rewrite *cksum* in assembly language. How does the speed compare to a version written in C?

5.3   Consider an implementation that uses a single input queue for all datagrams sent to IP. What is the chief disadvantage of such a solution?

5.4   Study the code in procedure *ipproc* carefully. Identify all instances where a datagram sent to/from the local machine is treated as a special case.

5.5   Can any of the special cases in the previous exercise be eliminated by requiring higher-level protocols to perform computation(s) when they enqueue a datagram for output?

5.6   Show that it is possible for *ipproc* to make one last iteration through all interfaces even though there are no datagrams waiting to be processed. Hint: consider the timing between the IP process and a device driver that deposits a datagram and sends IP a message.

5.7   Consider the AT&T *STREAMS* mechanism used to build device driver and protocol software. Can it be used to implement IP? How?

5.8   What is the chief advantage of implementing IP in an independent process? What is the chief disadvantage?

5.9   Procedure *ipsend* supplies a fixed value for the time-to-live field in the datagram header. Is this reasonable?

5.10 Look carefully at the initial value used for the datagram identification field. Argue that if a machine boots, sends a datagram, crashes, quickly reboots, and sends a different datagram to the same destination, fragmentation can cause severe errors.

6

IP: Routing Table And Routing Algorithm

6.1 Introduction

The previous chapter described the overall structure of Internet Protocol (IP) software and showed the code for the central procedure, *ipproc*. This chapter continues the discussion by presenting the details of routing. It examines the organization of an IP routing table and the definitions of data structures that implement it. It discusses the routing algorithm and shows how IP uses subnet masks when selecting a route. Finally, it shows how IP distinguishes between network-specific routes, subnet-specific routes, and host-specific routes.

6.2 Route Maintenance And Lookup

Conceptually, routing software can be divided into two groups. One group includes procedures used to determine the correct route for a datagram. The other group includes procedures used to add, change, or delete routes. Because a gateway must determine a route for each datagram it processes, the route lookup code determines the overall performance of the gateway. Thus, the lookup code is usually optimized for highest speed.

Route insertions, changes, or deletions usually occur at much slower rates than datagram routing. Programs that compute new routes communicate with other machines to establish reachability; they can take arbitrarily long before changing routes. Thus, route update procedures need not be as optimized as lookup operations. The fundamental idea is:

IP data structures and algorithms should be selected to optimize the cost of route lookup; the cost of route maintenance is not as important.

Although early TCP/IP software often used linear search for routing table lookup, most systems now use a hash table that permits arbitrarily large routing tables to be searched quickly.

Our software uses a form of bucket hashing. It partitions route table entries into many "buckets" and uses a hash function to find the appropriate bucket quickly.

6.3 Routing Table Organization

Figure 6.1 illustrates the data structure used for the route table.

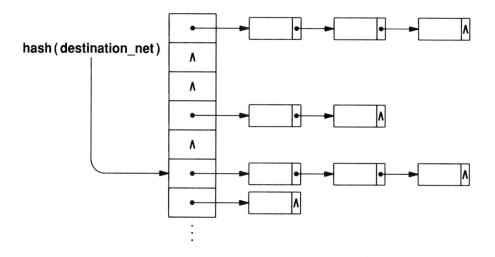

Figure 6.1 Implementation of a hashed route table using an array. Each entry in the array points to a linked list of records that each contain a destination address and a route to that destination.

The main data structure for storing routes is an array. Each entry in the array corresponds to a bucket and contains a pointer to a linked list of records for routes to destinations that hash into that bucket. Each record on the list contains a destination IP address, subnet mask, next-hop address for that destination, and the network interface to use for sending to the next-hop address, as well as other information used in route management. Because it cannot know subnet masks a priori, IP uses only the network portion of the destination IP address when computing the hash function. When searching entries on a linked list, however, IP uses the entire destination address to make comparisons. Later sections present the details.

6.4 Routing Table Data Structures

File *route.h* contains the declarations of routing table data structures.

```
/* route.h - RTFREE */

/* Routing Table Entries: */
struct route {
        IPaddr   rt_net;           /* network address for this route      */
        IPaddr   rt_mask;          /* mask for this route                 */
        IPaddr   rt_gw;            /* next IP hop                         */
        short    rt_metric;        /* distance metric                     */
        short    rt_ifnum;         /* interface number                    */
        short    rt_key;           /* sort key                            */
        short    rt_ttl;           /* time to live (seconds)              */
        struct   route *rt_next;   /* next entry for this hash value       */
/* stats */
        int      rt_refcnt;        /* current reference count             */
        int      rt_usecnt;        /* total use count so far              */
};

/* Routing Table Global Data: */
struct rtinfo {
        struct   route    *ri_default;
        int               ri_bpool;
        Bool              ri_valid;
        int               ri_mutex;
};

#define RT_DEFAULT ip_anyaddr    /* the default net                     */
#define RT_LOOPBACK ip_loopback  /* the loopback net                    */
#define RT_TSIZE        512      /* these are pointers; it's cheap      */
#define RT_INF          999      /* no timeout for this route           */

#define RTM_INF         16       /* an infinite metric                  */

/* rtget()'s second argument... */

#define RTF_REMOTE      0        /* traffic is from a remote host       */
#define RTF_LOCAL       1        /* traffic is locally generated        */
```

```
#define RT_BPSIZE        100      /* max number of routes                */

/* RTFREE - remove a route reference (assumes ri_mutex HELD)             */

#define RTFREE(prt)                                      \
        if (--prt->rt_refcnt <= 0) {                     \
                freebuf(prt);                            \
        }

extern  struct  rtinfo  Route;
extern  struct  route   *rttable[];
```

Structure *route* defines the contents of a node on the linked lists, and contains routing information for one possible destination. Field *rt_net* specifies the destination address (either a network, subnet, or complete host address); field *rt_mask* specifies the 32-bit mask used with that destination. The mask entries can cover the network portion, network plus subnet portion, or the entire 32 bits (i.e., they can include the host portion).

Field *rt_gw* specifies the IP address of the next-hop gateway for the route, and field *rt_metric* gives the distance of the gateway (measured in hops). Field *rt_ifnum* gives the internal number of the network interface used for the route (i.e., the network used to reach the next-hop gateway).

Remaining fields are used by the IP software. Field *rt_key* contains a sort key used when inserting the node on the linked list. Field *rt_refcnt* contains a reference count of processes that hold a pointer to the route, and field *rt_usecnt* records the number of times the route has been used. Finally, field *rt_next* contains a pointer to the next node on the linked list (the last node in a list contains *NULL*).

In addition to the *route* structure, file *route.h* defines the routing table, *rttable*. As Figure 6.1 shows, *rttable* is an array of pointers to *route* structures.

In addition to the routing table, IP requires a few other data items. The global structure *rtinfo* holds them. For example, the system provides a single *default route* that is used for any destination not contained in the table. Field *ri_default* points to a *route* structure that contains the next-hop address for the default route. Field *ri_valid* contains a Boolean variable that is *TRUE* if the routing data structures have been initialized.

6.5 Origin Of Routes And Persistence

Information in the routing table comes from several sources. When the system starts, initialization routines usually obtain an initial set of routes from secondary storage and install them in the table. During execution, incoming messages can cause ICMP or routing protocol software to change existing routes or install new routes. Finally, network managers can also add or change routes.

The volatility of a routing entry depends on its origin. For example, initial routes are usually chosen to be simplistic estimates, which should be replaced as soon as routing information arrives from any other source. However, network managers must be able to override any route and install permanent, unalterable routes that allow them to debug network routing problems without interference from routing protocols.

To accommodate flexibility in routes, field *rt_ttl* (*time-to-live*) in each routing entry specifies a time, in seconds, that the entry should remain valid. When *rt_ttl* reaches zero, the route is no longer considered valid and will be discarded. Routing protocols can install routes with time-to-live values computed according to the rules of the protocol, while managers can install routes with infinite time-to-live, guaranteeing that they will not be removed.

6.6 Routing A Datagram

6.6.1 Utility Procedures

Several utility procedures provide functions used in routing. Procedure *netnum* extracts the network portion of a given IP address, using the address class to determine which octets contain the network part and which contain the host part. It returns the specified address with all host bytes set to zero.

```
/* netnum.c - netnum */

#include <conf.h>
#include <kernel.h>
#include <network.h>

/*------------------------------------------------------------------
 *  netnum  -  compute the network portion of a given IP address
 *------------------------------------------------------------------
 */
int netnum(net, ipa)
IPaddr   net, ipa;
{
        int      bc;

        blkcopy(net, ipa, IP_ALEN);
        if (IP_CLASSA(net)) bc = 1;
        if (IP_CLASSB(net)) bc = 2;
        if (IP_CLASSC(net)) bc = 3;
        if (IP_CLASSD(net)) bc = 4;
        if (IP_CLASSE(net)) bc = 4;
        for (; bc < IP_ALEN; ++bc)
                net[bc] = 0;
        return OK;
}
```

IP uses procedure *netmatch* during routing to compare a destination (host) address to a routing entry. The routing entry contains the subnet mask and IP address for a given network. *Netmatch* uses the subnet mask to mask off the host bits in the destination address and compares the results to the network entry. If they match, *netmatch* returns *TRUE*; otherwise it returns *FALSE*.

Broadcasting is a special case because the action to be taken depends on the source of the datagram. Broadcast datagrams that arrive from network interfaces must be delivered to the local machine via the pseudo-network interface, while locally-generated broadcast datagrams must be sent to the appropriate network interface. To distinguish between the two, the software uses a host-specific route (a mask of all *1*s) to route arriving broadcast datagrams, and a network-specific route (the mask covers only the network portion) to route outgoing broadcasts. Thus, *netmatch* tests for a broadcast datagram explicitly, and uses the IP source address to decide whether the broadcast matches a given route.

```
/* netmatch.c - netmatch */

#include <conf.h>
#include <kernel.h>
#include <network.h>

/*------------------------------------------------------------------------
 * netmatch  -  Is "dst" on "net"?
 *------------------------------------------------------------------------
 */
Bool netmatch(dst, net, mask, islocal)
IPaddr  dst, net, mask;
Bool    islocal;
{
        int     i;

        for (i=0; i<IP_ALEN; ++i)
                if (mask[i] & dst[i] != net[i])
                        return FALSE;
        /*
         * local srcs should not match broadcast addresses (host routes)
         */
        if (islocal)
                if (isbrc(dst))
                        return !blkequ(mask, ip_maskall, IP_ALEN);
        return TRUE;
}
```

To route a datagram, IP must first see if it knows a valid subnet mask for the destination address. To do so, it calls procedure *netmask*.

```
/* netmask.c - netmask */

#include <conf.h>
#include <kernel.h>
#include <network.h>


/*-------------------------------------------------------------------------
 *  netmask  -  set the default mask for the given net
 *-------------------------------------------------------------------------
 */
int netmask(mask, net)
IPaddr  mask;
IPaddr  net;
{
        IPaddr  netpart;
        Bool    isdefault = TRUE;
        int     i, bc;

        for (i=0; i<IP_ALEN; ++i) {
                mask[i] = ~0;
                isdefault &= net[i] == 0;
        }
        if (isdefault) {
                blkcopy(mask, net, IP_ALEN);
                return OK;
        }
        /* check for net match (for subnets) */

        netnum(netpart, net);
        for (i=0; i<Net.nif; ++i) {
                if (nif[i].ni_svalid && nif[i].ni_ivalid &&
                    blkequ(nif[i].ni_net, netpart, IP_ALEN)) {
                        blkcopy(mask, nif[i].ni_mask, IP_ALEN);
                        return OK;
                }
        }
        if (IP_CLASSA(net)) bc = 1;
        if (IP_CLASSB(net)) bc = 2;
        if (IP_CLASSC(net)) bc = 3;
        if (IP_CLASSD(net)) bc = 4;
        if (IP_CLASSE(net)) bc = 4;
        for (; bc < IP_ALEN; ++bc)
                mask[bc] = 0;
        return OK;
}
```

Netmask takes the address of a subnet mask variable in its first argument and the address of a destination IP address in its second. It begins by setting the subnet mask to all 0's, and then checks several cases. By convention, if the destination address is all 0's, it specifies a default route, so *netmask* returns a subnet mask of all 0's. For other destinations, *netmask* calls *netnum* to extract the network portion of the destination address, and then checks each locally-connected network to see if it knows a subnet mask for that network. If the address of any locally-connected network matches the network portion of the destination, *netmask* extracts the subnet mask from the network interface structure for that network and returns it to the caller. Finally, if IP has no information about the subnet mask of the destination address, it sets the subnet mask to cover the network part of the address, depending on whether the address is class A, B, or C.

The routing function calls utility procedure *rthash* to hash a destination network address.

```
/* rthash.c - rthash */

#include <conf.h>
#include <kernel.h>
#include <network.h>

/*------------------------------------------------------------------------
 *  rthash  -  compute the hash for "net"
 *------------------------------------------------------------------------
 */
int rthash(net)
IPaddr  net;
{
        int     bc;     /* # bytes to count      */
        int     hv;     /* hash value            */

        hv = 0;
        if (IP_CLASSA(net)) bc = 1;
        if (IP_CLASSB(net)) bc = 2;
        if (IP_CLASSC(net)) bc = 3;
        if (IP_CLASSD(net)) bc = 4;
        if (IP_CLASSE(net)) bc = 4;
        while (bc--)
                hv += net[bc] & 0xff;
        return hv % RT_TSIZE;
}
```

The hash function used is both simple and efficient to compute. *Rthash* sums the individual octets of the network address, divides by the hash table size, and returns the remainder.

6.6.2 Obtaining A Route

Given a destination address, procedure *rtget* searches the routing table and returns a pointer to the entry for that route.

```
/* rtget.c - rtget */

#include <conf.h>
#include <kernel.h>
#include <network.h>


/*------------------------------------------------------------------
 *  rtget  -  get the route for a given IP destination
 *------------------------------------------------------------------
 */
struct route *rtget(dest, local)
IPaddr  dest;
Bool    local;            /* TRUE <=> locally generated traffic */
{
        struct  route   *prt;
        int             hv;

        if (!Route.ri_valid)
                rtinit();
        wait(Route.ri_mutex);
        hv = rthash(dest);
        for (prt=rttable[hv]; prt; prt=prt->rt_next) {
                if (prt->rt_ttl <= 0)
                        continue;              /* route has expired */
                if (netmatch(dest, prt->rt_net, prt->rt_mask, local))
                        if (prt->rt_metric < RTM_INF)
                                break;
        }
        if (prt == 0)
                prt = Route.ri_default; /* may be NULL too... */
        if (prt != 0 && prt->rt_metric >= RTM_INF)
                prt = 0;
        if (prt) {
                prt->rt_refcnt++;
                prt->rt_usecnt++;
        }
```

```
        signal(Route.ri_mutex);
        return prt;
}
```

The global variable *Route.ri_valid* specifies whether the table has been initialized. If it has not, *rtget* calls *rtinit*. Once the routing table and associated data structures have been initialized, *rtget* waits on the mutual exclusion semaphore to insure that only one process accesses the table at any time. It then computes the hash value of the destination address, uses it as an index into the table, and follows the linked list of routing entries.

At each entry, *rtget* calls *netmatch* to see if the destination specified by its argument matches the address in the entry. If no explicit match is found during the search, *rtget* uses the default route found in *Route.ri_default*.

Of course, it is possible that there is no default route and no explicit match. Thus, after performing route lookup, *rtget* must still check to see if it found a valid pointer. If it has, *rtget* increments the reference count and use count fields of the route entry before returning to the caller. Maintenance software uses the reference count field to determine whether it is safe to delete storage associated with the route. The reference count will remain nonzero as long as the procedure that called *rtget* needs to use the route entry. The use count provides a way for network administrators to find out how often each entry has been used to route datagrams.

6.6.3 Data Structure Initialization

Procedure *rtinit* initializes the routing table and default route, creates the mutual exclusion semaphore, allocates storage for nodes on the linked lists of routes, and links the storage onto a free list. The implementation is straightforward.

```
/* rtinit.c - rtinit */

#include <conf.h>
#include <kernel.h>
#include <sleep.h>
#include <network.h>

struct  rtinfo  Route;
struct  route   *rttable[RT_TSIZE];

/*------------------------------------------------------------------
 *  rtinit  -  initialize the routing table
 *------------------------------------------------------------------
 */
void rtinit()
{
        int i;

        for (i=0; i<RT_TSIZE; ++i)
                rttable[i] = 0;
        Route.ri_bpool = mkpool(sizeof(struct route), RT_BPSIZE);
        Route.ri_valid = TRUE;
        Route.ri_mutex = screate(1);
        Route.ri_default = NULL;
}
```

6.7 Periodic Route Table Maintenance

The system initiates a periodic sweep of the routing table to decrement time-to-live values and dispose of routes that have expired. Procedure *rttimer.c* implements the periodic update.

```
/* rttimer.c - rttimer */

#include <conf.h>
#include <kernel.h>
#include <network.h>

extern  Bool    dorip;          /* TRUE if we're running RIP output   */
extern  int     rippid;         /* RIP output pid, if running         */

/*------------------------------------------------------------------
 * rttimer - update ttls and delete expired routes
 *------------------------------------------------------------------
 */
```

```
int rttimer(delta)
{
        struct  route    *prt, *prev;
        Bool             ripnotify;
        int              i;

        if (!Route.ri_valid)
                return;
        wait(Route.ri_mutex);

        ripnotify = FALSE;
        for (i=0; i<RT_TSIZE; ++i) {
                if (rttable[i] == 0)
                        continue;
                for (prev = NULL, prt = rttable[i]; prt != NULL;) {
                        if (prt->rt_ttl != RT_INF)
                                prt->rt_ttl -= delta;
                        if (prt->rt_ttl <= 0) {
                                if (dorip && prt->rt_metric < RTM_INF) {
                                        prt->rt_metric = RTM_INF;
                                        prt->rt_ttl = RIPZTIME;
                                        ripnotify = TRUE;
                                        continue;
                                }
                                if (prev) {
                                        prev->rt_next = prt->rt_next;
                                        RTFREE(prt);
                                        prt = prev->rt_next;
                                } else {
                                        rttable[i] = prt->rt_next;
                                        RTFREE(prt);
                                        prt = rttable[i];
                                }
                                continue;
                        }
                        prev = prt;
                        prt = prt->rt_next;
                }
        }
        prt = Route.ri_default;
        if (prt && (prt->rt_ttl<RT_INF) && (prt->rt_ttl -= delta) <= 0)
                if (dorip && prt->rt_metric < RTM_INF) {
                        prt->rt_metric = RTM_INF;
                        prt->rt_ttl = RIPZTIME;
                } else {
                        RTFREE(Route.ri_default);
```

```
                              Route.ri_default = 0;
                    }
            signal(Route.ri_mutex);
            if (dorip && ripnotify)
                    send(rippid, 0);              /* send anything but TIMEOUT    */
            return;
}
```

The timer process (executing *slowtimer*) calls *rttimer* approximately once per second, passing in argument *delta*, the time that has elapsed since the last call. After waiting for the mutual exclusion semaphore, *rttimer* iterates through the routing table. For each entry, it traverses the linked list of routes, and examines each. For normal routes, *rttimer* decrements the time-to-live counter, and unlinks the node from the list if the counter reaches zero. However, if the gateway runs RIP, *rttimer* marks the expired route as having infinite cost, so it cannot be used for routing, and retains the expired route in the table for a short period†. Finally, *rttimer* decrements the time-to-live counter on the default route.

6.7.1 Adding A Route

Network management software and routing information protocols call functions that add, delete, or change routes. For example, procedure *rtadd* adds a new route to the table.

```
/* rtadd.c - rtadd */

#include <conf.h>
#include <kernel.h>
#include <network.h>

struct  route *rtnew();

/*------------------------------------------------------------------------
 *  rtadd  -  add a route to the routing table
 *------------------------------------------------------------------------
 */
int rtadd(net, mask, gw, metric, intf, ttl)
IPaddr  net, mask, gw;
int     metric, intf, ttl;
{
        struct  route   *prt, *srt, *prev;
        Bool            isdup;
        int             hv, i, j;

        if (!Route.ri_valid)
```

---

†Chapter 17 describes RIP, and explains how it uses the routing table.

```
                rtinit();

        prt = rtnew(net, mask, gw, metric, intf, ttl);
        if (prt == (struct route *)SYSERR)
                return SYSERR;

        /* compute the queue sort key for this route */
        for (prt->rt_key = 0, i=0; i<IP_ALEN; ++i)
                for (j=0; j<8; ++j)
                        prt->rt_key += (mask[i] >> j) & 1;
        wait(Route.ri_mutex);

        /* special case for default routes */
        if (blkequ(net, RT_DEFAULT, IP_ALEN)) {
                if (Route.ri_default)
                        RTFREE(Route.ri_default);
                Route.ri_default = prt;
                signal(Route.ri_mutex);
                return OK;
        }
        prev = NULL;
        hv = rthash(net);
        isdup = FALSE;
        for (srt=rttable[hv]; srt; srt = srt->rt_next) {
                if (prt->rt_key > srt->rt_key)
                        break;
                if (blkequ(srt->rt_net, prt->rt_net, IP_ALEN) &&
                    blkequ(srt->rt_mask, prt->rt_mask, IP_ALEN)) {
                        isdup = TRUE;
                        break;
                }
                prev = srt;
        }
        if (isdup) {
                struct  route   *tmprt;

                if (blkequ(srt->rt_gw, prt->rt_gw, IP_ALEN)) {
                        /* just update the existing route */
                        if (dorip) {
                                srt->rt_ttl = ttl;
                                if (srt->rt_metric != metric) {
                                        if (metric == RTM_INF)
                                                srt->rt_ttl = RIPZTIME;
                                        send(rippid, 0);
                                }
                        }
```

```
                        srt->rt_metric = metric;
                        RTFREE(prt);
                        signal(Route.ri_mutex);
                        return OK;
                }
                /* else, someone else has a route there... */
                if (srt->rt_metric <= prt->rt_metric) {
                        /* no better off to change; drop the new one */

                        RTFREE(prt);
                        signal(Route.ri_mutex);
                        return OK;
                } else if (dorip)
                        send(rippid, 0);
                tmprt = srt;
                srt = srt->rt_next;
                RTFREE(tmprt);
        } else if (dorip)
                send(rippid, 0);
        prt->rt_next = srt;
        if (prev)
                prev->rt_next = prt;
        else
                rttable[hv] = prt;
        signal(Route.ri_mutex);
        return OK;

}
```

Rtadd calls procedure rtnew to allocate a new node and initialize the fields. It then checks for the default route as a special case. For non-default routes, rtadd uses rthash to compute the index in the routing table for the new route, and follows the linked list of routes starting at that location. Once it finds the position in the list at which the new route should be inserted, it checks to see if the list contains an existing route for the same destination. If so, rtadd compares the metrics for the old and new route to see if the new route is better, and discards the new route if it is not. Finally, rtadd either inserts the new node on the list or copies information into an existing node for the same address.

Procedure rtnew allocates and initializes a new routing table entry. It calls getbuf to allocate storage for the new node, and then fills in the header.

```
/* rtnew.c - rtnew */

#include <conf.h>
#include <kernel.h>
#include <network.h>

/*-----------------------------------------------------------------------
 *  rtnew  -  create a route structure
 *-----------------------------------------------------------------------
 */
struct route *rtnew(net, mask, gw, metric, ifnum, ttl)
IPaddr  net, mask, gw;
int     metric, ifnum, ttl;
{
        struct  route *prt;

        prt = (struct route *)getbuf(Route.ri_bpool);
        if (prt == (struct route *)SYSERR)
                return (struct route *)SYSERR;

        blkcopy(prt->rt_net, net, IP_ALEN);
        blkcopy(prt->rt_mask, mask, IP_ALEN);
        blkcopy(prt->rt_gw, gw, IP_ALEN);
        prt->rt_metric = metric;
        prt->rt_ifnum = ifnum;
        prt->rt_ttl = ttl;
        prt->rt_refcnt = 1;       /* our caller */
        prt->rt_usecnt = 0;
        prt->rt_next = NULL;
        return prt;
}
```

6.7.2 Deleting A Route

Procedure *rtdel* takes a destination address as an argument and deletes the route to that destination by removing the node from the routing table.

```
/* rtdel.c - rtdel */

#include <conf.h>
#include <kernel.h>
#include <network.h>

/*------------------------------------------------------------------
 * rtdel  -  delete the route with the given net, mask
 *------------------------------------------------------------------
 */
int rtdel(net, mask)
IPaddr  net, mask;                      /* destination network and mask       */
{
        struct  route   *prt, *prev;
        int             hv, i;

        if (!Route.ri_valid)
                return SYSERR;
        wait(Route.ri_mutex);
        if (Route.ri_default &&
            blkequ(net, Route.ri_default->rt_net, IP_ALEN)) {
                RTFREE(Route.ri_default);
                Route.ri_default = 0;
                signal(Route.ri_mutex);
                return OK;
        }
        hv = rthash(net);

        prev = NULL;
        for (prt = rttable[hv]; prt; prt = prt->rt_next) {
                if (blkequ(net, prt->rt_net, IP_ALEN) &&
                    blkequ(mask, prt->rt_mask, IP_ALEN))
                        break;
                prev = prt;
        }
        if (prt == NULL) {
                signal(Route.ri_mutex);
                return SYSERR;
        }
        if (prev)
                prev->rt_next = prt->rt_next;
        else
                rttable[hv] = prt->rt_next;
        RTFREE(prt);
```

```
        signal(Route.ri_mutex);
        return OK;
}
```

As usual, the code checks for the default route as a special case. If no match oc-curs, *rtdel* hashes the destination address and searches the linked list of routes. Once it finds the correct route, *rtdel* unlinks the node from the linked list, and uses macro RTFREE to decrement the reference count. Recall that if the reference count reaches zero, *RTFREE* returns the node to the free list. If the reference count remains positive, some other process or processes must still be using the node; the node will be returned to the free list when the last of those processes decrements the reference count to zero.

Macro *RTFREE* assumes that the executing process has already obtained exclusive access to the routing table. Thus, it can be used in procedures like *rtdel*. Arbitrary pro-cedures that need to decrement the reference count on a route call procedure *rtfree*. When invoked, *rtfree* waits on the mutual exclusion semaphore, invokes macro *RTFREE*, and then signals the semaphore.

```
/* rtfree.c - rtfree */

#include <conf.h>
#include <kernel.h>
#include <network.h>

/*------------------------------------------------------------------
 *  rtfree  -  remove one reference to a route
 *------------------------------------------------------------------
 */
int rtfree(prt)
struct   route   *prt;
{
        if (!Route.ri_valid)
                return SYSERR;
        wait(Route.ri_mutex);
        RTFREE(prt);
        signal(Route.ri_mutex);
        return OK;
}
```

6.8 IP Options Processing

IP supports several options that control the way IP handles datagrams in hosts and gateways. To keep the example code simple and easy to understand, we have elected to omit option processing. However, the code contains a skeleton of two routines that scan options in the IP header. Gateways call procedure *ipdoopts*, which merely returns to its caller, leaving the options untouched in case the gateway forwards the datagram.

```
/* ipdoopts.c - ipdoopts */

#include <conf.h>
#include <kernel.h>
#include <network.h>


/*------------------------------------------------------------------------
 *  ipdoopts - do gateway handling of IP options
 *------------------------------------------------------------------------
 */
int ipdoopts(pni, pep)
struct  netif   *pni;
struct  ep      *pep;
{
        return OK;       /* not implemented yet */
}
```

Hosts call procedure *ipdstopts* to handle options in arriving datagrams. Although our procedure does not implement option processing, it parses the option length octets and deletes the options field from the IP header.

```
/* ipdstopts.c - ipdstopts */

#include <conf.h>
#include <kernel.h>
#include <network.h>


/*------------------------------------------------------------------------
 *  ipdstopts - do host handling of IP options
 *------------------------------------------------------------------------
 */
int ipdstopts(pni, pep)
struct  netif   *pni;
struct  ep      *pep;
{
```

```
struct  ip        *pip = (struct ip *)pep->ep_data;
char              *popt, *popend;
int               len;

if (IP_HLEN(pip) == IPMHLEN)
        return OK;
popt = pip->ip_data;
popend = &pep->ep_data[IP_HLEN(pip)];

/* NOTE: options not implemented yet */

/* delete the options */
len = pip->ip_len-IP_HLEN(pip); /* data length  */
if (len)
        blkcopy(pip->ip_data, &pep->ep_data[IP_HLEN(pip)], len);
pip->ip_len = IPMHLEN + len;
pip->ip_verlen = (pip->ip_verlen&0xf0) | IP_MINHLEN;
return OK;
}
```

6.9 Summary

The IP routing table serves as a central data structure. When routing datagrams the IP process uses the routing table to find a next-hop route for the datagram's destination. Because route lookup must be performed frequently, the table is organized to make lookup efficient. Meanwhile, the high-level protocol software that learns about new routes will insert, delete, or change routes.

This chapter examined the procedures for both lookup and table maintenance. It showed how a routing table can use hashing to achieve efficiency, and how reference counts allow one process to use a route while another process deletes it concurrently.

FOR FURTHER STUDY

Postel [RFC 791] gives the standard for the Internet Protocol, Hornig [RFC 894] specifies the standard for the transmission of IP datagrams across an Ethernet, and Mogul and Postel et. al. [RFCs 950 and 940] discuss subnetting. Specific constants used throughout IP can be found in Reynolds and Postel [RFC 1010].

Braden and Postel [RFC 1009] provides a summary of how Internet gateways handle IP datagrams. Postel [RFC 791] describes IP option processing, and Su [RFC 781] comments on the timestamp option. Mills [RFC 981] considers multipath routing, while Braun [RFC 1104] discusses policy-based routing.

EXERCISES

6.1 Consider the automatic initialization of the routing table by two processes at system startup. Is it possible for the two processes to interfere with one another? Explain.

6.2 The number of buckets used determines the efficiency of a bucket hashing scheme because it determines the average length of the linked lists. How much memory would be required to store 1000 routes if one wanted the average list to have no more than 3 entries?

6.3 What happens if procedure *rtdel* calls *rtfree* instead of using macro *RTFREE*?

6.4 ICMP redirect messages only allow gateways to specify destinations as host redirects or network redirects. How can the code in this chapter help one deduce that an address is a subnet address?

6.5 Assume that in the next version of IP, all addresses are self-identifying (e.g., each address comes with a correct subnet mask). How would you redesign the routing table data structures to make them more efficient?

6.6 Consider the routing of broadcast datagrams (see *netmatch*). The code carefully distinguishes between locally-generated broadcasts and incoming broadcasts. Why?

6.7 The special case that arises when routing broadcast datagrams can be eliminated by adding an extra field to each route entry that specifies whether the entry should be used for inbound traffic, outbound traffic, or both. How does adding such a field make network management more difficult?

6.8 We said that implementing the local host interface as a pseudo-network helped eliminate special cases. How many times do routines in this chapter make an explicit test for the local machine?

6.9 Does it make sense to design a routing table that stores *backup* routes (i.e., a table that keeps several routes to a given destination)? Explain.

6.10 Add type-of-service routing to the IP routing table in this chapter by allowing the route to be chosen as a function of the datagram's type of service, as well as its destination address.

6.11 Add security routing to the IP routing table in this chapter by allowing the route to be chosen as a function of the datagram's source address and protocol type as well as its destination address.

```
                freebuf(pep);
                return SYSERR;
        }
        pip = (struct ip *)pep->ep_data;
        if (pip->ip_len <= pni->ni_mtu) {
                blkcopy(pep->ep_nexthop, nh, IP_ALEN);
                iph2net(pip);
                return netwrite(pni, pep, EP_HLEN+net2hs(pip->ip_len));
        }
        /* else, we need to fragment it */

        if (pip->ip_fragoff & IP_DF) {
                IpFragFails++;
                icmp(ICT_DESTUR, ICC_FNADF, pip->ip_src, pep);
                return OK;
        }
        maxdlen = (pni->ni_mtu - IP_HLEN(pip)) &~ 7;
        offset = 0;
        offindg = (pip->ip_fragoff & IP_FRAGOFF)<<3;
        tosend = pip->ip_len - IP_HLEN(pip);

        while (tosend > maxdlen) {
                if (ipfsend(pni,nh,pep,offset,maxdlen,offindg) != OK) {
                        IpOutDiscards++;
                        freebuf(pep);
                        return SYSERR;
                }
                IpFragCreates++;
                tosend -= maxdlen;
                offset += maxdlen;
                offindg += maxdlen;
        }
        IpFragOKs++;
        IpFragCreates++;
        hlen = ipfhcopy(pep, pep, offindg);
        pip = (struct ip *)pep->ep_data;
        /* slide the residual down */
        blkcopy(&pep->ep_data[hlen], &pep->ep_data[IP_HLEN(pip)+offset],
                tosend);
        /* keep MF, if this was a frag to start with */
        pip->ip_fragoff = (pip->ip_fragoff & IP_MF)|(offindg>>3);
        pip->ip_len = tosend + hlen;
        pip->ip_cksum = 0;
        iph2net(pip);
```

```
    pip->ip_cksum = cksum(pip, hlen>>1);
    blkcopy(pep->ep_nexthop, nh, IP_ALEN);
    return netwrite(pni, pep, EP_HLEN+net2hs(pip->ip_len));
}
```

Arguments to *ipputp* give the interface number over which to route, the next-hop address, and a packet. If the packet length is less than the network MTU, *ipputp* calls *netwrite* to send the datagram and returns to its caller. If the datagram cannot be sent in one packet, *ipputp* divides the datagram into a sequence of fragments that each fit into one packet. To do so, *ipputp* computes the maximum possible fragment length, which must be a multiple of 8, and divides the datagram into a sequence of maximum-sized fragments plus a final fragment of whatever remains. Once it has computed a maximum fragment size, *ipputp* iterates through the datagram, calling procedure *ipfsend* to send each fragment.

The code contains a few subtleties. First, because each fragment must contain an IP header, the maximum amount of data that can be sent equals the MTU minus the IP header length, truncated to the nearest multiple of 8. Second, the iteration proceeds only while the data remaining in the datagram is strictly greater than the maximum that can be sent. Thus, the iteration will stop before sending the last fragment, even in the case where all fragments happen to be of equal size. Third, to send the final fragment, *ipputp* modifies the original datagram and does not copy the fragment into a new buffer. Fourth, the *more fragments* (MF) bit is not usually set in the final fragment of a datagram. However, in the case where a gateway happens to further fragment a non-final fragment, it must leave MF set in all fragments.

7.3.1 Sending One Fragment

Procedure *ipfsend* creates and sends a single fragment. It allocates a new buffer for the copy, calls *ipfhcopy* to copy the header and IP options, copies the data for this fragment into the new datagram, and passes the result to *netwrite*.

```
/* ipfsend.c - ipfsend */

#include <conf.h>
#include <kernel.h>
#include <network.h>

/*------------------------------------------------------------------------
 *  ipfsend  -  send one fragment of an IP datagram
 *------------------------------------------------------------------------
 */
int ipfsend(pni, nexthop, pep, offset, maxdlen, offindg)
struct  netif   *pni;
```

```
IPaddr              nexthop;
struct   ep         *pep;
int                 offset, maxdlen, offindg;
{
         struct   ep         *pepnew;
         struct   ip         *pip, *pipnew;
         int                 hlen, len;

         pepnew = (struct ep *)getbuf(Net.netpool);
         if (pepnew == (struct ep *)SYSERR)
                 return SYSERR;
         hlen = ipfhcopy(pepnew, pep, offindg);   /* copy the headers */

         pip = (struct ip *)pep->ep_data;
         pipnew = (struct ip *)pepnew->ep_data;
         pipnew->ip_fragoff = IP_MF | (offindg>>3);
         pipnew->ip_len = len = maxdlen + hlen;
         pipnew->ip_cksum = 0;

         iph2net(pipnew);
         pipnew->ip_cksum = cksum(pipnew, hlen>>1);

         blkcopy(&pepnew->ep_data[hlen],
                 &pep->ep_data[IP_HLEN(pip)+offset], maxdlen);
         blkcopy(pepnew->ep_nexthop, nexthop, IP_ALEN);

         return netwrite(pni, pepnew, EP_HLEN+len);
}
```

7.3.2 Copying A Datagram Header

Procedure *ipfhcopy* copies a datagram header. Much of the code is concerned with the details of IP options. According to the protocol standard, some options should only appear in the first fragment, while others must appear in all fragments. *Ipfhcopy* iterates through the options, and examines each to see whether it should be copied into all fragments. Finally, when *ipfhcopy* returns, *ipfsend* calls *netwrite* to send the fragment.

```
/* ipfhcopy.c - ipfhcopy */

#include <conf.h>
#include <kernel.h>
#include <network.h>

/*------------------------------------------------------------------------
 *  ipfhcopy - copy the hardware, IP header, and options for a fragment
 *------------------------------------------------------------------------
 */
int ipfhcopy(pepto, pepfrom, offindg)
struct  ep       *pepto, *pepfrom;
{
        struct  ip       *pipto = (struct ip *)pepto->ep_data;
        struct  ip       *pipfrom = (struct ip *)pepfrom->ep_data;
        unsigned         i, maxhlen, olen, otype;
        unsigned         hlen = (IP_MINHLEN<<2);

        if (offindg == 0) {
                blkcopy(pepto, pepfrom, EP_HLEN+IP_HLEN(pipfrom));
                return IP_HLEN(pipfrom);
        }
        blkcopy(pepto, pepfrom, EP_HLEN+hlen);

        /* copy options */

        maxhlen = IP_HLEN(pipfrom);
        i = hlen;
        while (i < maxhlen) {
                otype = pipfrom->ip_data[i];
                olen = pipfrom->ip_data[++i];
                if (otype & IPO_COPY) {
                        blkcopy(&pipto->ip_data[hlen],
                                pipfrom->ip_data[i-1], olen);
                        hlen += olen;
                } else if (otype == IPO_NOP || otype == IPO_EOOP) {
                        pipto->ip_data[hlen++] = otype;
                        olen = 1;
                }
                i += olen-1;

                if (otype == IPO_EOOP)
                        break;
        }
```

```
        /* pad to a multiple of 4 octets */
        while (hlen % 4)
                pipto->ip_data[hlen++] = IPO_NOP;
        return hlen;
}
```

7.4 Datagram Reassembly

Reassembly requires IP on the receiving machine to accumulate incoming fragments until a complete datagram can be reassembled. Once reassembled, IP routes the datagram on toward its destination. Because IP does not guarantee order of delivery, the protocol requires IP to accept fragments that arrive out of order or after delay. Furthermore, fragments for a given datagram may arrive intermixed with fragments from other datagrams.

7.4.1 Data Structures

To make the implementation efficient, the data structure used to store fragments must permit: quick location of the group of fragments that comprise a given datagram, fast insertion of a new fragment into a group, efficient test of whether a complete datagram has arrived, timeout of fragments, and eventual removal of fragments if the timer expires before reassembly can be completed.

Our example code uses an array of lists to store fragments. Each item in the array corresponds to a single datagram for which one or more fragments have arrived, and contains a pointer to a list of fragments for that datagram. File *ipreass.h* declares the data structures.

```
/* ipreass.h */

/* Internet Protocol (IP)  reassembly support */

#define IP_FQSIZE       10      /* max number of frag queues              */
#define IP_MAXNF        10      /* max number of frags/datagram           */
#define IP_FTTL         60      /* time to live (secs)                    */

/* ipf_state flags */

#define IPFF_VALID      1       /* contents are valid                     */
#define IPFF_BOGUS      2       /* drop frags that match                  */
#define IPFF_FREE       3       /* this queue is free to be allocated     */

struct  ipfq    {
        char    ipf_state;              /* VALID, FREE or BOGUS           */
        IPaddr  ipf_src;                /* IP address of the source       */
        short   ipf_id;                 /* datagram id                    */
        int     ipf_ttl;                /* countdown to disposal          */
        int     ipf_q;                  /* the queue of fragments         */
};

extern  int     ipfmutex;               /* mutex for ipfqt[]              */
extern  struct  ipfq    ipfqt[];        /* IP frag queue table            */
```

Array *ipfqt* forms the main data structure for fragments; each entry in the array corresponds to a single datagram. Structure *ipfq* defines the information kept. In addition to the datagram source address and identification fields (*ipf_src* and *ipf_id*), the entry contains a *time-to-live* counter (*ipf_ttl*) that specifies how long (in seconds) before the entry will expire if not all fragments arrive. Field *ipf_q* points to a linked list of all fragments that have arrived for the datagram.

Reassembly software must test whether all fragments have arrived for a given datagram. To make the test efficient, each fragment list is stored in sorted order. In particular, the fragments on a given list are ordered by their offset in the original datagram. The protocol design makes the choice of sort key easy because even fragmented fragments have offsets measured from the original datagram. Thus, it is possible to insert any fragment in the list without knowing whether it resulted from a single fragmentation or multiple fragmentations.

7.4.2 Mutual Exclusion

To guarantee that processes do not interfere with one another while accessing the list of fragments, the reassembly code uses a single mutual exclusion semaphore, *ipfmutex*. File *ipreass.h* declares the value to be an external integer, accessible to all the code. As we will see, mutual exclusion is particularly important because it allows the system to use separate processes for timeout and reassembly.

7.4.3 Adding A Fragment To A List

IP uses information in the header of an incoming fragment to identify the appropriate list. Fragments belong to the same datagram if they have identical values in both their source address and IP identification fields. Procedure *ipreass* takes a fragment, finds the appropriate list, and adds the fragment to the list. Given a fragment, it searches the fragment table to see if it contains an existing entry for the datagram to which the fragment belongs. At each entry, it compares the source and identification fields, and calls *ipfadd* to add the fragment to the list if it finds a match. It then calls *ipfjoin* to see if all fragments can be reassembled into a datagram. If no match is found, *ipreass* allocates the first unused entry in the array, copies in the source and identification fields, and places the fragment on a newly allocated queue.

Our implementation uses a linear search to locate the appropriate list for an incoming fragment, and may seem too inefficient for production use. Of course, some computers do receive fragments from many datagrams simultaneously and will require a faster search method. However, because most computers communicate frequently with machines in the local environment, they rarely receive fragments. Furthermore, because reassembly only happens for datagrams destined for the local machine and not for transit traffic, gateways do not need to reassemble datagrams as fast as they need to route them. So, for typical computer systems, a linear search suffices.

```
/* ipreass.c - ipreass */

#include <conf.h>
#include <kernel.h>
#include <network.h>
#include <q.h>

struct  ep      *ipfjoin();

/*-------------------------------------------------------------------------
 *  ipreass  -  reassemble an IP datagram, if necessary
 *      returns packet, if complete; 0 otherwise
 *-------------------------------------------------------------------------
 */
struct ep *ipreass(pep)
struct  ep      *pep;
{
        struct  ep      *pep2;
        struct  ip      *pip;
        int             firstfree;
        int             i;

        pip = (struct ip *)pep->ep_data;

        wait(ipfmutex);

        if ((pip->ip_fragoff & (IP_FRAGOFF|IP_MF)) == 0) {
                signal(ipfmutex);
                return pep;
        }
        IpReasmReqds++;
        firstfree = -1;
        for (i=0; i<IP_FQSIZE; ++i) {
                struct  ipfq    *piq = &ipfqt[i];

                if (piq->ipf_state == IPFF_FREE) {
                        if (firstfree == -1)
                                firstfree = i;
                        continue;
                }
                if (piq->ipf_id != pip->ip_id)
                        continue;
                if (!blkequ(piq->ipf_src, pip->ip_src, IP_ALEN))
                        continue;
```

```
                /* found a match */
                if (ipfadd(piq, pep) == 0) {
                        signal(ipfmutex);
                        return 0;
                }
                pep2 = ipfjoin(piq);
                signal(ipfmutex);
                return pep2;


        }
        /* no match */

        if (firstfree < 0) {
                /* no room-- drop */
                freebuf(pep);
                signal(ipfmutex);
                return 0;
        }
        ipfqt[firstfree].ipf_q = newq(IP_FQSIZE, QF_WAIT);
        if (ipfqt[firstfree].ipf_q < 0) {
                freebuf(pep);
                signal(ipfmutex);
                return 0;
        }
        blkcopy(ipfqt[firstfree].ipf_src, pip->ip_src, IP_ALEN);
        ipfqt[firstfree].ipf_id = pip->ip_id;
        ipfqt[firstfree].ipf_ttl = IP_FTTL;
        ipfqt[firstfree].ipf_state = IPFF_VALID;
        ipfadd(&ipfqt[firstfree], pep);
        signal(ipfmutex);
        return 0;
}


int     ipfmutex;
struct  ipfq    ipfqt[IP_FQSIZE];
```

7.4.4 Discarding During Overflow

Procedure *ipfadd* inserts a fragment on a given list. For the normal case, the procedure is trivial – *ipfadd* merely calls *enq* to enqueue the fragment and resets the time-to-live field for the datagram.

In the case where the fragment list has reached its capacity, the new fragment cannot be added to the list. When that occurs, *ipfadd* discards *all* fragments that correspond to the datagram, and frees the entry in array *ipfqt*. At first this may seem strange. However, the reason for discarding the entire list is simple: a single missing fragment will prevent IP from ever reassembling and processing the datagram, so freeing the memory used by the remaining fragments may make it possible to complete other datagrams. Furthermore, once the list reaches capacity, it cannot grow. Therefore, keeping the list consumes memory resources but does not contribute to the success of reassembling the datagram.

```
/* ipfadd.c - ipfadd */

#include <conf.h>
#include <kernel.h>
#include <proc.h>
#include <network.h>

/*------------------------------------------------------------------
 *  ipfadd  -  add a fragment to an IP fragment queue
 *------------------------------------------------------------------
 */
Bool ipfadd(iq, pep)
struct  ipfq    *iq;
struct  ep      *pep;
{
        struct  ip      *pip;
        int             fragoff;

        if (iq->ipf_state != IPFF_VALID) {
                freebuf(pep);
                return FALSE;
        }
        pip = (struct ip *)pep->ep_data;
        fragoff = pip->ip_fragoff & IP_FRAGOFF;

        if (enq(iq->ipf_q, pep, -fragoff) < 0) {
                /* overflow-- free all frags and drop */
                freebuf(pep);
                IpReasmFails++;
                while (pep = (struct ep *)deq(iq->ipf_q)) {
                        freebuf(pep);
                        IpReasmFails++;
                }
                freeq(iq->ipf_q);
                iq->ipf_state = IPFF_BOGUS;
                return FALSE;
        }
```

```
        iq->ipf_ttl = IP_FTTL;              /* restart timer */
        return TRUE;
}
```

7.4.5 Testing For A Complete Datagram

When adding a new fragment to a list, IP must check to see if it has all the fragments that comprise a datagram. Procedure *ipfjoin* examines a list of fragments to see
if they form a complete datagram.

```
/* ipfjoin.c - ipfjoin */

#include <conf.h>
#include <kernel.h>
#include <proc.h>
#include <network.h>

struct  ep      *ipfcons();

/*------------------------------------------------------------------
 *  ipfjoin  -  join fragments, if all collected
 *------------------------------------------------------------------
 */
struct ep *ipfjoin(iq)
struct  ipfq    *iq;
{
        struct  ep      *pep;
        struct  ip      *pip;
        int             off, packoff;

        if (iq->ipf_state == IPFF_BOGUS)
                return 0;
        /* see if we have the whole datagram */

        off = 0;
        while (pep=(struct ep *)seeq(iq->ipf_q)) {
                pip = (struct ip *)pep->ep_data;
                packoff =  (pip->ip_fragoff & IP_FRAGOFF)<<3;
                if (off < packoff) {
                        while(seeq(iq->ipf_q))
                                /*empty*/;
                        return 0;
                }
```

```
                 off = packoff + pip->ip_len - IP_HLEN(pip);
        }
        if (off > MAXLRGBUF) {              /* too big for us to handle */
                while (pep = (struct ep *)deq(iq->ipf_q))
                        freebuf(pep);
                freeq(iq->ipf_q);
                iq->ipf_state = IPFF_FREE;
                return 0;
        }
        if ((pip->ip_fragoff & IP_MF) == 0)
                return ipfcons(iq);

        return 0;
}
```

After verifying that the specified fragment list is in use, *ipfjoin* enters a loop that iterates through the fragments. It starts variable *off* at zero, and uses it to see if the current fragment occurs at the expected location in the datagram. First, *ipfjoin* checks to see that the offset in the current fragment matches *off*. If the offset of the current fragment exceeds *off*, there must be a missing fragment, so *ipfjoin* returns zero (which means that the fragments cannot be joined). If the fragment matches, *ipfjoin* computes the expected offset of the next fragment by adding the current fragment length to *off*.

Once *ipfjoin* verifies that all fragments have been collected, it tests to make sure the datagram will fit into a large buffer. The software can only handle datagrams that fit into large buffers because the datagram must be reassembled into contiguous memory before it can be passed to an application program. Thus, if the datagram cannot fit into a single buffer, *ipfjoin* discards the fragments. Finally, for datagrams that do fit, *ipfjoin* calls *ipfcons* to collect the fragments and rebuild a complete datagram.

7.4.6 Building A Datagram From Fragments

Procedure *ipfcons* reassembles fragments into a complete datagram. In addition to copying the data from each fragment into place, it builds a valid datagram header. Information for the datagram header comes from the header in the first fragment, modified to reflect the full datagram's size. *Ipfcons* turns off the fragment bit to show that the reconstructed datagram is not a fragment and sets the offset field to zero. If it reassembles the datagram, *ipfcons* releases the buffers that hold individual fragments. When it finishes reassembly, *ipfcons* releases the entry in the fragment table *ipfqt*.

```c
/* ipfcons.c - ipfcons */

#include <conf.h>
#include <kernel.h>
#include <network.h>

/*------------------------------------------------------------------------
 *  ipfcons  -  construct a single packet from an IP fragment queue
 *------------------------------------------------------------------------
 */
struct ep *ipfcons(iq)
struct  ipfq    *iq;
{
        struct  ep      *pep, *peptmp;
        struct  ip      *pip;
        int             off, seq;

        pep = (struct ep *)getbuf(Net.lrgpool);
        if (pep == (struct ep *)SYSERR) {
                while (peptmp = (struct ep *)deq(iq->ipf_q)) {
                        IpReasmFails++;
                        freebuf(peptmp);
                }
                freeq(iq->ipf_q);
                iq->ipf_state = IPFF_FREE;
                return 0;
        }
        /* copy the Ether and IP headers */

        peptmp = (struct ep *)deq(iq->ipf_q);
        pip = (struct ip *)peptmp->ep_data;
        off = IP_HLEN(pip);
        seq = 0;
        blkcopy(pep, peptmp, EP_HLEN+off);

        /* copy the data */
        while (peptmp != 0) {
                int dlen, doff;

                pip = (struct ip *)peptmp->ep_data;
                doff = IP_HLEN(pip) + seq
                        - ((pip->ip_fragoff&IP_FRAGOFF)<<3);
                dlen = pip->ip_len - doff;
                blkcopy(pep->ep_data+off, peptmp->ep_data+doff, dlen);
```

```
                    off += dlen;
                    seq += dlen;
                    freebuf(peptmp);
                    peptmp = (struct ep *)deq(iq->ipf_q);
            }

            /* fix the large packet header */
            pip = (struct ip *)pep->ep_data;
            pip->ip_len = off;
            pip->ip_fragoff = 0;

            /* release resources */
            freeq(iq->ipf_q);
            iq->ipf_state = IPFF_FREE;
            IpReasmOKs++;
            return pep;
    }
```

7.5 Maintenance Of Fragment Lists

Because IP is an unreliable delivery mechanism, datagrams can be lost as they
traverse an internet. If a fragment is lost, the IP software on the receiving end cannot
reassemble the original datagram. Furthermore, because IP does not provide an acknowledgement facility, no fragment retransmissions are possible. Thus, once a fragment
is lost, IP will never recover the datagram to which it belonged. Instead, higher-level
protocols, like TCP, use a new datagram to retransmit†.

To keep lost fragments from consuming memory resources and to keep IP from
becoming confused by reuse of the identification field, IP must periodically check the
fragment lists and discard an old list when reception of the remaining fragments is un-
likely. Procedure *ipftimer* performs the periodic sweep.

```
/* ipftimer.c - ipftimer */

#include <conf.h>
#include <kernel.h>
#include <network.h>

/*------------------------------------------------------------------------
 * ipftimer - update time-to-live fields and delete expired fragments
 *------------------------------------------------------------------------
 */
void ipftimer(gran)
int     gran;                   /* granularity of this run */
```

---

†Each retransmission of a TCP segment uses a datagram that has a unique IP identification, so IP cannot
intermix fragments from two transmissions when reassembling.

```
{
        struct  ep       *pep;
        struct  ip       *pip;
        int              i;

        wait(ipfmutex);
        for (i=0; i<IP_FQSIZE; ++i) {
                struct ipfq *iq = &ipfqt[i];

                if (iq->ipf_state == IPFF_FREE)
                        continue;
                iq->ipf_ttl -= gran;
                if (iq->ipf_ttl <= 0) {
                        if (iq->ipf_state == IPFF_BOGUS) {
                                /* resources already gone */
                                iq->ipf_state = IPFF_FREE;
                                continue;
                        }
                        if (pep = (struct ep *)deq(iq->ipf_q)) {
                                IpReasmFails++;
                                pip = (struct ip *)pep->ep_data;
                                icmp(ICT_TIMEX, ICC_FTIMEX,
                                        pip->ip_src, pep);
                        }
                        while (pep = (struct ep *)deq(iq->ipf_q)) {
                                IpReasmFails++;
                                freebuf(pep);
                        }
                        freeq(iq->ipf_q);
                        iq->ipf_state = IPFF_FREE;
                }
        }
        signal(ipfmutex);
}
```

Ipftimer iterates through the fragment lists each time it is called (usually once per second). It decrements the time-to-live field in each entry and discards the list if the timer reaches zero. When discarding a list, *ipftimer* extracts the first node, and uses the packet buffer to send an *ICMP time exceeded* message back to the source. After sending the ICMP message, *ipftimer* frees the list of fragments and marks the entry in *ipfqt* free for use again.

7.6 Initialization

Initialization of the data structures used for fragment reassembly is trivial. Procedure *ipfinit* creates the mutual exclusion semaphore and marks each entry in the fragment array available for use.

```
/* ipfinit.c - ipfinit */

#include <conf.h>
#include <kernel.h>
#include <network.h>

/*------------------------------------------------------------------
 * ipfinit  -  initialize IP fragment queue data structures
 *------------------------------------------------------------------
 */
void ipfinit()
{
        int     i;

        ipfmutex = screate(1);
        for (i=0; i<IP_FQSIZE; ++i)
                ipfqt[i].ipf_state = IPFF_FREE;
}
```

7.7 Summary

All machines that implement IP must be able to fragment outgoing datagrams and to reassemble fragmented datagrams that arrive.

In practice, gateways usually fragment datagrams when they encounter a datagram that is too large for the network MTU over which it must travel. Fragmentation consists of duplicating the datagram header for each fragment, setting the offset and fragment bits, copying part of the data, and sending the resulting fragments one at a time. The software fragments a datagram after IP routes it, but before IP deposits it on the output queue associated with a particular network interface. Compared to reassembly, fragmentation is straightforward.

To perform reassembly, IP uses a data structure that collects together fragments from a given datagram. Once all fragments have been collected, the datagram can be reassembled (reconstructed) and processed.

Reassembly works in parallel with a maintenance process. Each time a new fragment arrives for a datagram, IP resets the time-to-live field in the fragment table for that datagram. The separate maintenance process periodically checks the lists of fragments and decrements the time-to-live field in each entry. If the time-to-live reaches zero before all fragments arrive, the maintenance process discards the entire datagram.

FOR FURTHER STUDY

Many textbooks describe algorithms and data structures that apply to storage of linked lists. More information on fragment management can be found in the IP specification [RFC 791] and the host requirements document [RFC 1122].

EXERCISES

7.1 Read the IP specification carefully. Can two fragments from different datagrams ever have the same values for IP source and identification fields? Explain. (Hint: consider machine reboot.)

7.2 Look carefully at *ipputp* and *ipfhcopy*. Can *ipputp* ever underestimate the maximum size fragment that can be sent? Why or why not?

7.3 The example code chooses the maximum possible fragment size and divides a datagram into many pieces of that size followed by an odd piece. Is there any advantage to making all fragments as close to the same size as possible? Explain.

7.4 Procedure *ipreass* assigns each newly created fragment list a fixed value for time-to-live. Is there a better way to choose an initial time-to-live value? Explain.

7.5 Modify the fragment data structure to use hashing instead of sequential lookup and measure the improvement in performance. What can you conclude? Under what circumstances will hashing save time?

7.6 Use the *ping* command to generate datagrams of various sizes destined for a remote machine. See if you can detect the threshold of fragmentation from a discontinuity in the round trip delay. What does the result tell you about fragmentation cost?

7.7 Read the IP specification carefully. Does the example code correctly handle the *do not fragment* bit? Explain.

7.8 Consider a network capable of accepting 1000 datagrams per second. What constraint does such a network place on the choice of a fragment time-to-live (assuming IP uses a constant timeout for all fragments)?

7.9 What are the advantages and disadvantages of resetting the time-to-live for a datagram whenever a fragment arrives, as opposed to setting the timer once when the first fragment arrives?

8

IP: Error Processing (ICMP)

8.1 Introduction

The *Internet Control Message Protocol* (*ICMP*) is an integral part of IP that provides error reporting. ICMP handles several types of error conditions and always reports errors back to the original source. Any computer using IP must accept ICMP messages and change behavior in response to the reported error. Gateways must also be prepared to generate ICMP error messages when incoming datagrams cause problems.

This chapter reviews the details of ICMP processing. It shows code for generating error messages as well as the code for handling such messages when they arrive.

8.2 ICMP Message Formats

Unlike protocols that have a fixed message format, ICMP messages are *type-dependent*. The number of fields in a message, the interpretation of each field, and the amount of data the message carries depend on the message type.

8.3 Implementation Of ICMP Messages

File *icmp.h*, shown below, contains the declarations used for ICMP error messages. Type-dependent messages make the declaration of ICMP message formats more complex than those of other protocols. Structure *icmp* defines the message format. All ICMP messages begin with a fixed header, defined by fields *ic_type* (message type), *ic_code* (message subtype), and *ic_cksum* (message checksum). The next 32 bits in an ICMP message depend on the message type, and are declared in C using a *union*. In

ICMP echo requests and replies, the message contains a 16-bit identification and 16-bit sequence number. In an ICMP redirect, the 32 bits specify the IP address of a gateway. In parameter problem messages, the 32 bits contain an 8-bit pointer and three octets of padding. In other messages, the 32 bits contain zeroes. Finally, field *ic_data* defines the data area of an ICMP message. As with the protocols we have seen earlier, the structure only declares the first octet of data even though a message will contain multiple octets of data.

In addition to symbolic constants needed for all ICMP messages, *icmp.h* defines abbreviations that can be used to refer to short names in the union. For example, using an abbreviation, a programmer can specify the gateway address subfield using *something.ic_gw* instead of the fully qualified *something.icu.ic2_gw*.

```
/* icmp.h */


/* Internet Control Message Protocol Constants and Packet Format */


/* ic_type field */
#define ICT_ECHORP      0       /* Echo reply                         */
#define ICT_DESTUR      3       /* Destination unreachable            */
#define ICT_SRCQ        4       /* Source quench                      */
#define ICT_REDIRECT    5       /* Redirect message type              */
#define ICT_ECHORQ      8       /* Echo request                       */
#define ICT_TIMEX       11      /* Time exceeded                      */
#define ICT_PARAMP      12      /* Parameter Problem                  */
#define ICT_TIMERQ      13      /* Timestamp request                  */
#define ICT_TIMERP      14      /* Timestamp reply                    */
#define ICT_INFORQ      15      /* Information request                */
#define ICT_INFORP      16      /* Information reply                  */
#define ICT_MASKRQ      17      /* Mask request                       */
#define ICT_MASKRP      18      /* Mask reply                         */


/* ic_code field */
#define ICC_NETUR       0       /* dest unreachable, net unreachable   */
#define ICC_HOSTUR      1       /* dest unreachable, host unreachable  */
#define ICC_PROTOUR     2       /* dest unreachable, proto unreachable */
#define ICC_PORTUR      3       /* dest unreachable, port unreachable  */
#define ICC_FNADF       4       /* dest unr, frag needed & don't frag  */
#define ICC_SRCRT       5       /* dest unreachable, src route failed  */

#define ICC_NETRD       0       /* redirect: net                      */
#define ICC_HOSTRD      1       /* redirect: host                     */
#define IC_TOSNRD       2       /* redirect: type of service, net     */
#define IC_TOSHRD       3       /* redirect: type of service, host    */
```

```
#define ICC_TIMEX        0          /* time exceeded, ttl              */
#define ICC_FTIMEX       1          /* time exceeded, frag             */


#define IC_HLEN          8          /* octets                          */
#define IC_PADLEN        3          /* pad length (octets)             */


#define IC_RDTTL         300        /* ttl for redirect routes         */


/* ICMP packet format (following the IP header)                        */

struct  icmp    {                          /* ICMP packet              */
        char    ic_type;                   /* type of message (ICT_* above)*/
        char    ic_code;                   /* code (ICC_* above)       */
        short   ic_cksum;                  /* checksum of ICMP header+data */

        union   {
                struct {
                        short   ic1_id; /* for echo type, a message id  */
                        short   ic1_seq;/* for echo type, a seq. number */
                } ic1;
                IPaddr  ic2_gw;            /* for redirect, gateway     */
                struct {
                        char    ic3_ptr;/* pointer, for ICT_PARAMP      */
                        char    ic3_pad[IC_PADLEN];
                } ic3;
                int     ic4_mbz;          /* must be zero               */
        } icu;
        char    ic_data[1];                /* data area of ICMP message */
};

/* format 1 */
#define ic_id   icu.ic1.ic1_id
#define ic_seq  icu.ic1.ic1_seq

/* format 2 */
#define ic_gw   icu.ic2_gw

/* format 3 */
#define ic_ptr  icu.ic3.ic3_ptr
#define ic_pad  icu.ic3.ic3_pad

/* format 4 */
#define ic_mbz  icu.ic4_mbz
```

8.4 Handling Incoming ICMP Messages

When an IP datagram carrying an ICMP message arrives destined for the local machine, the IP process passes it to procedure *icmp_in*.

```c
/* icmp_in.c - icmp_in */

#include <conf.h>
#include <kernel.h>
#include <network.h>

/*------------------------------------------------------------------------
 *  icmp_in  -  handle ICMP packet coming in from the network
 *------------------------------------------------------------------------
 */
int icmp_in(pni, pep)
struct  netif   *pni;              /* not used */
struct  ep      *pep;
{
        struct  ip      *pip;
        struct  icmp    *pic;
        int             i, len;

        pip = (struct ip *)pep->ep_data;
        pic = (struct icmp *) pip->ip_data;

        len = pip->ip_len - IP_HLEN(pip);
        if (cksum(pic, len>>1)) {
                IcmpInErrors++;
                freebuf(pep);
                return SYSERR;
        }
        IcmpInMsgs++;
        switch(pic->ic_type) {
        case ICT_ECHORQ:
                IcmpInEchos++;
                return icmp(ICT_ECHORP, 0, pip->ip_src, pep, 0);
        case ICT_MASKRQ:
                IcmpInAddrMasks++;
                if (!gateway) {
                        freebuf(pep);
                        return OK;
                }
                pic->ic_type = (char) ICT_MASKRP;
```

```
                    netmask(pic->ic_data, pip->ip_dst);
                    break;
        case ICT_MASKRP:
                    IcmpInAddrMaskReps++;
                    for (i=0; i<Net.nif; ++i)
                            if (blkequ(nif[i].ni_ip, pip->ip_dst, IP_ALEN))
                                    break;
                    if (i != Net.nif) {
                            setmask(i, pic->ic_data);
                            send(pic->ic_id, ICT_MASKRP);
                    }
                    freebuf(pep);
                    return OK;
        case ICT_ECHORP:
                    IcmpInEchoReps++;
                    if (send(pic->ic_id, pep) != OK)
                            freebuf(pep);
                    return OK;
        case ICT_REDIRECT:
                    IcmpInRedirects++;
                    icredirect(pep);
                    return OK;
        case ICT_DESTUR:        IcmpInDestUnreachs++;    return OK;
        case ICT_SRCQ:          IcmpInSrcQuenchs++;      return OK;
        case ICT_TIMEX:         IcmpInTimeExcds++;       return OK;
        case ICT_PARAMP:        IcmpInParmProbs++;       return OK;
        case ICT_TIMERQ:        IcmpInTimestamps++;      return OK;
        case ICT_TIMERP:        IcmpInTimestampReps++;   return OK;
        default:
                    IcmpInErrors++;
                    freebuf(pep);
                    return OK;
        }
        icsetsrc(pip);

        len = pip->ip_len - IP_HLEN(pip);

        pic->ic_cksum = 0;
        pic->ic_cksum = cksum(pic, len>>1);

        IcmpOutMsgs++;
        ipsend(pip->ip_dst, pep, len);
        return OK;
}
```

The second argument to *icmp_in* is a pointer to a buffer that contains an IP datagram. *Icmp_in* locates the ICMP message in the datagram, and uses the ICMP *type* field to select one of six ICMP message types. The code handles each type separately.

To handle an ICMP *echo request* message, *icmp_in* calls *icmp* (discussed below) to generate an ICMP *echo reply* message. By contrast, to handle an ICMP *echo reply* message, ICMP extracts the message id field, assumes it is the process id of the process that sent the echo request, and sends the reply packet to that process.

In response to an ICMP *address mask request*, *icmp_in* changes the message to an *address mask reply*, uses *netmask* to find the appropriate subnet mask, and breaks out of the *switch* statement to send the reply.

For an ICMP *address mask reply*, *icmp_in* iterates through the interfaces until it finds one that matches the network address in the reply packet, and then calls procedure *setmask* (shown below) to set the subnet mask for that interface. It passes *setmask* the subnet mask found in the reply.

Icmp_in calls procedure *icredirect* to handle an incoming ICMP *redirect message*. The next section shows how *icredirect* changes the routing table.

In all cases, even for ICMP messages that it does not handle, *icmp_in* accumulates a count of incoming messages. As later chapters show, SNMP uses these counts.

8.5 Handling An ICMP Redirect Message

Procedure *icredirect* handles a request to change a route.

```
/* icredirect.c - icredirect */

#include <conf.h>
#include <kernel.h>
#include <network.h>

struct  route   *rtget();

/*------------------------------------------------------------------
 * icredirect - handle an incoming ICMP redirect
 *------------------------------------------------------------------
 */
int icredirect(pep)
struct  ep      *pep;
{
        struct  route   *prt;
        struct  ip      *pip, *pip2;
        struct  icmp    *pic;
        IPaddr          mask;
```

```
pip = (struct ip *)pep->ep_data;
pic = (struct icmp *)pip->ip_data;
pip2 = (struct ip *)pic->ic_data;

if (pic->ic_code == ICC_HOSTRD)
        blkcopy(mask, ip_maskall, IP_ALEN);
else
        netmask(mask, pip2->ip_dst);
prt = rtget(pip2->ip_dst, RTF_LOCAL);
if (prt == 0) {
        freebuf(pep);
        return OK;
}
if (blkequ(pip->ip_src, prt->rt_gw, IP_ALEN)) {
        rtdel(pip2->ip_dst, mask);
        rtadd(pip2->ip_dst, mask, pic->ic_gw, prt->rt_metric,
                prt->rt_ifnum, IC_RDTTL);
}
rtfree(prt);
freebuf(pep);
return OK;
}
```

Icredirect extracts the specified destination address from the redirect message, calls *netmask* to compute the appropriate subnet mask, and uses *rtget* to lookup the existing route. If the current route points to the gateway that sent the redirect message, *icredirect* deletes the existing route, and adds a new route that uses the new gateway specified in the redirect message.

8.6 Setting A Subnet Mask

When *icmp_in* receives a subnet mask reply, it calls procedure *setmask* to record the subnet mask in the network interface structure.

```
/* setmask.c - setmask */

#include <conf.h>
#include <kernel.h>
#include <network.h>

extern  int      bsdbrc;              /* use Berkeley (all-0's) broadcast    */
/*-------------------------------------------------------------------------
 *  setmask - set the net mask for an interface
 *-------------------------------------------------------------------------
 */
int setmask(inum, mask)
int     inum;
IPaddr  mask;
{
        IPaddr  aobrc;           /* all 1's broadcast */
        IPaddr  defmask;
        int     i;

        if (nif[inum].ni_svalid) {
                /* one set already-- fix things */

                rtdel(nif[inum].ni_subnet, nif[inum].ni_mask);
                rtdel(nif[inum].ni_brc, ip_maskall);
                rtdel(nif[inum].ni_subnet, ip_maskall);
        }
        blkcopy(nif[inum].ni_mask, mask, IP_ALEN);
        nif[inum].ni_svalid = TRUE;
        netmask(defmask, nif[inum].ni_ip);

        for (i=0; i<IP_ALEN; ++i) {
                nif[inum].ni_subnet[i] =
                        nif[inum].ni_ip[i] & nif[inum].ni_mask[i];
                if (bsdbrc) {
                        nif[inum].ni_brc[i] = nif[inum].ni_subnet[i];
                        aobrc[i] = nif[inum].ni_subnet[i] |
                                ~nif[inum].ni_mask[i];
                } else
                        nif[inum].ni_brc[i] = nif[inum].ni_subnet[i] |
                                ~nif[inum].ni_mask[i];
                /* set network (not subnet) broadcast */
                nif[inum].ni_nbrc[i] =
                        nif[inum].ni_ip[i] | ~defmask[i];
        }
```

```
        /* install routes */
        /* net */
        rtadd(nif[inum].ni_subnet, nif[inum].ni_mask, nif[inum].ni_ip,
                0, inum, RT_INF);
        if (bsdbrc)
                rtadd(aobrc, ip_maskall, nif[inum].ni_ip, 0,
                        NI_LOCAL, RT_INF);
        else    /* broadcast (all 1's) */
                rtadd(nif[inum].ni_brc, ip_maskall, nif[inum].ni_ip, 0,
                        NI_LOCAL, RT_INF);
        /* broadcast (all 0's) */
        rtadd(nif[inum].ni_subnet, ip_maskall, nif[inum].ni_ip, 0,
                NI_LOCAL, RT_INF);
        return OK;
}


IPaddr  ip_maskall = { 255, 255, 255, 255 };
```

Because changing the subnet mask should also change routes that correspond to the network address, *setmask* begins by calling *rtdel* to delete existing routes for the current interface address, broadcast address, and subnet broadcast address. It then copies the new subnet mask to field *ni_mask*, and sets *ni_svalid* to *TRUE*.

After the new mask has been recorded, *setmask* computes a new subnet address and subnet broadcast address for the interface. Finally, it calls *rtadd* to install new routes to the subnet and subnet broadcast addresses.

8.7 Choosing A Source Address For An ICMP Packet

For those cases that require a reply (e.g., ICMP echo request), ICMP must reverse the datagram source and destination addresses. To do so, procedure *icmp*, shown below, calls *icsetsrc*.

```
/* icsetsrc.c - icsetsrc */

#include <conf.h>
#include <kernel.h>
#include <network.h>

/*------------------------------------------------------------------------
 * icsetsrc -  set the source address on an ICMP packet
 *------------------------------------------------------------------------
 */
void icsetsrc(pip)
struct  ip      *pip;
{
        int     i;

        for (i=0; i<Net.nif; ++i) {
                if (i == NI_LOCAL)
                        continue;
                if (netmatch(pip->ip_dst,nif[i].ni_ip,nif[i].ni_mask,0))
                        break;
        }
        if (i == Net.nif)
                blkcopy(pip->ip_src, ip_anyaddr, IP_ALEN);
        else
                blkcopy(pip->ip_src, nif[i].ni_ip, IP_ALEN);
}
```

Icsetsrc iterates through each network interface and compares the network or sub-net IP address associated with that interface to the destination IP address of the ICMP message. If it finds a match, *icsetsrc* copies the local machine address for that interface network into the source field of the datagram. In the event that no match can be found, *icsetsrc* fills the datagram source field with *ip_anyaddr* (all 0's), allowing the routing routines to replace it with the address of the interface over which it is routed.

8.8 Generating ICMP Error Messages

Gateways generate ICMP error messages in response to congestion, time-to-live expiration, and other error conditions. They call procedure *icmp* to create and send one message.

```
/* icmp.c - icmp */

#include <conf.h>
#include <kernel.h>
#include <network.h>

struct  ep       *icsetbuf();

/*
 * ICT_REDIRECT - pa2 == gateway address
 * ICT_PARAMP   - pa2 == (packet) pointer to parameter error
 * ICT_MASKRP   - pa2 == mask address
 * ICT_ECHORQ   - pa1 == seq, pa2 == data size
 */

/*------------------------------------------------------------------------
 *  icmp -  send an ICMP message
 *------------------------------------------------------------------------
 */
icmp(type, code, dst, pa1, pa2)
short   type, code;
IPaddr  dst;
char    *pa1, *pa2;
{
        struct  ep       *pep;
        struct  ip       *pip;
        struct  icmp     *pic;
        Bool             isresp, iserr;
        IPaddr           src, tdst;
        int              i, datalen;

        IcmpOutMsgs++;
        blkcopy(tdst, dst, IP_ALEN);     /* worry free pass by value     */

        pep = icsetbuf(type, pa1, &isresp, &iserr);
        if (pep == SYSERR) {
                IcmpOutErrors++;
                return SYSERR;
        }
        pip = (struct ip *)pep->ep_data;
        pic = (struct icmp *) pip->ip_data;

        datalen = IC_HLEN;
```

```
        /* we fill in the source here, so routing won't break it */

        if (isresp) {
                if (iserr) {
                        if (!icerrok(pep)) {
                                freebuf(pep);
                                return OK;
                        }
                        blkcopy(pic->ic_data, pip, IP_HLEN(pip)+8);
                        datalen += IP_HLEN(pip)+8;
                }
                icsetsrc(pip);
        } else
                blkcopy(pip->ip_src, ip_anyaddr, IP_ALEN);
        blkcopy(pip->ip_dst, tdst, IP_ALEN);

        pic->ic_type = (char) type;
        pic->ic_code = (char) code;
        if (!isresp) {
                if (type == ICT_ECHORQ)
                        pic->ic_seq = (int) pa1;
                else
                        pic->ic_seq = 0;
                pic->ic_id = getpid();
        }
        datalen += icsetdata(type, pip, pa2);

        pic->ic_cksum = 0;
        pic->ic_cksum = cksum(pic, (datalen+1)>>1);

        pip->ip_proto = IPT_ICMP;        /* for generated packets */
        ipsend(tdst, pep, datalen);
        return OK;
}
```

Icmp takes the ICMP message *type* and *code* as arguments, along with a destination IP address and two final arguments that usually contain pointers. The exact meaning and type of the two final arguments depends on the ICMP message type. For example, for an ICMP *echo request*, the argument *pa1* contains an (integer) sequence
number, while argument *pa2* contains the (integer) data size. For an ICMP *echo
response*, argument *pa1* contains a pointer to a packet containing the ICMP *echo request* that caused the reply, while argument *pa2* is not used (it contains zero).

To build an ICMP message, procedure *icmp* calls *icsetbuf* to allocate a buffer. To insure compliance with the protocol, it fills in the datagram source address before sending the message to IP. For responses, *icmp* uses the destination address to which the request was sent; otherwise, it fills the source field with *ip_anyaddr* and allows the IP routing procedures to choose an outgoing address. For responses, *icmp* also calls *icerrok* to verify that it is not generating an error message about an error message.

Icmp then fills in remaining header fields, including the *type* and *code* fields. For an echo request, it sets the identification field to the process id of the sending process. Finally, it calls *icsetdata* to fill in the data area, computes the ICMP checksum, and calls *ipsend* to send the datagram.

8.9 Avoiding Errors About Errors

Procedure *icerrok* checks a datagram that caused a problem to verify that the gateway is allowed to send an error message about it. The rules are straightforward: a gateway should never generate an error message about an error message, or for any fragment other than the first, or for broadcast datagrams. The code checks each condition and returns *FALSE* if an error message is prohibited and *TRUE* if it is allowed.

```c
/* icerrok.c - icerrok */

#include <conf.h>
#include <kernel.h>
#include <network.h>

/*------------------------------------------------------------------------
 *  icerrok - is it ok to send an error response?
 *------------------------------------------------------------------------
 */
Bool icerrok(pep)
struct ep        *pep;
{
        struct  ip      *pip = (struct ip *)pep->ep_data;
        struct  icmp    *pic = (struct icmp *)pip->ip_data;

        /* don't send errors about error packets... */

        if (pip->ip_proto == IPT_ICMP)
                switch(pic->ic_type) {
                case ICT_DESTUR:
                case ICT_REDIRECT:
                case ICT_SRCQ:
                case ICT_TIMEX:
                case ICT_PARAMP:
                        return FALSE;
                default:
                        break;
                }
        /* ...or other than the first of a fragment */

        if (pip->ip_fragoff & IP_FRAGOFF)
                return FALSE;
        /* ...or broadcast packets */

        if (isbrc(pip->ip_dst))
                return FALSE;
        return TRUE;
}
```

8.10 Allocating A Buffer For ICMP

Procedure *icsetbuf* allocates a buffer for an ICMP error message, and sets two Boolean variables, one that tells whether the message is an error message (or an information request), and another that tells whether this message type is a response to a previous request.

```
/* icsetbuf.c - icsetbuf */

#include <conf.h>
#include <kernel.h>
#include <network.h>


/*------------------------------------------------------------------
 *  icsetbuf -  set up a buffer for an ICMP message
 *------------------------------------------------------------------
 */
struct ep *icsetbuf(type, pal, pisresp, piserr)
int     type;
char    *pal;                       /* old packet, if any   */
Bool    *pisresp,                   /* packet is a response */
        *piserr;                    /* packet is an error   */
{
        struct  ep      *pep;

        *pisresp = *piserr = FALSE;

        switch (type) {
        case ICT_REDIRECT:
                pep = (struct ep *)getbuf(Net.netpool);
                if (pep == SYSERR)
                        return SYSERR;
                blkcopy(pep, pal, MAXNETBUF);
                pal = (char *)pep;
                *piserr = TRUE;
                break;
        case ICT_DESTUR:
        case ICT_SRCQ:
        case ICT_TIMEX:
        case ICT_PARAMP:
                pep = (struct ep *)pal;
                *piserr = TRUE;
                break;
        case ICT_ECHORP:
```

```
        case ICT_INFORP:
        case ICT_MASKRP:
                pep = (struct ep *)pal;
                *pisresp = TRUE;
                break;
        case ICT_ECHORQ:
        case ICT_TIMERQ:
        case ICT_INFORQ:
        case ICT_MASKRQ:
                pep = (struct ep *)getbuf(Net.lrgpool);
                if (pep == SYSERR)
                        return SYSERR;
                break;
        case ICT_TIMERP:                    /* Not Implemented */
                /* IcmpOutTimestampsReps++; */
                IcmpOutErrors--;            /* Kludge: we increment above */
                freebuf(pal);
                return SYSERR;
        }
        switch (type) {          /* Update MIB Statistics */
        case ICT_ECHORP:         IcmpOutEchos++;          break;
        case ICT_ECHORQ:         IcmpOutEchoReps++;       break;
        case ICT_DESTUR:         IcmpOutDestUnreachs++;   break;
        case ICT_SRCQ:           IcmpOutSrcQuenchs++;     break;
        case ICT_REDIRECT:       IcmpOutRedirects++;      break;
        case ICT_TIMEX:          IcmpOutTimeExcds++;      break;
        case ICT_PARAMP:         IcmpOutParmProbs++;      break;
        case ICT_TIMERQ:         IcmpOutTimestamps++;     break;
        case ICT_TIMERP:         IcmpOutTimestampReps++;  break;
        case ICT_MASKRQ:         IcmpOutAddrMasks++;      break;
        case ICT_MASKRP:         IcmpOutAddrMaskReps++;   break;
        }
        return pep;
}
```

The code is straightforward and divides into four basic cases. For most replies, *icsetbuf* reuses the buffer in which the request arrived (i.e., returns the address supplied in argument *pal*). For unimplemented message types, *icsetbuf* deallocates the datagram that caused the problem and returns *SYSERR*. For ICMP messages that could contain large amounts of data (e.g., an *echo reply*), *icsetbuf* allocates a large buffer. For other messages that cannot use the original buffer, *icsetbuf* allocates a standard buffer.

8.11 The Data Portion Of An ICMP Message

Procedure *icsetdata* creates the data portion of an ICMP message. The action taken depends on the message *type*, which *icsetdata* receives as an argument.

```
/* icsetdata.c - icsetdata */

#include <conf.h>
#include <kernel.h>
#include <network.h>

/* ECHOMAX must be an even number */
#define ECHOMAX(pip)    (MAXLRGBUF-IC_HLEN-IP_HLEN(pip)-EP_HLEN-EP_CRC)

/*------------------------------------------------------------------------
 *  icsetdata -  set the data section. Return value is data length
 *------------------------------------------------------------------------
 */
int icsetdata(type, pip, pa2)
int             type;
struct  ip      *pip;
char            *pa2;
{
        struct  icmp    *pic = (struct icmp *)pip->ip_data;
        int             i, len;

        switch (type) {
        case ICT_ECHORP:
                len = pip->ip_len - IP_HLEN(pip) - IC_HLEN;
                if (isodd(len))
                        pic->ic_data[len] = 0;   /* so cksum works */
                return len;
        case ICT_DESTUR:
        case ICT_SRCQ:
        case ICT_TIMEX:
                pic->ic_mbz = 0;                        /* must be 0 */
                break;
        case ICT_REDIRECT:
                blkcopy(pic->ic_gw, pa2, IP_ALEN);
                break;
        case ICT_PARAMP:
                pic->ic_ptr = (char) pa2;
                for (i=0; i<IC_PADLEN; ++i)
                        pic->ic_pad[i] = 0;
```

```
                break;
        case ICT_MASKRP:
                blkcopy(pic->ic_data, pa2, IP_ALEN);
                break;
        case ICT_ECHORQ:
                if (pa2 > ECHOMAX(pip))
                        pa2 = ECHOMAX(pip);
                for (i=0; i<(int)pa2; ++i)
                        pic->ic_data[i] = i;
                if (isodd(pa2))
                        pic->ic_data[(int)pa2] = 0;
                return (int)pa2;
        case ICT_MASKRQ:
                blkcopy(pic->ic_data, ip_anyaddr, IP_ALEN);
                return IP_ALEN;
        }
        return 0;
}
```

For replies, *icmp* has created the outgoing message from the incoming request, so there is no need to copy data. However, *icsetdata* must compute and return the correct data length. For most messages, the data length is zero because the header contains all necessary information. *Icsetdata* fills in the appropriate fields. For example, in an ICMP *redirect* message, the caller supplies a pointer to the new gateway address in argument *pa2*, and *icsetdata* copies it into the message.

For ICMP *echo reply* messages, *icsetdata* computes the length from the incoming request message. To do so, it subtracts the IP header length and the ICMP header length from the datagram length. In addition, for odd-length *echo reply* messages, *icsetdata* must place an additional zero octet after the message, so the 16-bit checksum algorithm works correctly. For ICMP *echo request* messages, argument *pa2* specifies the data length.

8.12 Generating An ICMP Redirect Message

With the above ICMP procedures in place, it becomes easy to generate an ICMP error message. For example, procedure *ipredirect* generates an ICMP *redirect* message.

```
/* ipredirect.c - ipredirect */

#include <conf.h>
#include <kernel.h>
#include <network.h>

struct   route    *rtget();

/*-----------------------------------------------------------------------
 *  ipredirect  -  send redirects, if needed
 *-----------------------------------------------------------------------
 */
void ipredirect(pep, ifnum, prt)
struct    ep      *pep;             /* the current IP packet              */
int               ifnum;           /* the input interface                */
struct    route   *prt;            /* where we want to route it          */
{
        struct    ip      *pip = (struct ip *)pep->ep_data;
        struct    route   *tprt;
        int               rdtype, isonehop;
        IPaddr            nmask;  /* network part's mask                  */

        if (ifnum == NI_LOCAL || ifnum != prt->rt_ifnum)
                return;
        tprt = rtget(pip->ip_src, RTF_LOCAL);
        if (!tprt)
                return;
        isonehop = tprt->rt_metric == 0;
        rtfree(tprt);
        if (!isonehop)
                return;
        /* got one... */

        netmask(nmask, prt->rt_net);      /* get the default net mask     */
        if (blkequ(prt->rt_mask, nmask, IP_ALEN))
                rdtype = ICC_NETRD;
        else
                rdtype = ICC_HOSTRD;
        icmp(ICT_REDIRECT, rdtype, pip->ip_src, pep, prt->rt_gw);
}
```

The three arguments to *ipredirect* specify a pointer to a buffer that contains a packet, an interface number over which the packet arrived, and a pointer to a new route. After checking to insure that the interface does not refer to the local host and that the new route specifies an interface other than the one over which the packet arrived, *ipredirect* calls *rtget* to compute the route to the machine that sent the datagram.

Because the protocol specifies that a gateway can only send an ICMP redirect to a host on a directly connected network, *ipredirect* checks the metric on the route it found to the destination. A metric greater than zero means the host is not directly connected and causes *ipredirect* to return without sending a message. Once *ipredirect* finds that the offending host is on a directly connected network, it must examine the new route to determine whether it is a host-specific route or network-specific route. To do so, it examines the subnet mask associated with the route. If the mask covers more than the network portion, *ipredirect* declares the message to be a *host redirect*; otherwise, it declares the message a *network redirect*.

8.13 Summary

Conceptually, ICMP can be divided into two parts: one that handles incoming ICMP messages and another that generates outgoing ICMP messages. While both hosts and gateways must handle incoming messages, most outgoing messages are restricted to gateways. Thus, ICMP code is usually more complex in gateways than in hosts.

In practice, many details and the interaction between incoming and outgoing messages make ICMP code complex. Our design uses two primary procedures: *icmp_in* to handle incoming messages, and *icmp* to generate outgoing messages. Each of these calls several subprocedures to handle the details of creation of buffers, setting subnet masks, filling the header and data fields, and computing correct source addresses.

FOR FURTHER STUDY

Postel [RFC 792] describes the ICMP protocol. Mogul and Postel [RFC 950] adds subnet mask request and reply messages, while Braden *et al.* specifies many refinements [RFC 1122]. The gateway requirements document [RFC 1009] discusses how gateways should generate and handle ICMP messages.

EXERCISES

8.1   Consider procedure *icsetsrc*. Under what circumstances can the loop iterate through all interfaces without finding a match?

8.2 When it forms a reply, can ICMP merely reverse the source and destination address fields from the request? Explain. (Hint: read the protocol specification.)

8.3 What should a host do when it receives an ICMP *time exceeded* message?

8.4 What should a host do when it receives an ICMP *source quench* message?

8.5 Suppose a gateway generates an ICMP redirect message for a destination that it knows has a subnet address (i.e., the subnet mask extends past the network portion of the address). Should it specify the redirect as a *host redirect* or as a *network redirect*? Explain. (Hint: see RFC 1009.)

8.6 What does the example code do in response to an ICMP *source quench* message? What other messages are handled the same way?

8.7 Look carefully at *setmask*. It handles two types of broadcast address (all 0's and all 1's). Find pertinent statement(s) in the protocol standard that specify whether using two types of broadcast address is required, allowed, or forbidden.

9

UDP: User Datagrams

9.1 Introduction

The *User Datagram Protocol* (UDP) provides connectionless communication among application programs. It allows a program on one machine to send datagrams to program(s) on other machine(s) and to receive replies. This chapter discusses the implementation of UDP, concentrating on how UDP uses protocol port numbers to identify the endpoints of communication. It discusses two possible approaches to the problem of binding protocol port numbers, and shows the implementation of one approach in detail. Finally, it describes the UDP *pseudo-header* and examines how procedures that compute the UDP checksum use it.

9.2 UDP Ports And Demultiplexing

Conceptually, communication with UDP is quite simple. The protocol standard specifies an abstraction known as the *protocol port number* that application programs use to identify the endpoints of communication. When an application program on machine *A* wants to communicate with an application on machine *B* , each application must obtain a UDP protocol port number from its local operating system. Both must use these protocol port numbers when they communicate. Using protocol port numbers instead of system-specific identifiers like process, task, or job identifiers keeps the protocols independent of a specific system and allows communication between applications on a heterogeneous set of computer systems.

Although the idea of UDP protocol port numbers seems straightforward, there are two basic approaches to its implementation. Both approaches are consistent with the protocol standard, but they provide slightly different interfaces for application programs.

The next sections describe how clients and servers use UDP, and show how the two approaches accommodate each.

9.2.1 Ports Used For Pairwise Communication

As Figure 9.1a illustrates, some applications use UDP for pairwise communication. To do so, each of the two applications obtains a UDP port number from its local operating system, and they both use the pair of port numbers when they exchange UDP messages. In such cases, the ideal interface between the application programs and the protocol software separates the address specification operation from the operations for sending and receiving datagrams. That is, the interface allows an application to specify the local and remote protocol port numbers to be used for communication once, and then sends and receives datagrams many times. Of course, when specifying a protocol port on another machine, an application must also specify the IP address of that machine. Once the protocol port numbers have been specified, the application can send and receive an arbitrary number of datagrams.

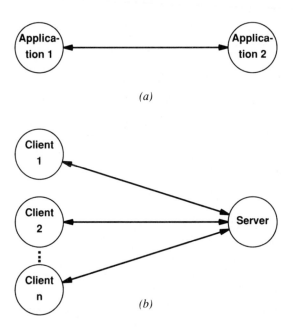

Figure 9.1 The two styles of interaction between programs using UDP. Clients and some other programs use pairwise interaction (*a*). Servers use many-one interaction (*b*), in which a single application may send datagrams to many destinations.

9.2.2 Ports Used For Many-One Communication

Most applications use the client-server model of interaction that Figure 9.1b illustrates. A single server application receives UDP messages from many clients. When the server begins, it cannot specify an IP address or a UDP port on another machine because it needs to allow arbitrary machines to send it messages. Instead, it specifies only a local UDP port number. Each message from a client to the server specifies the client's UDP port as well as the server's UDP port. The server extracts the source port number from the incoming UDP datagram, and uses that number as the destination port number when sending a reply. Of course, the server must also obtain the IP address of the client machine when a UDP datagram arrives, so it can specify the IP address when sending a reply.

Because servers communicate with many clients, they cannot permanently assign a destination IP address or UDP protocol port number. Instead, the interface for many-one communication must allow the server to specify information about the destination each time it sends a datagram. Thus, unlike the ideal interface for pairwise communication, the ideal interface for servers does not separate address specification and datagram transmission.

9.2.3 Modes Of Operation

To accommodate both pairwise communication and many-one communication, most interfaces to UDP use parameters to control the *mode* of interaction. One mode accommodates the pairwise interaction typical of clients. It allows an application to specify both the local and foreign protocol port numbers once, and then send and receive UDP datagrams without specifying the port numbers each time. Another mode accommodates servers. It allows the server to specify only a local port and then receive from arbitrary clients. The system may require an application program to explicitly declare the mode of interaction, or it may deduce the mode from the port bindings that the application specifies.

9.2.4 The Subtle Issue Of Demultiplexing

In addition to the notion of an interaction mode, a UDP implementation provides an interpretation for protocol port demultiplexing. There are two possibilities:

- Demultiplex using only the destination protocol port number, or

- Demultiplex using source address as well as destination protocol port number.

The choice affects the way application programs interact with the protocol software in a subtle way. To understand the subtlety, consider the two styles of demultiplexing Figure 9.2 illustrates.

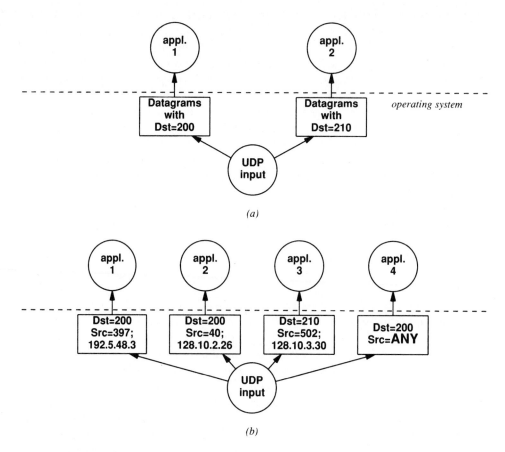

Figure 9.2 The two styles of UDP demultiplexing: (a) using only destination
port, and (b) using (source, destination) port pairs. In style (a), an
application receives all datagrams to a given destination port. In
style (b) it only receives datagrams from the specified source.

In one style of demultiplexing, the system sends all datagrams for a given destination protocol port to the same queue. In the second style of demultiplexing, the system
uses the source address (source protocol port number as well as the source IP address)
when demultiplexing datagrams. Thus, in the second style, each queue contains datagrams from a given site.

Each style has advantages and disadvantages. For example, in the first style, creating a server is trivial because an application receives all datagrams sent to a given protocol port number, independent of their origin. However, because the system does not
distinguish among multiple sources, the system cannot filter erroneously addressed datagrams. Thus, if a datagram arrives addressed to a given port, the application program
using that port will receive it, even if it was sent in error. In the second style, creating a

client is trivial because a given application receives only those datagrams from the application program with which it has elected to communicate. However, if a single application needs to communicate with two remote applications simultaneously, it must allocate two queues, one for each remote application. Furthermore, the system may need to provide additional mechanisms that allow a program to wait for I/O activity on either queue†.

Despite the apparent difficulties, it is possible to accommodate both clients and servers with both styles of demultiplexing. In the first style, a client that communicates with only one remote application must choose a local protocol port number not used by any other local program. In the second style, a server must use a *wildcard*‡ facility as Figure 9.2 illustrates. The source specification labeled *ANY* represents a wildcard that matches any source (any IP address and any protocol port number). At a given time, the system allows at most one wildcard for a given destination port. When a datagram arrives, the implementation checks to see if the source and destination matches a specified source-destination pair before checking the wildcard. Thus, in the example, if a datagram arrives with destination port *200*, source port *397*, and source IP address *192.5.48.3*, the system will place it in the queue for application *1*. Similarly, the system will place datagrams with destination port *220*, source port *40*, and source IP address *128.10.2.26* in the queue for application *2*. The system uses the wildcard specification to match other datagrams sent to port *200* and places them in the queue for application *4*.

9.3 UDP

Our example implementation uses the style of demultiplexing that chooses a queue for incoming datagrams using only the destination protocol port. We selected this style because it keeps demultiplexing efficient and allows application programs to communicate with multiple remote sites simultaneously. After reviewing the definition of data structures used for UDP, we will examine how the software processes arriving datagrams, and how it sends outgoing datagrams.

9.3.1 UDP Declarations

Structure *udp* in file *udp.h* defines the UDP datagram format. In addition to the 16-bit source and destination protocol port numbers, the UDP header contains a 16-bit datagram length field and a 16-bit checksum.

---

†Berkeley UNIX provides a *select* system call to permit an application to await activity on any one of a set of I/O descriptors.

‡Adding a wildcard facility makes the second style functionally equivalent to the first style.

```
/* udp.h */

/* User Datagram Protocol (UDP) constants and formats */

#define U_HLEN  8                    /* UDP header length in bytes           */

/* maximum data in UDP packet    */
#define U_MAXLEN        (IP_MAXLEN-(IP_MINHLEN<<2)-U_HLEN)

struct  udp {                                /* message format of DARPA UDP  */
        unsigned short  u_src;               /* source UDP port number       */
        unsigned short  u_dst;               /* destination UDP port number  */
        unsigned short  u_len;               /* length of UDP data           */
        unsigned short  u_cksum;             /* UDP checksum (0 => none)      */
        char    u_data[U_MAXLEN];            /* data in UDP message          */
};

/* UDP constants */

#define ULPORT          2050    /* initial UDP local "port" number       */

/* assigned UDP port numbers */

#define UP_ECHO         7       /* echo server                           */
#define UP_DISCARD      9       /* discard packet                        */
#define UP_USERS        11      /* users server                          */
#define UP_DAYTIME      13      /* day and time server                   */
#define UP_QOTD         17      /* quote of the day server               */
#define UP_CHARGEN      19      /* character generator                   */
#define UP_TIME         37      /* time server                           */
#define UP_WHOIS        43      /* who is server (user information)       */
#define UP_DNAME        53      /* domain name server                    */
#define UP_TFTP         69      /* trivial file transfer protocol server*/
#define UP_RWHO         513     /* remote who server (ruptime)           */
#define UP_RIP          520     /* route information exchange (RIP)       */

#ifndef Ndg
#define UPPS            1       /* number of xinu ports used to          */
#else                          /*   demultiplex udp datagrams           */
#define UPPS            Ndg
#endif
#define UPPLEN          50      /* size of a demux queue                 */
```

```
/* mapping of external network UDP "port" to internal Xinu port */

struct   upq    {                          /* UDP demultiplexing info     */
         Bool             up_valid;        /* is this entry in use?       */
         unsigned short   up_port;         /* local UDP port number       */
         int              up_pid;          /* port for waiting reader     */
         int              up_xport;        /* corresponding Xinu port on  */
};                                         /*  which incoming pac. queued */


extern   struct  upq     upqs[];
extern   int     udpmutex;          /* for UDP port searching mutex       */
```

In addition to the declaration of the UDP datagram format, *udp.h* contains symbolic constants for values assigned to the most commonly used UDP protocol port numbers. For example, a TFTP server always operates on port *69*, while RIP uses port *520*.

9.3.2 Incoming Datagram Queue Declarations

UDP software divides the data structures that store incoming datagrams into two conceptual pieces: the first piece consists of queues for arriving datagrams, while the second piece contains mapping information that UDP uses to select a queue. The first piece is part of the interface between UDP and application programs that need to extract arriving datagrams. The second piece is part of the operating system – UDP software uses it to select a queue, but application programs cannot access it. File *dgram.h* contains the declaration of the queues used by application programs.

```
/* dgram.h */

/* datagram pseudo-device control block */

struct  dgblk   {                               /* datagram device control block*/
        int     dg_dnum;                        /* device number of this device */
        int     dg_state;                       /* whether this device allocated*/
        int     dg_lport;                       /* local datagram port number   */
        int     dg_fport;                       /* foreign datagram port number */
        IPaddr  dg_fip;                         /* foreign machine IP address   */
        int     dg_xport;                       /* incoming packet queue        */
        int     dg_upq;                         /* index of our upq entry       */
        int     dg_mode;                        /* mode of this interface       */
};

/* datagram psuedo-device state constants */

#define DGS_FREE        0                       /* this device is available     */
#define DGS_INUSE       1                       /* this device is in use        */


#define DG_TIME         30                      /* read timeout (tenths of sec) */

/* constants for dg pseudo-device control functions */

#define DG_SETMODE      1                       /* set mode of device           */
#define DG_CLEAR        2                       /* clear all waiting datagrams  */

/* constants for dg pseudo-device mode bits */

#define DG_NMODE        001                     /* normal (datagram) mode       */
#define DG_DMODE        002                     /* data-only mode               */
#define DG_TMODE        004                     /* timeout all reads            */
#define DG_CMODE        010                     /* generate checksums (default) */

/* structure of xinugram as dg interface delivers it to user */

struct  xgram   {                               /* Xinu datagram (not UDP)      */
        IPaddr  xg_fip;                         /* foreign host IP address      */
        unsigned short  xg_fport;               /* foreign UDP port number      */
        unsigned short  xg_lport;               /* local UDP port number        */
        char    xg_data[U_MAXLEN];              /* maximum data to/from UDP     */
};

#define XGHLEN  8        /* error in ( (sizeof(struct xgram)) - U_MAXLEN)*/
```

```
/* constants for port specifications on UDP open call */

#define ANYFPORT          0                /* accept any foreign UDP port  */
#define ANYLPORT          0                /* assign a fresh local port num*/


extern  struct  dgblk   dgtab[Ndg];
extern  int     dgmutex;
```

Although the file contains many details beyond the scope of this chapter, two de-clarations are pertinent. The basic data structure used to store incoming datagrams con-sists of an array, *dgtab*. Each entry in the array is of type *dgblk*. Think of *dgtab* as a set of queues; there will be one active entry in *dgtab* for each local UDP protocol port in use. Field *dg_lport* specifies the local UDP protocol port number, and field *dg_xport* defines the queue of datagrams that have arrived destined for that port. Field *dg_state* specifies whether the entry is in use (*DGS_INUSE*) or currently unallocated (*DGS_FREE*).

In addition to defining the structure used for demultiplexing, *dgram.h* also specifies the format of datagrams transferred between an application program and the UDP proto-col software. Instead of passing the UDP datagram to applications, our software defines a new format in structure *xgram*. Recall that we use the style of demultiplexing where an application that opens a given protocol port number receives all datagrams sent to that port. The system passes datagrams to the application in *xgram* format, so the appli-cation can determine the sender's IP address as well as the sender's protocol port number.

9.3.3 Mapping UDP port numbers To Queues

UDP uses the destination port number on an incoming datagram to choose the correct entry in *dgtab*. It finds the mapping in array *upqs*, declared in file *udp.h*. Pro-cedure *udp_in*, shown later, compares the destination protocol port number to field *up_port* in each entry of the *upqs* array until it finds a match. It then uses field *up_xport* to determine the identity of the Xinu port used to enqueue the datagram.

Separating the mapping in *upqs* from the queues in *dgtab* may seem wasteful be-cause the current implementation uses a linear search for the mapping. However, linear search only suffices for systems that have few active UDP ports. Systems with many ports need to use a more efficient lookup scheme like *hashing*. Separating the data structure used to map ports from the data structure used for datagram queues makes it possible to modify the mapping algorithm without changing the data structures in the application interface. The separation also makes it possible for the operating system to use UDP directly, without relying on the same interface as application programs.

9.3.4 Allocating A Free Queue

Because our example code uses a sequential search of the *upqs* array, allocation of an entry is straightforward.

```
/* upalloc.c - upalloc */

#include <conf.h>
#include <kernel.h>
#include <proc.h>
#include <network.h>


/*------------------------------------------------------------------------
 *  upalloc  -  allocate a UDP port demultiplexing queue
 *------------------------------------------------------------------------
 */
int upalloc()
{
        struct  upq      *pup;
        int              i;

        wait(udpmutex);
        for (i=0 ; i<UPPS ; i++) {
                pup = &upqs[i];
                if (!pup->up_valid) {
                        pup->up_valid = TRUE;
                        pup->up_port = -1;
                        pup->up_pid = BADPID;
                        pup->up_xport = pcreate(UPPLEN);
                        signal(udpmutex);
                        return i;
                }
        }
        signal(udpmutex);
        return SYSERR;
}


struct  upq      upqs[UPPS];
```

Procedure *upalloc* searches the array until it finds an entry not currently used, fills in the fields, creates a Xinu port to serve as the queue of incoming datagrams, and re-turns the index of the entry to the caller.

9.3.5 Converting To And From Network Byte Order

Two utility procedures handle conversion of UDP header fields between network byte order and local machine byte order. Procedure *udpnet2h* handles conversion to the local machine order for incoming datagrams. The code is self-explanatory.

```
/* udpnet2h.c - udpnet2h */

#include <conf.h>
#include <kernel.h>
#include <network.h>

/*------------------------------------------------------------------------
 *  udpnet2h -  convert UDP header fields from net to host byte order
 *------------------------------------------------------------------------
 */
udpnet2h(pudp)
struct   udp      *pudp;
{
        pudp->u_src = net2hs(pudp->u_src);
        pudp->u_dst = net2hs(pudp->u_dst);
        pudp->u_len = net2hs(pudp->u_len);
}
```

A related procedure, *udph2net*, converts header fields from the local host byte order to standard network byte order.

```
/* udph2net.c - udph2net */

#include <conf.h>
#include <kernel.h>
#include <network.h>

/*------------------------------------------------------------------------
 *  udph2net -  convert UDP header fields from host to net byte order
 *------------------------------------------------------------------------
 */
udph2net(pudp)
struct  udp     *pudp;
{
        pudp->u_src = hs2net(pudp->u_src);
        pudp->u_dst = hs2net(pudp->u_dst);
        pudp->u_len = hs2net(pudp->u_len);
}
```

9.3.6 Processing An Arriving Datagram

A procedure in the pseudo-network interface calls procedure *udp_in* when a UDP datagram arrives destined for the local machine. It passes arguments that specify the index of the network interface on which the packet arrived and the address of a buffer containing the packet.

```
/* udp_in.c - udp_in */

#include <conf.h>
#include <kernel.h>
#include <proc.h>
#include <network.h>

/*------------------------------------------------------------------------
 *  udp_in -  handle an inbound UDP datagram
 *------------------------------------------------------------------------
 */
int udp_in(pni, pep)
struct  netif   *pni;
struct  ep      *pep;
{
        struct  ip      *pip = (struct ip *)pep->ep_data;
        struct  udp     *pudp = (struct udp *)pip->ip_data;
        struct  upq     *pup;
```

```
        unsigned short  dst;
        int             i;

        if (pudp->u_cksum && udpcksum(pip)) {
                freebuf(pep);
                return SYSERR;                        /* checksum error */
        }
        udpnet2h(pudp);             /* convert UDP header to host order */
        dst = pudp->u_dst;
        wait(udpmutex);
        for (i=0 ; i<UPPS ; i++) {
                pup = &upqs[i];
                if (pup->up_port == dst) {
                        /* drop instead of blocking on psend */
                        if (pcount(pup->up_xport) >= UPPLEN) {
                                signal(udpmutex);
                                freebuf(pep);
                                UdpInErrors++;
                                return SYSERR;
                        }
                        psend(pup->up_xport, pep);
                        UdpInDatagrams++;
                        if (!isbadpid(pup->up_pid)) {
                                send(pup->up_pid, OK);
                                pup->up_pid = BADPID;
                        }
                        signal(udpmutex);
                        return OK;
                }
        }
        signal(udpmutex);
        UdpNoPorts++;
        icmp(ICT_DESTUR, ICC_PORTUR, pip->ip_src, pep);
        return OK;
}

int     udpmutex;
```

Udp_in first checks to see whether the sender supplied the optional checksum (by testing to see if the checksum field is nonzero). It calls *udpcksum* to verify the checksum if one is present. The call will result in zero if the packet contains a valid checksum. If the checksum is both nonzero and invalid, *udp_in* discards the UDP datagram without further processing. *Udp_in* also calls *udpnet2h* to convert all header fields to the local machine byte order.

After converting the header, *udp_in* demultiplexes the datagram, and it searches the set of datagram queues (array *upqs*) until it finds one for the destination UDP port. If the port is not full, *udp_in* calls *psend* to deposit the datagram and then calls *send* to send a message to whichever process is awaiting the arrival. If the queue is full, *udp_in* records an overflow error and discards the datagram.

If *udp_in* searches the entire set of datagram queues without finding one reserved for the destination port on the incoming datagram, it means that no application program has agreed to receive datagrams for that port. In such cases, *udp_in* must call *icmp* to send an ICMP *destination unreachable* message back to the original source.

9.3.7 UDP Checksum Computation

Procedure *udpcksum* computes the checksum of a UDP datagram. Like the procedure *cksum* described earlier, it can be used to generate a checksum (by setting the checksum header field to zero), or to verify an existing checksum. However, the UDP checksum differs from earlier checksums in one important way:

> *The UDP checksum covers the UDP datagram plus a pseudo-header that includes the IP source and destination addresses, UDP length, and UDP protocol type identifier.*

When computing the checksum for an outgoing datagram, the protocol software must find out what values will be used when the UDP message is encapsulated in an IP datagram. When verifying the checksum for a message that has arrived, UDP extracts values from the IP datagram that carried the message. Including the IP source and destination addresses in the checksum provides protection against misrouted datagrams.

Procedure *udpcksum* does not assemble a pseudo-header in memory. Instead, it picks up individual fields from the IP header and includes them in the checksum computation. For example, *udpcksum* assigns *psh* the address of the IP source field in the datagram and adds the four 16-bit quantities starting at that address, which include the IP source and destination addresses.

```
/* udpcksum.c - udpcksum */

#include <conf.h>
#include <kernel.h>
#include <network.h>

#define UDP_ALEN        IP_ALEN         /* length of src+dst, in shorts */

/*------------------------------------------------------------------
 *  udpcksum -  compute a UDP pseudo-header checksum
 *------------------------------------------------------------------
 */
```

```
unsigned short udpcksum(pip)
struct   ip        *pip;
{
        struct   udp        *pudp = (struct udp *)pip->ip_data;
        unsigned            short  *psh;
        unsigned            long   sum;
        int                 len    = pudp->u_len;
        int                 i;

        sum = 0;

        psh = (unsigned short *) pip->ip_src;
        for (i=0; i<UDP_ALEN; ++i)
                sum += *psh++;

        psh = (unsigned short *)pudp;
        sum += pip->ip_proto + len;
        if (len & 0x1) {
                ((char *)pudp)[len] = 0;          /* pad */
                len += 1;          /* for the following division */
        }
        len /= 2;          /* convert to length in shorts */

        for (i=0; i<len; ++i)
                sum += *psh++;
        sum = (sum >> 16) + (sum & 0xffff);
        sum += (sum >> 16);

        return (short)(~sum & 0xffff);
}
```

9.4 UDP Output Processing

Before an application program can communicate using UDP, it needs a local UDP port number. Servers, which use well-known ports, request a specific port assignment from the operating system. Usually, clients do not need a specific port – they can use an arbitrary port number. However, because our system demultiplexes using only destination port numbers, a client must be assigned a unique port number. Procedure *udpnxtp* generates a UDP port number that is not in use.

```
/* udpnxtp.c - udpnxtp */

#include <conf.h>
#include <kernel.h>
#include <network.h>

/*------------------------------------------------------------------
 *  udpnxtp  -  return the next available UDP local "port" number
 *       N.B.: assumes udpmutex HELD
 *------------------------------------------------------------------
 */
unsigned short udpnxtp()
{
        static  unsigned short  lastport = ULPORT;
        Bool                    inuse = TRUE;
        struct  upq             *pup;
        int                     i;

        while (inuse) {
                lastport++;
                if (lastport == 0)
                        lastport = ULPORT;
                inuse = FALSE;
                for (i=0; !inuse && i<UPPS ; i++) {
                        pup = &upqs[i];
                        inuse = pup->up_valid && pup->up_port == lastport;
                }
        }
        return lastport;
}
```

To generate an unused port number, *udpnxtp* first increments the global counter *lastport*. It then iterates through the set of UDP input queues to see if any application program has already been assigned *lastport*. Usually, the iteration does not find a match, and *udpnxtp* returns *lastport* to the caller. If it does find a match, *udpnxtp* increments *lastport* and tries again.

9.4.1 Sending A UDP Datagram

When an application program generates UDP output, it transfers control to the operating system and eventually calls procedure *udpsend* to send the UDP datagram.

```
/* udpsend.c - udpsend */

#include <conf.h>
#include <kernel.h>
#include <network.h>

/*------------------------------------------------------------------------
 *  udpsend  -  send one UDP datagram to a given IP address
 *------------------------------------------------------------------------
 */
int
udpsend(fip, fport, lport, pep, datalen, docksum)
IPaddr          fip;
unsigned short  fport, lport;
struct  ep      *pep;
int             datalen;
Bool            docksum;
{
        struct  ip      *pip = (struct ip *) pep->ep_data;
        struct  udp     *pudp = (struct udp *) pip->ip_data;
        struct  route   *prt, *rtget();

        pip->ip_proto = IPT_UDP;
        pudp->u_src = lport;
        pudp->u_dst = fport;
        pudp->u_len = U_HLEN+datalen;
        pudp->u_cksum = 0;
        if (docksum) {
                prt = rtget(fip, RTF_LOCAL);
                if (prt == NULL) {
                        IpOutNoRoutes++;
                        freebuf(pep);
                        return SYSERR;
                }
                blkcopy(pip->ip_src, nif[prt->rt_ifnum].ni_ip, IP_ALEN);
                rtfree(prt);
                blkcopy(pip->ip_dst, fip, IP_ALEN);
                pudp->u_cksum = udpcksum(pip);
                if (pudp->u_cksum == 0)
                        pudp->u_cksum = ~0;
        }
        UdpOutDatagrams++;
        udph2net(pudp);
        return ipsend(fip, pep, U_HLEN+datalen);
}
```

Because gateways have multiple network connections, they have multiple IP addresses. Before *udpsend* can compute the UDP checksum, it needs to know which address IP will use as the source address for the IP datagram that carries the message. To find out, *udpsend* calls procedure *rtget*, passing it the destination IP address as an argument. Once it determines a route, *udpsend* extracts the network interface, from which it obtains the IP datagram source address.

Once it has computed the source address for the IP datagram, *udpsend* fills in the remaining fields of the UDP header, calls *udpcksum* to compute the checksum, and calls *ipsend* to pass the resulting IP datagram to IP for routing and transmission.

9.5 Summary

UDP provides both pairwise communication between peer programs and many-one communication between clients and a server. While the two basic styles of demultiplexing both support clients and servers, each has advantages and disadvantages. The example code demultiplexes using only the destination protocol port number, and makes the creation of servers trivial. To help support clients, the system includes a procedure that generates a unique (unused) protocol port number on demand.

Both UDP input and UDP output are straightforward. The IP process executes the UDP input procedure, which demultiplexes datagrams and deposits each on a queue associated with the destination protocol port. Application programs allocate a port used for transmission and then call the output procedures to create and send UDP datagrams.

The UDP checksum includes fields from a pseudo-header that are used to verify that the IP datagram carrying UDP contained the correct IP source and destination addresses. For input, UDP can obtain values for pseudo-header fields from the IP datagram that carries the UDP message. For output, the pseudo-header processing complicates the UDP checksum computation because it forces UDP to determine which address IP will use as the source address for the datagram.

FOR FURTHER STUDY

Postel [RFC 768] defines the UDP protocol and specifies the message format. The host requirements document [RFC 1122] provides further clarification. Leffler, McKusick, Karels, and Quarterman [1989] presents details of the BSD UNIX implementation.

EXERCISES

9.1 Read the RFC carefully to determine whether all pseudo-header fields used to verify the UDP checksum must be taken from the IP datagram that carries the UDP datagram. Can constants ever be used? Explain.

9.2 Read the 4BSD UNIX documentation. Which style of demultiplexing does it use?

9.3 Does your local system allow you to specify the size of a UDP input queue? If so, how can you choose a reasonable size?

9.4 Look at *udpcksum* carefully. What does it do if the computed checksum happens to be zero? Why?

9.5 Explain why *udpnxtp* skips ports between *0* and *ULPORT* (*2050*) when it generates a local port number.

9.6 How many UDP ports does a typical timesharing system use simultaneously? How many does a typical scientific workstation use?

9.7 Our example code uses sequential search to find a UDP port for demultiplexing. Devise a hashing scheme that lowers lookup time. Will your scheme ever *increase* lookup time? (Hint: consider the previous exercise).

10

TCP: Data Structures And Input Processing

10.1 Introduction

TCP is the most complex of all protocols in the suite of Internet protocols. It provides reliable, flow-controlled, end-to-end, stream service between two machines of arbitrary processing speed using the unreliable IP mechanism for communication. Like most reliable transport protocols, TCP uses *timeout with retransmission* to achieve reliability. However, unlike most other transport protocols, TCP is carefully constructed to work correctly even if datagrams are delayed, duplicated, lost, delivered out of order, or delivered with the data corrupted or truncated. Furthermore, TCP allows communicating machines to reboot and reestablish connections at arbitrary times without causing confusion about which connections are open and which are new.

This chapter examines the global organization of TCP software and describes the data structures TCP uses to manage information about connections. Chapter 11 describes the details of connection management and implementation of the TCP finite state machine used for input. Chapter 12 discusses output and the finite state machine used to control it. Chapters 13 through 15 discuss the details of timer management, estimation of round trip times, retransmission, and miscellaneous details such as urgent data processing.

10.2 Overview Of TCP Software

Recall from Chapter 2 that our implementation of TCP uses three processes. One process handles incoming segments, another manages outgoing segments, and the third is a timer that manages delayed events such as retransmission timeout. In theory, using separate processes isolates the input, output, and event timing parts of TCP and permits us to design each piece independently. In practice, however, the processes interact closely. For example, the input and output processes must cooperate to match incoming acknowledgements with outgoing segments and cancel the corresponding timer retransmission event. Similarly, the output and timer processes interact when the output process schedules a retransmission event or when the timer triggers a retransmission.

10.3 Transmission Control Blocks

TCP coordinates the activities of transmission, reception, and retransmission for each TCP connection through a data structure shared by all processes. The data structure is known as a *transmission control block* or *TCB*. TCP maintains one TCB for each active connection. The TCB contains all information about the TCP connection, including the addresses and port numbers of the connection endpoints, the current round-trip time estimate, data that has been sent or received, whether acknowledgement or retransmission is needed, and any statistics TCP gathers about the use of the connection.

Although the protocol standard defines the notion of the TCB and suggests some of the contents, it does not dictate all the details. Thus, a designer must choose the exact contents. Our example implementation places the information in structure *tcb*. In most cases field names match the names used in the protocol standard.

```
/* tcb.h - RUDK, SUDK, RUHK, SUHK */

/* TCP endpoint types */

#define TCPT_SERVER             1
#define TCPT_CONNECTION         2
#define TCPT_MASTER             3

/* TCP process info */
extern  int             tcpinp();
#define TCPISTK         4096            /* stack size for TCP input      */
#define TCPIPRI         100             /* TCP runs at high priority     */
#define TCPINAM         "tcpinp"        /* name of TCP input process     */
#define TCPIARGC        0               /* count of args to tcpin        */

extern  int             tcpout();
```

```
#define TCPOSTK         4096            /* stack size for TCP output    */
#define TCPOPRI         100             /* TCP runs at high priority    */
#define TCPONAM         "tcpout"        /* name of TCP output process   */
#define TCPOARGC        0               /* count of args to tcpout      */


#define TCPQLEN         20          /* TCP process port queue length        */


#define TCPMAXURG   MAXNETBUF       /* maximum urgent data buffer size      */
#define TCPUQLEN        5           /* TCP urgent queue lengths             */

/* TCP exceptional conditions */

#define TCPE_RESET              -1
#define TCPE_REFUSED            -2
#define TCPE_TOOBIG             -3
#define TCPE_TIMEDOUT           -4
#define TCPE_URGENTMODE         -5
#define TCPE_NORMALMODE         -6

/* string equivalents of TCPE_*, in "tcpswitch.c" */
extern   char     *tcperror[];

#define READERS         1
#define WRITERS         2

/* tcb_flags */

#define TCBF_NEEDOUT    0x01     /* we need output                       */
#define TCBF_FIRSTSEND  0x02     /* no data to ACK                       */
#define TCBF_GOTFIN     0x04     /* no more to receive                   */
#define TCBF_RDONE      0x08     /* no more receive data to process      */
#define TCBF_SDONE      0x10     /* no more send data allowed            */
#define TCBF_DELACK     0x20     /* do delayed ACK's                     */
#define TCBF_BUFFER     0x40     /* do TCP buffering (default no)        */
#define TCBF_PUSH       0x80     /* got a push; deliver what we have     */
#define TCBF_SNDFIN     0x100    /* user process has closed; send a FIN  */

/* aliases, for user programs */

#define TCP_BUFFER      TCBF_BUFFER
#define TCP_DELACK      TCBF_DELACK

/* receive segment reassembly data */
```

```
#define NTCPFRAG        10

/* URG queue element data */

#define UQTSIZE (2*Ntcp)          /* (total) max # pending urgent segs    */

#define UQS_FREE        0
#define UQS_ALLOC       1

struct uqe {
        int      uq_state;        /* UQS_* above                         */
        tcpseq   uq_seq;          /* start sequence of this buffer        */
        int      uq_len;          /* length of this buffer                */
        char     *uq_data;        /* data (0 if on urgent hole queue)     */
};

/* compute urgent data send and receive queue keys                        */
#define SUDK(ptcb, seq) (ptcb->tcb_sudseq - (seq))
#define SUHK(ptcb, seq) (ptcb->tcb_suhseq - (seq))
#define RUDK(ptcb, seq) (ptcb->tcb_rudseq - (seq))
#define RUHK(ptcb, seq) (ptcb->tcb_ruhseq - (seq))

extern  Bool     uqidone;
extern  struct   uqe uqtab[];
extern  int      uqmutex;

struct tcb {
        short    tcb_state;       /* TCP state                           */
        short    tcb_ostate;      /* output state                        */
        short    tcb_type;        /* TCP type (SERVER, CLIENT)           */
        int      tcb_mutex;       /* tcb mutual exclusion                */
        short    tcb_code;        /* TCP code for next packet            */
        short    tcb_flags;       /* various TCB state flags             */
        short    tcb_error;       /* return error for user side          */

        IPaddr   tcb_rip;         /* remote IP address                   */
        short    tcb_rport;       /* remote TCP port                     */
        IPaddr   tcb_lip;         /* local IP address                    */
        short    tcb_lport;       /* local TCP port                      */
        struct   netif  *tcb_pni; /* pointer to our interface            */

        tcpseq   tcb_suna;        /* send unacked                        */
        tcpseq   tcb_snext;       /* send next                           */
        tcpseq   tcb_slast;       /* sequence of FIN, if TCBF_SNDFIN     */
```

```
    long     tcb_swindow;    /* send window size (octets)          */
    tcpseq   tcb_lwseq;      /* sequence of last window update     */
    tcpseq   tcb_lwack;      /* ack seq of last window update      */
    int      tcb_cwnd;       /* congestion window size (octets)    */
    int      tcb_ssthresh;   /* slow start threshold (octets)      */
    int      tcb_smss;       /* send max segment size (octets)     */
    tcpseq   tcb_iss;        /* initial send sequence              */

    int      tcb_srt;        /* smoothed Round Trip Time           */
    int      tcb_rtde;       /* Round Trip deviation estimator     */
    int      tcb_persist;    /* persist timeout value              */
    int      tcb_keep;       /* keepalive timeout value            */
    int      tcb_rexmt;      /* retransmit timeout value           */
    int      tcb_rexmtcount; /* number of rexmts sent              */

    tcpseq   tcb_rnext;      /* receive next                       */

    tcpseq   tcb_rudseq;     /* base sequence for rudq entries     */
    int      tcb_rudq;       /* receive urgent data queue          */
    tcpseq   tcb_ruhseq;     /* base sequence for ruhq entries     */
    int      tcb_ruhq;       /* receive urgent hole queue          */
    int      tcb_sudseq;     /* base sequence for sudq entries     */
    int      tcb_sudq;       /* send urgent data queue             */
    int      tcb_suhseq;     /* base sequence for suhq entries     */
    int      tcb_suhq;       /* send urgent hole queue             */

    int      tcb_lqsize;     /* listen queue size (SERVERs)        */
    int      tcb_listenq;    /* listen queue port (SERVERs)        */
    struct tcb *tcb_pptcb;   /* pointer to parent TCB (for ACCEPT) */
    int      tcb_ocsem;      /* open/close semaphore               */
    int      tcb_dvnum;      /* TCP slave pseudo device number     */

    int      tcb_ssema;      /* send semaphore                     */
    char     *tcb_sndbuf;    /* send buffer                        */
    int      tcb_sbstart;    /* start of valid data                */
    int      tcb_sbcount;    /* data character count               */
    int      tcb_sbsize;     /* send buffer size (bytes)           */

    int      tcb_rsema;      /* receive semaphore                  */
    char     *tcb_rcvbuf;    /* receive buffer (circular)          */
    int      tcb_rbstart;    /* start of valid data                */
    int      tcb_rbcount;    /* data character count               */
    int      tcb_rbsize;     /* receive buffer size (bytes)        */
    int      tcb_rmss;       /* receive max segment size           */
```

```
        tcpseq  tcb_cwin;           /* seq of currently advertised window  */
        int     tcb_rsegq;          /* segment fragment queue              */
        tcpseq  tcb_finseq;         /* FIN sequence number, or 0           */
        tcpseq  tcb_pushseq;        /* PUSH sequence number, or 0          */
};
/* TCP fragment structure */

struct tcpfrag {
        tcpseq  tf_seq;
        int     tf_len;
};
/* TCP control() functions */

#define TCPC_LISTENQ    0x01      /* set the listen queue length          */
#define TCPC_ACCEPT     0x02      /* wait for connect after passive open  */
#define TCPC_STATUS     0x03      /* return status info (all, for master) */
#define TCPC_SOPT       0x04      /* set user-selectable options          */
#define TCPC_COPT       0x05      /* clear user-selectable options        */
#define TCPC_SENDURG    0x06      /* write urgent data                    */


/* global state information */

extern int tcps_oport;   /* Xinu port to start TCP output              */
extern int tcps_iport;   /* Xinu port to send TCP input packets        */
extern int tcps_lqsize;  /* default SERVER queue size                  */
extern int tcps_tmutex;  /* tcb table mutex                            */


extern int       (*tcpswitch[])(), (*tcposwitch[])();


#ifdef  Ntcp
extern struct   tcb     tcbtab[];
#endif
```

   While it is not possible to understand all fields in the TCB without looking at the procedures that use them, the meaning of some fields should be obvious. For example, in addition to fields that specify the current input and output states of the connection (*tcb_state* and *tcb_ostate*), the *tcb* structure includes fields that specify: a mutual exclusion semaphore (*tcb_mutex*), the local and remote IP addresses (*tcb_lip* and *tcb_rip*), the local and remote port numbers (*tcb_lport* and *tcb_rport*), and the network interface used (*tcb_pni*).

   Of course, the *tcb* structure contains information used when sending segments: the receiver's current window size (tcb_swindow), the next sequence number to send (*tcb_snext*), the lowest unacknowledged byte in the sequence (*tcb_suna*), the congestion window size (*tcb_cwnd*), the slow-start threshold (*tcb_ssthresh*), and the maximum allowable segment size (*tcb_smss*).

For retransmission, the *tcb* structure maintains the smoothed round trip time estimate (*tcb_srt*), an estimate of the deviation in round trip times (*tcb_rtde*), the retransmission timeout value (*tcb_rexmt*), and a count of consecutive retransmissions (*tcb_rexmtcount*).

Additional fields in *tcb* contain values used for reception. In addition to the address of the receive buffer (*tcb_rcvbuf*), the *tcb* contains fields that specify the start of valid data (*tcb_rbstart*), a count of characters in the receive buffer (*rbcount*), the allowable maximum segment size (*tcb_rmss*), and the sequence number of the last advertised window (*tcb_cwin*). We will discuss the remaining fields later.

Because segments can arrive out of order, TCP must store information about blocks of data as they arrive until it can assemble them into a contiguous stream. TCP keeps the information on a linked list, using structure *tcpfrag*, defined in *tcb.h*, to store the starting sequence number and length of each block.

10.4 TCP Segment Format

Structure *tcp* defines the TCP segment format. File *tcp.h* contains the declaration along with symbolic constants that define the meaning of bits in field *tcp_code*.

```
/* tcp.h - TCP_HLEN, SEQCMP */

typedef long    tcpseq;

/*
 * SEQCMP - sequence space comparator
 *      This handles sequence space wrap-around. Overlow/Underflow makes
 * the result below correct ( -, 0, + ) for any a, b in the sequence
 * space. Results:        result   implies
 *                          -        a < b
 *                          0        a = b
 *                          +        a > b
 */
#define SEQCMP(a, b)    ((a) - (b))

/* tcp packet format */

struct tcp {
        unsigned short  tcp_sport;      /* source port               */
        unsigned short  tcp_dport;      /* destination port          */
                tcpseq tcp_seq;         /* sequence                  */
                tcpseq tcp_ack;         /* acknowledged sequence     */
                char    tcp_offset;
                char    tcp_code;       /* control flags             */
        unsigned short  tcp_window;     /* window advertisement      */
        unsigned short  tcp_cksum;      /* check sum                 */
```

```
        unsigned short  tcp_urgptr;      /* urgent pointer                */
                 char   tcp_data[1];
};


/* TCP Control Bits */


#define TCPF_URG        0x20    /* urgent pointer is valid               */
#define TCPF_ACK        0x10    /* acknowledgement field is valid        */
#define TCPF_PSH        0x08    /* this segment requests a push          */
#define TCPF_RST        0x04    /* reset the connection                  */
#define TCPF_SYN        0x02    /* synchronize sequence numbers          */
#define TCPF_FIN        0x01    /* sender has reached end of its stream */


#define TCPMHLEN          20    /* minimum TCP header length             */
#define TCPHOFFSET      0x50    /* tcp_offset value for TCPMHLEN         */
#define TCP_HLEN(ptcp)          (((ptcp)->tcp_offset & 0xf0)>>2)


/* TCP Options */


#define TPO_EOOL           0    /* end Of Option List                    */
#define TPO_NOOP           1    /* no Operation                          */
#define TPO_MSS            2    /* maximum Segment Size                  */
```

File *tcp.h* also defines the macro function *TCP_HLEN* that computes the length of a TCP segment header in octets. The header length, measured in 32-bit words, is stored in the high-order 4 bits of the 8-bit offset field. To compute the header length in bytes, the macro must multiply the length in 32-bit words by *4*. To do so, it references the entire octet, computes a logical *and* to extract the length bits, and shifts them into position.

10.5 Sequence Space Comparison

TCP assigns integers, called *sequence numbers* (or *sequence values*) to octets in the data stream. When it sends data in a segment, TCP includes the sequence number in the segment header. The receiving TCP uses the sequence numbers to detect when segments arrive out of order, and to reorder them into the correct linear sequence. TCP chooses the initial starting sequence number for each connection at random to prevent delayed or duplicated packets from confusing the 3-way handshake.

The set of all possible sequence integers is known as the TCP *sequence space*. Because the sequence field in the TCP segment header has fixed size (*32* bits), it is possible for sequence numbers to reach the end of the sequence space and wrap around to zero. TCP software needs to make comparisons between sequence values so it can determine whether the sequence number in one segment is greater or less than the sequence number in another. If one uses conventional comparisons, small values like zero will always compare less than large values, even though zero "follows" the largest possible integer when sequence numbers wrap around the end of the sequence space.

Surprisingly, conventional computer arithmetic can be used to establish a correct relationship between two sequence values, as long as the sequence space size equals the range of integer values on the machine, and the values being compared do not differ by more than one-half the integer space. With current computers and networks, TCP never needs to compare two sequence numbers that differ by more than one-half the largest integer because computers cannot generate output fast enough to wrap around the sequence space before datagrams timeout.

If the two sequence numbers compared are close together, simple integer subtraction yields the desired result. Integer underflow takes care of the case where a very large number is subtracted from a very small number. That is, if a and b are two sequence numbers that differ by no more than one-half the largest possible integer value, the following is true:

result of $a - b$	relationship in Sequence Space
−	a precedes b
0	a equals b
+	a follows b

Figure 10.1 The result of subtracting two sequence values that differ by no more than one-half the largest sequence space value.

We can summarize:

> *TCP uses integer subtraction to compare two sequence values because it can assume they never differ by more than one-half of the sequence space. In such cases, integer underflow produces the desired result when comparing a very large integer with a very small one.*

Macro *SEQCMP* in file *tcp.h* implements sequence space comparison. The TCP code uses *SEQCMP* when doing comparisons to help the reader clearly distinguish between conventional subtraction and sequence space comparison.

10.6 TCP Finite State Machine

Conceptually, TCP uses a finite state machine to control all interactions. Each end of a TCP connection implements a copy of the state machine and uses it to control actions taken when a segment arrives. Figure 10.2 shows the TCP finite state machine and transitions among states.

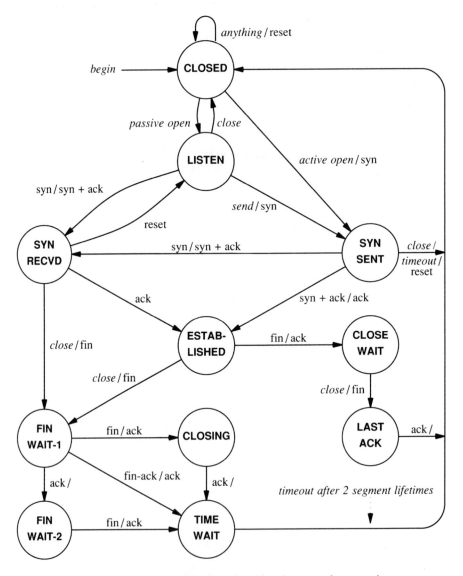

Figure 10.2 The TCP Finite State Machine that controls processing.

In theory, the finite state machine completely specifies how TCP on one machine interacts with TCP on another. In practice, however, the finite state machine does not fully specify interactions. Instead, the machine specifies only the *macroscopic state* of TCP, while additional variables further specify the details or *microscopic state*. More important, because the macroscopic transitions specified by the state machine do not control output or retransmission, such events must be handled separately. We can summarize:

> *The finite state machine specifies how TCP makes macroscopic state transitions in response to input or user commands; an implementation contains a separate mechanism that makes microscopic state transitions to control output and retransmission.*

10.7 Example State Transition

To understand the TCP finite state machine, consider an example of the three-way handshake used to establish a connection between a client and a server. Both the client and server will create an endpoint for communication, and both will have a copy of the finite state machine. The server begins first by issuing a *passive open* operation, which causes the server's finite state machine to enter the *listen* state. The server waits in the *LISTEN* state until a client contacts it. When a client issues an *active open*, it causes TCP software on its machine to send a *SYN* segment to the server and to enter the *SYN-SENT* state.

When the server, which is waiting in the *LISTEN* state, receives the *SYN* segment, it replies with a *SYN* plus an *ACK* segment, creates a new TCB, and places the new TCB in the *SYN-RECEIVED* state. When the *SYN* plus *ACK* segment arrives at the client, the client TCP replies with an *ACK*, and moves from the *SYN-SENT* state to the *ESTABLISHED* state. Finally, when the client's *ACK* arrives at the newly created TCB, it also moves to the *ESTABLISHED* state, which allows data transfer to proceed.

10.8 Declaration Of The Finite State Machine

File *tcpfsm.h* contains the symbolic constants for states in the TCP finite state machine.

```
/* tcpfsm.h - TCB, EVENT, MKEVENT */

/* TCP states */

#define TCPS_FREE               0
#define TCPS_CLOSED             1
#define TCPS_LISTEN             2
#define TCPS_SYNSENT            3
#define TCPS_SYNRCVD            4
#define TCPS_ESTABLISHED        5
#define TCPS_FINWAIT1           6
#define TCPS_FINWAIT2           7
#define TCPS_CLOSEWAIT          8
#define TCPS_LASTACK            9
#define TCPS_CLOSING            10
#define TCPS_TIMEWAIT           11

#define NTCPSTATES              12

/* Output States */

#define TCPO_IDLE               0
#define TCPO_PERSIST            1
#define TCPO_XMIT               2
#define TCPO_REXMT              3

#define NTCPOSTATES             4

/* event processing */

#define SEND            0x1
#define PERSIST         0x2
#define RETRANSMIT      0x3
#define DELETE          0x4
#define TMASK           0x7

#define EVENT(x)        (x & TMASK)
#define TCB(x)          (x >> 3)
#define MKEVENT(timer, tcb)     ((tcb<<3) | (timer & TMASK))

/* implementation parameters */

#define TCP_MAXRETRIES    12    /* max retransmissions before giving up */
#define TCP_TWOMSL        12000 /* 2 minutes (2 * Max Segment Lifetime) */
```

```
#define TCP_MAXRXT      2000    /* 20 seconds max rexmt time              */
#define TCP_MINRXT        50    /* 1/2 second min rexmt time             */
#define TCP_ACKDELAY      20    /* 1/5 sec ACK delay, if TCBF_DELACK     */

#define TCP_MAXPRS      6000    /* 1 minute max persist time             */

/* second argument to tcpsend(): */

#define TSF_NEWDATA        0    /* send all new data                     */
#define TSF_REXMT          1    /* retransmit the first pending segment */

/* third argument to tcpwr():    */

#define TWF_NORMAL         0    /* normal data write                     */
#define TWF_URGENT         1    /* urgent data write                     */
```

10.9 TCB Allocation And Initialization

10.9.1 Allocating A TCB

Procedures that implement the TCP finite state machine must allocate and initialize a TCB when TCP establishes a connection. To do so they call procedure *tcballoc*.

```
/* tcballoc.c - tcballoc */

#include <conf.h>
#include <kernel.h>
#include <network.h>

/*------------------------------------------------------------------------
 * tcballoc - allocate a Transmission Control Block
 *------------------------------------------------------------------------
 */
struct tcb *tcballoc()
{
        struct   tcb        *ptcb;
        int                 slot;

        wait(tcps_tmutex);
        /* look for a free TCB */

        for (ptcb=&tcbtab[0], slot=0; slot<Ntcp; ++slot, ++ptcb)
                if (ptcb->tcb_state == TCPS_FREE)
                        break;
        if (slot < Ntcp) {
                ptcb->tcb_state = TCPS_CLOSED;
                ptcb->tcb_mutex = screate(0);
        } else
                ptcb = (struct tcb *)SYSERR;
        signal(tcps_tmutex);
        return ptcb;
}
```

Tcballoc searches array tcbtab until it finds an unused entry (i.e., an entry with
state equal to *TCPS_FREE*). If such an entry exists, tcballoc changes the state to
CLOSED (the initial state of a connection), creates a mutual exclusion semaphore for
the TCB, and returns the address of the newly allocated entry to the caller. The call returns with *tcb_mutex* held. That is, the call returns with exclusive access to the new
TCB. If no unused TCB exists, tcballoc returns *SYSERR* to indicate that an error occurred.

10.9.2 Deallocating A TCB

When a connection terminates, TCP software calls procedure *tcbdealloc* to free the
TCB and allow it to be used again.

```
/* tcbdealloc.c - tcbdealloc */

#include <conf.h>
#include <kernel.h>
#include <network.h>

/*------------------------------------------------------------------------
 *  tcbdealloc - deallocate a TCB and free its resources
 *       ASSUMES ptcb->tcb_mutex HELD
 *------------------------------------------------------------------------
 */
int tcbdealloc(ptcb)
struct   tcb      *ptcb;
{
        if (ptcb->tcb_state == TCPS_FREE)
                return OK;
        switch (ptcb->tcb_type) {
        case TCPT_CONNECTION:
                tcpkilltimers(ptcb);
                sdelete(ptcb->tcb_ocsem);
                sdelete(ptcb->tcb_ssema);
                sdelete(ptcb->tcb_rsema);
                freemem(ptcb->tcb_sndbuf, ptcb->tcb_sbsize);
                freemem(ptcb->tcb_rcvbuf, ptcb->tcb_rbsize);
                if (ptcb->tcb_rsegq >= 0)
                        freeq(ptcb->tcb_rsegq);
                break;
        case TCPT_SERVER:
                pdelete(ptcb->tcb_listenq, 0);
        default:
                signal(ptcb->tcb_mutex);
                return SYSERR;
        }
        ptcb->tcb_state = TCPS_FREE;
        sdelete(ptcb->tcb_mutex);
        return OK;
}
```

Two special cases complicate the deallocation. As we will see, if a connection has been in progress, *tcbdealloc* must first call *tcpkilltimers* to delete any outstanding timer events. It must then delete the send and receive semaphores as well as the memory used to buffer incoming or outgoing data. For a server, *tcbdealloc* must delete the queue of incoming connection requests. Finally, in all cases, *tcbdealloc* must delete the mutual exclusion semaphore. We will see how TCP software allocates and uses the semaphores and buffers later.

10.10 Implementation Of The Finite State Machine

A designer must choose between two basic implementations of the TCP finite state machine:

- *Table-Driven*
- *Procedure-Driven*

A purely table-driven approach uses a two-dimensional array in which each row corresponds to one state, and each column corresponds to one possible input event or operation that causes transition. Thus, each table entry corresponds to an input event in a particular state. The entry contains the address of a procedure to call to process the event, as well as the integer value of the state to which a transition should occur. A state field in the TCB specifies the current state. When an input event occurs, TCP translates it into one of the possible columns and uses the translated input event and current state to select an entry from the table. TCP uses the entry to select and invoke a procedure, and then updates the state variable.

A procedure-driven approach uses one procedure for each input state. When an event occurs, TCP uses the current state to choose the correct procedure. The procedure processes the input event and updates the state variable.

The table-driven approach works well for implementing a finite state machine that has regular structure, simple semantics, and a relatively complex transition graph. The procedure-driven approach works well for implementing a finite state machine that has few transitions and complex semantics. We have chosen the latter.

> *Because the TCP state machine contains few states, specifies few transitions among the states, provides complex operations, and includes many exceptions to handle errors, our example implementation uses a procedure-driven implementation.*

Thus, our implementation has one procedure for each of the states shown in Figure 10.2, and it has a field in the TCB that specifies the current state. TCP calls the procedure for the current state whenever an input segment arrives. In addition, our implementation provides a separate procedure for each local operation (e.g., a server uses a separate procedure to issue a *passive open*).

10.11 Handling An Input Segment

When IP receives a TCP segment destined for the local machine, it eventually calls *tcp_in* to deliver the segment.

```
/* tcp_in.c - tcp_in */

#include <conf.h>
#include <kernel.h>
#include <network.h>

/*-----------------------------------------------------------------------
 *  tcp_in - deliver an inbound TCP packet to the TCP process
 *-----------------------------------------------------------------------
 */
int tcp_in(pni, pep)
struct   netif   *pni;
struct   ep      *pep;
{
        /* drop instead of blocking on psend */

        TcpInSegs++;
        if (pcount(tcps_iport) >= TCPQLEN) {
                freebuf(pep);
                return SYSERR;
        }
        psend(tcps_iport, pep);
        return OK;
}
```

As the code shows, *tcp_in* sends the incoming segment to the TCP input port, from which the TCP input process extracts it.

The TCP input process executes procedure *tcpinp*.

```
/* tcpinp.c - tcpinp */

#include <conf.h>
#include <kernel.h>
#include <network.h>

/*------------------------------------------------------------------------
 *  tcpinp  -  handle TCP segment coming in from IP
 *------------------------------------------------------------------------
 */
PROCESS tcpinp()
{
        struct  ep      *pep;
        struct  ip      *pip;
        struct  tcp     *ptcp;
        struct  tcb     *ptcb;

        tcps_iport = pcreate(TCPQLEN);
        signal(Net.sema);
        while (TRUE) {
                pep = (struct ep *)preceive(tcps_iport);
                if (pep == SYSERR)
                        break;
                pip = (struct ip *)pep->ep_data;
                if (tcpcksum(pip)) {
                        freebuf(pep);
                        continue;
                }
                ptcp = (struct tcp *)pip->ip_data;
                tcpnet2h(ptcp); /* convert all fields to host order */
                ptcb = tcpdemux(pep);
                if (ptcb == 0) {
                        tcpreset(pep);
                        freebuf(pep);
                        continue;
                }
                if (!tcpok(ptcb, pep))
                        tcpackit(ptcb, pep);
                else {
                        tcpopts(ptcb, pep);
                        tcpswitch[ptcb->tcb_state](ptcb, pep);
                }
                if (ptcb->tcb_state != TCPS_FREE)
                        signal(ptcb->tcb_mutex);
```

```
                          freebuf(pep);
                }
}
```

```
int tcps_oport, tcps_iport, tcps_lqsize, tcps_tmutex;
```

Tcpinp repeatedly extracts a segment from the input port, calls *tcpcksum* to verify the checksum, and calls *tcpnet2h* to convert header fields to local byte order. It uses *tcpdemux* to find the correct TCB for the segment (calling *tcpreset* to send a *RESET* if no TCB exists). It then calls *tcpok* to verify that the segment is acceptable for the current window, and calls *tcpackit* to send an acknowledgment if it is not.† Finally, *tcpinp* uses *tcpopts* to handle options in the segment, and then uses array *tcpswitch* to choose a procedure corresponding to the current input state. The next sections review individual procedures that *tcpinp* uses.

10.11.1 Converting A TCP Header To Local Byte Order

Procedure *tcpnet2h* converts integer fields in the TCP header from network standard byte order to local machine byte order.

---

†According to the protocol standard, the acknowledgement does not confirm receipt of the unacceptable segment; it merely reports the correctly received sequence and the current window size.

```
/* tcpnet2h.c - tcpnet2h */

#include <conf.h>
#include <kernel.h>
#include <network.h>


/*------------------------------------------------------------------------
 *  tcpnet2h -  convert TCP header fields from net to host byte order
 *------------------------------------------------------------------------
 */
struct tcp *tcpnet2h(ptcp)
struct   tcp      *ptcp;
{
        /* NOTE: does not include TCP options */

        ptcp->tcp_sport = net2hs(ptcp->tcp_sport);
        ptcp->tcp_dport = net2hs(ptcp->tcp_dport);
        ptcp->tcp_seq = net2hl(ptcp->tcp_seq);
        ptcp->tcp_ack = net2hl(ptcp->tcp_ack);
        ptcp->tcp_window = net2hs(ptcp->tcp_window);
        ptcp->tcp_urgptr = net2hs(ptcp->tcp_urgptr);
        return ptcp;
}
```

10.11.2 Computing The TCP Checksum

TCP computes a checksum the same as UDP. Initially, *tcpcksum* computes the checksum of a pseudo-header that includes the source and destination IP addresses, segment length, and protocol type value used by IP (the value used in field *ip_proto*). It then treats the segment as an array of 16-bit values and adds each of them to the checksum. Finally, *tcpcksum* handles overflow and returns the complement of the checksum to the caller.

```
/* tcpcksum.c - tcpcksum */

#include <conf.h>
#include <kernel.h>
#include <network.h>


/*------------------------------------------------------------------------
 *  tcpcksum -  compute a TCP pseudo-header checksum
 *------------------------------------------------------------------------
 */
```

```
unsigned short tcpcksum(pip)
struct   ip        *pip;
{
          struct  tcp      *ptcp = (struct tcp *)pip->ip_data;
          unsigned         short   *sptr, len;
          unsigned         long tcksum;
          int              i;

          tcksum = 0;

          sptr = (unsigned short *) pip->ip_src;
          /* 2*IP_ALEN octets = IP_ALEN shorts... */
          /* they are in net order.                 */
          for (i=0; i<IP_ALEN; ++i)
                  tcksum += *sptr++;
          sptr = (unsigned short *)ptcp;
          len = pip->ip_len - IP_HLEN(pip);
          tcksum += IPT_TCP + len;
          if (len % 2) {
                  ((char *)ptcp)[len] = 0;        /* pad */
                  len += 1;         /* for the following division */
          }
          len >>= 1;      /* convert to length in shorts */

          for (i=0; i<len; ++i)
                  tcksum += *sptr++;
          tcksum = (tcksum >> 16) + (tcksum & 0xffff);
          tcksum += (tcksum >> 16);

          return (short)(~tcksum & 0xffff);
}
```

10.11.3 Finding The TCB For A Segment

Procedure *tcpdemux* finds the correct TCB for an incoming segment. The code searches array *tcbtab* sequentially. For TCBs that correspond to established connections, *tcpdemux* makes four comparisons to check both connection endpoints. In addition to comparing the source and destination protocol port numbers in the segment to those in the entry, it compares the source and destination IP addresses in the IP datagram to those in the entry. However, because servers do not specify a foreign IP address or protocol port number, *tcpdemux* cannot compare the source addresses on these entries. Thus, for TCBs in the *LISTEN* state, *tcpdemux* compares only the destination protocol port number.

If a connection exists for the incoming segment, *tcpdemux* returns a pointer to the entry for the segment after acquiring its mutual exclusion semaphore. If no connection exists, *tcpdemux* examines the segment type. For most segment types, *tcpdemux* returns an error code (*0*). However, if the incoming segment contains a synchronization (*SYN*) request and a server has issued a passive open, *tcpdemux* returns a pointer to the TCB entry for the server. Of course, if no server has created a TCB for the specified destination address, *tcpdemux* returns an error for the *SYN* request.

To make searching efficient, *tcpdemux* searches the set of possible connections once. During the search, it looks for an exact match (i.e., a connection for which both endpoints in the TCB match both endpoints in the incoming segment) and also keeps a record of partial matches (server connections for which the destination matches). After completing the search, it tests to see if the segment consisted of a *SYN* request. If so, it returns any partial match that may have been found.

```
/* tcpdemux.c - tcpdemux */

#include <conf.h>
#include <kernel.h>
#include <network.h>

/*------------------------------------------------------------------------
 *  tcpdemux -  do TCP port demultiplexing
 *------------------------------------------------------------------------
 */
struct tcb *tcpdemux(pep)
struct  ep      *pep;
{
        struct  ip      *pip = (struct ip *)pep->ep_data;
        struct  tcp     *ptcp = (struct tcp *)pip->ip_data;
        struct  tcb     *ptcb;
        int             tcbn, lstcbn;

        wait(tcps_tmutex);
        for (tcbn=0, lstcbn = -1; tcbn<Ntcp; ++tcbn) {
                if (tcbtab[tcbn].tcb_state == TCPS_FREE)
                        continue;
                if (ptcp->tcp_dport == tcbtab[tcbn].tcb_lport &&
                    ptcp->tcp_sport == tcbtab[tcbn].tcb_rport &&
                    blkequ(pip->ip_src, tcbtab[tcbn].tcb_rip, IP_ALEN) &&
                    blkequ(pip->ip_dst, tcbtab[tcbn].tcb_lip, IP_ALEN)) {
                        break;
                }
```

```
            if (tcbtab[tcbn].tcb_state == TCPS_LISTEN &&
                ptcp->tcp_dport == tcbtab[tcbn].tcb_lport)
                        lstcbn = tcbn;
    }
    if (tcbn >= Ntcp)
            if (ptcp->tcp_code & TCPF_SYN)
                    tcbn = lstcbn;
            else
                    tcbn = -1;
    signal(tcps_tmutex);
    if (tcbn < 0)
            return 0;
    wait(tcbtab[tcbn].tcb_mutex);
    if (tcbtab[tcbn].tcb_state == TCPS_FREE)
            return 0;                           /* OOPS! Lost it... */
    return &tcbtab[tcbn];
}
```

10.11.4 Checking Segment Validity

We saw that *tcpinp* calls function *tcpok* to check the validity of a segment before following transitions of the finite state machine. *Tcpok* compares the incoming segment to information in the TCB to see whether data in the segment lies in the receive window.

```
/* tcpok.c - tcpok */

#include <conf.h>
#include <kernel.h>
#include <network.h>

/*------------------------------------------------------------------------
 *  tcpok -  determine if a received segment is acceptable
 *------------------------------------------------------------------------
 */
int tcpok(ptcb, pep)
struct   tcb      *ptcb;
struct   ep       *pep;
{
        struct   ip       *pip = (struct ip *)pep->ep_data;
        struct   tcp      *ptcp = (struct tcp *) pip->ip_data;
        int               seglen, wlast, slast, rwindow;
        Bool              rv;

        if (ptcb->tcb_state < TCPS_SYNRCVD)
                return TRUE;
        seglen = pip->ip_len - IP_HLEN(pip) - TCP_HLEN(ptcp);

        /* add SYN and FIN */
        if (ptcp->tcp_code & TCPF_SYN)
                ++seglen;
        if (ptcp->tcp_code & TCPF_FIN)
                ++seglen;
        rwindow = ptcb->tcb_rbsize - ptcb->tcb_rbcount;
        if (rwindow == 0 && seglen == 0)
                return ptcp->tcp_seq == ptcb->tcb_rnext;
        if (ptcp->tcp_code & TCPF_URG)
                (void) tcprcvurg(ptcb, pep);
        wlast = ptcb->tcb_rnext + rwindow - 1;
        rv = (ptcp->tcp_seq - ptcb->tcb_rnext) >= 0 &&
                (ptcp->tcp_seq - wlast) <= 0;
        if (seglen == 0)
                return rv;
        slast = ptcp->tcp_seq + seglen - 1;
        rv |= (slast - ptcb->tcb_rnext) >= 0 && (slast - wlast) <= 0;

        /* If no window, strip data but keep ACK, RST and URG          */
        if (rwindow == 0)
                pip->ip_len = IP_HLEN(pip) + TCP_HLEN(ptcp);
        return rv;
}
```

Tcpok allows all segments in the *unsynchronized states* (*CLOSED*, *LISTEN*, and *SYN-SENT*). For others, it computes the segment length. Conceptually, *SYN* and *FIN* occupy one position in the sequence space, so *tcpok* adds one to the length if either the *SYN* or *FIN* bits are set. Once it has determined the segment length, *tcpok* calls *tcprcvurg* to handle urgent data, computes the receiver window size (*rwindow*) and the highest possible sequence number that lies in the window (*wlast*). If data in the segment lies in the acceptable range (i.e., lies below or within the window), *tcpok* returns *TRUE*. Even if the window size is zero, some segment processing should still occur. Therefore, *tcpok* changes the IP header length when the window size is zero to make it appear that the segment arrived without data. *Tcpinp* has already verified the checksum, so it need not be recomputed.

10.11.5 Choosing A Procedure For the Current State

Once *tcpinp* has found a TCB for an incoming segment and verified that data in the segment is within the advertised window, it uses the current connection state (found in *ptcb->tcb_state*) to select a procedure to handle the segment. Array *tcpswitch* merely contains the addresses of procedures in one-to-one correspondence with states. As we will see, each procedure takes two arguments: a pointer to the TCB entry and a pointer to an incoming packet. File *tcpswitch.c* contains a declaration of the *tcpswitch* array.

```
/* tcpswitch.c */

#include <conf.h>
#include <kernel.h>
#include <network.h>


char    *tcperror[] = {
        "no error",
        "connection reset",             /* TCPE_RESET        */
        "connection refused",           /* TCPE_REFUSED      */
        "not enough buffer space",      /* TCPE_TOOBIG       */
        "connection timed out",         /* TCPE_TIMEDOUT     */
        "urgent data pending",          /* TCPE_URGENTMODE   */
        "end of urgent data",           /* TCPE_NORMALMODE   */
        };
/* SEGMENT ARRIVES state processing */

int     tcpclosed(), tcplisten(),tcpsynsent(), tcpsynrcvd(),
        tcpestablished(), tcpfin1(), tcpfin2(), tcpclosewait(),
        tcpclosing(), tcplastack(), tcptimewait();

int     (*tcpswitch[NTCPSTATES])() = {
        ioerr,                          /* TCPS_FREE         */
        tcpclosed,                      /* TCPS_CLOSED       */
        tcplisten,                      /* TCPS_LISTEN       */
```

```
        tcpsynsent,                     /* TCPS_SYNSENT        */
        tcpsynrcvd,                     /* TCPS_SYNRCVD        */
        tcpestablished,                 /* TCPS_ESTABLISHED    */
        tcpfin1,                        /* TCPS_FINWAIT1       */
        tcpfin2,                        /* TCPS_FINWAIT2       */
        tcpclosewait,                   /* TCPS_CLOSEWAIT      */
        tcplastack,                     /* TCPS_LASTACK        */
        tcpclosing,                     /* TCPS_CLOSING        */
        tcptimewait,                    /* TCPS_TIMEWAIT       */
};
/* Output event processing */


int     tcpidle(), tcppersist(), tcpxmit(), tcprexmt();

int     (*tcposwitch[NTCPOSTATES])() = {
        tcpidle,                        /* TCPO_IDLE           */
        tcppersist,                     /* TCPO_PERSIST        */
        tcpxmit,                        /* TCPO_XMIT           */
        tcprexmt,                       /* TCPO_REXMT          */
};
```

10.12 Summary

TCP uses three separate processes to handle input, output, and timer functions. The processes coordinate through a data structure known as the *transmission control block* (TCB). TCP maintains a separate TCB for each active connection.

Our example implementation uses a procedure-driven implementation of the finite state machine in which one procedure corresponds to each state. This chapter showed how the TCP input process handles an incoming segment, using the connection endpoints to demultiplex it among active TCBs and using a table to switch it to the appropriate state procedure.

FOR FURTHER STUDY

Postel [RFC 793] outlines the general idea underlying the TCB structure and describes many of the fields. The host requirements document [RFC 1122] contains further refinements. Many of the remaining fields in the TCB have been derived from RFCs discussed in the next chapters.

EXERCISES

10.1 Procedure *tcballoc* uses a sequential search to find a free TCB, which means the overhead of searching is proportional to the number of concurrent active TCP connections. Describe an implementation that can allocate a TCB in constant time.

10.2 Consider the order of fields in the example TCB. Have they been grouped according to function? Explain.

10.3 The code declares array *tcpswitch* to be an array of pointers to functions that return integers. How could one implement *tcpswitch* in a language like Pascal that does not provide pointers to procedures? What are the advantages and disadvantages of each implementation?

10.4 The code declares some integer fields in the TCP header to be *short* and others to be *long*. Will this declaration work on all machines? Explain why or why not.

10.5 File *tcpfsm.h* defines *12* to be the maximum number of retransmissions TCP makes before giving up. Discuss whether this is a reasonable limit.

10.6 File *tcpfsm.h* defines two times the *maximum segment lifetime* to be two minutes. Can you imagine an internet where datagrams survive more than two minutes? Explain.

10.7 If applications use TCP to carry a sequence of 16-bit integers from one machine to another, will they have the same value when they arrive? Why or why not?

10.8 Array *tcperror* (declared in file *tcpswitch.c*) contains pointers to strings that give an explanation of each possible TCP error message. What is the advantage of collecting all the messages into one array?

11

TCP: Finite State Machine Implementation

11.1 Introduction

Chapter 10 discussed the general organization of TCP software in which individual procedures correspond to states of the TCP finite state machine. It showed how the TCP input process demultiplexes the incoming segment among TCBs, and how it uses the state variable from a TCB to select one of the procedures that correspond to machine states. This chapter examines each of the state procedures in detail.

11.2 CLOSED State Processing

The *CLOSED* state represents a TCB that has been allocated but not used in any way. In particular, the application program that allocated the TCB has neither completed an *active open* operation nor has it completed a *passive open* operation. As a result, any incoming segment generates a TCP *RESET*. Procedure *tcpclosed* implements the *CLOSED* state. It calls one of the output procedures, *tcpreset*, to generate and send the *RESET* message.

```
/* tcpclosed.c - tcpclosed */

#include <conf.h>
#include <kernel.h>
#include <network.h>

/*------------------------------------------------------------------
 *  tcpclosed -  do CLOSED state processing
 *------------------------------------------------------------------
 */
int tcpclosed(ptcb, pep)
struct  tcb      *ptcb;
struct  ep       *pep;
{
        tcpreset(pep);
        return  SYSERR;
}
```

11.3 Graceful Shutdown

TCP uses a modified 3-way handshake to shut down connections. One side, call it *A*, initiates the shutdown by issuing a *close* operation. TCP on side *A* sends a *FIN* segment and moves to the *FIN-WAIT-1* state. When it receives the *FIN*, the other side, call it *B*, sends an *ACK*, moves to the *CLOSE-WAIT* state, and waits for the application to close the connection. Back at side *A*, receipt of the *ACK* causes TCP to move to the *FIN-WAIT-2* state.

When the application on side *B* executes a *close* operation, TCP sends a *FIN* and moves to the *LAST-ACK* state. Side *A* receives the *FIN*, moves to the *TIME-WAIT* state, sends the final *ACK*, and shuts down the connection. When the last *ACK* arrives on side *B*, that side shuts down as well. The next sections examine the procedures that handle graceful shutdown.

11.4 Timed Delay After Closing

Because the Internet Protocol is a best-effort delivery system, datagrams can be duplicated, delayed, or delivered out of order. Duplication and delay pose a potential problem for protocols like TCP that use IP for delivery because TCP allows applications to reuse protocol port numbers. In particular, a lost acknowledgement will cause a *RESET*, and will lead the sender to believe its last packet (including the *FIN* and data) was not delivered. Furthermore, if TCP allowed immediate reuse of port numbers after a connection terminated, a duplicated *FIN* request from the previous connection could cause termination of a later one that used the same ports.

To prevent duplicated segments from interfering with later connections, TCP does not delete a TCB immediately after a connection closes. Instead, it leaves the TCB in place for a short time. The standard specifies that TCP should wait twice the *maximum segment lifetime*† before deleting the record of a connection. In our implementation, procedure *tcpwait* schedules the delayed deletion of a TCB. Unlike most procedures in this chapter, *tcpwait* does not correspond to an input state. Instead, other input state procedures call it to schedule delayed deletion.

```
/* tcpwait.c - tcpwait */

#include <conf.h>
#include <kernel.h>
#include <network.h>

/*------------------------------------------------------------------------
 *  tcpwait - (re)schedule a DELETE event for 2MSL from now
 *------------------------------------------------------------------------
 */
int tcpwait(ptcb)
struct  tcb      *ptcb;
{
        int      tcbnum = ptcb - &tcbtab[0];

        tcpkilltimers(ptcb);
        tmset(tcps_oport, TCPQLEN, MKEVENT(DELETE, tcbnum), TCP_TWOMSL);
        return OK;
}
```

Tcpwait uses the timer process described in Chapter 13. It calls *tcpkilltimers* to delete any pending events associated with the TCB (e.g., retransmission events), and *tmset* to create a *deletion event* that will occur *TCP_TWOMSL* time units in the future. When the deletion event occurs, it causes the timer process to delete the TCB.

11.5 TIME-WAIT State Processing

TCP leaves a connection in the *TIME-WAIT* state after successful completion of graceful shutdown. Procedure *tcptimewait* implements *TIME-WAIT* state processing.

---

†The maximum segment lifetime is defined to be the maximum time a segment can survive in the underlying delivery system before it must be discarded.

```
/* tcptimewait.c - tcptimewait */

#include <conf.h>
#include <kernel.h>
#include <network.h>

/*------------------------------------------------------------------
 *  tcptimewait -  do TIME_WAIT state input processing
 *------------------------------------------------------------------
 */
int tcptimewait(ptcb, pep)
struct   tcb      *ptcb;
struct   ep       *pep;
{
        struct  ip       *pip = (struct ip *)pep->ep_data;
        struct  tcp      *ptcp = (struct tcp *)pip->ip_data;

        if (ptcp->tcp_code & TCPF_RST)
                return tcbdealloc(ptcb);
        if (ptcp->tcp_code & TCPF_SYN) {
                tcpreset(pep);
                return tcbdealloc(ptcb);
        }
        tcpacked(ptcb, pep);
        tcpdata(ptcb, pep);                     /* just ACK any packets */
        tcpwait(ptcb);
        return OK;
}
```

If a *RESET* arrives, the other side of the connection must have reinitialized, so *tcptimewait* deallocates the TCB. To prevent delayed *SYN* requests from causing a new connection, *tcptimewait* sends a *RESET* if a *SYN* segment arrives. Finally, if any other segment arrives, it could mean that an acknowledgment was lost, so TCP responds to the segment as usual. It calls *tcpacked* to handle acknowledgements, and *tcpdata* to process data in the segment. Finally, it calls *tcpwait* to remove the old deletion event and schedule a new one. The consequence of restarting the timer for each new segment can be surprising.

> *Because TCP restarts the TCB deletion timeout after each non-SYN segment, the TCB will not expire as long as the other side continues to send segments.*

The advantage of leaving the TCB in place is that TCP will correctly handle delayed messages. The disadvantage is that an implementation that never stops sending segments can keep resources reserved in another machine indefinitely.

11.6 CLOSING State Processing

TCP reaches the *CLOSING* state after receiving a *FIN* in response to a *FIN*. Thus, both sides have agreed to shut down, and TCP has entered the *CLOSING* state to await an acknowledgment of its *FIN*. Procedure *tcpclosing* implements the *CLOSING* state.

```
/* tcpclosing.c - tcpclosing */

#include <conf.h>
#include <kernel.h>
#include <network.h>

/*------------------------------------------------------------------
 * tcpclosing -  do CLOSING state input processing
 *------------------------------------------------------------------
 */
int tcpclosing(ptcb, pep)
struct  tcb     *ptcb;
struct  ep      *pep;
{
        struct  ip      *pip = (struct ip *)pep->ep_data;
        struct  tcp     *ptcp = (struct tcp *)pip->ip_data;

        if (ptcp->tcp_code & TCPF_RST)
                return tcbdealloc(ptcb);
        if (ptcp->tcp_code & TCPF_SYN) {
                tcpreset(pep);
                return tcbdealloc(ptcb);
        }
        tcpacked(ptcb, pep);
        if ((ptcb->tcb_code & TCPF_FIN) == 0) {
                ptcb->tcb_state = TCPS_TIMEWAIT;
                tcpwait(ptcb);
        }
        return OK;
}
```

If a *RESET* arrives, *tcpclosing* deallocates the TCB. If a *SYN* request arrives, *tcpclosing* responds by sending a *RESET* and deallocating the TCB. For other segments, *tcpclosing* calls *tcpacked* to handle acknowledgements. Bit *TCPF_FIN* in the code field of the TCB records whether an acknowledgment has arrived for the *FIN* that was sent. When a segment arrives acknowledging the *FIN*, *tcpacked* clears the bit. *Tcpclosing* checks the bit and causes a transition to the *TIME-WAIT* state if the bit has been cleared. When it makes the transition, *tcpclosing* calls *tcpwait* to erase any pending events and start the TCB deletion timer.

11.7 FIN-WAIT-2 State Processing

Usually, when one side sends a *FIN*, the other side acknowledges it immediately and delays before sending the second *FIN*. The state machine handles the delay with state *FIN-WAIT-2*, implemented by procedure *tcpfin2*.

```
/* tcpfin2.c - tcpfin2 */

#include <conf.h>
#include <kernel.h>
#include <network.h>

/*------------------------------------------------------------------------
 *  tcpfin2 -  do FIN_WAIT_2 state input processing
 *------------------------------------------------------------------------
 */
int tcpfin2(ptcb, pep)
struct  tcb      *ptcb;
struct  ep       *pep;
{
        struct  ip       *pip = (struct ip *)pep->ep_data;
        struct  tcp      *ptcp = (struct tcp *)pip->ip_data;

        if (ptcp->tcp_code & TCPF_RST)
                return tcpabort(ptcb, TCPE_RESET);
        if (ptcp->tcp_code & TCPF_SYN) {
                tcpreset(pep);
                return tcpabort(ptcb, TCPE_RESET);
        }
        if (tcpacked(ptcb, pep) == SYSERR)
                return OK;
        tcpdata(ptcb, pep);      /* for data + FIN ACKing */

        if (ptcb->tcb_flags & TCBF_RDONE) {
                ptcb->tcb_state = TCPS_TIMEWAIT;
```

```
            tcpwait(ptcb);
    }
    return OK;
}
```

If a *RESET* arrives, *tcpfin2* calls *tcpabort* to abort the connection and deallocate the TCB. It sends a *RESET* in response to an arriving *SYN*. If the other side sent data or a *FIN* in the segment, *tcpfin2* calls *tcpacked* to acknowledge the input and *tcpdata* to process it.

The finite state machine specifies that TCP should change to the *TIME-WAIT* state when a *FIN* arrives. However, it is important to understand that TCP does not follow such state transitions merely because a segment arrives with the *FIN* bit set. Instead, to accommodate datagrams that arrive out of order, it waits until the entire sequence of data has been received up to and including the *FIN*. That is,

> *Because TCP must handle out-of-order delivery, it does not make all state transitions instantly. In particular, it delays transitions that occur for a* FIN *segment until all data has been received and acknowledged.*

In terms of the implementation, if all the data plus a *FIN* arrives, the call to *tcpdata* sets bit *TCBF_RDONE* in the TCB. Thus, when checking to see whether it should move to the *TIME-WAIT* state, *tcpfin2* checks the *TCBF_RDONE* bit in the TCB instead of the *FIN* bit in the segment. When making a transition to *TIME-WAIT*, *tcpfin2* calls *tcpwait* to remove existing timer events and create a TCB deletion event.

11.8 FIN-WAIT-1 State Processing

TCP enters state *FIN-WAIT-1* when the user issues a *close* operation, causing TCP to send a *FIN*. The other side can respond with an *ACK* of the *FIN* or with its own *FIN* or both. If a *FIN* arrives alone, the other side must have started to close the connection, so TCP responds with an *ACK* and moves to the *CLOSING* state. If an *ACK* arrives alone, TCP moves to the *FIN-WAIT-2* state to await the *FIN*. Finally, if both a *FIN* and an *ACK* arrive, TCP moves to the *TIME-WAIT* state. Procedure *tcpfin1* implements these transitions.

```
/* tcpfin1.c - tcpfin1 */

#include <conf.h>
#include <kernel.h>
#include <network.h>

/*------------------------------------------------------------------------
 *  tcpfin1 -  do FIN_WAIT_1 state input processing
 *------------------------------------------------------------------------
 */
int tcpfin1(ptcb, pep)
struct tcb      *ptcb;
struct ep       *pep;
{
        struct  ip      *pip    = (struct ip *)pep->ep_data;
        struct  tcp     *ptcp   = (struct tcp *)pip->ip_data;

        if (ptcp->tcp_code & TCPF_RST)
                return tcpabort(ptcb, TCPE_RESET);
        if (ptcp->tcp_code & TCPF_SYN) {
                tcpreset(pep);
                return tcpabort(ptcb, TCPE_RESET);
        }
        if (tcpacked(ptcb, pep) == SYSERR)
                return OK;
        tcpdata(ptcb, pep);
        tcpswindow(ptcb, pep);

        if (ptcb->tcb_flags & TCBF_RDONE) {
                if (ptcb->tcb_code & TCPF_FIN)          /* FIN not ACKed*/
                        ptcb->tcb_state = TCPS_CLOSING;
                else {
                        ptcb->tcb_state = TCPS_TIMEWAIT;
                        signal(ptcb->tcb_ocsem);        /* wake closer  */
                        tcpwait(ptcb);
                }
        } else if ((ptcb->tcb_code & TCPF_FIN) == 0) {
                signal(ptcb->tcb_ocsem);                /* wake closer  */
                ptcb->tcb_state = TCPS_FINWAIT2;
        }
        return OK;
}
```

As expected, *tcpfin1* aborts the connection immediately if a *RESET* arrives, and sends a *RESET* in response to a *SYN*. In general, TCP must still process incoming data, so it calls *tcpacked* to handle incoming acknowledgements, *tcpdata* to process data in the segment, and *tcpswindow* to adjust its sending window size. Once the input has been processed, *tcpfin1* checks to see if it should make a state transition. If the *TCBF_RDONE* bit is set, a *FIN* has arrived and so has all data in the sequence up to the *FIN*. If the *TCPF_FIN* bit is cleared, an *ACK* has arrived for the outgoing *FIN*. *Tcpfin1* uses these two bits to determine whether to make a transition to the *CLOSING*, *FIN-WAIT-2*, or *TIME-WAIT* states. When making the transition to *TIME-WAIT*, it must call *tcpwait* to schedule a TCB deletion event. When the outgoing *FIN* has been acknowledged, *tcpfin1* signals semaphore *ocsem*, allowing the application program that has closed the connection to complete the *close* operation. If multiple application programs have access to the TCB, it will be deleted when the last one issues a *close*.

11.9 CLOSE-WAIT State Processing

The shutdown states we have seen so far handle transitions when an application program initiates shutdown with a *close* operation. By contrast, when a *FIN* arrives before the application issues a *close*, TCP enters the *CLOSE-WAIT* state. It uses end-of-file to inform the application program that the other side has shut down the connection, and waits for the application to issue a *close* operation before moving to the *LAST-ACK* state.

TCP uses procedure *tcpclosewait* to process incoming segments while it waits in the *CLOSE-WAIT* state.

```
/* tcpclosewait.c - tcpclosewait */

#include <conf.h>
#include <kernel.h>
#include <network.h>

/*------------------------------------------------------------------
 *  tcpclosewait -  do CLOSE_WAIT state input processing
 *------------------------------------------------------------------
 */
int tcpclosewait(ptcb, pep)
struct  tcb     *ptcb;
struct  ep      *pep;
{
        struct  ip      *pip = (struct ip *)pep->ep_data;
        struct  tcp     *ptcp = (struct tcp *)pip->ip_data;

        if (ptcp->tcp_code & TCPF_RST) {
                TcpEstabResets++;
                TcpCurrEstab--;
                return tcpabort(ptcb, TCPE_RESET);
        }
        if (ptcp->tcp_code & TCPF_SYN) {
                TcpEstabResets++;
                TcpCurrEstab--;
                tcpreset(pep);
                return tcpabort(ptcb, TCPE_RESET);
        }
        tcpacked(ptcb, pep);
        tcpswindow(ptcb, pep);
        return OK;
}
```

If a *RESET* arrives, *tcpclosewait* calls *tcpabort* to abort the connection and remove the TCB. If a *SYN* arrives, *tcpclosewait* generates a *RESET* and aborts the connection. Finally, it calls *tcpacked* to handle acknowledgements and *tcpswindow* to update the sending window size.

11.10 LAST-ACK State Processing

The transition from *CLOSE-WAIT* to *LAST-ACK* occurs when an application issues a *close* operation. During the transition, TCP schedules a *FIN* to be sent and enters the *LAST-ACK* state to await acknowledgement. The *FIN* will be sent after remaining data, which may be delayed if the receiver has closed its window. Once it sends the *FIN*, TCP schedules retransmission. If an acknowledgement does not arrive within the normal retransmission timeout, TCP will retransmit the *FIN*. Procedure *tcplastack* implements *LAST-ACK* state processing.

```
/* tcplastack.c - tcplastack */

#include <conf.h>
#include <kernel.h>
#include <network.h>


/*------------------------------------------------------------------------
 *  tcplastack -  do LAST_ACK state input processing
 *------------------------------------------------------------------------
 */
int tcplastack(ptcb, pep)
struct  tcb     *ptcb;
struct  ep      *pep;
{
        struct  ip      *pip = (struct ip *)pep->ep_data;
        struct  tcp     *ptcp = (struct tcp *)pip->ip_data;

        if (ptcp->tcp_code & TCPF_RST)
                return tcpabort(ptcb, TCPE_RESET);
        if (ptcp->tcp_code & TCPF_SYN) {
                tcpreset(pep);
                return tcpabort(ptcb, TCPE_RESET);
        }
        tcpacked(ptcb, pep);
        if ((ptcb->tcb_code & TCPF_FIN) == 0)
                signal(ptcb->tcb_ocsem);            /* close() deallocs    */
        return OK;
}
```

If a *RESET* arrives, *tcplastack* calls *tcpabort* to abort the connection. If a *SYN* arrives, it sends a *RESET* and then aborts the connection. For other cases, *tcplastack* calls *tcpacked* to handle incoming acknowledgements, and signals the open/close semaphore to allow applications to complete their *close* operations once the outgoing *FIN* has been acknowledged.

11.11 ESTABLISHED State Processing

Once a connection has been established, both sides remain in the *ESTABLISHED* state while they exchange data and acknowledgments. TCP calls procedure *tcpestablished* to handle any segment that arrives while in the *ESTABLISHED* state.

```c
/* tcpestablished.c - tcpestablished */

#include <conf.h>
#include <kernel.h>
#include <network.h>

/*------------------------------------------------------------------------
 *  tcpestablished -  do ESTABLISHED state input processing
 *------------------------------------------------------------------------
 */
int tcpestablished(ptcb, pep)
struct  tcb     *ptcb;
struct  ep      *pep;
{
        struct  ip      *pip = (struct ip *)pep->ep_data;
        struct  tcp     *ptcp = (struct tcp *)pip->ip_data;

        if (ptcp->tcp_code & TCPF_RST) {
                TcpEstabResets++;
                TcpCurrEstab--;
                return tcpabort(ptcb, TCPE_RESET);
        }
        if (ptcp->tcp_code & TCPF_SYN) {
                TcpEstabResets++;
                TcpCurrEstab--;
                tcpreset(pep);
                return tcpabort(ptcb, TCPE_RESET);
        }
        if (tcpacked(ptcb, pep) == SYSERR)
                return OK;
        tcpdata(ptcb, pep);
        tcpswindow(ptcb, pep);
        if (ptcb->tcb_flags & TCBF_RDONE)
                ptcb->tcb_state = TCPS_CLOSEWAIT;
        return OK;
}
```

If a *RESET* arrives, it means the other endpoint must have restarted and has no knowledge of the connection. Therefore, *tcpestablished* calls *tcpabort* to abort the connection immediately. If a *SYN* segment arrives, *tcpestablished* sends a *RESET* and aborts the connection. Otherwise, it calls *tcpacked* to handle incoming acknowledgements, *tcpdata* to check the *FIN* bit and extract data from the segment, and *tcpswindow* to update the sending window size if the segment contains a new window advertisement. If a *FIN* has arrived and all data up through the *FIN* has been received, the call to *tcpdata* will set bit *TCBF_RDONE* of the TCB flags field. *Tcpestablished* uses this bit to determine whether it should move to the *CLOSE-WAIT* state.

11.12 Processing Data In A Segment

In the *ESTABLISHED* state, TCP must accept data from incoming segments, use it to fill in the receive buffer, compute a new window size, and send an acknowledgement. Procedure *tcpdata* handles the details of receiving data.

```
/* tcpdata.c - tcpdata */

#include <conf.h>
#include <kernel.h>
#include <network.h>

/*------------------------------------------------------------------------
 *  tcpdata - process an input segment's data section
 *------------------------------------------------------------------------
 */
int tcpdata(ptcb, pep)
struct  tcb     *ptcb;
struct  ep      *pep;
{
        struct  ip      *pip = (struct ip *)pep->ep_data;
        struct  tcp     *ptcp = (struct tcp *)pip->ip_data;
        tcpseq          first, last, wlast;
        int             datalen, rwindow, i, pp, pb;

        if (ptcp->tcp_code & TCPF_SYN) {
                ptcb->tcb_rnext++;
                ptcb->tcb_flags |= TCBF_NEEDOUT;
                ++ptcp->tcp_seq;        /* so we start with data */
        }
        datalen = pip->ip_len - IP_HLEN(pip) - TCP_HLEN(ptcp);
        rwindow = ptcb->tcb_rbsize - ptcb->tcb_rbcount;
        wlast = ptcb->tcb_rnext + rwindow-1;
```

```
        first = ptcp->tcp_seq;
        last = first + datalen - 1;
        if (SEQCMP(ptcb->tcb_rnext, first) > 0) {
                datalen -= ptcb->tcb_rnext - first;
                first = ptcb->tcb_rnext;
        }
        if (SEQCMP(last, wlast) > 0) {
                datalen -= last - wlast;
                ptcp->tcp_code &= ~TCPF_FIN;     /* cutting it off */
        }
        pb = ptcb->tcb_rbstart + ptcb->tcb_rbcount; /* == rnext, in buf */
        pb += first - ptcb->tcb_rnext;          /* distance in buf      */
        pb %= ptcb->tcb_rbsize;                 /* may wrap             */
        pp = first - ptcp->tcp_seq;             /* distance in packet   */
        for (i=0; i<datalen; ++i) {
                ptcb->tcb_rcvbuf[pb] = ptcp->tcp_data[pp++];
                if (++pb >= ptcb->tcb_rbsize)
                        pb = 0;
        }
        tcpdodat(ptcb, ptcp, first, datalen);   /* deal with it         */
        if (ptcb->tcb_flags & TCBF_NEEDOUT)
                tcpkick(ptcb);
        return OK;
}
```

Tcpdata begins by checking the *SYN* bit in the incoming segment. Conceptually, a *SYN* occupies one position in the arriving data sequence, so if the segment contains a *SYN*, *tcpdata* adds one to the sequence number in the TCB.

To handle data in the incoming segment, *tcpdata* computes its length (*datalen*) as well as the space remaining in the buffer (*rwindow*). It then computes an index in the receive buffer where the data starts (*pb*) and an index in the data area of the segment (*pp*). It treats the receive buffer as a circular array and copies *datalen* octets from the segment into the buffer, wrapping around if the buffer index exceeds the buffer size. After copying data into the receive buffer, *tcpdata* calls procedure *tcpdodat* to finish processing, and procedure *tcpkick* to start output if output is needed (e.g., to return an acknowledgement).

Procedure *tcpdodat* handles several details.

```
/* tcpdodat.c - tcpdodat */

#include <conf.h>
#include <kernel.h>
#include <network.h>
```

```
/*------------------------------------------------------------------------
 *  tcpdodat  -   do input data processing
 *------------------------------------------------------------------------
 */
int tcpdodat(ptcb, ptcp, first, datalen)
struct  tcb      *ptcb;
struct  tcp      *ptcp;
tcpseq           first;
int              datalen;
{
        int      wakeup = 0;

        if (ptcb->tcb_rnext == first) {
                if (datalen > 0) {
                        tfcoalesce(ptcb, datalen, ptcp);
                        ptcb->tcb_flags |= TCBF_NEEDOUT;
                        wakeup++;
                }
                if (ptcp->tcp_code & TCPF_FIN) {
                        ptcb->tcb_flags |= TCBF_RDONE|TCBF_NEEDOUT;
                        ptcb->tcb_rnext++;
                        wakeup++;
                }
                if (ptcp->tcp_code & TCPF_PSH) {
                        ptcb->tcb_flags |= TCBF_PUSH;
                        wakeup++;
                }
                if (wakeup)
                        tcpwakeup(READERS, ptcb);
        } else {
                /* process delayed controls */
                if (ptcp->tcp_code & TCPF_FIN)
                        ptcb->tcb_finseq = ptcp->tcp_seq + datalen;
                if (ptcp->tcp_code & TCPF_PSH)
                        ptcb->tcb_pushseq = ptcp->tcp_seq + datalen;
                ptcp->tcp_code &= ~(TCPF_FIN|TCPF_PSH);
                tfinsert(ptcb, first, datalen);
        }
        return OK;
}
```

For the case where data in the incoming segment extends the sequence of contiguous data that has been received successfully, *tcpdodat* must process control flags immediately. First, it sets the output flags field in the TCB (*tcb_flags*) so an acknowledgement will be generated. It calls procedure *tfcoalesce* to determine whether the data fills in holes in the sequence space that were formed when segments arrived out of order. Second, if the segment contains a *FIN* in addition to data, *tcpdodat* counts the *FIN* as an item in the sequence space, and sets the output flags to show that a *FIN* has arrived and an *ACK* is needed. Third, if the incoming segment has the *push bit* set, *tcpdodat* sets a flag to show that *push* has been requested. In any case, if *tcpdodat* determines that new data is available, it calls *tcpwakeup* to awaken any application processes that may be blocked awaiting data arrival.

If a segment arrives out of order, *tcpdodat* must handle delayed controls. For example, it could happen that a segment carrying a *FIN* arrives before the last segment carrying data. In such cases, TCP has stored information about the *FIN* in the TCB, so if the missing data arrives, *tcpdodat* can perform processing that was delayed. It calls *tfinsert* to record the octets received.

11.13 Keeping Track Of Received Octets

Recall that TCP must accommodate out-of-order delivery. Because the window advertisement limits incoming data to the buffer that has been allocated, TCP can always copy the arriving data directly into the buffer (except for urgent data, which is stored separately). However, TCP must also keep a record of which octets from the sequence have been received. To do so, it maintains a list of (*sequence, length*) pairs received for each active TCB.

Borrowing terminology used by IP, our example implementation calls items on the list *fragments*. Each item on the TCP fragment list represents a single segment of data that has been received. The entry contains the sequence number of the first octet and a length as defined by structure *tcpfrag* in file *tcb.h*. Whenever data arrives out of order, *tcpdodat* calls procedure *tfinsert* to insert an entry on the fragment list.

```
/* tfinsert.c - tfinsert */

#include <conf.h>
#include <kernel.h>
#include <network.h>
#include <q.h>

/*------------------------------------------------------------------------
 * tfinsert - add a new TCP segment fragment to a TCB sequence queue
 *------------------------------------------------------------------------
 */
int     tfinsert(ptcb, seq, datalen, gotfin)
struct  tcb     *ptcb;
tcpseq          seq;
int             datalen;
```

```
{
        struct  tcpfrag *tf;

        if (datalen == 0)
                return OK;
        tf = (struct tcpfrag *)getmem(sizeof(struct tcpfrag));
        tf->tf_seq = seq;
        tf->tf_len = datalen;
        if (ptcb->tcb_rsegq < 0)
                ptcb->tcb_rsegq = newq(NTCPFRAG, QF_WAIT);
        if (enq(ptcb->tcb_rsegq, tf, -tf->tf_seq) < 0)
                freemem(tf, sizeof(struct tcpfrag));
        return OK;
}
```

Tfinsert takes four arguments that describe the sequence of data that has arrived. It allocates a new node for the data and links the node into the fragment list. The arguments consist of a pointer to a TCB, a starting sequence number, data length, and a Boolean that specifies whether a *FIN* has arrived. When data first arrives out of order for a connection, no queue exists, so *tfinsert* calls *newq* to create one. In any case, it calls *enq* to enqueue the new node.

In addition to adding entries that record the sequence numbers of data received, TCP must advance the counter that tells how many contiguous octets of the sequence space have been received successfully. In essence, it moves a pointer along the sequence space until it finds the next "hole." Procedure *tfcoalesce* implements the operation.

```c
/* tfcoalesce.c - tfcoalesce */

#include <conf.h>
#include <kernel.h>
#include <network.h>

/*------------------------------------------------------------------------
 *  tfcoalesce -  join TCP fragments
 *------------------------------------------------------------------------
 */
int tfcoalesce(ptcb, datalen, ptcp)
struct   tcb      *ptcb;
int               datalen;
struct   tcp      *ptcp;
{
        struct tcpfrag  *tf;
        int     new;

        ptcb->tcb_rnext += datalen;
        ptcb->tcb_rbcount += datalen;
        if (ptcb->tcb_rnext == ptcb->tcb_finseq)
                goto alldone;
        if ((ptcb->tcb_rnext - ptcb->tcb_pushseq) >= 0) {
                ptcp->tcp_code |= TCPF_PSH;
                ptcb->tcb_pushseq = 0;
        }
        if (ptcb->tcb_rsegq < 0)          /* see if this closed a hole */
                return OK;
        tf = (struct tcpfrag *)deq(ptcb->tcb_rsegq);
        while ((tf->tf_seq - ptcb->tcb_rnext) <= 0) {
                new = tf->tf_len - (ptcb->tcb_rnext - tf->tf_seq);
                if (new > 0) {
                        ptcb->tcb_rnext += new;
                        ptcb->tcb_rbcount += new;
                }
                if (ptcb->tcb_rnext == ptcb->tcb_finseq)
                        goto alldone;
                if ((ptcb->tcb_rnext - ptcb->tcb_pushseq) >= 0) {
                        ptcp->tcp_code |= TCPF_PSH;
                        ptcb->tcb_pushseq = 0;
                }
                freemem(tf, sizeof(struct tcpfrag));
                tf = (struct tcpfrag *)deq(ptcb->tcb_rsegq);
                if (tf == 0) {
```

```
                        freeq(ptcb->tcb_rsegq);
                        ptcb->tcb_rsegq = EMPTY;
                        return OK;
                }
        }
        enq(ptcb->tcb_rsegq, tf, -tf->tf_seq);  /* got one too many     */
        return OK;
alldone:
        do
                freemem(tf, sizeof(struct tcpfrag));
        while (tf=deq(ptcb->tcb_rsegq));
        freeq(ptcb->tcb_rsegq);
        ptcb->tcb_rsegq = EMPTY;
        ptcp->tcp_code |= TCPF_FIN;
        return OK;
}
```

The central loop in *tfcoalesce* iterates through the entire TCP fragment list. It removes the first entry before starting, and then removes another entry each time the loop iterates. On each iteration, it checks to see if the entry it removed extends the currently received sequence space. The test is straightforward: a new entry only extends the sequence space if its starting sequence lies within or exactly adjacent to the existing sequence (field *tcb_rnext*).

During the iteration, if field *tcb_rnext* reaches the sequence number of the *FIN*, *tfcoalesce* declares that input is complete and branches to label *alldone* to remove the list. If the loop completes without exhausting the list, *tfcoalesce* must reinsert the last unlinked entry back into the list.

11.14 Aborting A TCP Connection

We have seen that several of the state procedures need to abort a TCP connection immediately. To do so, they call procedure *tcpabort*, passing as an argument a pointer to the TCB that must be deallocated, as well as an integer that encodes the cause of the abort.

```
/* tcpabort.c - tcpabort */

#include <conf.h>
#include <kernel.h>
#include <network.h>

/*------------------------------------------------------------------------
 *  tcpabort -  abort an active TCP connection
 *------------------------------------------------------------------------
 */
int tcpabort(ptcb, error)
struct   tcb      *ptcb;
int               error;
{
        tcpkilltimers(ptcb);
        ptcb->tcb_flags |= TCBF_RDONE|TCBF_SDONE;
        ptcb->tcb_error = error;
        tcpwakeup(READERS|WRITERS, ptcb);
        return OK;
}
```

Tcpabort uses *tcpkilltimers* to delete all pending events for the connection. In addition, it sets bits in the flags field to show that both reception and transmission have completed. It stores the argument *error* in the TCB to show what kind of error caused the problem. Finally, *tcpabort* calls *tcpwakeup* to awaken any readers or writers that may be blocked awaiting I/O. Each of the application programs waiting to read or write will awaken and find the error type stored in the TCB.

11.15 Establishing A TCP Connection

Recall that TCP uses a 3-way handshake to establish a connection. A server issues a *passive open* and waits in the *LISTEN* state, while a client issues an *active open* and enters the *SYN-SENT* state. The server moves to the *SYN-RECEIVED* state. Eventually, both client and server enter the *ESTABLISHED* state. The next sections present the procedures associated with the states used to establish a connection.

11.16 Initializing A TCB

TCP calls procedure *tcpsync* to initialize a TCB whenever an application issues an active or passive *open* operation.

```
/* tcpsync.c - tcpsync */

#include <conf.h>
#include <kernel.h>
#include <network.h>

/*------------------------------------------------------------------------
 * tcpsync - initialize TCB for a new connection request
 *------------------------------------------------------------------------
 */
int tcpsync(ptcb)
struct  tcb     *ptcb;
{
        ptcb->tcb_state = TCPS_CLOSED;
        ptcb->tcb_type = TCPT_CONNECTION;

        ptcb->tcb_iss = ptcb->tcb_suna = ptcb->tcb_snext = tcpiss();
        ptcb->tcb_lwack = ptcb->tcb_iss;

        ptcb->tcb_sndbuf = (char *)getmem(TCPSBS);
        ptcb->tcb_sbsize = TCPSBS;
        ptcb->tcb_sbstart = ptcb->tcb_sbcount = 0;
        ptcb->tcb_ssema = screate(1);

        ptcb->tcb_rcvbuf = (char *)getmem(TCPRBS);
        ptcb->tcb_rbsize = TCPRBS;
        ptcb->tcb_rbstart = ptcb->tcb_rbcount = 0;
        ptcb->tcb_rsegq = EMPTY;
        ptcb->tcb_rsema = screate(0);

        ptcb->tcb_rudq = ptcb->tcb_ruhq = EMPTY;
        ptcb->tcb_sudq = ptcb->tcb_suhq = EMPTY;

        ptcb->tcb_ocsem = screate(0);

        /* timer stuff */

        ptcb->tcb_srt = 0;                      /* in sec/100   */
        ptcb->tcb_rtde = 0;                     /* in sec/100   */
```

```
        ptcb->tcb_rexmt = 50;              /* in sec/100    */
        ptcb->tcb_rexmtcount = 0;
        ptcb->tcb_keep = 12000;            /* in sec/100    */

        ptcb->tcb_code = TCPF_SYN;
        ptcb->tcb_flags = 0;
        return OK;
}
```

Tcpsync initializes the connection to the *CLOSED* state, allocates send and receive buffers, creates send and receive semaphores, and initializes miscellaneous counters and retransmission estimates. Finally, it sets the *TCPF_SYN* bit in the *tcb_code* field to indicate that a *SYN* should be sent.

11.17 SYN-SENT State Processing

Once TCP has sent a *SYN* request, it moves to the *SYN-SENT* state. Procedure *tcpsynsent* implements *SYN-SENT* state processing.

```
/* tcpsynsent.c - tcpsynsent */

#include <conf.h>
#include <kernel.h>
#include <network.h>


/*------------------------------------------------------------------------
 *  tcpsynsent  -  do SYN_SENT state processing
 *------------------------------------------------------------------------
 */
int tcpsynsent(ptcb, pep)
struct  tcb       *ptcb;
struct  ep        *pep;
{
        struct  ip        *pip = (struct ip *)pep->ep_data;
        struct  tcp       *ptcp = (struct tcp *)pip->ip_data;

        if ((ptcp->tcp_code & TCPF_ACK) &&
            ((ptcp->tcp_ack - ptcb->tcb_iss <= 0) ||
            (ptcp->tcp_ack - ptcb->tcb_snext) > 0))
                return tcpreset(pep);
        if (ptcp->tcp_code & TCPF_RST) {
                ptcb->tcb_state = TCPS_CLOSED;
```

```
                ptcb->tcb_error = TCPE_RESET;
                TcpAttemptFails++;
                tcpkilltimers(ptcb);
                signal(ptcb->tcb_ocsem);
                return OK;
        }
        if ((ptcp->tcp_code & TCPF_SYN) == 0)
                return OK;
        ptcb->tcb_swindow = ptcp->tcp_window;
        ptcb->tcb_lwseq = ptcp->tcp_seq;
        ptcb->tcb_rnext = ptcp->tcp_seq;
        ptcb->tcb_cwin = ptcb->tcb_rnext + ptcb->tcb_rbsize;
        tcpacked(ptcb, pep);
        tcpdata(ptcb, pep);
        ptcp->tcp_code &= ~TCPF_FIN;
        if (ptcb->tcb_code & TCPF_SYN)          /* our SYN not ACKed    */
                ptcb->tcb_state = TCPS_SYNRCVD;
        else {
                TcpCurrEstab++;
                ptcb->tcb_state = TCPS_ESTABLISHED;
                signal(ptcb->tcb_ocsem);        /* return in open       */
        }
        return OK;
}
```

If an *ACK* arrives, *tcpsynsent* checks to insure the *ACK* specifies the correct sequence number and sends a *RESET* if it does not. If a *RESET* arrives, *tcpsynsent* moves to the *CLOSED* state and calls *tcpkilltimers* to delete any pending events. If the incoming segment contains a *SYN*, it can also carry data or an acknowledgement for a *SYN* that was sent previously, so *tcpsynsent* calls *tcpacked* and *tcpdata* to process the segment. Finally, *tcpsynsent* examines the *TCPF_SYN* bit in the TCB to see if the *SYN* for this connection has been acknowledged. If the *SYN* has been acknowledged, *tcpsynsent* moves the connection to the *ESTABLISHED* state. Otherwise, it moves to the *SYN-RECEIVED* state.

11.18 SYN-RECEIVED State Processing

TCP places a connection in the *SYN-RECEIVED* state either when a *SYN* arrives from the other end to initiate a 3-way handshake, or when a *SYN* arrives without an *ACK* and the connection is in the *SYN-SENT* state. Procedure *tcpsynrcvd* handles incoming segments for the *SYN-RECEIVED* state.

```c
/* tcpsynrcvd.c - tcpsynrcvd */

#include <conf.h>
#include <kernel.h>
#include <network.h>

/*------------------------------------------------------------------------
 *  tcpsynrcvd -  do SYN_RCVD state input processing
 *------------------------------------------------------------------------
 */
int tcpsynrcvd(ptcb, pep)
struct  tcb      *ptcb;
struct  ep       *pep;
{
        struct  ip       *pip = (struct ip *)pep->ep_data;
        struct  tcp      *ptcp = (struct tcp *)pip->ip_data;
        struct  tcb      *pptcb;

        if (ptcp->tcp_code & TCPF_RST) {
                TcpAttemptFails++;
                if (ptcb->tcb_pptcb != 0)
                        return tcbdealloc(ptcb);
                else
                        return tcpabort(ptcb, TCPE_REFUSED);
        }
        if (ptcp->tcp_code & TCPF_SYN) {
                TcpAttemptFails++;
                tcpreset(pep);
                return tcpabort(ptcb, TCPE_RESET);
        }
        if (tcpacked(ptcb, pep) == SYSERR)
                return OK;
        if (ptcb->tcb_pptcb != 0) {
                pptcb = ptcb->tcb_pptcb;
                if (wait(pptcb->tcb_mutex) != OK) {
                        TcpAttemptFails++;
                        tcpreset(pep);
                        return tcbdealloc(ptcb);
                }
                if (pptcb->tcb_state != TCPS_LISTEN) {
                        TcpAttemptFails++;
                        tcpreset(pep);
                        signal(pptcb->tcb_mutex);
```

```
                        return tcbdealloc(ptcb);
                }
                if (pcount(pptcb->tcb_listenq) >= pptcb->tcb_lqsize) {
                        TcpAttemptFails++;
                        signal(pptcb->tcb_mutex);
                        return tcbdealloc(ptcb);
                }
                psend(pptcb->tcb_listenq, ptcb->tcb_dvnum);
                signal(pptcb->tcb_mutex);
        } else
                signal(ptcb->tcb_ocsem);          /* from an active open */
        TcpCurrEstab++;
        ptcb->tcb_state = TCPS_ESTABLISHED;
        tcpdata(ptcb, pep);
        if (ptcb->tcb_flags & TCBF_RDONE)
                ptcb->tcb_state = TCPS_CLOSEWAIT;
        return OK;
}
```

If a *RESET* arrives, *tcpsynrcvd* aborts the connection and deallocates the TCB. For passively opened connections, the TCB is a separate copy of the parent TCB, so it merely calls *tcpdealloc* to remove the orphan TCB. For actively opened connections, however, it calls *tcpabort*, which records the error in the TCB. It also aborts the connection if a *SYN* arrives.

Because TCP only enters the *SYN-RECEIVED* state after responding to a *SYN*, any incoming segment other than *RESET* or *SYN* means the other side views the connection as established. Thus, when a segment arrives, *tcpsynrcvd* calls *tcpacked* to handle acknowledgements, moves to the *ESTABLISHED* state, and calls *tcpdata* to extract data from the segment.

Tcpsynrcvd also handles part of the transition between a server and the process that executes for a particular connection. As we will see, when a server issues a passive open, it creates a *listen queue*. The server then enters a loop, extracting the next connection from the listen queue and creating a process to handle the connection. We can summarize:

> *Using a passive open, a server creates a queue of connections for a given TCP port. TCP allocates a new TCB for each new connection, places a connection identifier in the listen queue for the port, and awakens the server process so it can handle the new connection.*

For passive opens, *tcpsynrcvd* enqueues *tcb_dvnum*, the descriptor the server will use for the connection, on the listen queue for the server. To avoid blocking the input process, it uses *pcount* to insure that space remains on the queue, and *psend* to enqueue the connection identifier on the listen queue. For active connections, *tcpsynrcvd* signals the open-close semaphore, allowing the active *open* to proceed. In either case, *tcpsynrcvd* moves the state of the connection to the *ESTABLISHED* state, and calls *tcpdata* to extract data from the segment, if it exists. Finally, it checks the *tcb_flags* field to see if a *FIN* has arrived (possibly out of sequence or possibly in the same segment that carried the *SYN*), and transfers to the *CLOSE-WAIT* state if it has.

11.19 LISTEN State Processing

The *LISTEN* state, used by servers to await connections from clients, is among the most complex because it creates a new TCB for each incoming connection. Procedure *tcplisten* provides the implementation.

```
/* tcplisten.c - tcplisten */

#include <conf.h>
#include <kernel.h>
#include <network.h>


/*------------------------------------------------------------------------
 *  tcplisten -  do LISTEN state processing
 *------------------------------------------------------------------------
 */
int tcplisten(ptcb, pep)
struct   tcb      *ptcb;
struct   ep       *pep;
{
        struct   tcb     *newptcb;
        struct   ip      *pip = (struct ip *)pep->ep_data;
        struct   tcp     *ptcp = (struct tcp *)pip->ip_data;

        if (ptcp->tcp_code & TCPF_RST)
                return OK;                    /* "parent" TCB still in LISTEN */
        if ((ptcp->tcp_code & TCPF_ACK) ||
            (ptcp->tcp_code & TCPF_SYN) == 0)
                return tcpreset(pep);
        newptcb = tcballoc();
        if (newptcb == SYSERR || tcpsync(newptcb) == SYSERR)
                return SYSERR;
        newptcb->tcb_state = TCPS_SYNRCVD;
        newptcb->tcb_ostate = TCPO_IDLE;
        newptcb->tcb_error = 0;
```

```
        newptcb->tcb_pptcb = ptcb;                          /* for ACCEPT   */

        blkcopy(newptcb->tcb_rip, pip->ip_src, IP_ALEN);
        newptcb->tcb_rport = ptcp->tcp_sport;
        blkcopy(newptcb->tcb_lip, pip->ip_dst, IP_ALEN);
        newptcb->tcb_lport = ptcp->tcp_dport;

        tcpwinit(ptcb, newptcb, pep);    /* initialize window data     */

        newptcb->tcb_finseq = newptcb->tcb_pushseq = 0;
        newptcb->tcb_flags = TCBF_NEEDOUT;
        TcpPassiveOpens++;
        ptcp->tcp_code &= ~TCPF_FIN;     /* don't process FINs in LISTEN */
        tcpdata(newptcb, pep);
        signal(newptcb->tcb_mutex);
}
```

Tcplisten begins as expected. It ignores *RESET* requests because no connection exists. It sends a *RESET* for any incoming segment other than a *SYN* segment.

Once it receives a *SYN*, *tcplisten* must call *tcballoc* to create a TCB for the new connection. We call the original TCB the *parent* and the new TCB the *child*. *Tcplisten* calls *tcpsync* to initialize fields in the child TCB and then places the child in the *SYN-RECEIVED* state. Meanwhile, the parent TCB remains in the *LISTEN* state. An important step in initializing the new TCB consists of copying the sender's IP address and protocol port number from the arriving segment into the newly created TCB. Afterward, *tcplisten* calls *tcpwinit* to finish initializing window information for the new TCB.

Tcplisten does not explicitly generate the *SYN* and *ACK* response for the new connection. Instead, it sets bit *TCBF_NEEDOUT* in the *tcb_flags* field to indicate that output is needed, and calls *tcpdata* to process any data from the segment and to start output. Finally, *tcplisten* signals the mutual exclusion semaphore for the new TCB, allowing other parts of TCP to begin using it (e.g., to accept input or generate acknowledgements).

11.20 Initializing Window Variables For A New TCB

Procedure *tcpwinit* initializes variables used to control window and segment sizes.

```
/* tcpwinit.c - tcpwinit */

#include <conf.h>
#include <kernel.h>
#include <network.h>

/*------------------------------------------------------------------
 *  tcpwinit - initialize window data for a new connection
 *------------------------------------------------------------------
 */
int tcpwinit(ptcb, newptcb, pep)
struct  tcb       *ptcb, *newptcb;
struct  ep        *pep;
{
        struct  ip        *pip = (struct ip *)pep->ep_data;
        struct  tcp       *ptcp = (struct tcp *)pip->ip_data;
        struct  route     *prt, *rtget();
        Bool              local;
        int               mss;

        newptcb->tcb_swindow = ptcp->tcp_window;
        newptcb->tcb_lwseq = ptcp->tcp_seq;
        newptcb->tcb_lwack = newptcb->tcb_iss;  /* set in tcpsync()      */

        prt = (struct route *)rtget(pip->ip_src, RTF_REMOTE);
        local = prt && prt->rt_metric == 0;
        newptcb->tcb_pni = &nif[prt->rt_ifnum];
        rtfree(prt);
        if (local)
                mss = newptcb->tcb_pni->ni_mtu-IPMHLEN-TCPMHLEN;
        else
                mss = 536;       /* RFC 1122 */
        if (ptcb->tcb_smss) {
                newptcb->tcb_smss = min(ptcb->tcb_smss, mss);
                ptcb->tcb_smss = 0;                    /* reset server smss    */
        } else
                newptcb->tcb_smss = mss;
        newptcb->tcb_rmss = mss;                       /* receive mss          */
        newptcb->tcb_cwnd = newptcb->tcb_smss;  /* 1 segment              */
        newptcb->tcb_ssthresh = 65535;               /* IP max window        */
        newptcb->tcb_rnext = ptcp->tcp_seq;
        newptcb->tcb_cwin = newptcb->tcb_rnext + newptcb->tcb_rbsize;
}
```

Because Chapter 14 discusses congestion control and the window size limits used to implement it, most of the initialization cannot be understood before reading that chapter. However, the maximum segment size selection is interesting and can be understood easily.

The TCP standard specifies that TCP should use a default *maximum segment size* (MSS) of *536* octets† when communicating with destinations that do not lie on a directly connected network. For destinations on directly connected networks, however, TCP can use the network MTU to compute an optimal MSS. To do so, *tcpwinit* calls *rtget* to find a route to the remote endpoint. If the route has a metric of zero, the destination lies on a directly connected network, so TCP computes the MSS by subtracting the TCP and IP header sizes from the network MTU. If TCP on the remote machine specifies an MSS, *tcpwinit* uses the smaller of the specified MSS and the MSS computed from the network MTU. In any case, *tcpwinit* uses the MSS computed from the network MTU for input.

11.21 Summary

We examined an implementation that uses a single procedure to represent each state of the TCP finite state machine. This chapter reviewed the eleven state procedures as well as the utility procedures they use. Each state procedure handles incoming segments. It must accommodate requests to abort (e.g., *RESET*) and special requests to start (*SYN*) and shutdown (*FIN*).

The requirement that TCP accept segments out of order complicates most state procedures. For example, TCP may receive a request for shutdown (*FIN*) before all data arrives. Or it may receive a segment carrying data before a segment that completes the 3-way handshake used to establish the connection. Our implementation accommodates out-of-order delivery by recording startup and shutdown events in the TCB and checking them as each segment arrives.

FOR FURTHER STUDY

The TCP standard [RFC 793] specifies the finite state machine and gives details about making transitions. The host requirements document [RFC 1122] discusses changes and clarifications.

---

†The maximum segment size is computed by subtracting the minimum size of an IP header (*20* octets), and the minimum size of a TCP header (*20* octets) from the default IP datagram size (*576* octets).

EXERCISES

11.1   The state diagram in Figure 10.2 shows a direct transition from *SYN-RECEIVED* to *FIN-WAIT-1* if the user issues a *close*. Explain why our implementation of TCP cannot make such a transition.

11.2   Suppose an underlying network exhibits extremely bad behavior and reorders datagrams completely. Can a *FIN* for a connection ever arrive before the *SYN* for that connection? Why or why not?

11.3   Read the protocol standard carefully. How should TCP respond if an acknowledgement arrives for data that has not been sent yet?

11.4   Describe what happens if TCP enters state *FIN-WAIT-2* and then the remote site crashes. Hint: Are there any timers running locally? Explain how the problem can be resolved.

12

TCP: Output Processing

12.1 Introduction

Chapters 10 and 11 discussed the use of a finite state machine to control TCP input processing. Although the standard specifies finite state machine transitions used for input, an implementation is much more complex than the simple diagram implies. This chapter discusses the output side of TCP and shows how it also uses a finite state machine to control processing. It discusses output of data segments that originate when an application program on the local machine sends information, output of acknowledgements sent in response to arriving segments, and output triggered when retransmission timers expire.

12.2 Controlling TCP Output Complexity

TCP output is complex because it interacts closely with TCP input and timer events, all of which occur concurrently. For example, when the output process sends a segment, it must schedule a retransmission event. Later, if the retransmission timer expires, the timer process must send the segment. Meanwhile, the application program may generate new data, causing TCP to send more segments, or acknowledgements may arrive, causing TCP to cancel previous retransmission events. However, because the underlying IP protocol may drop, delay, or deliver segments out of order, events may not occur in the expected order. Even if data arrives at the remote site, an acknowledgement may be lost. Because the remote site may receive data out of order, a single *ACK* may acknowledge receipt of many segments. Furthermore, a site may receive the *FIN* for a connection before it has received all data segments, so retransmission may be necessary even after an application closes a connection. Thus, the correct response to an input or output event depends on the history of previous events and cannot easily be specified in isolation.

To help control the complexity of interactions among the TCP input, output, and timer processes, our implementation uses a simple finite state machine to control output operations. Unlike the finite state machine used for input, the output state machine is not part of the TCP standard. Instead, it is part of our design, and other implementations may use slightly different strategies to control output. In general, all implementations need some technique to handle the details of output because the input state machine does not distinguish among output operations.

> We think of the output state machine as defining microscopic transitions that occur within a single state of the input state machine.

Thus, once the input state machine reaches its *ESTABLISHED* state, the output state machine makes transitions that control transmission, retransmission, and idling when there is nothing to send.

12.3 The Four TCP Output States

In principle, the output state machine is simpler than the input machine. Conceptually, it contains only four possible states and the transitions among them are quite simple, as Figure 12.1 shows. For example, when an application program produces new data and needs TCP to form and send a segment, it places the data in a buffer, moves the output state to *TRANSMIT*, and signals the output process, allowing it to execute. The output process calls an appropriate procedure to generate and send a segment, and then moves the output state machine back to the *IDLE* state.

The state diagram only provides a model from which the designer builds software. As with the input side, exceptions and special cases complicate the implementation, and no simple state transition diagram can explain all the subtleties.

12.4 TCP Output As A Process

Using a separate TCP output process helps separate execution of the input, timer, and output functions, and allows them to operate concurrently. For example, a retransmission timer may expire and trigger retransmission, while the input process is sending an acknowledgement in response to an incoming segment. The interaction can be especially complex because a TCP segment can carry acknowledgements along with data. If each procedure that needs output acts independently, TCP generates unnecessary traffic. To coordinate output, our example implementation uses a single process to handle output, and makes all interaction *message-driven*. When a procedure needs to generate output, it places information in the TCB and sends a message to the TCP output process. Thus, there is little interaction among processes generating output, and little need for mutual exclusion.

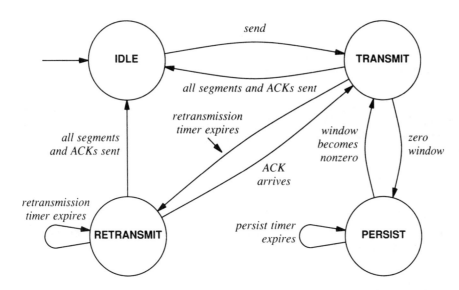

Figure 12.1 Conceptual transitions among the four TCP output states. Unlike the finite state machine used for input, the output state machine is not specified by the TCP protocol standard – it was defined for our implementation.

12.5 TCP Output Messages

Figure 12.2 lists the message types that can be sent to the TCP output process.

Number	Message	Meaning
1	SEND	Send data and/or ACK
2	PERSIST	Send probe to test receiver's zero window
3	RETRANSMIT	Retransmit data segment
4	DELETE	Delete a TCB that has expired

Figure 12.2 The five message types that can be sent to the TCP output process.

Although two of the message types have the same names as states in the finite state machine used for output, they should not be confused. A message specifies an action that is required, while a state specifies the current status of the connection. For example, a message that specifies *RETRANSMIT* may occur while the connection is in the *TRANSMIT* state.

12.6 Encoding Output States And TCB Numbers

Conceptually, whenever a process passes a message to the TCP output process, it must send two items: the index of the TCB to which the message applies and a value that identifies the message type. In our example code, the operating system only provides message passing facilities for passing a single integer value. To accommodate the restriction on message passing, our example TCP encodes both the TCB and message to be delivered into a single integer.

In addition to symbolic constants for the output states, file *tcpfsm.h* (shown in Chapter 10) contains declarations of three in-line macro functions used to encode and decode messages. Function *MKEVENT* takes a TCB number and message type (called a *timer event*), and encodes them in an integer by using the low-order *3* bits to represent the event, and the higher-order bits to store the TCB index. Function *TCB* takes an encoded integer value and extracts the TCB index; function *EVENT* takes an encoded integer value and extracts the event.

12.7 Implementation Of The TCP Output Process

Our implementation of the finite state machine used for output follows the pattern used for input. A single procedure handles each state; the output process uses the current output state, found in the TCB, to choose the appropriate procedure. The code can be found in procedure *tcpout*.

```
/* tcpout.c - tcpout */

#include <conf.h>
#include <kernel.h>
#include <network.h>


/*------------------------------------------------------------------------
 * tcpout - handle events affecting TCP output processing
 *------------------------------------------------------------------------
 */
PROCESS tcpout()
{
        struct  tcb     *ptcb;
        int             i;

        tcps_oport = pcreate(TCPQLEN);
        signal(Net.sema);                   /* synchronize on startup      */

        while (TRUE) {
```

```
            i = preceive(tcps_oport);
            ptcb = &tcbtab[TCB(i)];
            if (ptcb->tcb_state <= TCPS_CLOSED)
                    continue;                       /* a rogue; ignore it   */
            wait(ptcb->tcb_mutex);
            if (ptcb->tcb_state <= TCPS_CLOSED)
                    continue;                       /* TCB deallocated      */
            if (EVENT(i) == DELETE)                 /* same for all states  */
                    tcbdealloc(ptcb);
            else
                    tcposwitch[ptcb->tcb_ostate](TCB(i), EVENT(i));
            if (ptcb->tcb_state != TCPS_FREE)
                    signal(ptcb->tcb_mutex);
        }
}
```

Tcpout begins by calling *pcreate* to create a port on which messages can be queued. It records the port identifier in global variable *tcps_oport*, so other processes can know where to send messages. *Tcpout* then enters an infinite loop, waiting for the next message to arrive at the port, extracting the message, and handling it.

After receiving a message from the port, *tcpout* uses functions *TCB* and *EVENT* to decode the TCB number and event type. It then uses the output state variable from the TCB (*tcb_ostate*) and array *tcposwitch* to select the procedure for the current output.

Tcpout contains two optimizations. First, because state processing does not make sense if the TCB is closed, *tcpout* tests explicitly for a closed TCB. If it is closed, *tcpout* continues processing without calling any state procedures. Second, because all states deallocate the TCB in response to a *DELETE* event, *tcpout* tests for the *DELETE* event explicitly, and calls *tcbdealloc* directly whenever it arrives.

12.8 Mutual Exclusion

To guarantee that it has exclusive use of the TCB, *tcpout* waits on the mutual exclusion semaphore, *tcb_mutex*. Thus, each state procedure is called with exclusive access to the TCB. As a consequence, the state procedures should not wait on the mutual exclusion semaphore. We can summarize:

> *The TCP output process obtains exclusive use of a TCB before calling*
> *a state procedure. The state procedure must not wait on the mutual*
> *exclusion semaphore again, or deadlock will result.*

12.9 Implementation Of The IDLE State

Procedure *tcpidle* implements *IDLE* state processing. It is called whenever an event occurs for an idle connection.

```
/* tcpidle.c - tcpidle */

#include <conf.h>
#include <kernel.h>
#include <network.h>

/*------------------------------------------------------------------
 *  tcpidle - handle events while a connection is idle
 *------------------------------------------------------------------
 */
int tcpidle(tcbnum, event)
int     tcbnum;
int     event;
{
        if (event == SEND)
                tcpxmit(tcbnum, event);
        return OK;
}
```

Remember that *tcpout* explicitly tests for a *DELETE* event. Of the remaining events, *PERSIST* and *RETRANSMIT* cannot occur for an idle connection. Therefore, only *SEND* messages make sense in the *IDLE* state. *Tcpidle* calls *tcpxmit* to send data or an acknowledgement.

12.10 Implementation Of The PERSIST State

The *PERSIST* state handles events when the remote receiver has advertised a zero window. To avoid having a lost window update prevent TCP from ever sending, the protocol standard requires a sender to probe the receiver periodically by sending a segment. The receiver will return its latest window size in the *ACK*.

Procedure *tcppersist* implements the *PERSIST* state.

```
/* tcppersist.c - tcppersist */

#include <conf.h>
#include <kernel.h>
#include <network.h>
```

```
/*------------------------------------------------------------------------
 *  tcppersist - handle events while the send window is closed
 *------------------------------------------------------------------------
 */
int tcppersist(tcbnum, event)
int     tcbnum, event;
{
        struct  tcb     *ptcb = &tcbtab[tcbnum];

        if (event != PERSIST)
                return OK;       /* ignore everything else */
        tcpsend(tcbnum, TSF_REXMT);
        ptcb->tcb_persist = min(ptcb->tcb_persist<<1, TCP_MAXPRS);
        tmset(tcps_oport, TCPQLEN, MKEVENT(PERSIST, tcbnum),
                ptcb->tcb_persist);
        return OK;
}
```

While in the *PERSIST* state, only the periodic events to test the window are allowed. Therefore, *tcppersist* discards all other events. It uses *tcpsend* to send a segment and calls *tmset* to reschedule another *PERSIST* event in the future.

12.11 Implementation Of The TRANSMIT State

Procedure *tcpxmit* handles the details of transmission.

```
/* tcpxmit.c - tcpxmit */

#include <conf.h>
#include <kernel.h>
#include <network.h>

/*------------------------------------------------------------------------
 *  tcpxmit - handle TCP output events while we are transmitting
 *------------------------------------------------------------------------
 */
int tcpxmit(tcbnum, event)
{
        struct  tcb     *ptcb = &tcbtab[tcbnum];
        int             tosend, tv, pending, window;

        if (event == RETRANSMIT) {
                tmclear(tcps_oport, MKEVENT(SEND, tcbnum));
                tcprexmt(tcbnum, event);
                ptcb->tcb_ostate = TCPO_REXMT;
                return OK;
        } /* else SEND */
        tcpsndurg(tcbnum);                      /* send urgent data, if any    */
        tosend = tcphowmuch(ptcb);
        if (tosend == 0) {
                if (ptcb->tcb_flags & TCBF_NEEDOUT)
                        tcpsend(tcbnum, TSF_NEWDATA);    /* just an ACK */
                return OK;
        } else if (ptcb->tcb_swindow == 0) {
                ptcb->tcb_ostate = TCPO_PERSIST;
                ptcb->tcb_persist = ptcb->tcb_rexmt;
                tcpsend(tcbnum, TSF_NEWDATA);
                tmset(tcps_oport, TCPQLEN, MKEVENT(PERSIST,tcbnum),
                        ptcb->tcb_persist);
                return OK;
        }       /* else, we have data and window */
        ptcb->tcb_ostate = TCPO_XMIT;
        window = min(ptcb->tcb_swindow, ptcb->tcb_cwnd);
        pending = ptcb->tcb_snext - ptcb->tcb_suna;
        while (tcphowmuch(ptcb) > 0 && pending <= window) {
                tcpsend(tcbnum, TSF_NEWDATA);
                pending = ptcb->tcb_snext - ptcb->tcb_suna;
        }
        tv = MKEVENT(RETRANSMIT, tcbnum);
        if (!tmleft(tcps_oport, tv))
```

```
                    tmset(tcps_oport, TCPQLEN, tv, ptcb->tcb_rexmt);
            return OK;
}
```

If a retransmission event caused the call, *tcpxmit* moves the connection to the *RE-TRANSMIT* state and calls *tcprexmt* to send the segment.

For normal transmissions, *tcpxmit* checks several possibilities. First, it calls *tcpsndurg* to send pending urgent data. Second, it calls *tcphowmuch* to compute the number of octets of data that should be sent. If no more data remains to be sent, *tcpxmit* checks the *TCBF_NEEDOUT* bit in field *tcb_flags* to see if output is needed (e.g., an acknowledgement, *pushed* data, or a window update), and calls *tcpsend* if output is pending.

If the output buffer contains data that is ready for transmission, *tcpxmit* checks the send window (*tcb_swindow*). If the receiver has specified a zero window size, *tcpxmit* moves to the *PERSIST* state, uses the current retransmission timer period (*tcb_rexmt*) as the persist period, and schedules a *PERSIST* event for that time interval.

Finally, *tcpxmit* handles the case where data is ready and the receiver has advertised a nonzero window. It moves to the *TRANSMIT* state, and uses *tcphowmuch* to determine how much data can be sent. It repeatedly calls *tcpsend* to transmit a segment. To handle the case where one or more of the transmitted segments are lost, *tcpxmit* schedules a single retransmission event for the first segment in the window.

12.12 Implementation Of The RETRANSMIT State

Because the implementation of the *RETRANSMIT* state involves estimation of round-trip delays and backoff heuristics, the code appears in Chapter 14.

12.13 Sending A Segment

When *tcpxmit* needs to send a segment, it calls *tcpsend* to perform the task. *Tcpsend* allocates a buffer, assembles a segment, and sends it in an IP datagram.

```
/* tcpsend.c - tcpsend */

#include <conf.h>
#include <kernel.h>
#include <network.h>

/*------------------------------------------------------------------
 *  tcpsend  -  compute and send a TCP segment for the given TCB
 *------------------------------------------------------------------
 */
int tcpsend(tcbnum, rexmt)
int     tcbnum;
Bool    rexmt;
{
        struct  tcb     *ptcb = &tcbtab[tcbnum];
        struct  ep      *pep;
        struct  ip      *pip;
        struct  tcp     *ptcp;
        char            *pch;
        int             i, datalen, tocopy, off, newdata;

        pep = (struct ep *)getbuf(Net.netpool);
        if (pep == SYSERR)
                return SYSERR;
        pip = (struct ip *)pep->ep_data;
        blkcopy(pip->ip_src, ptcb->tcb_lip, IP_ALEN);
        blkcopy(pip->ip_dst, ptcb->tcb_rip, IP_ALEN);
        pip->ip_proto = IPT_TCP;
        datalen = tcpsndlen(ptcb, rexmt, &off); /* get length & offset  */
        ptcp = (struct tcp *)pip->ip_data;
        ptcp->tcp_sport = ptcb->tcb_lport;
        ptcp->tcp_dport = ptcb->tcb_rport;
        if (!rexmt) {
                if (ptcb->tcb_code & TCPF_URG)
                        ptcp->tcp_seq = ptcb->tcb_suna + off;
                else
                        ptcp->tcp_seq = ptcb->tcb_snext;
        } else
                ptcp->tcp_seq = ptcb->tcb_suna;
        ptcp->tcp_ack = ptcb->tcb_rnext;

        if ((ptcb->tcb_flags & TCBF_SNDFIN) &&
            SEQCMP(ptcp->tcp_seq+datalen, ptcb->tcb_slast) == 0)
                ptcb->tcb_code |= TCPF_FIN;
        ptcp->tcp_code = ptcb->tcb_code;
```

```
          ptcp->tcp_offset = TCPHOFFSET;
          if ((ptcb->tcb_flags & TCBF_FIRSTSEND) == 0)
                  ptcp->tcp_code |= TCPF_ACK;
          if (ptcp->tcp_code & TCPF_SYN)
                  tcprmss(ptcb, pip);
          pip->ip_verlen = (IP_VERSION<<4) | IP_MINHLEN;
          pip->ip_len = IP_HLEN(pip) + TCP_HLEN(ptcp) + datalen;
          if (datalen > 0)
                  ptcp->tcp_code |= TCPF_PSH;
          ptcp->tcp_window = tcprwindow(ptcb);
          if (ptcb->tcb_code & TCPF_URG)
#ifdef  BSDURG
                  ptcp->tcp_urgptr = datalen;       /* 1 past end          */
#else   /* BSDURG */
                  ptcp->tcp_urgptr = datalen-1;
#endif  /* BSDURG */
          else
                  ptcp->tcp_urgptr = 0;
          pch = &pip->ip_data[TCP_HLEN(ptcp)];
          i = (ptcb->tcb_sbstart+off) % ptcb->tcb_sbsize;
          for (tocopy=datalen; tocopy > 0; --tocopy) {
                  *pch++ = ptcb->tcb_sndbuf[i];
                  if (++i >= ptcb->tcb_sbsize)
                          i = 0;
          }
          ptcb->tcb_flags &= ~TCBF_NEEDOUT;         /* we're doing it      */
          if (rexmt) {
                  newdata = ptcb->tcb_suna + datalen - ptcb->tcb_snext;
                  if (newdata < 0)
                          newdata = 0;
                  TcpRetransSegs++;
          } else {
                  newdata = datalen;
                  if (ptcb->tcb_code & TCPF_SYN)
                          newdata++; /* SYN is part of the sequence        */
                  if (ptcb->tcb_code & TCPF_FIN)
                          newdata++; /* FIN is part of the sequence        */
          }
          ptcb->tcb_snext += newdata;
          if (newdata >= 0)
                  TcpOutSegs++;
          if (ptcb->tcb_state == TCPS_TIMEWAIT)     /* final ACK           */
                  tcpwait(ptcb);
          datalen += TCP_HLEN(ptcp);
          tcph2net(ptcp);
```

```
        ptcp->tcp_cksum = 0;
        ptcp->tcp_cksum = tcpcksum(pip);
        return ipsend(pip->ip_dst, pep, datalen);
}
```

Although the idea behind sending a segment is straightforward, many details make the code complex. Conceptually, TCP maintains the sequence space as Figure 12.3 illustrates.

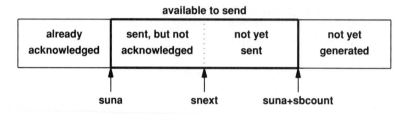

Figure 12.3 The conceptual sequence space and fields in the TCB that maintain pointers into it. Sequence numbers increase from left to right.

Because TCP uses a circular output buffer to hold the data, *tcpsend* must translate the sequence space computation into corresponding buffer addresses when it accesses data. Figure 12.4 explains how the available data maps into a circular buffer.

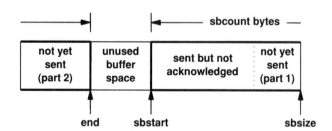

Figure 12.4 Available data wrapped around a circular TCP output buffer. Variable *sbcount* tells the number of available bytes and *end* gives the location of the last byte of data. *End* can be computed as *(sbstart+sbcount)* mod *sbsize*.

Tcpsend begins by allocating a buffer that will hold an IP datagram as well as a complete TCP segment. It copies the local and remote IP addresses into the IP datagram, and calls *tcpsndlen* to compute the length of data to send as well as the se-

quence number of the first octet being sent. If the call occurred because retransmission
is needed, *tcpsend* uses the sequence number of the first unacknowledged data octet in
place of the computed value.

Tcpsend places the sequence number of the next expected incoming octet
(*tcb_rnext*) in the *acknowledgement* field of the segment. After filling in other values in
the header, *tcpsend* calls *tcprwindow* to compute a window advertisement, and checks
for urgent data. Finally, it copies data octets into the segment from the sending buffer,
fills in the remaining header fields, calls *tcph2net* to convert integers to network byte
order, calls *tcpcksum* to compute the segment checksum, and passes the resulting IP datagram to *ipsend* for transmission.

12.14 Computing The TCP Data Length

Procedure *tcpsndlen* computes the amount of data to be sent.

```
/* tcpsndlen.c - tcpsndlen */

#include <conf.h>
#include <kernel.h>
#include <network.h>
#include <q.h>

struct   uqe      *uqalloc();

/*------------------------------------------------------------------------
 *  tcpsndlen - compute the packet length and offset in sndbuf
 *------------------------------------------------------------------------
 */
int tcpsndlen(ptcb, rexmt, poff)
struct   tcb      *ptcb;
Bool     rexmt;
int      *poff;
{
        struct   uqe      *puqe, *puqe2;
        int               datalen;

        if (rexmt || ptcb->tcb_sudq == EMPTY) {
                if (rexmt || (ptcb->tcb_code & TCPF_SYN))
                        *poff = 0;
                else
                        *poff = ptcb->tcb_snext - ptcb->tcb_suna;
                datalen = ptcb->tcb_sbcount - *poff;
                /* remove urgent data holes */
```

```
        if (!rexmt) {
                datalen = tcpshskip(ptcb, datalen, poff);
                datalen = min(datalen, ptcb->tcb_swindow);
        }
        return min(datalen, ptcb->tcb_smss);
}
/* else, URGENT data */

puqe = (struct uqe *)deq(ptcb->tcb_sudq);
*poff = ptcb->tcb_sbstart + puqe->uq_seq - ptcb->tcb_suna;
if (*poff > ptcb->tcb_sbsize)
        *poff -= ptcb->tcb_sbsize;
datalen = puqe->uq_len;
if (datalen > ptcb->tcb_smss) {
        datalen = ptcb->tcb_smss;
        puqe2 = uqalloc();
        if (puqe2 == SYSERR) {
                uqfree(puqe);               /* bail out and        */
                return ptcb->tcb_smss;  /* try as normal data  */
        }
        puqe2->uq_seq = puqe->uq_seq;
        puqe2->uq_len = datalen;

        /* put back what we can't use */
        puqe->uq_seq += datalen;
        puqe->uq_len -= datalen;
} else {
        puqe2 = puqe;
        puqe = (struct uqe *)deq(ptcb->tcb_sudq);
}
if (puqe == 0) {
        freeq(ptcb->tcb_sudq);
        ptcb->tcb_sudq = -1;
} else if (enq(ptcb->tcb_sudq, puqe,
                SUDK(ptcb, puqe->uq_seq)) < 0)
        uqfree(puqe);    /* shouldn't happen */
if (ptcb->tcb_suhq == EMPTY) {
        ptcb->tcb_suhq = newq(TCPUQLEN, QF_WAIT);
        ptcb->tcb_suhseq = puqe2->uq_seq;
}
if (enq(ptcb->tcb_suhq, puqe2, SUHK(ptcb, puqe2->uq_seq)) < 0)
        uqfree(puqe2);
return datalen;

}
```

The normal case is straightforward. If the length is needed for retransmission of a segment, or for the first segment in a stream, *tcpsndlen* starts the offset at zero (i.e., the offset from the first unacknowledged byte of data), and sets the data length equal to the count of octets in the output buffer. For other cases, *tcpsndlen* computes the offset of the first unsent byte of data, and computes the length of data to be sent by finding the difference between that sequence and the highest sequence of octets in the sending buffer. Of course, for non-retransmitted data, *tcpsndlen* must honor the receiver's advertised window, so if the window is smaller, it limits the data length.

Most of *tcpsndlen* computes the data length for *urgent data*, which is discussed in Chapter 15.

12.15 Computing Sequence Counts

Procedure *tcpxmit* uses function *tcphowmuch* to determine whether it needs to generate a segment. *Tcphowmuch* determines how much data is waiting.

```
/* tcphowmuch.c.c - tcphowmuch */

#include <conf.h>
#include <kernel.h>
#include <network.h>

/*------------------------------------------------------------------------
 *  tcphowmuch.c - compute how much data is available to send
 *------------------------------------------------------------------------
 */
int tcphowmuch(ptcb)
struct  tcb     *ptcb;
{
        int     tosend;

        tosend = ptcb->tcb_suna + ptcb->tcb_sbcount - ptcb->tcb_snext;
        if (ptcb->tcb_code & TCPF_SYN)
                ++tosend;
        if (ptcb->tcb_flags & TCBF_SNDFIN)
                ++tosend;
        return tosend;
}
```

Tcphowmuch differs from procedures like *tcpsndlen* because it handles an important detail: it counts the *SYN* and *FIN* codes, as well as data. Thus, it may report a positive count, when procedures that compute data length report zero.

12.16 Other TCP Procedures

12.16.1 Sending A Reset

The input procedures call *tcpreset* to generate and send a *RESET* segment whenever segments arrive unexpectedly (e.g., when no connection exists). The argument is a pointer to the input packet that caused the error.

```
/* tcpreset.c - tcpreset */

#include <conf.h>
#include <kernel.h>
#include <network.h>

/*------------------------------------------------------------------------
 *  tcpreset - generate a reset in response to a bad packet
 *------------------------------------------------------------------------
 */
int tcpreset(pepin)
struct    ep      *pepin;
{
        struct    ep      *pepout;
        struct    ip      *pipin = (struct ip *)pepin->ep_data, *pipout;
        struct    tcp     *ptcpin = (struct tcp *)pipin->ip_data, *ptcpout;
        int               datalen;

        if (ptcpin->tcp_code & TCPF_RST)
                return OK;                    /* no RESETs on RESETs */
        pepout = (struct ep *)getbuf(Net.netpool);
        if (pepout == SYSERR)
                return SYSERR;
        pipout = (struct ip *)pepout->ep_data;
        blkcopy(pipout->ip_src, pipin->ip_dst, IP_ALEN);
        blkcopy(pipout->ip_dst, pipin->ip_src, IP_ALEN);
        pipout->ip_proto = IPT_TCP;
        pipout->ip_verlen = (IP_VERSION<<4) | IP_MINHLEN;
        pipout->ip_len = IPMHLEN + TCPMHLEN;

        ptcpout = (struct tcp *)pipout->ip_data;
        ptcpout->tcp_sport = ptcpin->tcp_dport;
        ptcpout->tcp_dport = ptcpin->tcp_sport;
        if (ptcpin->tcp_code & TCPF_ACK) {
                ptcpout->tcp_seq = ptcpin->tcp_ack;
```

```
                ptcpout->tcp_code = TCPF_RST;
        } else {
                ptcpout->tcp_seq = 0;
                ptcpout->tcp_code = TCPF_RST|TCPF_ACK;
        }
        datalen = pipin->ip_len - IP_HLEN(pipin) - TCP_HLEN(ptcpin);
        if (ptcpin->tcp_code & TCPF_FIN)
                datalen++;
        ptcpout->tcp_ack = ptcpin->tcp_seq + datalen;
        ptcpout->tcp_offset = TCPHOFFSET;
        ptcpout->tcp_window = ptcpout->tcp_urgptr = 0;
        tcph2net(ptcpout);
        ptcpout->tcp_cksum = 0;
        ptcpout->tcp_cksum = tcpcksum(pipout);
        TcpOutSegs++;
        return ipsend(pipout->ip_dst, pepout, TCPMHLEN);
}
```

Tcpreset tests the *TCPF_RST* bit in the segment that caused the problem to avoid generating *RESET* messages in response to *RESET* messages. It then proceeds to allocate a buffer that will hold an IP datagram and a *RESET* segment, and fills in the IP header.

When filling in the TCP header, *tcpreset* checks to see if the segment that caused the problem contained an ACK. If it does, *tcpreset* takes the sequence number for the *RESET* from the incoming acknowledgement field. Otherwise, it uses zero for the sequence number.

After filling in all the header fields, *tcpreset* calls *tcph2net* to convert integers in the TCP header to network byte order. It then calls *tcpcksum* to compute the checksum, and *ipsend* to send the resulting datagram.

12.16.2 Converting To Network Byte Order

Procedure *tcph2net* converts fields in the TCP header to network byte order. The code is straightforward.

```
/* tcph2net.c - tcph2net */

#include <conf.h>
#include <kernel.h>
#include <network.h>


/*------------------------------------------------------------------------
 *  tcph2net -  convert TCP header fields from host to net byte order
 *------------------------------------------------------------------------
 */
struct tcp *tcph2net(ptcp)
struct  tcp      *ptcp;
{
        /* NOTE: does not include TCP options */

        ptcp->tcp_sport = hs2net(ptcp->tcp_sport);
        ptcp->tcp_dport = hs2net(ptcp->tcp_dport);
        ptcp->tcp_seq = hl2net(ptcp->tcp_seq);
        ptcp->tcp_ack = hl2net(ptcp->tcp_ack);
        ptcp->tcp_window = hs2net(ptcp->tcp_window);
        ptcp->tcp_urgptr = hs2net(ptcp->tcp_urgptr);
        return ptcp;
}
```

12.16.3 Waiting For Space In The Output Buffer

Application programs that generate output may need to block if insufficient space remains in the buffer associated with a given TCB. To allocate space, they call procedure *tcpgetspace*.

```
/* tcpgetspace.c - tcpgetspace */

#include <conf.h>
#include <kernel.h>
#include <proc.h>
#include <network.h>


/*------------------------------------------------------------------------
 *  tcpgetspace  -  wait for space in the send buffer
 *       N.B. - returns with tcb_mutex HELD
 *------------------------------------------------------------------------
 */
int tcpgetspace(ptcb, len)
```

```
struct  tcb       *ptcb;
int               len;
{
        if (len > ptcb->tcb_sbsize)
                return TCPE_TOOBIG;      /* we'll never have this much   */
        while (1) {
                wait(ptcb->tcb_ssema);
                wait(ptcb->tcb_mutex);
                if (ptcb->tcb_state == TCPS_FREE)
                        return SYSERR;                          /* gone       */
                if (ptcb->tcb_error) {
                        tcpwakeup(WRITERS, ptcb);       /* propagate it */
                        signal(ptcb->tcb_mutex);
                        return ptcb->tcb_error;
                }
                if (len < ptcb->tcb_sbsize - ptcb->tcb_sbcount)
                        return len;
                signal(ptcb->tcb_mutex);
        }
}
```

If an application needs more space than the entire buffer can hold, *tcpgetspace* returns an error code. Otherwise, it signals the mutual exclusion semaphore and waits on
the ''send'' semaphore again. *Tcpgetspace* tests field *tcb_error* to see if an error has
occurred (e.g., a *RESET* caused TCP to abort the connection). If so, *tcpgetspace* calls
tcpwakeup to awaken other processes that are waiting to write, signals the mutual exclusion semaphore, and returns the error to its caller.

If no error has occurred, *tcpgetspace* computes the available space by subtracting
the count of used bytes from the buffer size. If the available space is sufficient to satisfy the request, *tcpgetspace* returns to its caller. Otherwise, it signals the mutual exclusion semaphore, and waits on the send semaphore again. Note that when *tcpgetspace*
finds sufficient space, it returns to its caller with the mutual exclusion semaphore held.
Thus, no other process can take space in the buffer until the caller uses the space it requested and signals the semaphore.

12.16.4 Awakening Processes Waiting For A TCB

Application programs block while waiting to transfer data through a TCP connection. If an abnormal condition causes TCP to break the connection, it must unblock all
waiting processes before it can deallocate the TCB. Each process will resume execution, usually in a *read* or *write* procedure, which will find the error condition recorded
in the TCB and report the error to its caller. Procedure *tcpwakeup* unblocks waiting
processes. It takes two arguments: the first specifies the type of process that should be
awakened (either *READERS* or *WRITERS*), and the second gives a pointer to the appropriate TCB.

```
/* tcpwakeup.c - tcpwakeup */

#include <conf.h>
#include <kernel.h>
#include <network.h>

/*------------------------------------------------------------------------
 * tcpwakeup -  wake up processes sleeping for TCP, if necessary
 *      NB: Called with tcb_mutex HELD
 *------------------------------------------------------------------------
 */
int tcpwakeup(type, ptcb)
int             type;
struct  tcb     *ptcb;
{
        int     freelen;

        if (type & READERS) {
                if (((ptcb->tcb_flags & TCBF_RDONE) ||
                    ptcb->tcb_rbcount > 0 || ptcb->tcb_rudq >= 0) &&
                    scount(ptcb->tcb_rsema) <= 0)
                        signal(ptcb->tcb_rsema);
        }
        if (type & WRITERS) {
                freelen = ptcb->tcb_sbsize - ptcb->tcb_sbcount;
                if (((ptcb->tcb_flags & TCBF_SDONE) || freelen > 0) &&
                    scount(ptcb->tcb_ssema) <= 0)
                        signal(ptcb->tcb_ssema);
                /* special for abort */
                if (ptcb->tcb_error && ptcb->tcb_ocsem > 0)
                        signal(ptcb->tcb_ocsem);
        }
        return OK;
}
```

Two semaphores control reading and writing. When no data remains for processes to read, and no processes are waiting to read, the count of the reader's semaphore remains zero. Thus, any new process that attempts to read will be blocked. *Tcpwakeup* examines the input buffer, and if data is available, it signals the reader's semaphore. If one or more processes remain blocked, one of them will proceed. If not, the call to *signal* will increment the semaphore count, which will allow the next process that issues a *read* to continue. Thus, the name *wakeup* is a slight misnomer because it might not awaken any processes when called.

Tcpwakeup examines the TCB to decide whether readers or writers should be allowed to proceed. If the remote side has sent all data, *tcpwakeup* will find bit *TCBF_RDONE* set. It also examines the buffer to see if data has arrived, and a separate list to see if urgent data is present. In such cases, it checks to see if the semaphore currently allows access, and calls *signal* if it does not.

Tcpwakeup also participates in error propagation. If processes remain blocked waiting on the semaphore when an error occurs, the call to *signal* will allow the first process to proceed. When that process finds the error code, it signals the semaphore again, allowing the next process to read. After each process executes, it signals the semaphore to allow one more process to execute, until all waiting processes have resumed and found the error code.

Tcpwakeup behaves similarly when awakening processes waiting to write. It signals the writers' semaphore to unblock the first one, which will execute and unblock the next, and so on. *Tcpwakeup* also checks for the special case where the connection has been aborted and either an open or close is pending. In that case, it signals the open-close semaphore. The call to *open* or *close* returns an error code and deletes the TCB.

12.16.5 Choosing An Initial Sequence Number

To make TCP work in an environment where segments can be lost, duplicated, or delivered out of order, it must choose a unique starting sequence number each time it attempts to create a new connection. Procedure *tcpiss* generates an initial starting sequence by using the current time-of-day clock.

```
/* tcpiss.c - tcpiss */

#include <conf.h>
#include <kernel.h>
#include <network.h>


#define TCPINCR          904


/*------------------------------------------------------------------------
 *  tcpiss - set the ISS for a new connection
 *------------------------------------------------------------------------
 */
int tcpiss()
{
        static  int     seq = 0;
        extern  long    clktime;                        /* the system ticker    */

        if (seq == 0)
                seq = clktime;
        seq += TCPINCR;
        return seq;
}
```

Tcpiss maintains a static variable and uses the clock to initialize the variable only once. After initialization, *tcpiss* merely increments the starting sequence by a small amount (*904*) for each new connection.

12.17 Summary

TCP output uses an extremely simple finite state machine; it can be thought of as controlling microscopic transitions within a single state of the input finite state machine. The output machine has four states that correspond to an idle connection, a connection on which data is being transmitted, a connection for which data is waiting but the receiver has closed its window, and a connection on which data is being retransmitted.

To help separate the interactions between input, output, and timer functions, our example implementation uses a separate process for each. All normal TCP output occurs from the output process, which performs only one operation at any time. Thus, there is never a problem controlling the concurrent interaction of transmission, retransmission, and acknowledgements. Other processes use message passing to inform the output process that output is needed; the output process uses a single message queue in which each message includes both a TCB number and a request for that TCB. Requests can specify transmission of data or acknowledgement, retransmission, deletion of the TCB, or the probe of a closed window.

The example implementation uses a separate procedure to implement each state of the output finite state machine. We saw that although the ideas are straightforward, details, exceptions, and special cases complicate the code.

FOR FURTHER STUDY

Postel [RFC 793] specifies the TCP protocol, and [RFC 1122] contains further refinements.

EXERCISES

12.1   Explain what happens to the TCP checksum if routes change *after* a TCP connection has been opened. (Hint: consider the pseudo header and the IP addresses used by *tcpsend*.)

12.2   Suppose a low priority process is waiting to write to a TCP connection, a medium priority process is executing, and a high priority process needs to create a new connection. Explain how *tcpwakeup* and the TCB deallocation scheme can allow the medium priority process to prevent the high priority process from forming a connection.

12.3   Ask David Stevens (dls@cs.purdue.edu) why the example code increments the starting sequence number by *904*.

12.4   Read the specification to find out how long TCP should persist in attempting to probe a closed window. How long does our example implementation persist?

13

TCP: Timer Management

13.1 Introduction

Real-time delay processing forms an essential part of TCP. In addition to the obvious need for timers that handle retransmissions, TCP uses timers for the 2 MSL delay following connection close, for probing after a receiver advertises a zero-size window, and, in some implementations, to delay acknowledgements.

This chapter considers an implementation of software that handles real-time delays. It shows how a single data structure can efficiently store a variety of delay requests, and how a single timer process can manage all the delays TCP requires. Earlier chapters have already shown how input and output software calls the timer routines to schedule delays and how the output process manages events when they occur. Later chapters will complete the investigation by showing how TCP estimates round trip delays and uses the round-trip estimates to compute retransmission delays.

13.2 A General Data Structure For Timed Events

The key to efficient management of timed events lies in a data structure known as a *delta list*. Each item on a delta list corresponds to an event scheduled to occur in the future. Because each scheduled event may occur at a different time, each item on a delta list has a field that gives the time at which the event should occur. To make updates efficient, a delta list stores events ordered by the time at which they will occur, and uses *relative* times, not *absolute* times. For example, Figure 13.1 shows a delta list that contains four items scheduled to occur 16, 20, 21, and 30 time units in the future. Items on the list have time values of *16, 4, 1*, and *9* because the first item occurs *16* time units from the present, the second occurs *4* time units after the first, the third occurs *1* time unit after the second, and the fourth occurs *9* time units beyond the third.

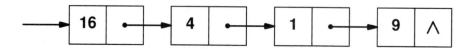

Figure 13.1 A delta list of events that occur *16, 20, 21*, and *30* time units in the future. Stored values give times relative to the previous event.

The chief advantage of a delta list lies in its efficiency. Because all times are relative, a periodic timer process only needs to decrement the time in the first item on the list. When the time in the first item reaches zero, the event occurs and the timer removes the item from the list. It then begins periodically decrementing the count in the next item on the list. The simplicity and efficiency will become clear as we consider software that manages a delta list.

13.3 A Data Structure For TCP Events

Items on the TCP delta list must contain more than a time field and a pointer to the next item. They must identify the action to be taken when the event expires. Structure *tqent* specifies the exact format of items on the TCP delta list. The declaration can be found in file *tcptimer.h*.

```
/* tcptimer.h */

/* A timer delta list entry */

struct  tqent {
        int     tq_timeleft;        /* time to expire (1/100 secs)  */
        long    tq_time;            /* time this entry was queued   */
        int     tq_port;            /* port to send the event       */
        int     tq_portlen;         /* length of "tq_port"          */
        int     tq_msg;             /* data to send when expired    */
        struct  tqent   *tq_next;   /* next in the list             */
};
/* timer process declarations and definitions */
```

```
extern   int              tcptimer();
#define TMSTK            512              /* stack size for fast timer   */
#define TMPRI            100              /* timer process priority      */
#define TMNAM            "tcptimer"       /* name of fast timer process  */
#define TMARGC           0                /* count of args to TCP timer  */


extern   long    ctr100;                  /* 1/100th of a second clock   */

extern   int     tqmutex;
extern   int     tqpid;
extern   struct  tqent   *tqhead;
```

Field *tq_next* contains a pointer to the next item on the list. Field *tq_timeleft* specifies the time at which the item should occur. Values in *tq_timeleft* are relative times measured in hundredths of seconds, and follow the rule for delta lists:

> *Time in the first item on the list is measured relative to the current time, while time in other items is measured relative to the previous item on the list.*

13.4 Timers, Events, And Messages

TCP timer management software can follow one of two basic designs: items on the timer delta list can store commands that the timer process interprets when the event occurs, or items on the list can store messages that the timer process delivers when the event occurs. The chief advantage of the former design lies in its ability to permit each timer event to trigger an arbitrarily complex operation. The chief advantage of the latter design lies in its simplicity. The timer process does not need to know the meaning of each message – it can take the same action whenever an event occurs.

To keep the timer process simple and efficient, we have chosen the latter design. Each event on the delta list includes a message (field *tq_msg*) and the identifier of a port to which the message should be sent when the event occurs (field *tq_port*). The timer mechanism sends the message in *tq_msg* to the port given by *tq_port*. To summarize:

> *The example TCP timer mechanism does not understand or interpret the messages stored in events. When the event occurs, the timer merely sends the specified message to the specified port.*

13.5 The TCP Timer Process

When the system first starts, protocol initialization software creates a TCP timer process that executes procedure *tcptimer*.

```
/* tcptimer.c - tcptimer */

#include <conf.h>
#include <kernel.h>
#include <network.h>
#include <tcptimer.h>

int     tqmutex;
int     tqpid;
struct  tqent   *tqhead;

/*------------------------------------------------------------------
 *  tcptimer -  TCP timer process
 *------------------------------------------------------------------
 */
PROCESS tcptimer()
{
        long    now, lastrun;           /* times from system clock    */
        int     delta;                  /* time since last iteration  */
        struct  tqent   *tq;            /* temporary delta list ptr   */

        lastrun = ctr100;               /* initialize to "now"        */
        tqmutex = screate(1);           /* mutual exclusion semaphore */
        tqpid = getpid();               /* record timer process id    */
        signal(Net.sema);               /* start other network processes*/

        while (TRUE) {
                sleep10(TIMERGRAN);      /* real-time delay            */
                if (tqhead == 0)         /* block timer process if delta */
                        suspend(tqpid);  /*   list is empty            */

                wait(tqmutex);
                now = ctr100;
                delta = now - lastrun;   /* compute elapsed time       */

                /* Note: check for possible clock reset (time moved    */
                /* backward or delay was over an order of magnitude too */
                /* long)                                               */
```

```
                if (delta < 0 || delta > TIMERGRAN*100)
                        delta = TIMERGRAN*10;   /* estimate the delay   */
                lastrun = now;
                while (tqhead != 0  &&  tqhead->tq_timeleft <= delta) {
                        delta -= tqhead->tq_timeleft;
                        if (pcount(tqhead->tq_port) <= tqhead->tq_portlen)
                                psend(tqhead->tq_port, tqhead->tq_msg);
                        tq = tqhead;
                        tqhead = tqhead->tq_next;
                        freemem(tq, sizeof(struct tqent));
                }
                if (tqhead)
                        tqhead->tq_timeleft -=delta;
                signal(tqmutex);
        }
}
```

The timer process begins by creating a mutual exclusion semaphore and storing its id in variable *tqmutex*. It also stores its own process id in variable *tqpid*, and signals the network semaphore to allow packets to flow. Finally, *tcptimer* enters an infinite loop.

In each iteration of the main loop, *tcptimer* calls *sleep10* to delay for *TIMERGRAN* tenths of seconds. It then checks the head of the delta list. If no item remains on the list, the timer calls *suspend* to block itself until some other process deposits an item. Although the call to *suspend* is not necessary, it eliminates having the timer process continue periodic execution when there is nothing for it to do.

As long as the delta list remains nonempty, *tcptimer* continues to iterate. On each iteration, it waits on the mutual exclusion semaphore (*tqmutex*) to obtain exclusive use of the delta list, processes items on the list, and then signals the mutual exclusion semaphore to allow other processes to access the list again. Note that the list is always available while *tcptimer* is blocked in the call to *sleep10*.

In the Xinu operating system, global variable *ctr100* contains the value of the real-time clock expressed as hundredths of seconds past an epoch date. *Tcptimer* references variable *ctr100* to obtain the current time, and uses variable *lastrun* to record the time of each iteration. Therefore, *tcptimer* can compute the elapsed time between iterations by subtracting the value of *lastrun* from the current time. The code checks to see if the system clock has been reset (e.g., time has moved backward or time has moved forward by more than ten times the expected delay). If it has, *tcptimer* substitutes a reasonable estimate for the delay and proceeds.

To process items on the delta list, *tcptimer* compares the time remaining for the item to the time that has expired between iterations. If the event should have occurred during the interval between the last iteration and the current iteration, *tcptimer* sends the message that the event contains (*tq_msg*) to the port that the message specifies (*tq_port*). It then removes the event from the delta list.

When removing an event, *tcptimer* updates the value of *delta* by decrementing the time for the event. Thus, like items on the list, *delta* always contains a relative time, making it possible to compare it directly to the time value stored in an individual item.

When *tcptimer* finishes removing items that have occurred, two possibilities exist: the list can be empty or nonempty. If the list is empty, no further processing is needed. However, if the list is nonempty, it must be true that the time remaining before the next item should occur is greater than *delta*. In such cases, *tcptimer* reduces the time of the remaining item by *delta* before beginning the next cycle of delay.

13.6 Deleting A TCP Timer Event

TCP software may need to cancel an event before it expires. For example, when it receives an acknowledgement, TCP might cancel a retransmission event. To cancel an event, TCP needs to remove the corresponding item from the timer delta list. Procedure *tmclear* provides the necessary function.

```
/* tmclear.c - tmclear */

#include <conf.h>
#include <kernel.h>
#include <network.h>
#include <tcptimer.h>


/*------------------------------------------------------------------
 *  tmclear - clear the indicated timer
 *------------------------------------------------------------------
 */
int tmclear(port, msg)
int     port, msg;
{
        struct  tqent   *prev, *ptq;
        int             timespent;

        wait(tqmutex);
        prev = 0;
        for (ptq = tqhead; ptq != NULL; ptq = ptq->tq_next) {
                if (ptq->tq_port == port && ptq->tq_msg == msg) {
                        timespent = ctr100 - ptq->tq_time;
                        if (prev)
                                prev->tq_next = ptq->tq_next;
                        else
                                tqhead = ptq->tq_next;
                        if (ptq->tq_next)
```

```
                           ptq->tq_next->tq_timeleft +=
                                           ptq->tq_timeleft;
                   signal(tqmutex);
                   freemem(ptq, sizeof(struct tqent));
                   return timespent;
               }
           prev = ptq;
       }
       signal(tqmutex);
       return SYSERR;
}
```

Tmclear takes a message (*msg*) and a port identifier (*port*) as arguments, and deletes a timer event with that message and port pair. The code is straightforward. *Tmclear* searches the delta list until it finds the item that matches the arguments. At each step, it keeps a pointer to an item on the list (*ptq*) and a pointer to the previous item (*prev*). When it finds a match, *tmclear* removes the item by unlinking it from the list and calling *freemem* to return the storage to the system's free memory pool.

Recall that times stored in items on the delta list are relative. Thus, whenever *tmclear* deletes an event, it must be careful to adjust the time remaining for events that follow it. To make the adjustment, *tmclear* checks field *tq_next* to see if any items follow the one being deleted. If so, *tmclear* adds the delay for the deleted item to the delay for the one following.

13.7 Deleting All Events For A TCB

We saw in Chapters 10 and 11 that before TCP can remove a TCB, it must delete all timer events associated with that TCB. Procedure *tcpkilltimers* performs the task. Because our TCP software only allows three possible message types, and only arranges to send messages to the TCP output port, *tcpkilltimers* can use three calls to *tmclear* to delete all TCP events for a given TCB.

```
/* tcpkilltimers.c - tcpkilltimers */

#include <conf.h>
#include <kernel.h>
#include <network.h>


/*-------------------------------------------------------------------
 * tcpkilltimers - kill all outstanding timers for a TCB
 *-------------------------------------------------------------------
 */
int tcpkilltimers(ptcb)
struct   tcb      *ptcb;
{
        int      tcbnum = ptcb - &tcbtab[0];

        /* clear all possible pending timers */

        tmclear(tcps_oport, MKEVENT(SEND, tcbnum));
        tmclear(tcps_oport, MKEVENT(RETRANSMIT, tcbnum));
        tmclear(tcps_oport, MKEVENT(PERSIST, tcbnum));
        return OK;
}
```

Most software that calls *tcpkilltimers* uses a pointer to refer to a TCB instead of the array index. To accommodate such software, argument *ptcb* is declared to be a pointer to the TCB. However, *tcpkilltimers* needs to use a TCB index number in the call to *MKEVENT*. To compute the index, *tcpkilltimers* uses pointer arithmetic, subtracting the address of the start of the TCB array (*tcbtab*) from the pointer to a given entry. Thus, variable *tcbnum* contains an integer index of the entry.

13.8 Determining The Time Remaining For An Event

Procedure *tmleft* determines the amount of time left before an event occurs. It returns zero if no such event exists.

```
/* tmleft.c - tmleft */

#include <conf.h>
#include <kernel.h>
#include <network.h>
#include <tcptimer.h>
```

```
/*-------------------------------------------------------------------
 *  tmleft  -  how much time left for this timer?
 *-------------------------------------------------------------------
 */
int tmleft(port, msg)
int     port, msg;
{
        struct  tqent   *tq;
        int             timeleft = 0;

        if (tqhead == NULL)
                return 0;
        wait(tqmutex);
        for (tq = tqhead; tq != NULL; tq = tq->tq_next) {
                if (tq->tq_port == port && tq->tq_msg == msg) {
                        timeleft += tq->tq_timeleft;
                        signal(tqmutex);
                        return timeleft;
                }
        }
        signal(tqmutex);
        return 0;
}
```

To determine the time remaining, *tmleft* must sum the relative times in all events up to and including the time on the specified event. It uses pointer *tq* to walk the linked list, starting at *tqhead* and following pointer *tq_next* in each item. As it moves along the list, *tmleft* accumulates the time delay in local variable *timeleft*. When it reaches the item for which the time was requested, it signals the mutual exclusion semaphore and returns the computed total to the caller. If the specified event does not exist, *tmleft* returns zero.

13.9 Inserting A TCP Timer Event

TCP software calls procedure *tmset* to create an event and insert it on the TCP delta list. *Tmset* takes arguments that specify a desired delay (*time*), a message to be sent when the event occurs (*msg*), the port to which the message should be sent (*port*), and the length of the port (*portlen*).

```
/* tmset.c - tmset */

#include <conf.h>
#include <kernel.h>
#include <network.h>
#include <tcptimer.h>

/*------------------------------------------------------------------
 *  tmset -  set a fast timer
 *------------------------------------------------------------------
 */
int tmset(port, portlen, msg, time)
int     port, portlen, msg, time;
{
        struct  tqent   *ptq, *newtq, *tq;

        newtq = (struct tqent *)getmem(sizeof(struct tqent));
        newtq->tq_timeleft = time;
        newtq->tq_time = ctr100;
        newtq->tq_port = port;
        newtq->tq_portlen = portlen;
        newtq->tq_msg = msg;
        newtq->tq_next = NULL;

        /* clear duplicates */
        (void) tmclear(port, msg);

        wait(tqmutex);
        if (tqhead == NULL) {
                tqhead = newtq;
                resume(tqpid);
                signal(tqmutex);
                return OK;
        }
        /* search the list for our spot */

        for (ptq=0, tq=tqhead; tq; tq=tq->tq_next) {
                if (newtq->tq_timeleft < tq->tq_timeleft)
                        break;
                newtq->tq_timeleft -= tq->tq_timeleft;
                ptq = tq;
        }
        newtq->tq_next = tq;
        if (ptq)
```

```
                ptq->tq_next = newtq;
        else
                tqhead = newtq;
        if (tq)
                tq->tq_timeleft -= newtq->tq_timeleft;
        signal(tqmutex);
        return OK;
}
```

Tmset calls *getmem* to allocate free memory for an event list item, and then fills in fields of the item from the arguments. It calls *tmclear* to remove the message from the list if it already exists. Finally, *tmset* waits on the mutual exclusion semaphore, inserts the new item in the list, and signals the mutual exclusion semaphore before returning.

Although the list insertion code in *tmset* is straightforward, a few details make it appear complicated. The timer process remains suspended as long as no events are pending. When *tmset* inserts an item into an empty list, it calls *resume* to restart the timer process. When it inserts into a nonempty list, *tmset* must search the list to find the correct insertion point.

During the search, *tmset* uses two variables that point to a node on the list (*tq*) and its predecessor (*ptq*). As it passes items on the list, *tmset* subtracts their delay from the delay for the new item to keep its delay relative to the current position in the list. When the *while* loop terminates, the new item belongs between the items to which *ptq* and *tq* point. *Tmset* links the new item into the list and decrements the time on the successor by the added delay.

13.10 Starting TCP Output Without Delay

The example timer software has been constructed to work correctly, even if the caller specifies a delay of zero clock ticks. *Tmset* will correctly add the new request to the beginning of the delta list. When the *tcptimer* process awakens, it will remove the item from the delta list and deposit the message on the TCP output port. When the TCP output process receives the message, it will proceed to handle it.

Although the mechanism works correctly, scheduling an event with zero delay is inefficient because it forces the operating system to context switch between the calling process, the TCP timer process, and the TCP output process in rapid succession. Furthermore, scheduling a *SEND* event with zero delay occurs often (whenever the input process needs to send an *ACK* or whenever an application program generates output). To eliminate the unnecessary context switch, our example software provides procedure *tcpkick* that can be used to schedule a *SEND* without delay.

```
/* tcpkick.c - tcpkick */

#include <conf.h>
#include <kernel.h>
#include <network.h>


/*------------------------------------------------------------------
 *  tcpkick -  make sure we send a packet soon
 *------------------------------------------------------------------
 */
int tcpkick(ptcb)
struct  tcb      *ptcb;
{
        int     tcbnum = ptcb - &tcbtab[0];      /* for MKEVENT() */
        int     tv;

        tv = MKEVENT(SEND, tcbnum);
        if (ptcb->tcb_flags & TCBF_DELACK && !tmleft(tcps_oport, tv))
                tmset(tcps_oport, TCPQLEN, tv, TCP_ACKDELAY);
        else if (pcount(tcps_oport) < TCPQLEN)
                psend(tcps_oport, tv);  /* send now */
        return OK;
}
```

After creating a needed event, *tcpkick* checks the TCB to see if it is using delayed *ACK*s (bit *TCBF_DELACK*). As long as *ACK*s are not delayed, *tcpkick* sends the message directly to the TCP output process. If it finds that *ACK*s should be delayed, *tcpkick* calls *tmset* to schedule the event in a short time.

13.11 Summary

TCP requires real-time processing to handle events like retransmission that must be scheduled to occur in the future. Our sample implementation stores delayed events on a delta list because it makes periodic updates efficient. Items on a delta list each correspond to a single event. The delta list arranges items by the time they will occur and stores time relative to the previous item on the list.

A single TCP process manages the delta list. It periodically decrements the remaining time in the first item on the list, and schedules the event when the time reaches zero. When an event occurs, the TCP timer process extracts an integer message and a port identifier from the event, and sends the message to that port. Thus, the timer process does not understand or interpret the messages stored in events.

FOR FURTHER STUDY

Comer [1987] describes delta list processing in more detail and gives invariants for maintaining times in relative form during the search.

EXERCISES

13.1   Devise a slightly different data structure that eliminates some or all of the special cases in *tmset*.

13.2   Step through the insertion of a new item on a delta list to see if you understand how the relative time is maintained during the search.

13.3   Rewrite *tcpkilltimers* to search the delta list and remove *all* items for a given TCB. How much more efficient is it than the current implementation?

13.4   How does the modification suggested in the previous exercise reduce the generality of the timing mechanism?

13.5   Would it be helpful to modify *tcpkick* to allow it to handle messages other than *SEND*? Why or why not?

14

TCP: Flow Control And Adaptive Retransmission

14.1 Introduction

TCP accommodates an extraordinary diversity of underlying physical networks by tolerating a wide range of delay, throughput, and packet loss rates. It handles each connection independently, allowing multiple connections from a single machine to each traverse a path with different underlying characteristics. More important, TCP adapts to changes in the round trip delay on a given connection, making it reliable even when the underlying packet switching system experiences congestion or temporary failures.

Adaptive retransmission lies at the heart of TCP and accounts for its success. In essence, adaptive retransmission uses recent past behavior to predict future behavior. It requires TCP to measure the round trip delay for each transmission, and to use statistical techniques to combine the individual measurements into a smoothed estimate of the mean round trip delay. Furthermore, TCP continually updates its round trip delay estimate as it acquires new measurements.

This chapter considers the implementation of software that provides adaptive retransmission. It discusses measurement of round trip times, statistical smoothing, retransmission timing, generation and processing of acknowledgements, and window-based flow control. It includes congestion-control and slow-start techniques as well as timer backoff and other optimizations.

Although the techniques discussed in this chapter require only a few lines of code to implement, their effect on TCP performance is dramatic. More important, they have arisen after much experimentation and careful analysis, so an average programmer is not likely to invent them independently. Finally, most of these techniques are now part of the TCP standard, so they must not be considered optional.

14.2 The Difficulties With Adaptive Retransmission

In principle, round trip estimation should be easy. However, problems in a practical internet impose several difficulties. Segments or acknowledgements can be lost or delayed, making individual round trip measurements inaccurate. Bursty traffic from multiple sources can cause delays to fluctuate wildly. Furthermore, the load imposed by even a single connection can congest a network or gateway. Finally, retransmission after segment loss can cause congestion, or add to it.

Although the original TCP specification contained many subtle weaknesses and omissions, most of the adaptive retransmission problems have been solved either through improvements in statistical smoothing methods or through the use of practical heuristics.

14.3 Tuning Adaptive Retransmission

To achieve efficiency and robustness, TCP adaptive retransmission must be tuned in five principle areas:

- Retransmission timer and backoff
- Window-based flow control
- Maximum segment size computation
- Congestion avoidance and control
- Round trip estimation

The next sections examine each of these areas in detail, and show the implementation of techniques to resolve these subtle problems.

14.4 Retransmission Timer And Backoff

TCP uses a *cumulative acknowledgement* scheme in which each acknowledgement carries a sequence number. The sequence number specifies how many contiguous octets from the data stream the remote site has received correctly. Because acknowledgements do not specify individual segments and because acknowledgements can be lost, the sender cannot distinguish whether a given acknowledgement arose from an original transmission or the retransmission of a segment. Thus, the sender cannot accurately measure the round trip delay for retransmitted segments.

14.4.1 Karn's Algorithm

The standard specifies that TCP should use a technique known as *Karn's algorithm* to control the retransmission timer value. During normal data transfer, acknowledgements arrive for each segment before the retransmission timer expires. In such cases, Karn's algorithm does not interfere with the usual process of measuring the round trip delay and computing a retransmission timeout for the next segment to be sent. However, because TCP cannot correctly associate acknowledgements with individual transmissions of a segment, Karn's algorithm specifies that TCP should ignore round trip measurements for all retransmitted segments. Furthermore, once retransmissions begin, Karn's algorithm separates the computation of retransmission timeouts from the previous estimate of round trip delay, doubling the timeout for each retransmission.

To implement Karn's algorithm, the software needs to store three pieces of information. First, it needs to store a value for retransmission timeout, which it computes from the current round trip estimate. Second, it needs to store an indication of whether TCP has begun retransmitting. Third, it needs to store a count of retransmissions. Our example code keeps all these values in fields of the TCB. Field *tcb_rexmt* stores the current value for the retransmission timer. If retransmission has begun, field *tcb_ostate* contains the value *TCPO_REXMT*. Finally, field *tcb_rexmtcount* records the current count of retransmissions.

14.4.2 Retransmit Output State Processing

Procedure *tcprexmt* implements the retransmission computation specified by Karn's algorithm.

```
/* tcprexmt.c - tcprexmt */

#include <conf.h>
#include <kernel.h>
#include <network.h>

/*------------------------------------------------------------------------
 *  tcprexmt - handle TCP output events while we are retransmitting
 *------------------------------------------------------------------------
 */
int tcprexmt(tcbnum, event)
{
        struct  tcb     *ptcb = &tcbtab[tcbnum];

        if (event != RETRANSMIT)
                return OK;         /* ignore others while retransmitting   */
        if (++ptcb->tcb_rexmtcount > TCP_MAXRETRIES) {
                tcpabort(ptcb, TCPE_TIMEDOUT);
                return OK;
        }
        tcpsend(tcbnum, TSF_REXMT);
        tmset(tcps_oport, TCPQLEN, MKEVENT(RETRANSMIT, tcbnum),
                min(ptcb->tcb_rexmt<<ptcb->tcb_rexmtcount, TCP_MAXRXT));
        if (ptcb->tcb_ostate != TCPO_REXMT)
                ptcb->tcb_ssthresh = ptcb->tcb_cwnd;    /* first drop    */
        ptcb->tcb_ssthresh = min(ptcb->tcb_swindow,ptcb->tcb_ssthresh)/2;
        if (ptcb->tcb_ssthresh < ptcb->tcb_smss)
                ptcb->tcb_ssthresh = ptcb->tcb_smss;
        ptcb->tcb_cwnd = ptcb->tcb_smss;
        return OK;
}
```

   Tcprexmt corresponds to the *RETRANSMIT* output state, and will be called by the
TCP output process whenever a timer event occurs during retransmission. Because the
connection has begun retransmission, events like *SEND* cannot be processed, so
tcprexmt ignores all events except the *RETRANSMIT* event.

   Tcprexmt increments the retransmission count in field *tcb_rexmtcount* and enforces
a maximum retransmission count by comparing it to the constant *TCP_MAXRETRIES*.
When it reaches the maximum allowed count, *tcprexmt* calls *tcpabort* to abort the connection, passing it the error code *TCPE_TIMEDOUT*. After *tcprexmt* has checked for
errors, it calls *tcpsend* to retransmit the unacknowledged data that remains in the output
buffer. The second argument to *tcpsend* specifies that this call is for retransmission.

Once *tcprexmt* retransmits the data, it needs to schedule another retransmission timeout in the future. The call to *tmset* implements timer control according to Karn's algorithm. It shifts the timeout in *tcb_rexmt* left *tcb_rexmtcount* bits to double the delay for each retransmission that has occurred. It then passes the computed delay as an argument to *tmset*, causing it to schedule a new *RETRANSMIT* event.

For small values of *TCP_MAXRETRIES*, doubling the timeout on each retransmission works well. However, if the system allows a large number of retries, doubling the timeout on each can result in severe delays before TCP decides to abort a connection. To prevent the timeout from becoming arbitrarily large, *tcprexmt* enforces a maximum timeout by choosing the minimum of the computed timeout and constant *TCP_MAXRXT*.

Section *14.7.1* discusses the final few statements in *tcprexmt*, which handle congestion control.

14.5 Window-Based Flow Control

When TCP on the receiving machine sends an acknowledgement, it includes a *window advertisement* in the segment to tell the sender how much buffer space the receiver has available for additional data. The window advertisement always specifies the data the receiver can accept beyond the data being acknowledged, and TCP mandates that once a receiver advertises a given window, it may never advertise a subset of that window (i.e., the window never shrinks). Of course, as the sender fills the advertised window, the value in the acknowledgement field increases and the value in the window field may become smaller until it reaches zero. However, the receiver may never decrease the point in the sequence space through which it has agreed to accept data. Thus, the window advertisement can only decrease if the sender supplies data and the acknowledgement number increases; it cannot decrease merely because the receiver decides to decrease its buffer size.

TCP uses window advertisements to control the flow of data across a connection. A receiver advertises small window sizes to limit the data a sender can generate. In the extreme case, advertising a window size of zero halts transmission altogether†.

14.5.1 Silly Window Syndrome

If a receiver advertises buffer space as soon as it becomes available, it may cause behavior known as the *silly window syndrome*. Silly window behavior is characterized as a situation in which the receiver's window oscillates between zero and a small positive value, while the sender transmits small segments to fill the window as soon as it opens. Such behavior leads to low network utilization because each segment transmitted contains little data compared to the overhead for TCP and IP headers.

To prevent a TCP peer from falling victim to the silly window syndrome when transmitting, TCP uses a technique known as *receiver-side silly window avoidance*. The silly window avoidance rule states that once a receiver advertises a zero window, it

---

†We say that the receiver "closes" the window.

should delay advertising a nonzero window until it has a nontrivial amount of space in its buffer. A nontrivial amount of buffer space is defined to be the space sufficient for one maximum-sized segment or the space equivalent to one quarter of the buffer, whichever is larger.

14.5.2 Receiver-Side Silly Window Avoidance

Procedure *tcprwindow* implements receiver-side silly window avoidance when it computes a window advertisement.

```
/* tcprwindow.c - tcprwindow */

#include <conf.h>
#include <kernel.h>
#include <network.h>


/*------------------------------------------------------------------------
 *  tcprwindow - do receive window processing for a TCB
 *------------------------------------------------------------------------
 */
int tcprwindow(ptcb)
struct  tcb     *ptcb;
{
        int     window;

        window = ptcb->tcb_rbsize - ptcb->tcb_rbcount;
        if (ptcb->tcb_state < TCPS_ESTABLISHED)
                return window;
        /*
         *      Receiver-Side Silly Window Syndrome Avoidance:
         *  Never shrink an already-advertised window, but wait for at
         *  least 1/4 receiver buffer and 1 max-sized segment before
         *  opening a zero window.
         */
        if (window*4 < ptcb->tcb_rbsize || window < ptcb->tcb_rmss)
                window = 0;
        window = max(window, ptcb->tcb_cwin - ptcb->tcb_rnext);
        ptcb->tcb_cwin = ptcb->tcb_rnext + window;
        return window;
}
```

Tcprwindow begins by computing a window size equal to the available buffer space (i.e., the size of the receive buffer minus the current count of characters in the buffer). If TCP has just begun a three-way handshake, but has not yet established a connection (the state is less than *TCPS_ESTABLISHED*), the receiver maximum segment size has not been initialized. Therefore, *tcprwindow* cannot apply receiver-side silly window avoidance – it merely stores the value computed for the window in field *tcb_window* of the TCB and returns to its caller. Once a connection has been established, *tcprwindow* applies the rule for receiver-side silly window avoidance, by reducing the window to zero unless a nontrivial amount of space is available.

The final statements of *tcprwindow* apply congestion avoidance to the window advertisement as discussed below.

14.5.3 Optimizing Performance After A Zero Window

Once a receiver advertises a zero window, the sender enters the *PERSIST* output state and begins to probe the receiver†. The receiver responds to each probe by sending an acknowledgement. As long as the window remains closed, the probes continue, and the acknowledgements contain a window advertisement of zero. Eventually, when sufficient space becomes available, the acknowledgements will carry a nonzero window, and the sender will start to transmit new data.

Although the sender bears ultimate responsibility for probing a zero window, a minor optimization can improve performance. The optimization consists of arranging for the receiver to generate a *gratuitous acknowledgement* that contains the new window size, without waiting for the next probe. Thus, in our implementation, whenever an application program extracts data from a TCP input buffer, it checks to see if the additional space causes the window to open, and sends a gratuitous acknowledgement if it does. As the sender processes the acknowledgement, it finds the nonzero window advertisement, moves back to the *TRANSMIT* state, and resumes transmission of data.

14.5.4 Adjusting The Sender's Window

Procedure *tcpswindow* computes the size of the sender's window. It handles window advertisements in incoming segments, and keeps track of the amount of data the peer TCP is willing to receive.

---

†Chapter 12 discusses output processing and the output state machine.

```
/* tcpswindow.c - tcpswindow */

#include <conf.h>
#include <kernel.h>
#include <network.h>

/*------------------------------------------------------------------
 *  tcpswindow -  handle send window updates from remote
 *------------------------------------------------------------------
 */
int tcpswindow(ptcb, pep)
struct  tcb     *ptcb;
struct  ep      *pep;
{
        struct ip       *pip = (struct ip *)pep->ep_data;
        struct tcp      *ptcp = (struct tcp *)pip->ip_data;
        tcpseq          wlast, owlast;

        if (SEQCMP(ptcp->tcp_seq, ptcb->tcb_lwseq) < 0)
                return OK;
        if (SEQCMP(ptcp->tcp_seq, ptcb->tcb_lwseq) == 0 &&
            SEQCMP(ptcp->tcp_ack, ptcb->tcb_lwack) < 0)
                return OK;
        /* else, we have a send window update */

        /* compute the last sequences of the new and old windows */

        owlast = ptcb->tcb_lwack + ptcb->tcb_swindow;
        wlast = ptcp->tcp_ack + ptcp->tcp_window;

        ptcb->tcb_swindow = ptcp->tcp_window;
        ptcb->tcb_lwseq = ptcp->tcp_seq;
        ptcb->tcb_lwack = ptcp->tcp_ack;
        if (SEQCMP(wlast, owlast) <= 0)
                return OK;
        /* else,  window increased */
        if (ptcb->tcb_ostate == TCPO_PERSIST) {
                tmclear(tcps_oport, MKEVENT(PERSIST, ptcb-&tcbtab[0]));
                ptcb->tcb_ostate = TCPO_XMIT;
        }
        tcpkick(ptcb);                          /* do something with it */
        return OK;
}
```

In the TCB, field *tcb_swindow* always contains the number of bytes that TCP can send beyond the currently acknowledged sequence. That is, it contains the value from the most recently received window advertisement. However, because segments can arrive out of order, TCP must be careful when updating *tcb_swindow*. It must verify that the incoming segment was generated after the segment that was last used to update the window. To do so, it keeps a record of the sequence (*tcb_lwseg*) and acknowledgement (*tcb_lwack*) fields from the segment whenever it updates the window.

When a segment arrives, *tcpswindow* compares the sequence and acknowledgement fields to the stored values. If the value in the sequence field is smaller than the stored sequence value, the segment has arrived out of order and the window advertisement must be ignored. Furthermore, if the sequence number in the segment matches the stored sequence value, but the acknowledgement in the segment is smaller than the stored acknowledgement, the acknowledgement has arrived out of order, so the window advertisement must be ignored. When *tcpswindow* determines that the segment contains a valid advertisement, it stores the new window size in field *tcb_swindow* and updates the stored sequence and acknowledgement values.

14.6 Maximum Segment Size Computation

We saw that when *tcprwindow* applies receiver-side silly window avoidance, it needs to know the size of the largest possible segment that can be expected to arrive. In addition, when TCP generates segments that carry data, it limits their size to the *maximum segment size* (*MSS*) allowed for the connection. TCP negotiates the MSS for both outgoing and incoming segments when it exchanges requests during the three-way handshake. Once it establishes a MSS in each direction, TCP never changes them.

14.6.1 The Sender's Maximum Segment Size

To understand how the example TCP software chooses a maximum segment size for output, look again at procedure *tcpwinit* in Chapter 11†. *Tcpwinit* computes an initial value for the maximum segment size (MSS), and stores it in field *tcb_smss* of the TCB. To help avoid IP fragmentation, the host requirements document specifies that TCP must use an initial maximum segment size of *536* octets if the connection passes through a gateway. For connections that lie on a directly connected network, TCP chooses an initial value such that the network packets will be as full as possible (i.e., it computes an initial maximum data size by subtracting the size of TCP and IP headers from the MTU for the local network used to reach the remote machine). *Tcpwinit* determines whether the connection will pass through a gateway by finding whether the route to the destination has a metric greater than zero.

After choosing an initial MSS, TCP processes the maximum segment size option found in incoming *SYN* segments. Procedure *tcpsmss* handles the details of processing the MSS option.

---

†*Tcpwinit* initializes the MSS when a remote client establishes a connection to a local server; a similar piece of code initializes the MSS when a local client forms a connection to a remote server.

```
/* tcpsmss.c - tcpsmss */

#include <conf.h>
#include <kernel.h>
#include <network.h>

/*------------------------------------------------------------------------
 *  tcpsmss - set sender MSS from option in incoming segment
 *------------------------------------------------------------------------
 */
int tcpsmss(ptcb, ptcp, popt)
struct  tcb      *ptcb;
struct  tcp      *ptcp;
char             *popt;
{
        unsigned         mss, len;

        len = *++popt;
        if ((ptcp->tcp_code & TCPF_SYN) == 0)
                return len;
        switch (len-2) {          /* subtract kind & len  */
        case sizeof(char):
                mss = *popt;
                break;
        case sizeof(short):
                mss = net2hs(*(unsigned short *)popt);
                break;
        case sizeof(long):
                mss = net2hl(*(unsigned long *)popt);
                break;
        default:
                mss = ptcb->tcb_smss;
                break;
        }
        mss -= TCPMHLEN;          /* save just the data buffer size */
        if (ptcb->tcb_smss)
                ptcb->tcb_smss = min(mss, ptcb->tcb_smss);
        else
                ptcb->tcb_smss = mss;
        return len;
}
```

A maximum segment size can only be negotiated during the three-way handshake, so *tcpsmss* ignores the option unless the segment carrying it has the *SYN* bit set. It then selects one of four cases, using the number of octets in the option value to choose a case. Our implementation supports MSS option values of 8, 16, or 32 bits†. *Tcpsmss* extracts the option value and converts it to local machine byte order. In other cases, *tcpsmss* substitutes the initial MSS from the TCB. Finally, after extracting a value for the MSS from the option, *tcpsmss* compares it to the initial MSS in the TCB, and uses the minimum of the two. Thus, *tcpsmss* never allows the MSS option on an incoming segment to increase the initial MSS value.

14.6.2 Option Processing

Procedure *tcpopts* handles option processing, and calls *tcpsmss* to extract the MSS option.

```c
/* tcpopts.c - tcpopts */

#include <conf.h>
#include <kernel.h>
#include <network.h>

/*------------------------------------------------------------------------
 * tcpopts - handle TCP options for an inbound segment
 *------------------------------------------------------------------------
 */
int tcpopts(ptcb, pep)
struct    tcb      *ptcb;
struct    ep       *pep;
{
        struct    ip       *pip = (struct ip *)pep->ep_data;
        struct    tcp      *ptcp = (struct tcp *)pip->ip_data;
        char               *popt, *popend;
        int                len;

        if (TCP_HLEN(ptcp) == TCPMHLEN)
                return OK;
        popt = ptcp->tcp_data;
        popend = &pip->ip_data[TCP_HLEN(ptcp)];
        do {
                switch (*popt) {
                case TPO_NOOP:  popt++;
                                /* fall through */
                case TPO_EOOL:  break;
                case TPO_MSS:
```

---

†Many implementations only support 16 bit values.

```
                        popt += tcpsmss(ptcb, ptcp, popt);
                        break;
                default:
                        break;
                }
        } while (*popt != TPO_EOOL && popt<popend);

        /* delete the options */
        len = pip->ip_len-IP_HLEN(pip)-TCP_HLEN(ptcp);
        if (len)
                blkcopy(ptcp->tcp_data,&pip->ip_data[TCP_HLEN(ptcp)],len);
        pip->ip_len = IP_HLEN(pip) + TCPMHLEN + len;
        ptcp->tcp_offset = TCPHOFFSET;
        return OK;
}
```

Because the current TCP standard specifies only one real option, MSS, the code is extremely simple. In addition to the MSS option, *tcpopts* must also handle option codes that denote *no-operation* and *end of options*.

Once *tcpopts* reaches the end-of-options code, it deletes the options field altogether by moving the data portion of the segment and adjusting the length field in the segment header. Removing the option field makes it possible for procedures throughout the TCP software to assume a fixed offset for the data.

14.6.3 Advertising An Input Maximum Segment Size

Procedure *tcprmss* creates the maximum segment size option in a *SYN* segment. It assumes the maximum segment size has already been computed and stored in the TCB.

```
/* tcprmss.c - tcprmss */

#include <conf.h>
#include <kernel.h>
#include <network.h>


/*------------------------------------------------------------------------
 *  tcprmss - set receive MSS option
 *------------------------------------------------------------------------
 */
int tcprmss(ptcb, pip)
struct  tcb     *ptcb;
struct  ip      *pip;
{
```

```
struct   tcp       *ptcp = (struct tcp *)pip->ip_data;
int                mss, hlen, olen, i;

hlen = TCP_HLEN(ptcp);
olen = 2 + sizeof(short);
pip->ip_data[hlen] = TPO_MSS;           /* option kind      */
pip->ip_data[hlen+1] = olen;            /* option length    */
mss = hs2net((short)ptcb->tcb_smss);
for (i=olen-1; i>1; i--) {
        pip->ip_data[hlen+i] = mss & LOWBYTE;
        mss >>= 8;
}
hlen += olen + 3;        /* +3 for proper rounding below */
/* header length is high 4 bits of tcp_offset, in longs */
ptcp->tcp_offset = ((hlen<<2) & 0xf0) | ptcp->tcp_offset & 0xf;
}
```

Option creation is straightforward. The option consists of a single octet containing *TPO_MSS*, a single octet that gives the option length, and a binary integer in network byte order that contains the maximum segment size. *Tcprmss* adjusts the TCP header length in the segment to include the option octets.

14.7 Congestion Avoidance And Control

When congestion occurs, delays increase, causing TCP to retransmit segments. In the worst case, retransmissions increase congestion and produce an effect known as *congestion collapse*. To avoid adding to congestion, the standard now specifies that TCP should use strategies that reduce retransmission when packet delay or loss occurs. The first strategy is known as *multiplicative decrease*.

14.7.1 Multiplicative Decrease

The idea behind multiplicative decrease is simple: the sender-side of TCP maintains an internal variable known as the *congestion window* that it uses to restrict the amount of data being sent. When transmitting, TCP uses the minimum of the receiver's advertised window and the internal congestion window to determine how much data to send.

To compute the congestion window size, assume the number of retransmissions provides a measure of congestion in the internet. While no congestion or loss occurs, set the congestion window size to the receiver's advertised window size. That is, use the receiver's advertised window to determine how much data to send. When congestion begins (i.e., when a retransmission occurs), reduce the congestion window size by a

multiplicative constant. In particular, reduce the congestion window by half each time retransmission occurs, but never reduce it to less than the size required for one segment.

Procedure *tcprexmt*, shown in section 14.4.2, implements multiplicative decrease. In the code, variable *tcb_cwnd* contains the congestion window size. *Tcprexmt* sets variable *tcb_ssthresh* to one half of either the advertised window (*tcb_swindow*) or the current congestion window (*tcb_cwnd*), whichever is smaller. It then checks to make sure that the computed value does not go below *1 MSS*.

Although the technique is called *multiplicative*, the congestion window threshold will decrease exponentially when measured in lost segments. The first loss drops it to one-half of the original window, the second to one-quarter, the third to one-eighth, and so on.

14.8 Slow-Start And Congestion Avoidance

14.8.1 Slow-start

We said that when an internet carrying TCP segments becomes congested, additional retransmissions can exacerbate the situation. To help recover from congestion, the standard now requires TCP to reduce its rate of transmission. In particular, TCP assumes that packet loss results from congestion, and immediately uses a technique known as *slow-start* during the recovery. To further improve performance and to avoid having new connections add to the congestion, TCP uses slow-start whenever it starts sending data on a newly established connection.

Slow-start is the reverse of multiplicative decrease – it provides multiplicative increase†. The idea is again simple: start the congestion window at the size of a single segment (the MSS) and send it. If communication is successful and an acknowledgement arrives before the retransmission timer expires, add one segment to the congestion window size (i.e., double it to two segments). Continue adding one segment to the congestion window each time an acknowledgement arrives. Thus, if both segments arrive successfully in the second round of transmissions, the congestion window will increase to *4* segments, and it will continue to increase exponentially until it reaches the threshold that has been set by multiplicative decrease.

14.8.2 Slower Increase After Threshold

Once the congestion window reaches the threshold, TCP slows down. Instead of adding a new segment to the congestion window every time an acknowledgement arrives, TCP increases the congestion window size by one segment for each round trip time. To estimate a round trip time, the code uses the time to send and receive acknowledgements for the data in one window. Of course, TCP does not wait for an entire window of data to be sent and acknowledged before increasing the congestion window size. Instead, it adds a small increment to the congestion window size each time an acknowledgement arrives. The small increment is chosen to make the increase average

---

†Slow-start is an unfortunate name because it starts flow quickly in the absence of loss; it only remains slow if loss continues.

approximately one segment over an entire window. To understand how the idea translates into code, think of TCP sending maximum size segments, and remember that we want to increase the congestion window by:

$$increase = segment / window$$

Because the system has experienced congestion, the current window is limited to the congestion window size, which means that the number of increments TCP makes is determined by the number of segments that fit in the congestion window.

$$segments\ per\ window = congestion\ window / max\ segment\ size$$

Let N denote the segments per window. To increment by one segment over the entire window, TCP increments by $1/N$ for each of the N acknowledgements. Thus, when an acknowledgement arrives, TCP increments by:

$$\begin{aligned} increment\ &= (one\ segment / N) \\ &= (MSS\ bytes / N) \\ &= MSS / (congestion\ window/MSS) \end{aligned}$$

or

$$increment = (\ MSS * MSS\ ) / congestion\ window$$

14.8.3 Implementation Of Congestion Window Increase

The last few lines of procedure *tcprtt* implement congestion window increase when acknowledgements arrive†.

---

† The remaining code in *tcprtt* participates in retransmission timer estimation, and is discussed in detail later.

```
/* tcprtt.c - tcprtt */

#include <conf.h>
#include <kernel.h>
#include <network.h>


/*------------------------------------------------------------------------
 *  tcprtt - do round trip time estimates & cong. window processing
 *------------------------------------------------------------------------
 */
int tcprtt(ptcb)
struct  tcb     *ptcb;
{
        int     rrt,            /* raw round trip              */
                delta;          /* deviation from smoothed     */

        rrt = tmclear(tcps_oport, MKEVENT(RETRANSMIT, ptcb-&tcbtab[0]));
        if (rrt != SYSERR && ptcb->tcb_ostate != TCPO_REXMT) {
                if (ptcb->tcb_srt == 0)
                        ptcb->tcb_srt = rrt<<3; /* prime the pump */
                /*
                 * "srt" is scaled X 8 here, so this is really:
                 *      delta = rrt - srt
                 */
                delta = rrt - (ptcb->tcb_srt>>3);
                ptcb->tcb_srt += delta;         /* srt = srt + delta/8  */
                if (delta < 0)
                        delta = -delta;
                /*
                 * "rtde" is scaled X 4 here, so this is really:
                 *      rtde = rtde + (|delta| - rtde)/4
                 */
                ptcb->tcb_rtde += delta - (ptcb->tcb_rtde>>2);
                /*
                 * "srt" is scaled X 8, rtde scaled X 4, so this is:
                 *      rto = 2*(srt + rtde)
                 */
                ptcb->tcb_rexmt = ((ptcb->tcb_srt>>2)+ptcb->tcb_rtde)>>1;
                if (ptcb->tcb_rexmt < TCP_MINRXT)
                        ptcb->tcb_rexmt = TCP_MINRXT;
        }
        if (ptcb->tcb_cwnd < ptcb->tcb_ssthresh)
                ptcb->tcb_cwnd += ptcb->tcb_smss;
        else
```

```
                 ptcb->tcb_cwnd += (ptcb->tcb_smss * ptcb->tcb_smss) /
                        ptcb->tcb_cwnd;

        return OK;
}
```

The final *if* statement of *tcprtt* handles congestion window increase. If variable *tcb_cwnd* is less than *tcb_ssthresh*, procedure *tcprtt* provides slow-start by incrementing the congestion window by the maximum segment size. If the congestion window has passed the threshold, *tcprtt* uses additive increase and increments the congestion window by MSS^2/tcb_cwnd.

14.9 Round Trip Estimation And Timeout

From the beginning, researchers recognized that TCP performance depends on its ability to estimate the mean of the round trip time on a connection. The best way to think of the problem is to imagine a sequence of round trip measurements that arrive over time. TCP uses the history of measurements to estimate the current round trip delay, and chooses a retransmission timeout derived from its estimate of round trip delay. Because the round trip delay varies over time, TCP weights recent measurements more heavily than older ones. However, because individual measurements of round trip delay can fluctuate wildly from the norm when congestion occurs, TCP cannot ignore the history of measurements completely.

Performance studies have shown that TCP can exhibit significantly higher throughput if it estimates the variance in round trip delay as well as the mean. Knowing the variance makes it possible to compute a timeout that accommodates expected fluctuations without retransmitting unnecessarily. The standard now specifies using the improved round trip estimation technique described here.

14.9.1 A Fast Mean Update Algorithm

It would be foolish for TCP to keep a history of round trip measurements for purposes of computing the mean and variance in round trip delay because good incremental algorithms exist. Thus, TCP keeps a "running average" which it updates each time it obtains a new measurement. For example, it updates the average by computing:

$$\text{error} = \text{measurement} - \text{average}$$

and

$$\text{average} = \text{average} + \delta * \text{error}$$

where δ is a fraction less than *1*. In fact, TCP can keep a "running mean deviation" and use the *error* term above to update the deviation:

$$\text{deviation} = \text{deviation} + (\lvert \text{error} \rvert - \text{deviation})$$

In practice, implementations achieve efficiency by scaling the computation by a power of two, and using integer arithmetic instead of floating point. For example, choosing:

$$\delta = 1/2^n$$

allows the code to perform division by shifting. The value $n = 3$ is convenient. If *average* stores a scaled form of the average, the code becomes:

```
error = measurement - (average >> 3);
average = average + error;
if (error < 0)
    error = -error;
error = error - (deviation >> 3);
deviation = deviation + error;
```

To further improve performance, TCP uses a slightly larger value for δ, making the final form:

```
error = measurement - (average >> 3);
average = average + error;
if (error < 0)
    error = -error;
error = error - (deviation >> 2);
deviation = deviation + error;
retransmission_timer = ( (average>>2)+ deviation) >> 1;
```

Procedure *tcprtt* implements round trip estimation. It is called whenever an acknowledgement arrives. Thus, a call to *tcprtt* signals the end of retransmissions, and the output state reverts to *TRANSMIT*.

Tcprtt first calls *tmclear*. The call accomplishes two things: it deletes the pending retransmission event for the connection, and it computes the time that has elapsed since the event was scheduled.

Recall that acknowledgement ambiguity makes round trip measurement impossible for retransmitted segments, and that Karn's algorithm specifies ignoring acknowledgements for retransmitted segments. *Tcprtt* implements Karn's algorithm by testing to make sure the round trip measurement is valid and that the acknowledgement does not correspond to a retransmitted segment (i.e., TCP is not in the *RETRANSMIT* state).

If the elapsed time, *rrt*, is valid, *tcprtt* assumes it provides a raw measure of round trip delay, and uses it to compute a new value for the smoothed round trip time, *tcb_srt*. It also produces a new estimate for the mean deviation (*tcb_rtde*). Finally, it computes a retransmission timeout from the new round trip estimate and stores it in *tcb_rexmt*. Note that our implementation uses constant *TCP_MINRXT* as a fixed minimum retransmission delay to insure that the computed value does not approach zero.

14.9.2 Handling Incoming Acknowledgements

Procedure *tcpacked* handles acknowledgements in incoming segments. It computes and returns to its caller the number of octets in the sequence space beyond those octets acknowledged by previous segments.

```
/* tcpacked.c - tcpacked */

#include <conf.h>
#include <kernel.h>
#include <network.h>


/*------------------------------------------------------------------------
 * tcpacked - handle in-bound ACKs and do round trip estimates
 *------------------------------------------------------------------------
 */
int tcpacked(ptcb, pep)
struct  tcb     *ptcb;
struct  ep      *pep;
{
        struct  ip      *pip = (struct ip *)pep->ep_data;
        struct  tcp     *ptcp = (struct tcp *)pip->ip_data;
        int             acked, tcbnum, cacked;

        if (!(ptcp->tcp_code & TCPF_ACK))
                return SYSERR;
        acked = ptcp->tcp_ack - ptcb->tcb_suna;
        cacked = 0;
        if (acked <= 0)
                return 0;         /* duplicate ACK */
        if (SEQCMP(ptcp->tcp_ack, ptcb->tcb_snext) > 0)
                if (ptcb->tcb_state == TCPS_SYNRCVD)
                        return tcpreset(pep);
                else
                        return tcpackit(ptcb, pep);
        tcprtt(ptcb);
        ptcb->tcb_suna = ptcp->tcp_ack;
        if (acked && ptcb->tcb_code & TCPF_SYN) {
                acked--;
                cacked++;
                ptcb->tcb_code &= ~TCPF_SYN;
                ptcb->tcb_flags &= ~TCBF_FIRSTSEND;
        }
        if ((ptcb->tcb_code & TCPF_FIN) &&
```

```
            SEQCMP(ptcp->tcp_ack, ptcb->tcb_snext) == 0) {
                acked--;
                cacked++;
                ptcb->tcb_code &= ~TCPF_FIN;
                ptcb->tcb_flags &= ~TCBF_SNDFIN;
        }
        ptcb->tcb_sbstart = (ptcb->tcb_sbstart+acked) % ptcb->tcb_sbsize;
        ptcb->tcb_sbcount -= acked;
        if (acked && scount(ptcb->tcb_ssema) <= 0)
                signal(ptcb->tcb_ssema);
        tcpostate(ptcb, acked+cacked);
        return acked;
}
```

If called with a segment that does not contain an acknowledgement bit, *tcpacked* returns an error value. If an acknowledgement is present, *tcpacked* computes the number of new octets acknowledged (*acked*) by subtracting the start of unacknowledged data stored in the TCB from the acknowledgement number in the segment. If the acknowledgement specifies a sequence number less than the currently recorded start of unacknowledged data, the segment must be a duplicate or have arrived out of order, so *tcpacked* returns zero to indicate that no additional octets were acknowledged.

Tcpacked includes a special check for acknowledgements that specify a sequence number beyond the sequence number of data that has been sent. For most states, the standard specifies that TCP must acknowledge such segments. Thus, *tcpacked* calls *tcpackit* to generate an acknowledgement. For the *SYN-RECEIVED* state, however, an acknowledgement beyond the current sequence number means an incorrect *3*-way handshake and must be answered by a *RESET*.

Once *tcpacked* has checked to see that the acknowledgement lies in the expected range, it calls *tcprtt* to update the smoothed round trip estimate and compute a new retransmission timeout. It also updates field *tcb_suna*, which contains the starting sequence number of unacknowledged data.

Tcpacked handles two special cases: *FIN* and *SYN* processing. Conceptually, both lie in the sequence space. *Tcpacked* records the presence of a *SYN* by clearing bit *TCBF_FIRSTSEND* in the TCB. It also decrements by *1* the count of acknowledged data returned to the caller, because the count specifies only data and should not include the *SYN*. Similarly, *tcpacked* clears bit *TCPF_FIN* in the TCB code flags if the segment acknowledges a *FIN* for the connection.

The final section of *tcpacked* updates variables in the TCB to reflect changes caused by the arrival of the acknowledgement. Basically, it manipulates counters and buffer pointers to discard outgoing data in the send buffer that has been acknowledged. First, it moves the buffer pointer (*tcb_sbstart*) forward *acked* positions, wrapping around to the start of the buffer if it passes the end. Second, it subtracts the number of octets acked from the count of data in the buffer (*tcb_sbcount*). Third, if acknowledged data has been removed from the buffer, and one or more application programs are blocked waiting for space in the buffer, *tcpacked* signals the send buffer semaphore, allowing the next program to write into the buffer.

14.9.3 Generating Acknowledgments For Data Outside The Window

We said that TCP was required to generate an acknowledgement in response to incorrect incoming acknowledgements. In particular, TCP sends an acknowledgement whenever the remote side acknowledges data that lies beyond the current output window. Procedure *tcpackit* generates such acknowledgements.

```
/* tcpackit.c - tcpackit */

#include <conf.h>
#include <kernel.h>
#include <network.h>

/*------------------------------------------------------------------
 *  tcpackit  -  generate an ACK for a received TCP packet
 *------------------------------------------------------------------
 */
int tcpackit(ptcb, pepin)
struct  tcb     *ptcb;
struct  ep      *pepin;
{
        struct ep       *pepout;
        struct ip       *pipin = (struct ip *)pepin->ep_data, *pipout;
        struct tcp      *ptcpin = (struct tcp *)pipin->ip_data, *ptcpout;

        if (ptcpin->tcp_code & TCPF_RST)
                return OK;
        if (pipin->ip_len <= IP_HLEN(pipin) + TCP_HLEN(ptcpin) &&
                        !(ptcpin->tcp_code & (TCPF_SYN|TCPF_FIN)))
                return OK;       /* duplicate ACK */
        pepout = (struct ep *)getbuf(Net.netpool);
        if (pepout == SYSERR)
                return SYSERR;
        pipout = (struct ip *)pepout->ep_data;
        blkcopy(pipout->ip_src, pipin->ip_dst, IP_ALEN);
        blkcopy(pipout->ip_dst, pipin->ip_src, IP_ALEN);
        pipout->ip_proto = IPT_TCP;
        pipout->ip_verlen = (IP_VERSION<<4) | IP_MINHLEN;
        pipout->ip_len = IP_HLEN(pipout) + TCPMHLEN;
        ptcpout = (struct tcp *)pipout->ip_data;
        ptcpout->tcp_sport = ptcpin->tcp_dport;
```

```
        ptcpout->tcp_dport = ptcpin->tcp_sport;
        ptcpout->tcp_seq = ptcb->tcb_snext;
        ptcpout->tcp_ack = ptcb->tcb_rnext;
        ptcpout->tcp_code = TCPF_ACK;
        ptcpout->tcp_offset = TCPHOFFSET;
        ptcpout->tcp_window = tcprwindow(ptcb);
        ptcpout->tcp_urgptr = 0;
        ptcpout->tcp_cksum = 0;
        ptcpout->tcp_cksum = tcpcksum(pipout);
        TcpOutSegs++;
        return ipsend(pipout->ip_dst, pepout, TCPMHLEN);
}
```

To prevent infinite loops, *tcpackit* does not respond to a *RESET* segment. For all others, it allocates a network buffer, fills in the TCP and IP headers, sets the *ACK* bit, and calls *ipsend* to forward the datagram on toward its destination.

14.10 Miscellaneous Notes And Techniques

Procedure *tcprtt* also aids *sender-side silly window avoidance*. It does so by checking for a pending *RETRANSMIT* event before scheduling another one. The idea is to avoid needless transmissions, because they trigger a sequence of acknowledgements. If the peer does not implement silly window avoidance, the acknowledgments may report small increments in window size, which, in turn, can cause the sender to transmit small segments. Thus, avoiding unnecessary acknowledgements helps conserve network bandwidth and prevent silly window behavior.

14.11 Summary

Adaptive retransmission lies at the heart of TCP, and makes it operate over a wide variety of underlying networks. To make TCP robust and efficient, adaptive retransmission algorithms must be tuned in several areas, including: retransmission timer backoff, window-based flow control, maximum segment size computation, congestion avoidance and control, and round trip estimation.

Experience and analysis have produced techniques and heuristics that are now either suggested or required by the TCP protocol standard. While each technique requires only a few lines of code, taken together they make a significant difference in raising throughput and lowering delay.

FOR FURTHER STUDY

Postel [RFC 793] contains the original standard for TCP that includes a description of adaptive retransmission; many of the techniques found in this chapter have been added by later RFCs. Braden [RFC 1122] incorporates significant changes in the standard. Clark [RFCs 813 and 816] describe window management and fault recovery. Postel [RFC 879] comments on maximum segment size. Nagle [RFC 865] gives the technique for silly window avoidance. Karn and Partridge [1987] reviews TCP performance improvements, including estimation of round trip times and Karn's algorithm. Jacobson [1988] gives the congestion control algorithms that are now a required part of the standard. Mills [RFC 889] discusses measurement of Internet round trip delays. Borman [April 1989] summarizes experiments with high-speed TCP on Cray computers.

EXERCISES

14.1 This chapter mentioned using both sender-side and receiver-side silly window avoidance techniques. Will the receiver-side technique perform well even if the sender does not use silly window avoidance? Explain.

14.2 To find out how much *slow-start* limits throughput on an Ethernet connection (MTU=1500 octets), assume a round trip delay of 3 milliseconds. Calculate the throughput of the first 32 packets sent (a) using *slow-start*, and (b) without *slow-start*.

14.3 If a sender has a 16K byte buffer and a 1K byte maximum segment size, how many lost acknowledgments does it take before the congestion window reaches 1 MSS?

14.4 Karn's algorithm specifies ignoring round trip estimates when segments must be retransmitted. What happens if TCP always associates ACKs with the original transmission? With the most recent retransmission?

14.5 Read Jacobson [1988], a paper on congestion avoidance. What does it suggest will happen if the multiplicative decrease uses a value of .8 instead of .5?

14.6 Consider the effect of buffer size on throughput. Suppose two different implementations of TCP use 16K byte and 64K byte output buffers, and both implementations transmit across a single, congested path to receivers with large receiver-side buffers. How does the loss of a single segment affect throughput on each of two connections? The loss of 10 successive segments?

14.7 Read about MTU discovery techniques. Explain how TCP can use them.

14.8 Argue that requiring an MSS of *536* for nonlocal connections places an unnecessary limit on TCP.

14.9 Will our example implementation work correctly on a local network that has an MTU just slightly less than the input (or output) buffer size? Explain.

14.10   Our implementation uses an aggressive acknowledgement policy (i.e., it does not delay sending acknowledgements to wait for window changes or data flowing in the opposite direction). How does aggressive acknowledgement improve performance? How can delayed acknowledgements affect *slow-start* and congestion control?

14.11   TCP does not provide a *keepalive* function in the protocol. However, some applications need to know when a connection fails even if they are not sending data. Extend our implementation to provide a *keepalive* function.

14.12   Some applications prefer to have TCP shutdown a connection that has been idle more than N minutes, where N is an argument specified by the application. Implement an automatic shutdown mechanism for idle connections.

14.13   Look at each state in the TCP finite state machine (Figure 10.2), and consider what happens to one side of a connection if the computer on the other side crashes and does not reboot. Determine which states need a long-term timeout to delete the TCB.

15

TCP: Urgent Data Processing And The Push Function

15.1 Introduction

Previous chapters considered conventional TCP input and output as well as heuristics to improve flow control and adaptive retransmission. This chapter considers two remaining aspects of TCP: its ability to send out-of-band data, and its ability to bypass normal buffering. Out-of-band data provides increased functionality and makes it possible to build programs that provide for *interruption* or a *program abort* function. Buffering is important because it makes TCP more efficient and lowers network overhead. However, buffering increases data transmission delays. Programs that need immediate delivery can force TCP to bypass buffering, so data will be delivered without delay. The next sections consider how TCP provides out-of-band communication and how an application can bypass buffering.

15.2 Out-Of-Band Signaling

TCP uses a *stream paradigm* for normal data transfer. An application at one end of a connection creates a data stream, which it passes to TCP on its local machine. TCP sends data from the stream across the internet to TCP on the machine at the other end of the connection, which delivers it to the application on that machine. The stream paradigm works well for many applications, but does not suffice for all communication because it forces the receiver to process all data in sequence. Sometimes, an application needs to communicate out-of-band messages that bypass the normal data stream. For example, remote login protocols use out-of-band messages to signal the remote site in cases when a program misbehaves and must be aborted. The signal to abort must be processed even if the program has stopped consuming data in the normal stream. Thus, it cannot be sent as part of the normal data stream.

15.3 Urgent Data

TCP uses the term *urgent data* to refer to out-of-band messages. When sending an out-of-band message, the sender sets the *urgent data bit (TCPF_URG)* in field *tcp_code* of the segment header, places the urgent data in the segment, and assigns the *urgent data pointer* field (*tcp_urgptr*) an offset in the data area of the segment at which the urgent data ends. Because the protocol standard provides only one pointer in the header, the segment does not contain an explicit pointer to the beginning of urgent data.

When a segment carrying urgent data arrives, the receiver must extract the urgent data and pass it to the receiving application immediately, bypassing any normal data that may be waiting. To do so, TCP places the application in *urgent mode*, which informs the application that urgent data exists. After the application has been placed in urgent mode, TCP returns the urgent data when the application reads from the connection. Finally, TCP informs the application that the end of urgent data has occurred.

15.4 Interpreting The Standard

The specification of urgent data is among the least understood and least documented parts of TCP. The original standard failed to provide complete answers for several questions. First, how can a receiver know where urgent data begins? Second, how can TCP inform an application that urgent data has arrived? Third, how does TCP inform an application when all urgent data has been processed? Fourth, what happens if multiple segments carrying urgent data arrive out of order? Fifth, does the urgent pointer point to the last octet of urgent data or to one location beyond the end of it†? More to the point, the standard assumes a message-passing interface, and fails to describe TCP semantics in the *open-read-write-close* paradigm most implementations use. Subsequent revisions have only provided partial solutions. To understand the subtleties underlying these questions, look at the conceptual diagram in Figure 15.1.

---

†While the current standard is quite explicit about this (the pointer specifies the last location of urgent data), most extant implementations, including 4BSD UNIX, have chosen to interpret the pointer as pointing one location beyond urgent data.

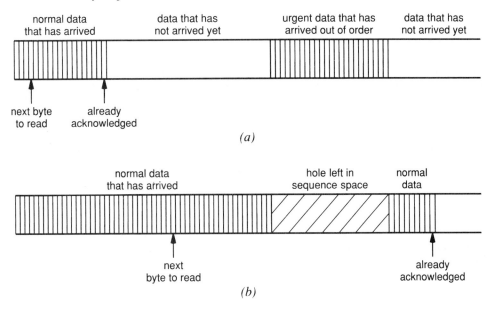

Figure 15.1 (a) The TCP sequence space when urgent data arrives before all
normal data, and (b) the same sequence space after urgent data
has been processed and additional normal data has arrived. The
space occupied by urgent data forms a hole in the space.

Urgent data occupies part of the sequence space used for normal data transfer. In most cases, urgent data arrives in order with other data, so the receiver has already received and acknowledged the sequence up to the start of the urgent message. However, as Figure 15.1a shows, because the underlying IP layer does not guarantee to deliver segments in order, a segment carrying urgent data may arrive earlier than some of the segments carrying normal data for lower values in the sequence space. In fact, because urgent messages are usually short, and because some gateways give short datagrams priority, out-of-order delivery is quite common.

Figure 15.1b shows a consequence of having urgent data occupy places in the sequence space. When the urgent data arrives, TCP immediately passes it to the application program reading from the connection. After processing the urgent data, the application returns to normal data processing and continues to acquire octets from the place it was reading when the urgent data arrived. As a consequence, a ''hole'' remains in the sequence space at those locations where urgent data resided. When the application reaches the hole, TCP must skip over it as if those locations did not exist.

Because the standard is vague on many points concerning urgent data processing, we have chosen an interpretation. First, we assume that if a segment arrives with the urgent bit set, the entire data area up to and including the octet specified by the urgent pointer contains urgent data.† Second, our code contains a configuration constant (*BSDURG*) that allows it to use either the standard interpretation or the Berkeley UNIX

---

†BSD UNIX and implementations derived from it assume only a single octet in the segment contains urgent data. They treat remaining octets as normal data.

interpretation of the urgent pointer (i.e., whether the urgent pointer points to the last octet of urgent data or one octet beyond it). Third, the standard says that if additional urgent data arrives while an application is in urgent mode, the application should receive the additional urgent data as well. It also states that, while inside urgent data, it is not necessary for TCP to tell the application when a segment boundary has been passed. We chose to extend this definition further by not informing the application about segment boundaries that lie between *noncontiguous* blocks of urgent data. That is,

> *From the application program's point of view, TCP treats all pending urgent data as a single consecutive sequence of octets. The application does not receive any information about which octets of urgent data came from which segment, nor does it receive a warning if segments carrying urgent data arrive out of order.*

The assumption here is that most applications use the urgent data facility to carry short messages. If a program sends large volumes of urgent data, it may be delivered out of order.

15.4.1 Informing The Application

Our implementation uses a *passive* method to inform an application that urgent data has arrived. It waits for the application to issue a *read* request. Once urgent data arrives, the next call to read will place the process in urgent mode and return the special return code *TCPE_URGENTMODE*. Subsequent calls to *read* return octets of urgent data. After all urgent data has been consumed, a call to *read* will reset the process back to normal mode, and will return the value zero to inform the application that it has reached the end of the urgent data. If no process ever calls *read*, the urgent data will not be consumed. To summarize:

> *Our implementation handles urgent data passively. It waits for an application to read from the connection before informing the application that urgent data has arrived. The TCP software never takes action to handle the urgent data, nor does it create a process to interpret urgent messages.*

15.4.2 Multiple Concurrent Application Programs

Although a concurrent processing system allows multiple processes to read from a single connection, the TCP standard does not specify the semantics of how they should process urgent data. We decided to implement the following scheme: each process has an independent record of whether it is in urgent mode. When a process calls *read* on a TCP connection for which urgent data has arrived, TCP places that process in urgent mode. Subsequent calls to *read* from that process will return octets from the urgent mode data. However, all processes share a single copy of urgent mode data, so the octets of urgent data read by one process will not be available to another.

In essence, our scheme for concurrent processing assumes that programmers take responsibility for reasonable use. It also means that two processes can both be in urgent mode simultaneously, and that one of them may call *read* and consume the urgent data before the other executes. Thus, any application program that allows concurrent use of a TCP connection should be prepared to expect zero octets of urgent data after it receives a message telling it to enter urgent mode.

15.5 A Data Structure For Urgent Mode Data

When thinking about urgent mode data, it is important to realize that:

> *Urgent mode data may reside at locations in the sequence space beyond the current window.*

To see why, consider a simple case that occurs when the receiver has advertised a window of zero octets. The sender may need to send urgent data without waiting for the receiver to open its window.

From an implementation point of view, the single most important consequence of allowing urgent mode data outside the current window is that the receiver cannot store it in the usual TCP input buffer, because the advertised window corresponds to buffer locations. Our implementation uses a dedicated data structure to hold urgent data for each TCB, and organizes each as a linked list. Structure *uqe*, declared in file *tcb.h*, defines the contents of an item on one of the lists.

Each item on an urgent data list corresponds to a block of urgent data that arrived in a single segment. It has fields that specify a starting sequence space number for the data (*uq_seq*), the data length (*uq_len*), and a pointer to a buffer that holds the data (*uq_data*). The list is sorted by sequence number, so an application always receives the urgent data that has arrived with the lowest sequence number first.

15.6 Extracting Urgent Data From An Incoming Segment

When an urgent segment arrives, *tcpok*† calls procedure *tcprcvurg* to extract the urgent data from it. *Tcprcvurg* allocates a node for the urgent data list, allocates a buffer to hold the urgent message, and copies the urgent data from the segment into the allocated buffer. Finally, it links the node into the urgent message list.

See page 188 for a listing of *tcpok*.

```
/* tcprcvurg.c - tcprcvurg */

#include <conf.h>
#include <kernel.h>
#include <network.h>
#include <q.h>

struct  uqe     *uqalloc();

/*-------------------------------------------------------------------
 *  tcprcvurg -  handle TCP urgent data
 *-------------------------------------------------------------------
 */
int tcprcvurg(ptcb, pep)
struct  tcb     *ptcb;
struct  ep      *pep;
{
        struct  ip      *pip = (struct ip *)pep->ep_data;
        struct  tcp     *ptcp = (struct tcp *)pip->ip_data;
        struct  uqe     *puqe;
        int             datalen, offset;

        datalen = pip->ip_len - IP_HLEN(pip) - TCP_HLEN(ptcp);
        /*
         * Berkeley machines treat the urgent pointer as "last+1", but
         * RFC 1122 says just "last." Defining "BSDURG" causes Berkeley
         * semantics.
         */
#ifdef  BSDURG
        ptcp->tcp_urgptr -= 1;
#endif  /* BSDURG */
        if (ptcp->tcp_urgptr >= datalen || ptcp->tcp_urgptr >= TCPMAXURG)
                ptcp->tcp_urgptr = datalen-1;   /* quietly fix it        */
        puqe = uqalloc();
        if (puqe == (struct uqe *)SYSERR)
                return SYSERR;                  /* out of buffer space!!! */
        puqe->uq_seq = ptcp->tcp_seq;
        puqe->uq_len = ptcp->tcp_urgptr + 1;
        puqe->uq_data = (char *)getbuf(Net.netpool);
        if (puqe->uq_data == (char *)SYSERR) {
                puqe->uq_data = 0;
                uqfree(puqe);
                return SYSERR;
        }
```

```
            blkcopy(puqe->uq_data, &pip->ip_data[TCP_HLEN(ptcp)],
                    puqe->uq_len);
        if (ptcb->tcb_rudq < 0) {
                ptcb->tcb_rudseq = ptcb->tcb_rnext;
                ptcb->tcb_rudq = newq(TCPUQLEN, QF_WAIT);
                if (ptcb->tcb_rudq < 0) {
                        uqfree(puqe);
                        return SYSERR;  /* treat it like normal data   */
                }
        }
        if (datalen > puqe->uq_len) {
                /* some non-urgent data left, edit the packet          */

                ptcp->tcp_seq += puqe->uq_len;
                offset = TCP_HLEN(ptcp) + puqe->uq_len;
                blkcopy(&pip->ip_data[TCP_HLEN(ptcp)],
                        &pip->ip_data[offset], datalen-puqe->uq_len);
                ptcp->tcp_urgptr = 0;
                pip->ip_len -= puqe->uq_len;
                /* checksums already checked, so no need to redo them   */
        }
        if (enq(ptcb->tcb_rudq,puqe,ptcb->tcb_rudseq-puqe->uq_seq) < 0) {
                uqfree(puqe);
                return SYSERR;
        }
        return OK;
}
```

Tcprcvurg begins by checking to make sure the urgent data pointer in the segment
is valid (i.e., it contains an offset that lies within the data area of the segment). It then
calls *uqalloc* to allocate a node for the urgent data list, fills in the sequence and length
fields, allocates buffer space for the urgent data, and copies it from the segment into the
allocated space. After creating a node for the list, *tcprcvurg* checks to see that an urgent list has been allocated for this TCB. To do so, it examines field *tcb_rudq*, and
calls *newq* to allocate a list if none is present. Before returning, it calls *enq* to insert the
new node on the list.

A single segment may carry *both* urgent and normal data. In such cases, *tcprcvurg*
adjusts the segment after extracting the urgent data. It increments the sequence number
(*tcp_seq*) to skip the urgent data, and moves the normal data to the beginning of the
data area. It also clears the urgent data pointer (*tcp_urgptr*) and decrements the IP data
length to reflect the changes.

15.7 Sequence Numbers, Keys, And List Order

We said that each list of urgent data entries was stored in sequence order. Thus, when *tcprcvurg* inserts an item on a list of urgent data, it must use an insertion key that retains the correct order. However, TCP uses a finite representation for sequence values, allowing them to wrap around as needed. Thus, *tcprcvurg* cannot use sequence values by themselves as keys for insertion or it might store urgent data items out of order.

To keep the order correct, *tcprcvurg* uses a base and offset technique. When it creates a new list, *tcprcvurg* records the current value of *tcb_rnext*, the sequence number of the octet it expects to receive next, in field *tcb_rudseq*, and uses it as a base value. Whenever it stores an entry in the urgent data list, it computes an insertion key by subtracting the stored base value from the sequence number of the item being inserted. Because conventional *32*-bit integer arithmetic produces underflow, the resulting key values are always comparable. Thus, even if the sequence numbers wrap around, using keys that are measured relative to a common base value keeps the items in the desired order.

15.8 Urgent Data Queue Manipulation Routines

To limit the amount of memory consumed by urgent data lists, our implementation places a fixed, maximum count on the total number of urgent data nodes available. To do so, it statically allocates the nodes in an array, *uqtab*. Procedure *uqalloc* allocates a new node from the array when one is needed.

```
/* uqalloc.c - uqalloc */

#include <conf.h>
#include <kernel.h>
#include <network.h>

/*------------------------------------------------------------------
 * uqalloc - allocate a TCP urgent queue entry
 *------------------------------------------------------------------
 */
struct uqe *uqalloc()
{
        static  int     last = 0;
        struct  uqe     *puqe;
        int             count;

        if (!uqidone)
                uqinit();
```

```
        wait(uqmutex);
        for (count=0; count<UQTSIZE; ++count) {
                if (++last >= UQTSIZE)
                        last = 0;
                puqe = &uqtab[last];
                if (puqe->uq_state == UQS_FREE) {
                        puqe->uq_state = UQS_ALLOC;
                        signal(uqmutex);
                        return puqe;
                }
        }
        signal(uqmutex);
        return (struct uqe *)SYSERR;
}


Bool    uqidone = FALSE;
int     uqmutex;
struct uqe uqtab[UQTSIZE];
```

If the list of available nodes has not been initialized, *uqalloc* calls procedure *uqinit*, which assigns *UQS_FREE* to the state field in each item of the array. In any case, it calls *wait* to obtain exclusive use of the array, and then searches it for an unused entry. The search always starts at the location given by variable *last* plus *1* and wraps completely around. Because *last* has been declared *static*, it will retain its value between procedure calls, making the search more efficient by not searching recently allocated locations.

If it finds an unused entry, *uqalloc* sets the state field of the node to *UQS_ALLOC*, signals the mutual exclusion semaphore, and returns the address of the newly allocated item to its caller. If it cannot find a free entry after searching the entire array, *uqalloc* returns *SYSERR*.

File *uqalloc.c* also contains declarations of the Boolean used to record whether the urgent data structures have been initialized (*uqidone*), the mutual exclusion semaphore (*uqmutex*), and the table of urgent data queues (*uqtab*).

15.8.1 Initialization Of Urgent Queue Nodes

Procedure *uqinit* creates the mutual exclusion semaphore, and initializes the set of free nodes by assigning their state fields the value *UQS_FREE*.

```
/* uqinit.c - uqinit */

#include <conf.h>
#include <kernel.h>
#include <network.h>


/*------------------------------------------------------------------
 *  uqinit -  initialize TCP urgent queue data
 *------------------------------------------------------------------
 */
int uqinit()
{
        int     i;

        uqidone = TRUE;
        uqmutex = screate(0);
        for (i=0; i<UQTSIZE; ++i)
                uqtab[i].uq_state = UQS_FREE;
        signal(uqmutex);
        return OK;
}
```

15.8.2 Deallocating An Urgent Queue Node

Procedure *uqfree* deallocates an urgent queue node and returns it to a state in which *uqalloc* can reallocate it. *Uqfree* deallocates the buffer used to hold urgent data, and then sets the state field.

```
/* uqfree.c - uqfree */

#include <conf.h>
#include <kernel.h>
#include <network.h>


/*------------------------------------------------------------------
 *  uqfree -  free an urgent queue entry
 *------------------------------------------------------------------
 */
int uqfree(puqe)
struct  uqe     *puqe;
{
        wait(uqmutex);
        if (puqe->uq_data)
```

```
                    freebuf(puqe->uq_data);
            puqe->uq_state = UQS_FREE;
            signal(uqmutex);
            return OK;
}
```

15.9 Reading Urgent Data

When an application reads input after urgent data has been received, the sequence
of calls eventually reaches procedure *tcprurg*.

```
/* tcprurg.c - tcprurg */

#include <conf.h>
#include <kernel.h>
#include <proc.h>
#include <network.h>
#include <q.h>

/*------------------------------------------------------------------------
 *  tcprurg  -  read pending urgent data
 *------------------------------------------------------------------------
 */
int tcprurg(ptcb, pch, len)
struct  tcb     *ptcb;
char            *pch;
int             len;
{
        struct  uqe     *puqe;
        int             cc, uc;
        tcpseq          cseq, eseq;

        puqe = (struct uqe *)deq(ptcb->tcb_rudq);
        cseq = puqe->uq_seq;
        for (cc=uc=0; cc < len && puqe;) {
                *pch++ = puqe->uq_data[uc++];
                ++cc;
                if (uc >= puqe->uq_len) {
                        while (puqe) {
                                eseq = puqe->uq_seq + puqe->uq_len - 1;
                                if (SEQCMP(cseq, eseq) < 0)
                                        break;
                                tcpaddhole(ptcb, puqe);
```

```
                              puqe = (struct uqe *)deq(ptcb->tcb_rudq);
                      }
                      if (puqe == 0)
                              break;
                      if (SEQCMP(cseq, puqe->uq_seq) < 0) {
                              cseq = puqe->uq_seq;
                              uc = 0;
                      } else
                              uc = cseq - puqe->uq_seq;
              } else
                      cseq++;
      }
      if (puqe == 0) {
              freeq(ptcb->tcb_rudq);
              ptcb->tcb_rudq = EMPTY;
              return cc;
      }
      if (uc) {
              /* we need to adjust puqe */

              puqe->uq_seq = cseq;
              puqe->uq_len -= uc;
              blkcopy(puqe->uq_data, &puqe->uq_data[uc], puqe->uq_len);
      }
      if (enq(ptcb->tcb_rudq, puqe, RUDK(ptcb, puqe->uq_seq)) < 0)
              uqfree(puqe);     /* shouldn't happen */
      return cc;
}
```

Once a process has been placed in urgent mode, calls to *tcprurg* extract octets of urgent data from the stored list and return it to the caller. The caller specifies three arguments: a TCB entry (*ptcb*), a buffer address (*pch*), and a buffer length (*len*). *Tcprurg* extracts up to *len* bytes of data from the urgent data list and places it in the caller's buffer. Finally, it returns the number of bytes read as the value of the function. The caller can use the returned count to determine whether all *len* bytes were read or less than *len* bytes of urgent data were available.

Recall that if multiple segments arrive carrying urgent data, each will occupy one entry on the urgent data list. To extract bytes of urgent data, *tcprurg* iterates through the list, extracting the data from each node in succession until it reaches the end of the list or it has found *len* octets. If it reaches the end of the data in a particular node during the iteration, it deallocates the node and moves to the next one on the list.

15.10 Collecting Holes

Recall from Figure 15.1b that when a process reads urgent data, it creates a "hole" in the sequence space. Later, when normal input processing reaches the location of the hole, it must increment the sequence counter to skip the locations that were occupied by urgent data. TCP needs a data structure to record the location of holes so it can find them when processing input,

Our design uses a linked list to record sequence space holes. Items on the list of holes have exactly the same format as items on the sequence list, except that they contain no data. Using the same node format for the list of urgent data and the list of holes makes recording holes easy. TCP can use the same node that records urgent data to record the hole left after an application program extracts the data. *Tcprurg* contains the code. After extracting all the data from a node on the urgent data list, *tcprurg* calls *tcpaddhole* to insert the node into the list of holes.

```
/* tcpaddhole.c - tcpaddhole */

#include <conf.h>
#include <kernel.h>
#include <network.h>
#include <q.h>

/*------------------------------------------------------------------------
 *  tcpaddhole  -  add an URGENT data hole to the receive hole queue
 *------------------------------------------------------------------------
 */
int tcpaddhole(ptcb, puqe)
struct  tcb     *ptcb;
struct  uqe     *puqe;
{
        freebuf(puqe->uq_data, puqe->uq_len);
        puqe->uq_data = 0;
        if (ptcb->tcb_ruhq < 0)
                ptcb->tcb_ruhq = newq(TCPUQLEN, QF_WAIT);
        if (enq(ptcb->tcb_ruhq, puqe, RUHK(ptcb, puqe->uq_seq)) < 0)
                uqfree(puqe);
        return OK;
}
```

Tcpaddhole accepts a node that has been removed from the urgent data list and inserts it on the list of holes (field *tcb_ruhq* of the TCB). The sequence and length fields, which were used to specify the location and length of urgent data, retain their values. They now specify the location of a hole in the sequence space from which urgent data has been extracted.

Before calling *enq* to insert the node on the list of holes, *tcpaddhole* discards the urgent data itself and keeps only the location information. To do so, it calls *freebuf* to release the buffer that holds the data. It also checks that the list of holes has been allocated before inserting the node, and calls *newq* if not.

Tcpaddhole uses macro *RUHK†* (Receiver Urgent Hole Key) to compute a key for the node. *RUHK* computes the key by subtracting the stored value for the urgent data base sequence from the sequence value for this segment.

15.11 Skipping Holes

When processing input in normal mode, an application must check for holes in the sequence space and skip them. Once it reaches the sequence number for the next hole, it calls procedure *tcprhskip* to skip by it.

```
/* tcprhskip.c - tcprhskip */

#include <conf.h>
#include <kernel.h>
#include <proc.h>
#include <network.h>


/*------------------------------------------------------------------
 * tcprhskip  -  skip a read hole in a TCP sequence
 *------------------------------------------------------------------
 */
struct uqe *tcprhskip(ptcb, puqe, seq)
struct  tcb     *ptcb;
struct  uqe     *puqe;
tcpseq          seq;
{
        if (seq < puqe->uq_seq + puqe->uq_len) {
                ptcb->tcb_rbcount -= puqe->uq_len;
                ptcb->tcb_rbstart += puqe->uq_len;
                ptcb->tcb_rbstart %= ptcb->tcb_rbsize;
        }
        uqfree(puqe);
        puqe = (struct uqe *)deq(ptcb->tcb_ruhq);
        if (puqe == 0) {
                freeq(ptcb->tcb_ruhq);
                ptcb->tcb_ruhq = -1;
        }
        return puqe;
}
```

---

†RUHK is defined in file *tcb.h* on page 166 . The file also contains related macros that handle computation of the receiver urgent data key (*RUDK*), the sender urgent data key (*SUDK*), and the sender urgent hole key (*SUHK*).

To keep our implementation manageable, we chose to allocate space in the input buffer for all locations in the sequence space, even if urgent data occupies some of the sequence values†. Thus, making the adjustment to skip a hole is easy. *Tcprhskip* only needs to adjust the variables that control the input buffer to bypass the hole. It decrements the count of characters in the buffer, increments the starting pointer, and if necessary, wraps it around to the beginning of the buffer. Finally, it calls *deq* to remove the entry from the list of holes, and calls *freeq* to delete the list if it becomes empty.

15.12 Reading Data From TCP

Now that we have seen all the pieces, it should be easy to understand how an application obtains input data from TCP. Procedure *tcpgetdata* handles the task.

```
/* tcpgetdata.c - tcpgetdata */

#include <conf.h>
#include <kernel.h>
#include <network.h>

/*------------------------------------------------------------------------
 *  tcpgetdata  -  copy data from a TCP receive buffer to a user buffer
 *------------------------------------------------------------------------
 */
int tcpgetdata(ptcb, pch, len)
struct   tcb      *ptcb;
char              *pch;
int               len;
{
        struct   uqe      *puqe, *tcprhskip();
        tcpseq            seq;
        int               cc;

        if (ptcb->tcb_ruhq >= 0)
                puqe = (struct uqe *)deq(ptcb->tcb_ruhq);
        else
                puqe = 0;
        seq = ptcb->tcb_rnext - ptcb->tcb_rbcount; /* start sequence    */
        for (cc=0; ptcb->tcb_rbcount && cc < len;) {
                /* see if we're at an urgent data hole */
                if (puqe && SEQCMP(puqe->uq_seq, seq) <= 0) {
                        puqe = tcprhskip(ptcb, puqe, seq);
                        continue;
                }
```

---

†Keep in mind that most urgent data messages consist of a single data octet.

```
                    /* ...now normal data processing */

                    *pch++ = ptcb->tcb_rcvbuf[ptcb->tcb_rbstart];
                    --ptcb->tcb_rbcount;
                    if (++ptcb->tcb_rbstart >= ptcb->tcb_rbsize)
                            ptcb->tcb_rbstart = 0;
                    ++cc;
            }
            if (puqe)
                    if (enq(ptcb->tcb_ruhq,puqe,RUHK(ptcb,puqe->uq_seq)) < 0)
                            uqfree(puqe);    /* shouldn't happen... */
            if (ptcb->tcb_rbcount == 0)
                    ptcb->tcb_flags &= ~TCBF_PUSH;
            /*
             * open the receive window, if it's closed and we've made
             * enough space to fit a segment.
             */
            if (SEQCMP(ptcb->tcb_cwin, ptcb->tcb_rnext) <= 0 &&
                            tcprwindow(ptcb)) {
                    ptcb->tcb_flags |= TCBF_NEEDOUT;
                    tcpkick(ptcb);
            }
            return cc;
    }
```

Tcpgetdata begins by obtaining a pointer to the first entry on the list of holes. It then calculates the sequence number of the first octet of data it will extract from the buffer (by subtracting the count of characters in the buffer from the sequence number of the highest octet received).

Once it has found the starting sequence number, *tcpgetdata* enters its main loop. The loop iterates while there are characters in the buffer and the number of characters obtained is less than the number the caller requested. On each iteration, *tcpgetdata* extracts one octet of data from the input buffer and copies it to the caller's buffer. Before doing so, however, it checks to see if it has reached a hole left in the sequence space by previously consumed urgent data. If it encounters a hole (i.e., its sequence number matches the sequence of the next hole), *tcpgetdata* calls *tcprhskip* to skip the hole, and then goes on to the next octet following the hole.

Tcpgetdata also contains the code that handles window manipulation described in Chapter 14. Before it returns, *tcpgetdata* checks to see if *tcb_rnext* has moved past the currently advertised window and if *tcprwindow* returns a nonzero window advertisement. If so, it sets bit *TCBF_NEEDOUT* in the TCB, and calls *tcpkick* to generate a gratuitous acknowledgement. Acknowledgements created by *tcpgetdata* do not correspond to arriving data at all – TCP uses them merely to report to the sender that the window size has increased without waiting for a probe. Of course, if *tcprwindow* computes a zero-size window, *tcpgetdata* will not send an unnecessary acknowledgement.

15.13 Sending Urgent Data

Generating and sending urgent data is somewhat simpler than processing incoming urgent data. In particular, three assumptions help simplify the code. First, we assume that application programs write an urgent message in a single call. That is, the program must assemble an entire urgent message and pass it to TCP through a single procedure call. Second, we assume that urgent data should be written in the sequence space starting at the next available sequence number. Third, we assume that urgent data will be placed in the TCP output buffer along with normal data.

These three assumptions help eliminate special cases and make it possible to use most of the code already designed for handling normal data output. Because TCP receives an entire urgent message in a single call, it does not need a special mechanism to collect pieces of the message before transmission. Because urgent data falls in the usual place in the sequence space and output buffer, it can be stored exactly like normal output data. Furthermore, because urgent data always occurs in the sequence space contiguous to normal data, the sender can handle retransmission as it does for normal data. The only special case occurs when transmitting urgent data: according to the standard, the sender must force transmission even if the receiver has closed the window.

15.14 Recording The Locations Of Urgent Data Messages

15.14.1 Possible Approaches

Because TCP sends urgent data immediately, even if the receiver has closed its window, it may send the urgent data out of sequence. Later, after the receiver opens its window, TCP returns to the output buffer and begins sending the normal data again. During normal data transmission, TCP must skip past locations that contain the urgent data it has already sent. To guarantee that TCP can correctly skip urgent messages during normal transmission, it needs a data structure that records which locations in the outgoing sequence space correspond to urgent data. One possible approach uses a bit-map for each active TCB in parallel with the output buffer for that TCB. Each bit in the bit-map corresponds to a single octet in the output buffer, and specifies whether that octet contains urgent data. Another approach, the one we have selected, keeps a separate linked list for each TCB, where each item on the list records the location of a contiguous block of urgent data. The items are kept in sequence order, and must be discarded when a segment arrives that acknowledges them. When transmitting a segment, the output routines check the list to find the boundaries between normal and urgent data, and avoid sending urgent messages along with normal data.

15.14.2 Adding A Node To The Urgent Data Output List

Procedure *tcpwurg* creates a node on an urgent data output list. It takes three arguments that specify the TCB to use, the starting sequence, and length of the urgent data. After allocating a node and filling in the fields that record the sequence number and length, *tcpwurg* calls *enq* to insert it on the output list given by field *tcb_sudq*. Before inserting the node, *tcpwurg* checks for the existence of a list. If no list has been allocated, *tcpwurg* calls *newq* to create it.

```
/* tcpwurg.c - tcpwurg */

#include <conf.h>
#include <kernel.h>
#include <network.h>
#include <q.h>


struct  uqe     *uqalloc();


/*------------------------------------------------------------------
 *  tcpwurg  -  keep track of urgent data boundaries on writes
 *------------------------------------------------------------------
 */
int tcpwurg(ptcb, sboff, len)
struct  tcb     *ptcb;
int             sboff;
int             len;
{
        struct  uqe     *puqe;

        puqe = uqalloc();
        if (puqe == (struct uqe *)SYSERR)
                return SYSERR;
        puqe->uq_seq = ptcb->tcb_suna + sboff;
        puqe->uq_len = len;
        puqe->uq_data = 0;
        if (ptcb->tcb_sudq < 0) {
                ptcb->tcb_sudq = newq(TCPUQLEN, QF_WAIT);
                ptcb->tcb_sudseq = puqe->uq_seq;
        }
        if (enq(ptcb->tcb_sudq, puqe, SUDK(ptcb, puqe->uq_seq)) < 0) {
                uqfree(puqe);
                return SYSERR;
        }
        return len;
}
```

15.15 Transmitting Urgent Data

Procedure *tcpsndurg* transmits urgent data.

```
/* tcpsndurg.c - tcpsndurg */

#include <conf.h>
#include <kernel.h>
#include <network.h>

/*------------------------------------------------------------------------
 *  tcpsndurg.c - send pending urgent data
 *------------------------------------------------------------------------
 */
int tcpsndurg(tcbnum)
int     tcbnum;
{
        int     ptcb = &tcbtab[tcbnum];
        int     tv;

        ptcb->tcb_code |= TCPF_URG;
        while (ptcb->tcb_sudq > 0)
                tcpsend(tcbnum, TSF_NEWDATA);
        ptcb->tcb_code &= ~TCPF_URG;
        return OK;
}
```

Because urgent data must be sent ahead of all normal data, *tcpsndurg* iterates through the entire list of urgent messages. For each urgent message on the list, it calls *tcpsend* to form and transmit a segment that carries the message.

15.16 TCP Push Function

Usually, TCP buffers both input and output. When processing output, it collects as much data as possible into each segment to improve throughput and lower overhead. When processing input, it collects incoming data from individual segments into the input buffer from which application programs extract it. Buffering improves overall efficiency. Inside a host or gateway, it lowers context switching and procedure call overhead. Outside of the computer system, buffering lowers network overhead by passing more data in each packet.

In general, buffering improves throughput by trading lower throughput for increased delay. Sometimes high delays caused by buffering create problems for communicating applications. To allow applications to bypass buffering, TCP supplies a *push* function. A sending application executes a *push request* to request that TCP send all existing data without delay. When TCP sends the data, it sets the *push bit* in the segment code field, so the receiver knows about the request as well. When data arrives in a segment that has the *push bit* set, TCP makes the data available to the receiving application without delay.

15.17 Interpreting Push With Out-Of-Order Delivery

In principle, honoring the push bit in an incoming segment should be simple: when a segment arrives with the push bit set, TCP should make the data available to the application immediately. However, because segments may arrive out of order, the notion of a push must be defined carefully. There are two extremes. First, a segment carrying the push bit may arrive before segments that carry data which appears earlier in the sequence space. Because TCP must deliver data to the application in sequence, it cannot deliver the data that arrived with the push bit set. The standard specifies that the push request refers to data in the buffer and not merely to a point in the sequence. Thus, TCP must remember that a push has been requested for specific data and switch to immediate delivery after intervening data arrives. Second, a segment with the push bit set may arrive later than segments carrying data with higher sequence numbers. That is, the segment carrying a push bit may fill in a gap in the sequence space. The protocol standard says that when a segment arrives with the push bit set, TCP must deliver *all* available data to the application program. Thus, the arrival of a segment with the push bit set may cause TCP to immediately deliver data *beyond* the data in the segment.

The idea underlying the definition of the push function is fundamental: TCP does not observe record boundaries. A programmer cannot depend on TCP to deliver data exactly to the point of a push operation because the amount delivered depends on the buffer contents and the timing of arrivals. To summarize:

> *Push does not mark record boundaries. When a sender invokes the push operation, TCP will transmit and deliver all data in its buffers. Thus, if a segment S with the push bit set arrives late, TCP on the receiving side may deliver additional data to the application beyond the data carried in S.*

However, even though push does not provide explicit record boundaries, the protocol does specify that a receiver must maintain some state information concerning the push. The rules are fairly simple: the receiver should immediately deliver all available data, or it should remember that a push has arrived, so it can begin immediate delivery as soon as it has received everything in the sequence up to and including the data in the segment that carries the push. TCP must remember how much data to deliver immediately so it can stop delivering in push mode when it reaches the appropriate point in the sequence space.

15.18 Implementation Of Push On Input

To record the arrival of a segment with the push bit set, our system uses two variables in the TCB. Field *tcb_pushseq* records the sequence number of the octet just past the end of the segment that arrived with the push bit set. Field *tcb_code* contains a bit that indicates whether a push has arrived. The bit in the code field can be thought of as a mode bit. When *TCBF_PUSH* is not set, TCP uses normal delivery. When *TCBF_PUSH* has been set, the input has received a push and will deliver data immediately until the buffer has been cleared.

We have already examined the procedures that implement the push operation. Procedure *tcpdodat*† processes the push bit when it extracts data from an incoming segment. Two cases arise. Either the arriving segment extends the currently acknowledged sequence (i.e., there are no gaps in the sequence space before the segment that contains the push), or the arriving segment has come out of order. In both cases *tcpdodat* sets the bit *TCBF_PUSH* in the TCB code field to indicate that TCP should deliver data in push mode. If the new segment extends the available sequence space, the data should be passed to waiting application programs immediately, so *tcpdodat* calls *tcpwakeup* to awaken them. If the sequence space contains gaps, *tcpdodat* cannot pass data to application programs immediately. Instead, it delays push processing until later. To do so, it computes the sequence number of the first octet beyond the data in the segment (by adding the length of data in the segment to the segment sequence number), and records the result in TCB field *tcb_pushseq*. It then turns *off* the push bit in the TCB to await segments that fill the gap.

Procedure *tfcoalesce*‡ handles delayed push processing. *Tfcoalesce* reconstructs the incoming data stream by inserting each arriving segment in a list ordered by sequence number. As it inserts a segment, *tfcoalesce* checks to see if the sequence number of received data has reached the stored value of the push sequence. If so, all data up through the segment that contains a push must be present, so *tfcoalesce* turns on the push bit and resets the push sequence field.

Once enabled, push mode continues until the receiving application has emptied the buffer. That occurs when the count of octets in the buffer reaches zero. The code to turn off push mode can be found in procedure *tcpgetdata*, covered earlier in this chapter.

---

†See page 206 for a listing of *tcpdodat.c*.
‡See page 210 for a listing of *tfcoalesce.c*.

15.19 Summary

TCP supports an urgent message facility that allows communicating application programs to send out-of-band messages. Because urgent messages may arrive outside the current window, TCP cannot use the normal input buffer to store them. Instead, it keeps a separate list of urgent messages. When an application reads input from a connection on which urgent data has arrived, TCP places the application in urgent mode until it consumes all available urgent data.

Urgent data output is simpler than input because TCP can store urgent messages in the standard output buffer and use the same acknowledgement mechanism it uses for normal data. However, it must send urgent data immediately, even if the receiver has closed its window, and it must keep a record of which locations contain urgent data so it can correctly skip them during normal data transmission.

The TCP push function allows a sender to specify that outgoing data should be transmitted and delivered without delay. Out-of-order delivery complicates push processing. If a segment arrives with the push bit set after segments that carry data for higher sequence values, the standard specifies TCP should push all available data. If a segment arrives with the push bit set before segments carrying data for lower sequence values, TCP records the sequence number of the segment that has the push bit set, and enables push when intervening data has arrived.

FOR FURTHER STUDY

Postel [RFC 793] specifies urgent data processing and the *push* operation. Braden [RFC 1122] refines the specification.

EXERCISES

15.1   Suppose a sender incorrectly transmits both urgent data *and* normal data for the same locations in the sequence space. How will the sample code behave? What will the application receive?

15.2   Suppose two segments carrying urgent data arrive out of order, such that the first segment to arrive specifies sequence *1000*, and the second segment to arrive specifies sequence *900*. What will an application program receive if it reads from the connection after the first segment arrives, but before the second arrives? What will it receive if it waits until both have arrived before reading?

15.3   One alternative to the design presented here arranges for an application to leave urgent mode after receiving a single urgent mode message, and then re-enter urgent mode if further messages are pending. Is this approach legitimate? Hint: read the protocol standard.

15.4   What happens if the sender sets the push sequence and then sends enough additional segments to always keep the receive buffer nonempty?

15.5   Suppose a receive buffer contains some data when a segment arrives with the push bit
set, but there is a gap in the sequence space between the data already received and the
new segment. Does the protocol standard forbid, recommend, or require TCP to deliver
the existing data in push mode?

15.6   In the previous question, what happens in our implementation if *tcpdodat* sets the push
bit in the TCB *on* when it assigns *tcb_pushseq*?

15.7   Suppose a segment carrying urgent data is lost. How does our implementation respond?
What does the protocol standard specify should happen?

16

Socket-Level Interface

16.1 Introduction

Each operating system defines the details of the interface between application programs and the protocol software. This chapter explores an interface from the Xinu operating system. Although the procedures and exact order of arguments are specific to the Xinu system, this interface contains the same basic structure found in other systems. Studying the interface procedures will help clarify the underlying protocol software and show how it interacts with application programs.

16.2 Interfacing Through A Device

Unlike UNIX systems, which incorporate services and devices into the file system, Xinu incorporates services and files into devices. It uses a *device paradigm* for all input and output operations, including communication between an application program and protocol software. To do so, the system provides a *device abstraction*, and defines a set of devices, most of which correspond to peripheral I/O hardware devices. For example, the system uses the device abstraction to provide a *CONSOLE* that application programs use to communicate with the console terminal. In addition to abstract devices that correspond directly to conventional hardware devices, Xinu provides many device definitions that permit applications to access system services. For example, Xinu provides devices used to access individual files on local disks, remote files, and protocol software.

Whether it uses an abstract device that corresponds to physical hardware or to a service, an application program follows the *open-read-write-close* paradigm to use it. The program calls *open* with three arguments:

```
d = open(device, name, other)
```

The first argument is an integer device identifier that specifies the device to be used, and the second argument specifies the name of an object associated with that device. The meaning of the third argument depends on the device being opened. For many devices, it specifies whether the object should be opened for reading, writing, or both. *Open* returns a device descriptor to be used for accessing the specified object.

Once an object has been opened and a device descriptor has been created for it, an application program uses functions *read* and *write* to transfer data from or to the object. Both take three arguments: a device descriptor for the object, a pointer to a buffer, and a transfer size (in bytes). Most devices interpret the transfer size as a maximum buffer length. A call to *read* specifies a maximum buffer length and returns the count of bytes read.

```
len = read(device, buffer, buflen);
```

A call to *write* returns a status code.

```
status = write(device, buffer, buflen);
```

When an application finishes using an object, it calls *close* to terminate use. Because Xinu uses a global device descriptor space and allows processes to exchange device descriptors through shared memory, it cannot know how many processes are currently using a given device. Thus, unlike many systems, Xinu does not close open devices automatically when an application terminates†. Instead, the application is responsible for calling *close* explicitly.

16.2.1 Single Byte I/O

Because some programs find it easier to transfer a single byte (character) at a time, the device system supports two additional functions. Function *getc*‡ reads a single byte from a device and returns it as the function value. It is most often used with terminal devices.

```
ch = getc(CONSOLE);
```

Procedure *putc* takes a device descriptor and a character as an argument and writes the character to the specified device.

```
putc(CONSOLE,'\n'); /* move Console to next line */
```

---

†Xinu does support the UNIX notions of *standard input*, *standard output*, and *standard error*, and it calls *close* on each of these three descriptors when a process terminates.

‡In Xinu *getc* and *putc* are system calls and not library routines.

16.2.2 Extensions For Non-Transfer Functions

In addition to the operations that *open* and *close* a device, and the operations that transfer data (*read*, *write*, *getc*, and *putc*), Xinu supports two functions used to control devices. Programs use the first function, *seek*, to position physical devices (especially disks) and abstract devices (especially files).

```
seek(device, position);
```

Argument *device* must be an integer device descriptor, while argument *position* is a long integer that gives an offset at which the device should be positioned.

A second, more generic function, *control* handles all other nontransfer operations†. *Control* takes a variable number of arguments.

```
control(device, FUNC, arg1, arg2, ... );
```

It always requires two arguments that specify the descriptor of a device to be controlled and a control function to be used on that device. Some control functions require additional arguments.

Control functions include any operation that does not specify data transfer, or operations that involve special handling (e.g., writing TCP urgent data). For example, *control* can be used to specify whether a terminal device echoes characters (applications usually turn off echo before prompting for a password or other secret information that should not be displayed). An application can also use *control* to change a device's mode of operation.

A programmer must consult the documentation to determine the set of *control* functions available for a given device and the exact meaning of each. If a specific *control* function requires additional arguments, the documentation specifies their types and meanings.

16.3 TCP Connections As Devices

The Xinu system uses two types of devices for TCP connections. It provides a *TCP master device* (used to create connections), and *TCP slave devices* (used to communicate once a connection has been established). Both clients and servers use the master device to create a connection.

When a client program wishes to make a TCP connection, it calls *open* on the TCP master device, specifying the remote destination with which it wishes to communicate. The call allocates a TCP slave device for the connection, initializes the internal data structures associated with it, and returns the slave device descriptor to the caller. The caller then uses the slave device descriptor with *read* or *write* to pass data across the connection. When the client finishes transferring data, it calls *close* on the slave device to shut down the connection and make the slave device available for reuse.

---

†Many of the Xinu TCP *control* functions parallel BSD UNIX system calls. For example, while BSD UNIX supports an *accept* system call, Xinu supports a *TCPC_ACCEPT* control function that has the same effect.

16.4 An Example TCP Client Program

It will be helpful to examine the code for an example client. When called, procedure *finger* implements a *finger* command. The finger function allows a user on one machine to find out which users are logged into another machine. To do so, the client opens a TCP connection to the remote server, sends one line of text, and then prints all data that comes back from the server. The line of text sent either gives the login name of a user to finger or consists of an empty line, which requests information on all users logged into the system.

```
/* finger.c - finger */

#include <conf.h>
#include <kernel.h>
#include <proc.h>
#include <network.h>


#define FINGERPORT      79              /* TCP port finger server uses  */


/*------------------------------------------------------------------------
 *  finger  -  client procedure to print information about remote users
 *------------------------------------------------------------------------
 */
finger(rhost, user, outdev)
char    *rhost;                 /* domain name of remote host to contact*/
char    *user;                  /* name of specific user or null pointer*/
int     outdev;                 /* device on which to print output      */
{
        IPaddr  addr;           /* holds IP address of remote host      */
        int     dd;             /* device descriptor for connection     */
        int     cc;             /* count of characters read             */
        char    buf[2048];      /* buffer to hold finger information     */

        /* convert domain name to IP address and place in dotted        */
        /* decimal string "xxx.xxx.xxx.xxx:port" for call to open        */

        name2ip(addr, rhost);
        sprintf(buf, "%u.%u.%u.%u:%d", BYTE(addr, 0), BYTE(addr, 1),
                BYTE(addr, 2), BYTE(addr, 3), FINGERPORT);

        /* open connection, write one line (so it works with any server */
        /* and then repeatedly read and print data that arrives over    */
        /* the connection.                                              */
```

```
        dd = open(TCP, buf, ANYLPORT);
        if (user)
                write(dd, user, strlen(user));
        write(dd, "\r\n", 2);
        while ( (cc = read(dd, buf, sizeof(buf))) > 0)
                write(outdev, buf, cc);
        close(dd);
        return(OK);
}
```

In the code, the call to *open* takes three arguments: the tcp master device descriptor (constant *TCP*), a string that specifies the remote machine's IP address and port number (*buf*), and an integer that specifies the local protocol port number to use. Because the client can use an arbitrary local port number, it uses constant *ANYLPORT*.

Once *finger* opens a connection, it writes a single line of text, and then repeatedly reads and prints information that the server returns. The call to *read* will block until the server replies and a full buffer of data is available. Of course, the call will also return if all data has arrived and the server has closed the connection, even if the buffer is not full.

16.5 An Example TCP Server Program

Servers are more complex than clients because a server must be able to queue an incoming connection request while servicing an existing connection. To do so, it calls *open* on the master device, specifying that it wants to create a TCP device in passive mode. It then uses two control calls to manipulate the passive device. First, it calls *control* using function code *TCPC_LISTENQ* to set the length of the incoming request queue. It then enters a loop in which it calls *control* using function code *TCPC_ACCEPT* to accept the next incoming connection. The system allocates a slave device for each new connection, and returns the slave device descriptor.

Consider the example *finger server* shown below. A finger service provides information about users logged into the computer. The server begins by opening the TCP device to obtain a passive descriptor that it uses to accept incoming connections. Each time it accepts a connection, the server reads one line of input from the connection, and responds by sending information about users logged into the local machine. After it finishes sending, the server closes the connection. To keep the example code simple, our server merely returns fixed information found in the strings declared at the beginning of the program.

```
/* fingerd.c - fingerd */

#include <conf.h>
#include <kernel.h>
#include <network.h>

#define FINGERPORT      79          /* TCP port finger server uses  */
#define BUFFERSIZ       120         /* size of input buffer         */
#define QUEUESIZE       5           /* size of conn. request queue  */

str1 = "Login          Name        \n";   /* fake information to return*/
str2 = "dls     David L. Stevens\n";
str3 = "comer   Douglas E. Comer\n";


/*-----------------------------------------------------------------------
 * fingerd  -  server to provide information about users logged in
 *-----------------------------------------------------------------------
 */
PROCESS fingerd()
{
        int     dd;                 /* descriptor for server        */
        int     dd2;                /* descriptor for a connection  */
        char    request[BUFFERSIZ]; /* space to read request        */

        /* Open TCP in passive mode (no connection) for the server  */
        /* and set maximum queue size for incoming connections      */

        dd = open(TCP, ANYFPORT, FINGERPORT);
        control(dd, TCPC_LISTENQ, QUEUESIZE);

        /* Continually wait for next connection, read one line from it */
        /* and respond to the request                                  */

        while (TRUE) {
                dd2 = control(dd, TCPC_ACCEPT);

                /* Fake version: read and then ignore what client sends */

                if (read(dd2, request, sizeof(request)) < 2) {
                        close(dd2);
                        continue;
                }
                write(dd2, str1, strlen(str1));
                write(dd2, str2, strlen(str2));
```

```
            write(dd2, str3, strlen(str3));
            close(dd2);
        }
}
```

In the code, the *control* call using function code *TCPC_ACCEPT* returns the device descriptor of a slave device for a given connection (*dd2*). The server then uses descriptor *dd2* to *read* and *write* information. Meanwhile, if new connection requests arrive, TCP will associate them with the original device and enqueue them. When the server finishes using a connection, it closes the slave device descriptor, making it available for use with new connections.

16.6 Implementation Of The TCP Master Device

To implement a device, a programmer must supply procedures that correspond to all of the high-level operations: *open*, *close*, *read*, *write*, *putc*, *getc*, *seek*, and *control*. For the TCP master device, only two of these operations are meaningful – the remainder merely return an error code if called. The meaningful operations consist of *open*, used to form a connection, and *control*, used to set default parameters that apply to all connections.

16.6.1 TCP Master Device Open Function

Tcpmopen implements the *open* operation for the master device.

```
/* tcpmopen.c - tcpmopen */

#include <conf.h>
#include <kernel.h>
#include <network.h>
#include <proc.h>


/*------------------------------------------------------------------
 *  tcpmopen  -  open a fresh TCP pseudo device and return descriptor
 *------------------------------------------------------------------
 */
int tcpmopen(pdev, fport, lport)
struct  devsw    *pdev;
char             *fport;
int              lport;
{
        struct  tcb      *ptcb;
        int              error;

        ptcb = (struct tcb *)tcballoc();
        if (ptcb == (struct tcb *)SYSERR)
                return SYSERR;
        ptcb->tcb_error = 0;
        proctab[currpid].ptcpumode = FALSE;
        if (fport == ANYFPORT)
                return tcpserver(ptcb, lport);

        if (tcpbind(ptcb, fport, lport) != OK ||
            tcpsync(ptcb) != OK) {
                ptcb->tcb_state = TCPS_FREE;
                sdelete(ptcb->tcb_mutex);
                return SYSERR;
        }
        if (error = tcpcon(ptcb))
                return error;
        return ptcb->tcb_dvnum;
}
```

To open a new connection, *tcpmopen* calls *tcballoc*† to allocate an unused TCB, and initializes the *urgent mode* Boolean in the process table entry of the calling process. It then examines the foreign port argument, *fport*, to see whether the caller requested a passive or active open. As the finger example shows, a server specifies the constant *ANYFPORT*, while a client specifies a particular foreign destination. If the foreign port argument indicates the caller is a server, *tcpmopen* passes control to procedure

---

†See page 178 for a listing of *tcballoc.c*.

tcpserver. Otherwise, it calls *tcpbind* to record the foreign address, *tcpsync*‡ to initialize fields of the TCB, and *tcpcon* to initiate an active connection.

16.6.2 Forming A Passive TCP Connection

Tcpmopen calls procedure *tcpserver* to handle the details of passive open.
Tcpserver fills in a previously allocated TCB so it is ready to receive and queue connection requests, and it returns the slave device descriptor corresponding to the TCB so a
server can use it.

```
/* tcpserver.c - tcpserver */

#include <conf.h>
#include <kernel.h>
#include <network.h>


/*------------------------------------------------------------------
 * tcpserver - do a TCP passive open
 *------------------------------------------------------------------
 */
int tcpserver(ptcb, lport)
struct  tcb     *ptcb;
int             lport;
{
        if (lport == ANYLPORT) {
                ptcb->tcb_state = TCPS_FREE;
                sdelete(ptcb->tcb_mutex);
                return SYSERR;
        }
        ptcb->tcb_type = TCPT_SERVER;
        ptcb->tcb_lport = lport;
        ptcb->tcb_state = TCPS_LISTEN;
        ptcb->tcb_lqsize = tcps_lqsize;
        ptcb->tcb_listenq = pcreate(ptcb->tcb_lqsize);
        ptcb->tcb_smss = 0;
        signal(ptcb->tcb_mutex);
        return ptcb->tcb_dvnum;
}
```

Tcpserver begins by examining the local port specification. While a passive connection can have an arbitrary, unspecified foreign port, it must have a specific local port
(i.e., the well-known port at which the server operates). If the caller requests an arbitrary local port, *tcpserver* deallocates the mutual exclusion semaphore and returns

---

‡See page 213 for a listing of *tcpsync.c*.

SYSERR to its caller. Otherwise, it assigns fields in the allocated TCB to make it ready
to accept connections, and it returns the device descriptor used to access the newly allocated TCB.

16.6.3 Forming An Active TCP Connection

We said that *tcpmopen* calls three procedures when it needs to form an active connection: *tcpbind*, *tcpsync*, and *tcpcon*. Procedure *tcpbind* stores the foreign and local
endpoint addresses in a TCB.

```
/* tcpbind.c - tcpbind */

#include <conf.h>
#include <kernel.h>
#include <network.h>


/*------------------------------------------------------------------------
 *  tcpbind - bind a TCP pseudo device to its addresses and port
 *------------------------------------------------------------------------
 */
int tcpbind(ptcb, fport, lport)
struct  tcb        *ptcb;
char               *fport;
int                lport;
{
        struct  route      *prt, *rtget();
        struct  tcb        *ptcb2;
        int                slot;

        if (dnparse(fport, ptcb->tcb_rip, &ptcb->tcb_rport) == SYSERR)
                return SYSERR;
        prt = rtget(ptcb->tcb_rip, RTF_LOCAL);
        if (prt == 0)
                return SYSERR;
        if (prt->rt_ifnum == NI_LOCAL)
                blkcopy(ptcb->tcb_lip, ptcb->tcb_rip, IP_ALEN);
        else
                blkcopy(ptcb->tcb_lip, nif[prt->rt_ifnum].ni_ip, IP_ALEN);
        ptcb->tcb_pni = &nif[prt->rt_ifnum];
        rtfree(prt);
        if (lport == ANYLPORT) {
                ptcb->tcb_lport = tcpnxtp();      /* pick one */
                return OK;
        }
```

```
        ptcb->tcb_lport = lport;
        for (slot=0, ptcb2=&tcbtab[0]; slot<Ntcp; ++slot, ++ptcb2) {
                if (ptcb == ptcb2 ||
                    ptcb2->tcb_state == TCPS_FREE ||
                    ptcb->tcb_rport != ptcb2->tcb_rport ||
                    ptcb->tcb_lport != ptcb2->tcb_lport ||
                    !blkequ(ptcb->tcb_rip, ptcb2->tcb_rip, IP_ALEN) ||
                    !blkequ(ptcb->tcb_lip, ptcb2->tcb_lip, IP_ALEN))
                        continue;
                return SYSERR;
        }
        return OK;
}
```

Tcpbind begins by calling procedure *dnparse* to parse the remote endpoint specification and break it into a remote protocol port number (field *tcb_rport*) and a remote IP address (field *tcb_rip*). It checks to make sure a route exists to the specified remote machine. It also checks to see if the route leads to the pseudo interface (i.e., for the case where two local processes are using TCP to communicate), and uses the IP address from that interface if it does.

After handling the remote machine endpoint, *tcpbind* handles the local port. If the caller specified an arbitrary local port, *tcpbind* calls function *tcpnxtp* to allocate an unused local port number. Otherwise, it must check the specified port to insure that no other connection is using it. To do so, it fills in the specified endpoint in the TCB, and iterates through all TCBs, comparing the connection endpoint to the endpoint specified for the new one. TCP allows multiple connections to use the same local port number as long as the remote endpoints differ. Therefore, *tcpnxt* must check the remote endpoint's IP address and protocol port in the comparison. If none are equal, *tcpbind* returns *OK*. If it finds that another connection already has the same endpoints allocated, it returns the error code *SYSERR*.

16.6.4 Allocating An Unused Local Port

Procedure *tcpnxtp* allocates an unused local port and returns it to the caller.

```
/* tcpnxtp.c - tcpnxtp */

#include <conf.h>
#include <kernel.h>
#include <network.h>


#define IPPORT_RESERVED          1024    /* from BSD */


/*------------------------------------------------------------------
 * tcpnxtp  -  return the next available TCP local "port" number
 *------------------------------------------------------------------
 */
short tcpnxtp()
{
        static  short   lastport=1;     /* #'s 1-1023 */
        int             i, start;

        wait(tcps_tmutex);
        for (start=lastport++; start != lastport; ++lastport) {
                if (lastport == IPPORT_RESERVED)
                        lastport = 1;
                for (i=0; i<Ntcp; ++i)
                        if (tcbtab[i].tcb_state != TCPS_FREE &&
                                        tcbtab[i].tcb_lport == lastport)
                                break;
                if (i == Ntcp)
                        break;
        }
        if (lastport == start)
                panic("out of TCP ports");
        signal(tcps_tmutex);
        return lastport;
}
```

Tcpnxtp uses static variable *lastport* to retain the integer index of the most recently assigned port across calls. Thus, when *tctpnxtp* begins, *lastport* has the same value as it had during the previous call.

Tcpnxtp uses a simple algorithm. It iterates through all possible local port numbers until it finds one not in use. On a given call, variable *start* records the starting value of variable *lastport*, and the iteration continues until *tcpnxtp* has tried all possible values once.

Although the TCP standard does not restrict TCP ports to small values, our example code follows a convention used by BSD UNIX systems. Such systems reserve ports *1* through *1024* for privileged programs. Thus, allocating a port in that range guarantees that the client can communicate effectively, even if the server requires it to use a privileged port.

16.6.5 Completing An Active Connection

Once *tcpbind* has stored the connection endpoints in a TCB and verified that no other connection has them assigned, *tcpmopen* calls *tcpsync*† to initialize most fields in the TCB, and then it calls procedure *tcpcon* to form a connection.

```
/* tcpcon.c - tcpcon */

#include <conf.h>
#include <kernel.h>
#include <network.h>

/*------------------------------------------------------------------------
 *  tcpcon - initiate a connection
 *------------------------------------------------------------------------
 */
int tcpcon(ptcb)
struct  tcb     *ptcb;
{
        struct  netif   *pni = ptcb->tcb_pni;
        struct  route   *prt, *rtget();
        Bool            local;
        int             error, mss;

        prt = (struct route *)rtget(ptcb->tcb_rip, RTF_REMOTE);
        local = prt && prt->rt_metric == 0;
        rtfree(prt);
        if (local)
                mss = ptcb->tcb_pni->ni_mtu-IPMHLEN-TCPMHLEN;
        else
                mss = 536;                      /* RFC 1122          */
        ptcb->tcb_smss = mss;                   /* default           */
        ptcb->tcb_rmss = ptcb->tcb_smss;
        ptcb->tcb_swindow = ptcb->tcb_smss;     /* conservative      */
        ptcb->tcb_cwnd = ptcb->tcb_smss;        /* 1 segment         */
        ptcb->tcb_ssthresh = 65535;             /* IP Max window size */
        ptcb->tcb_rnext = 0;
        ptcb->tcb_finseq = 0;
        ptcb->tcb_pushseq = 0;
        ptcb->tcb_flags = TCBF_NEEDOUT|TCBF_FIRSTSEND;
        ptcb->tcb_ostate = TCPO_IDLE;
```

†See page 213 for a listing of *tcpsync.c*.

```
        ptcb->tcb_state = TCPS_SYNSENT;
        tcpkick(ptcb);
        ptcb->tcb_listenq = SYSERR;
        TcpActiveOpens++;
        signal(ptcb->tcb_mutex);
        wait(ptcb->tcb_ocsem);
        if (error = ptcb->tcb_error)
                tcbdealloc(ptcb);
        return error;                           /* usually 0 */
}
```

Tcpcon initializes the maximum segment size, sequence space counters, and buffer pointers. It calls tcpkick to start the connection, and returns to its caller.

16.6.6 Control For The TCP Master Device

Procedure tcpmcntl implements the control operation for the TCP master device.

```
/* tcpmcntl.c - tcpmcntl */

#include <conf.h>
#include <kernel.h>
#include <network.h>

/*------------------------------------------------------------------------
 *  tcpmcntl - control function for the master TCP pseudo-device
 *------------------------------------------------------------------------
 */
int tcpmcntl(pdev, func, arg)
struct  devsw   *pdev;
int             func;
int             arg;
{
        int     rv;

        if (pdev != &devtab[TCP])
                return SYSERR;

        switch (func) {
        case TCPC_LISTENQ:
                tcps_lqsize = arg;
                rv = OK;
                break;
```

```
default:
        rv = SYSERR;
}
return rv;
```
}

The control operation for the master TCP device allows the caller to set parameters or control processing for all newly created slave devices. The current implementation of *tcpmcntl* provides only one possible control function – it allows the caller to set the default size of the listen queue for passive opens. After the default size has been set, all passive opens will begin with the new queue size.

16.7 Implementation Of A TCP Slave Device

Once the master device *open* operation has created a slave device and allocated a new TCB for a connection, the application uses the slave for input and output. Usually, the application invokes *read* and *write* operations on the slave device. It can also use *getc* or *putc* to transfer a single byte at a time, or *control* to control the individual device.

16.7.1 Input From A TCP Slave Device

Procedure *tcpread* implements the *read* operation for a TCP slave device.

```
/* tcpread.c - tcpread */

#include <conf.h>
#include <kernel.h>
#include <proc.h>
#include <network.h>

/*------------------------------------------------------------------------
 * tcpread  -  read one buffer from a TCP pseudo-device
 *------------------------------------------------------------------------
 */
tcpread(pdev, pch, len)
struct  devsw   *pdev;
char            *pch;
int             len;
{
        struct  tcb     *ptcb = (struct tcb *)pdev->dvioblk;
        int             state = ptcb->tcb_state;
        int             cc;

        if (state != TCPS_ESTABLISHED && state != TCPS_CLOSEWAIT)
                return SYSERR;
retry:
        wait(ptcb->tcb_rsema);
        wait(ptcb->tcb_mutex);

        if (ptcb->tcb_state == TCPS_FREE)
                return SYSERR;                  /* gone          */
        if (ptcb->tcb_error) {
                tcpwakeup(READERS, ptcb);       /* propagate it */
                signal(ptcb->tcb_mutex);
                return ptcb->tcb_error;
        }
        if (ptcb->tcb_rudq < 0) {
                if (proctab[currpid].ptcpumode) {
                        proctab[currpid].ptcpumode = FALSE;
                        cc = TCPE_NORMALMODE;
                } else if (len > ptcb->tcb_rbcount &&
                    ptcb->tcb_flags & TCBF_BUFFER &&
                    (ptcb->tcb_flags & TCBF_PUSH|TCBF_RDONE) == 0) {
                        signal(ptcb->tcb_mutex);
                        goto retry;
                } else
                        cc = tcpgetdata(ptcb, pch, len);
```

```
        } else {
                if (proctab[currpid].ptcpumode)
                        cc = tcprurg(ptcb, pch, len);
                else {
                        proctab[currpid].ptcpumode = TRUE;
                        cc = TCPE_URGENTMODE;
                }
        }
        if (cc == 0 && (ptcb->tcb_flags & TCBF_RDONE) == 0) {
                /*
                 * Have to block after all. Holes can cause
                 * rbcount != 0, but no real data available.
                 */
                signal(ptcb->tcb_mutex);
                goto retry;
        }
        tcpwakeup(READERS, ptcb);
        signal(ptcb->tcb_mutex);
        return cc;
}
```

If the TCB is not in the *ESTABLISHED* or *CLOSE-WAIT* states, input is not permitted, so *tcpread* returns *SYSERR*. Before extracting data from the input buffer, it waits on the read semaphore. When input arrives, *tcpwakeup* will signal the read semaphore, allowing the application to proceed. It then waits on the mutual exclusion semaphore to guarantee exclusive access to the TCB.

Once it has exclusive access, *tcpread* checks to see if the connection has disappeared (i.e., the TCB has moved to state *TCPS_FREE*), and returns *SYSERR* if it has. Next, it checks to see if an error has occurred, and calls *tcpwakeup* to unblock the next process waiting to read. It then returns the error code to its caller.

Otherwise, *tcpread* is ready to extract data from the buffer. It checks the head of the urgent data queue for this connection, *tcb_rudq*, and calls *tcprurg* to read urgent data if any is waiting. If no urgent data is waiting, *tcpread* checks to see if sufficient data remains in the buffer to satisfy the request. *Tcpread* will normally continue to block until sufficient data has been received (i.e., until the buffer contains at least *len* bytes). However, in three special cases *tcpread* does not block. First, if data has arrived with the push bit set, *tcpread* delivers the data immediately. Second, if the sender has finished transmission and closed the connection, *tcpread* must deliver the final data or it will block forever (no additional data will arrive). Third, if the application program specifies unbuffered delivery (i.e., clears the *TCBF_BUFFER* bit in the TCB flags field), *tcpread* delivers the data that has arrived without waiting. Thus, if sufficient data is available to satisfy the request, or if one of the three special cases occurs, *tcpread* delivers data without waiting for more to arrive. It calls *tcpgetdata* to extract the data and copy it into the application program's buffer.

Once it has finished extracting data, *tcpread* calls *tcpwakeup* to allow the next
waiting reader to determine whether additional data remains. It then signals the mutual
exclusion semaphore and returns. *Tcpread* either returns an error code (which is less
than zero), or the count of characters extracted as its function value. Thus, the application that called *read* knows exactly how many bytes of data were received.

16.7.2 Single Byte Input From A TCP Slave Device

Function *tcpgetc* implements the *getc* operation for a TCP slave device. It simply
calls *tcpread* to read a single character and returns the result to its caller.

```
/* tcpgetc.c - tcpgetc */

#include <conf.h>
#include <kernel.h>
#include <proc.h>
#include <network.h>


/*------------------------------------------------------------------------
 *  tcpgetc  -  read one character from a TCP pseudo-device
 *------------------------------------------------------------------------
 */
int tcpgetc(pdev)
struct   devsw    *pdev;
{
        char    ch;
        int     cc;

        cc = tcpread(pdev, &ch, 1);
        if (cc < 0)
                return SYSERR;
        else if (cc == 0)
                return EOF;
        /* else, valid data */
        return ch;
}
```

16.7.3 Output Through A TCP Slave Device

Procedure *tcpwrite* implements the *write* operation, and procedure *tcpputc* implements single character (byte) output. They both call a single underlying procedure,
tcpwr.

```
/* tcpwrite.c - tcpwrite */

#include <conf.h>
#include <kernel.h>
#include <network.h>

/*------------------------------------------------------------------------
 *  tcpwrite  -  write one buffer from a TCP pseudo-device
 *------------------------------------------------------------------------
 */
int tcpwrite(pdev, pch, len)
struct  devsw   *pdev;
char            *pch;
int             len;
{
        return tcpwr(pdev, pch, len, TWF_NORMAL);
}


/* tcpputc.c - tcpputc */

#include <conf.h>
#include <kernel.h>
#include <proc.h>
#include <network.h>

/*------------------------------------------------------------------------
 *  tcpputc  -  write one character to a TCP pseudo-device
 *------------------------------------------------------------------------
 */
int tcpputc(pdev, ch)
struct  devsw   *pdev;
char            ch;
{
        return tcpwr(pdev, &ch, 1, TWF_NORMAL);
}
```

```
/* tcpwr.c - tcpwr */

#include <conf.h>
#include <kernel.h>
#include <proc.h>
#include <network.h>


/*------------------------------------------------------------------------
 * tcpwr  -  write urgent and normal data to TCP buffers
 *------------------------------------------------------------------------
 */
int tcpwr(pdev, pch, len, isurg)
struct  devsw   *pdev;
char            *pch;
int             len;
Bool            isurg;
{
        struct  tcb     *ptcb = (struct tcb *)pdev->dvioblk;
        int             sboff, tocopy;

        if (ptcb->tcb_state != TCPS_ESTABLISHED)
                return SYSERR;
        tocopy = tcpgetspace(ptcb, len);          /* acquires tcb_mutex   */
        if (tocopy <= 0)
                return tocopy;
        sboff = (ptcb->tcb_sbstart+ptcb->tcb_sbcount) % ptcb->tcb_sbsize;
        if (isurg)
                len = tcpwurg(ptcb, sboff, len);
        while (tocopy--) {
                ptcb->tcb_sndbuf[sboff] = *pch++;
                ++ptcb->tcb_sbcount;
                if (++sboff >= ptcb->tcb_sbsize)
                        sboff = 0;
        }
        ptcb->tcb_flags |= TCBF_NEEDOUT;
        tcpwakeup(WRITERS, ptcb);
        signal(ptcb->tcb_mutex);

        if (isurg || ptcb->tcb_snext == ptcb->tcb_suna)
                tcpkick(ptcb);
        return len;
}
```

If the connection is not in the *ESTABLISHED* state, output is prohibited, so *tcpwr* returns *SYSERR*. Otherwise, it calls *tcpgetspace* to allocate space in the output buffer. If *tcpgetspace* returns an error, *tcpwr* returns the error to its caller. Otherwise, *tcpwr* computes the position in the output buffer for the data it is about to write (by adding the count of characters already in the send buffer to the starting position of those characters, and wrapping the pointer around the end of the buffer). It then copies the data into the buffer starting at that position.

Finally, after creating new output data to be sent, *tcpwr* sets bit *TCBF_NEEDOUT* to indicate that new data is awaiting output, and calls *tcpwakeup* to awaken other writers. If the caller requested urgent delivery or no output is in progress, *tcpwr* calls *tcpkick* to start output immediately (sender silly window avoidance).

16.7.4 Closing A TCP Connection

Once an application finishes using a TCP connection, it calls *tcpclose* on the slave device to shutdown the connection. *Tcpclose* also deallocates the slave device.

```
/* tcpclose.c - tcpclose */

#include <conf.h>
#include <kernel.h>
#include <network.h>

/*------------------------------------------------------------------------
 *  tcpclose - close a TCP connection
 *------------------------------------------------------------------------
 */
int tcpclose(pdev)
struct  devsw    *pdev;
{
        struct  tcb       *ptcb = (struct tcb *)pdev->dvioblk;
        int               error;

        wait(ptcb->tcb_mutex);
        switch (ptcb->tcb_state) {
        case TCPS_LISTEN:
        case TCPS_ESTABLISHED:
        case TCPS_CLOSEWAIT:
                break;
        case TCPS_FREE:
                return SYSERR;
        default:
                signal(ptcb->tcb_mutex);
                return SYSERR;
        }
```

```
if (ptcb->tcb_error || ptcb->tcb_state == TCPS_LISTEN)
        return tcbdealloc(ptcb);
/* to get here, we must be in ESTABLISHED or CLOSE_WAIT */

TcpCurrEstab--;
ptcb->tcb_flags |= TCBF_SNDFIN;
ptcb->tcb_slast = ptcb->tcb_suna + ptcb->tcb_sbcount;
if (ptcb->tcb_state == TCPS_ESTABLISHED)
        ptcb->tcb_state = TCPS_FINWAIT1;
else    /* CLOSE_WAIT */
        ptcb->tcb_state = TCPS_LASTACK;
ptcb->tcb_flags |= TCBF_NEEDOUT;
tcpkick(ptcb);
signal(ptcb->tcb_mutex);
wait(ptcb->tcb_ocsem);                  /* wait for FIN to be ACKed     */
error = ptcb->tcb_error;
if (ptcb->tcb_state == TCPS_LASTACK)
        tcbdealloc(ptcb);
return error;
}
```

One can only close a connection that is in the *ESTABLISHED, CLOSE_WAIT*, or *LISTEN* states. For other states, *tcpclose* returns *SYSERR*.

Closing a connection from the *LISTEN* state simply means deallocating the TCB (no connection is in progress). Similarly, if an application closes a connection after an error has occurred, *tcpclose* deallocates the TCB.

For the *ESTABLISHED* state, closing a connection means moving to state *FIN-WAIT-1*; for the *CLOSE-WAIT* state, it means moving to state *LAST-ACK*. In either case, *tcpclose* sets bit *TCBF_SNDFIN* to show that a *FIN* is needed, sets bit *TCBF_NEEDOUT* to cause the output process to send the *FIN*, and calls *tcpkick* to start the output process (which will send the *FIN*).

Finally, *tcpclose* blocks on the open-close semaphore associated with the TCB to await the acknowledgement of the *FIN*. When the *ACK* arrives, input procedure *tcpfin1* or input procedure *tcplastack* will signal the open-close semaphore. When *tcpclose* resumes execution, it deallocates the TCB and returns to its caller. If the connection terminates abnormally, before the *FIN* has been acknowledged, *close* returns an appropriate error code.

16.7.5 Control Operations For A TCP Slave Device

TCP allows applications to control parameters for individual connections by providing a *control* function for slave devices. Procedure *tcpcntl* implements the *control* operation.

```
/* tcpcntl.c - tcpcntl */

#include <conf.h>
#include <kernel.h>
#include <network.h>

/*------------------------------------------------------------------------
 *  tcpcntl - control function for TCP pseudo-devices
 *------------------------------------------------------------------------
 */
int tcpcntl(pdev, func, arg, arg2)
struct  devsw   *pdev;
int             func;
char            *arg, *arg2;
{
        struct  tcb     *ptcb = (struct tcb *)pdev->dvioblk;
        int             rv;

        if (ptcb == NULL || ptcb->tcb_state == TCPS_FREE)
                return SYSERR;

        wait(ptcb->tcb_mutex);
        if (ptcb->tcb_state == TCPS_FREE) /* verify no state change */
                return SYSERR;

        switch (func) {
        case TCPC_ACCEPT:       if (ptcb->tcb_type != TCPT_SERVER) {
                                        rv = SYSERR;
                                        break;
                                }
                                signal(ptcb->tcb_mutex);
                                return preceive(ptcb->tcb_listenq);
        case TCPC_LISTENQ:      rv = tcplq(ptcb, arg);
                                break;
        case TCPC_STATUS:       rv = tcpstat(ptcb, arg);
                                break;
        case TCPC_SOPT:
        case TCPC_COPT:         rv = tcpuopt(ptcb, arg);
                                break;
        case TCPC_SENDURG:      /*
                                 * tcpwr acquires and releases tcb_mutex
                                 * itself.
                                 */
                                signal(ptcb->tcb_mutex);
```

```
                                        return tcpwr(pdev, arg, arg2, TWF_URGENT);
        default:
                rv = SYSERR;
        }
        signal(ptcb->tcb_mutex);
        return rv;
}
```

When *tcpcntl* begins, it verifies that the TCB is valid and acquires exclusive access
to it. It then examines the *func* argument to see which control operation the caller requested.

16.7.6 Accepting Connections From A Passive Device

The example in section *16.5* illustrates how servers use the *TCPC_ACCEPT* function to accept an individual connection from a TCB in the *LISTEN* state. The implementation is trivial. *Tcpcntl* verifies that the TCB has been opened for use by a server,
signals the mutual exclusion semaphore, and calls *preceive* to acquire the slave descriptor for the next incoming connection request. It must signal the mutual exclusion semaphore to permit TCP software to process incoming *SYN* requests. However, it cannot
proceed until a new connection has been established. *Preceive* blocks until the connection succeeds and the slave device can be used.

16.7.7 Changing The Size Of A Listen Queue

Function *TCPC_LISTENQ* allows the caller to change the size of the queue of incoming connections. Recall that an application can use the same function on the master
device to change the default size that all servers receive when they issue a passive open.
The difference here is that *tcpcntl* only changes the size of the queue for a single slave
device. *Tcpcntl* calls procedure *tcplq* to make the change.

```
/* tcplq.c - tcplq */

#include <conf.h>
#include <kernel.h>
#include <network.h>
#include <mark.h>
#include <ports.h>


/*------------------------------------------------------------------
 *  tcplq - set the listen queue size for a TCP pseudo device
 *------------------------------------------------------------------
 */
```

```
int tcplq(ptcb, lqsize)
struct  tcb      *ptcb;
int              lqsize;
{
        if (ptcb->tcb_state == TCPS_FREE)
                return SYSERR;
        ptcb->tcb_lqsize = lqsize;
        if (ptcb->tcb_type == TCPT_SERVER) {
                pdelete(ptcb->tcb_listenq, PTNODISP);
                ptcb->tcb_listenq = pcreate(ptcb->tcb_lqsize);
        }
        return OK;
}
```

To change the size of a connection queue, *tcplq* replaces the queue size stored in the TCB with the new size, deletes the existing queue, and creates a new one.

16.7.8 Acquiring Statistics From A Slave Device

Often, network management software needs to extract and report about the status of individual connections. The control function *TCPC_STATUS* provides a mechanism for doing so. It calls procedure *tcpstat* to gather and report statistics about a connection to the caller.

```
/* tcpstat.c - tcpstat */

#include <conf.h>
#include <kernel.h>
#include <network.h>

/*------------------------------------------------------------------------
 *  tcpstat - return status information for a TCP pseudo device
 *------------------------------------------------------------------------
 */
int tcpstat(ptcb, tcps)
struct  tcb     *ptcb;
struct tcpstat  *tcps;
{
        tcps->ts_type = ptcb->tcb_type;
        switch (ptcb->tcb_type) {
        case TCPT_SERVER:
                /* should increase to entire TCP MIB */
                tcps->ts_connects = TcpActiveOpens;
                tcps->ts_aborts = TcpEstabResets;
                tcps->ts_retrans = TcpRetransSegs;
                break;
        case TCPT_CONNECTION:
                blkcopy(tcps->ts_laddr, ptcb->tcb_lip, IP_ALEN);
                tcps->ts_lport = ptcb->tcb_lport;
                blkcopy(tcps->ts_faddr, ptcb->tcb_rip, IP_ALEN);
                tcps->ts_fport = ptcb->tcb_rport;
                tcps->ts_rwin = ptcb->tcb_rbsize - ptcb->tcb_rbcount;
                tcps->ts_swin = ptcb->tcb_swindow;
                tcps->ts_state = ptcb->tcb_state;
                tcps->ts_unacked = ptcb->tcb_suna;
                tcps->ts_prec = 0;
                break;
        case TCPT_MASTER:
                break;
        }
        return OK;
}
```

Tcpstat assumes the caller has passed it the address of a *tcpstat* structure into which it must place various statistics. File *tcpstat.h* contains the declaration of the structure as well as the definitions of various shorthand identifiers used to access individual fields.

```
/* tcpstat.h */

/*      The union returned by the TCP STATUS control call              */
struct tcpstat {
        int     ts_type;        /* which kind of TCP status?           */
        union {
                struct {
                        long    tsu_connects;   /* # connections       */
                        long    tsu_aborts;     /* # aborts            */
                        long    tsu_retrans;    /* # retransmissions   */
                } T_unt;
                struct {
                        IPaddr  tsu_laddr;      /* local IP            */
                        short   tsu_lport;      /* local TCP port      */
                        IPaddr  tsu_faddr;      /* foreign IP          */
                        short   tsu_fport;      /* foreign TCP port    */
                        short   tsu_rwin;       /* receive window      */
                        short   tsu_swin;       /* peer's window       */
                        short   tsu_state;      /* TCP state           */
                        long    tsu_unacked;    /* bytes unacked       */
                        int     tsu_prec;       /* IP precedence       */
                } T_unc;
                struct {
                        long    tsu_requests;   /* # connect requests  */
                        long    tsu_qmax;       /* max queue length    */
                } T_uns;
        } T_un;
};

#define ts_connects     T_un.T_unt.tsu_connects
#define ts_aborts       T_un.T_unt.tsu_aborts
#define ts_retrans      T_un.T_unt.tsu_retrans

#define ts_laddr        T_un.T_unc.tsu_laddr
#define ts_lport        T_un.T_unc.tsu_lport
#define ts_faddr        T_un.T_unc.tsu_faddr
#define ts_fport        T_un.T_unc.tsu_fport
#define ts_rwin         T_un.T_unc.tsu_rwin
#define ts_swin         T_un.T_unc.tsu_swin
#define ts_state        T_un.T_unc.tsu_state
#define ts_unacked      T_un.T_unc.tsu_unacked
#define ts_prec         T_un.T_unc.tsu_prec

#define ts_requests     T_un.T_uns.tsu_requests
#define ts_qmax         T_un.T_uns.tsu_qmax
```

16.7.9 Setting Or Clearing TCP Options

The *control* operation also allows an application to clear or set option bits in the *tcb_flags* field. While most of these bits are intended for internal use, at least two of them can be pertinent to an application. First, bit *TCBF_BUFFER* determines whether *read* behaves synchronously or asynchronously. In particular, if the caller requests TCP to *read* n bytes of data, a synchronous call will block until n bytes of data arrive, while an asynchronous read will return as soon as any data arrives, even if it contains fewer than n bytes. (Of course, *read* always returns without waiting for n bytes if the sender shuts down the connection or specifies *push*.) Second, an application can set bit *TCBF_DELACK* to cause TCP to delay sending acknowledgements. Although delayed acknowledgements are not recommended for general use†, some connections use them to reduce traffic (because acknowledgements will be piggybacked in outgoing data segments).

To clear or set options bits, the application program calls *control* with *TCPC_COPT* or *TCPC_SOPT* as the function argument and a bit mask as the third argument. When *tcpcntl* finds either of the clear or set requests, it passes the request to procedure *tcpuopt*.

```
/* tcpuopt.c - tcpuopt, ISUOPT */

#include <conf.h>
#include <kernel.h>
#include <network.h>

#define ISUOPT(flags)    (!(flags & ~(TCBF_DELACK|TCBF_BUFFER)))

/*------------------------------------------------------------------------
 *  tcpuopt - set/clear TCP user option flags
 *------------------------------------------------------------------------
 */
int tcpuopt(ptcb, flags)
struct  tcb     *ptcb;
int             flags;
{
        if (!ISUOPT(flags))
                return SYSERR;
        if (TCPC_SOPT)
                ptcb->tcb_flags |= flags;
        else
                ptcb->tcb_flags &= ~flags;
        return OK;
}
```

---

†Unfortunately, the host requirements document, RFC 1122, does recommend delayed acknowledgements, even though many researchers agree that their use will confuse TCP round-trip estimation, and can lead to poor performance except in a few unusual cases.

Tcpuopt uses the macro *ISUOPT* to check whether the user has specified any bits other than *TCBF_DELACK* or *TCBF_BUFFER*. If so, it rejects the request. *Tcpuopt* then examines the function code to determine whether it should set or clear the specified bits. The bits will remain set as long as the TCB remains allocated.

16.8 Initialization Of A Slave Device

At system startup, the operating system initializes each device, including TCP slave devices used for connections. Procedure *tcpinit* handles initialization of a slave device.

```
/* tcpinit.c - tcpinit */

#include <conf.h>
#include <kernel.h>
#include <network.h>
#include <mark.h>

static MARKER tcpmark;

/*------------------------------------------------------------------------
 * tcpinit  -  initialize TCP slave pseudo device marking it free
 *------------------------------------------------------------------------
 */
int tcpinit(pdev)
struct   devsw   *pdev;
{
        struct   tcb      *tcb;

        if (unmarked(tcpmark)) {
                mark(tcpmark);
                tcps_tmutex = screate(1);
                tcps_lqsize = 5;         /* default listen Q size        */
        }
        pdev->dvioblk = (char *) (tcb = &tcbtab[pdev->dvminor]);
        tcb->tcb_dvnum = pdev->dvnum;
        tcb->tcb_state = TCPS_FREE;
        return OK;
}

#ifdef  Ntcp
struct  tcb      tcbtab[Ntcp];            /* tcp device control blocks    */
#endif
```

Initialization consists of assigning the constant *TCPS_FREE* to the state field in the corresponding TCB. Once the TCB has been initialized, it becomes available for allocation by procedure *tcballoc*.

16.9 Summary

TCP does not specify the exact details of the interface between protocol software and application programs. Instead, it allows the operating system to choose an interface. Many systems use the *socket* interface taken from BSD UNIX.

Our example interface uses the device abstraction along with the *open-read-write-close* paradigm. An application calls *open* on a TCP master device to allocate a device descriptor it can use for an individual connection. When a client *opens* the TCP master device, it receives a connected descriptor used for data transfer; when a server *opens* the TCP master device, it receives a stub descriptor used only to accept incoming connections. The server then repeatedly issues a *control* call on the stub descriptor to acquire descriptors for individual connections.

Once a connection has been established, applications use *read*, *write*, *getc*, or *putc* to transfer data. Finally, the application calls *close* to terminate use and make the descriptor available for new connections.

We examined the implementation of procedures that provide I/O operations on both the TCP master device as well as TCP slave devices.

FOR FURTHER STUDY

Comer [1988] presents an overview of the BSD UNIX socket interface, while Leffler, McKusick, Karels, and Quarterman [1989] discusses its implementation. Stevens [1990] examines how applications use various UNIX protocol interfaces. Comer [1984] presents details of the Xinu device structure, and shows how operations like *read* and *write* map into underlying functions like *tcpread* and *tcpwrite*.

EXERCISES

16.1   The remote machine specification used by the TCP master device may seem awkward. State several reasons why it might have been chosen.

16.2   As an alternative to the design presented here, consider a design in which the master TCP device passes all control operations on to all currently active slave devices. For example, one can imagine an *ABORT* control function which, when applied to a TCP slave device aborts the connection for that slave and, when applied to the TCP master device, aborts all connections in progress on all slave devices. What are the advantages and disadvantages of such a scheme?

16.3 Examine the code for mutual exclusion at the beginning of *tcpcntl* carefully. Can the call to *wait* ever result in an error? Will it affect the outcome in any way? Explain.

16.4 What happens if one or more connection requests have arrived before a server uses *control* to change the size of the listen queue for its slave device?

16.5 List additional control functions that an application program might find useful.

16.6 Our code uses *control* to implement all nontransfer operations. Compare this approach to one that uses separate system calls for each special operation (e.g., *accept*, *listen*, etc.). What are the advantages and disadvantages of each?

16.7 Large buffers generally imply higher throughput, but sometimes large buffers do not. Suppose multiple application programs continually attempt to *read* from a single TCP connection with the *TCBF_BUFFER* bit set. Argue that whichever of them uses the largest buffer will receive the least service.

16.8 In the question above, under what circumstances is it possible that if many applications attempt to read from a single connection one of them will not receive any data at all, while the others continue to receive data?

17

RIP: Active Route Propagation And Passive Acquisition

17.1 Introduction

Earlier chapters showed the structure of an IP routing table and the procedures IP uses when forwarding datagrams toward their destinations. Hosts or gateways, interconnected with simple internet topologies, initialize their IP routing tables at system startup by inserting a few entries that never change. In most environments, however, gateways propagate routing information dynamically to provide automated computation of minimal paths and automatic recovery from temporary network or gateway failures. Hosts and gateways that receive the propagated information update their routing table entries accordingly.

This chapter examines the *Routing Information Protocol* (*RIP*), one of the most popular protocols used to propagate routing information among gateways and hosts. Although RIP seems simple on the surface, we will see that there are many subtle rules that govern which routes to advertise and when to advertise them. The rules help prevent routing loops, and make route propagation both faster and more reliable.

Route propagation is among the most complex tasks in an internet. Small deviations from the standard or the omission of a few heuristics can lead to severe problems, such as nonoptimal routes or instabilities. Furthermore, while most errors in protocol software affect only the machine that runs the incorrect software, poorly written route propagation software is especially dangerous, because it can affect all machines on its internet. Thus, like all routing protocols, a correct implementation of RIP requires careful attention to detail.

17.2 Active And Passive Mode Participants

TCP/IP internets follow the premise that gateways know correct routes because they exchange routing information with other gateways. By contrast, hosts only learn routes from gateways; their routing information may not be complete or authoritative. Hence, hosts are forbidden from informing other machines about routes. In summary:

> *Gateways engage in active propagation of routing information, while hosts acquire routing information passively and never propagate it.*

The RIP protocol honors this rule by providing two basic modes of operation. Hosts use RIP in *passive mode*, to passively listen for RIP messages sent by gateways, extract routing information from them, and update their own routing tables. Passive RIP does not propagate information from the local routing table. Gateways use RIP in *active mode*. Active participants listen for RIP messages from other gateways, install new routes in their routing tables, and send messages that contain the updated routing table entries. Thus, active participants engage in two activities (transmission and reception), while passive participants engage in only one (reception). The next sections focus on active participants.

17.3 Basic RIP Algorithm And Cost Metric

RIP uses a *vector-distance* algorithm to propagate routes and local network broadcast to deliver messages. Each gateway periodically broadcasts routes from its current IP routing table on all network interfaces. Like other vector-distance protocols, the RIP message contains pairs that consist of a destination network and the distance to that network.

When a RIP update message arrives, the receiving machine examines each entry and compares the entry to its current route for the same destination, D. The receiver uses a triangle inequality to test whether the advertised route to D is superior to the existing route. That is, when examining an entry received from gateway G, the receiver asks whether the cost of going to G, plus the cost of going from G to D, is less than the current cost of going to D. Expressed in mathematical terms, the receiver R asks if

$$cost(R, G) + cost(G, D) < cost(R, D)$$

where *cost(i, j)* denotes the cost of the least expensive path from i to j. The receiver only updates its routing table entry for a destination if the cost of sending traffic through gateway G is less than the current cost. When changing a route, the receiver assigns it a cost equal to

$$cost(R, G) + cost(G, D)$$

Because the cost of reaching a neighboring gateway is *1*, the new cost becomes

$$cost(R, D) = cost(G, D) + 1$$

Although the above description seems simple, one final detail complicates it. Suppose R's current route to destination D goes through gateway G. When a new update arrives from G, R must change its cost for the route independent of whether G reports a decrease or an increase in cost. Thus, the final version of the algorithm becomes:

> *When a RIP update arrives with metric* M *for destination* D *from gateway* G, *compare it to the current route. If no route exists, create one with next hop equal to* G *and cost equal to* M+1. *If the current route specifies* G *as the next hop, set the cost in the route to* M+1. *Otherwise, if the cost of the current route is greater than* M+1, *set the cost to* M+1, *and set the next hop to* G.

17.4 Instabilities And Solutions

17.4.1 Count To Infinity

Most vector-distance algorithms share a common problem because they allow temporary routing loops. A routing loop occurs for destination D when two or more gateways become locked in a circular sequence, such that each gateway thinks the optimal path to destination D uses the next gateway in the sequence. The simplest routing loops involve two gateways that each think the other is the best next hop along a route to a given destination.

Gateways using RIP cannot easily detect routing loops. When a routing loop does occur for destination D, the RIP protocol causes the gateways involved to slowly increment their metrics one at a time. They will continue until the metric reaches *infinity*, a value so large that the routing software interprets it to mean, "no route exists for this destination." To help limit the damage routing loops cause, RIP defines infinity to be a small number. We can summarize:

> *To limit the time a routing loop can persist, RIP defines infinity to be 16. When a routing metric reaches that value, RIP interprets it to mean "no route exists."*

17.4.2 Gateway Crashes And Route Timeout

RIP requires all participating gateways and hosts to apply a timeout to all routes. A route must expire when its timeout occurs. To understand timeout, consider what happens when a gateway G, that has been actively participating in RIP, crashes. Neighboring gateways have received update messages from G, and have installed routes that use G as the next hop. When G crashes, neighbors have no way of knowing that the routes using it as a next hop have become invalid. In essence, the cost for the route has become infinity, but the neighbors have no way of learning about the change because the gateway responsible for broadcasting the routing updates has crashed. Thus, gateways that receive information from RIP take responsibility for insuring it remains correct.

> *When installing or changing a route, associate a timer with it. If no information arrives to revalidate the route before the timer expires, declare the route to be invalid.*

17.4.3 Split Horizon

One of the most common causes of routing loops arises if gateways advertise all routing information on all network interfaces. To understand the problem, consider three gateways, A, B, and C, attached to the same Ethernet. Suppose gateway A has a cost *1* path to destination D, and has advertised it by broadcasting a RIP update packet. Both B and C have received the update and have installed routes for destination D with cost *2*. If they advertise their routes, no problem occurs because their routes are more expensive than the route A advertises.

Now suppose that gateway A *crashes*. If B or C continue to advertise their cost *2* route to D long enough, machines on the network will eventually time out the route that A advertised, and will adopt a cost *2* route. In fact, as soon as the route A advertised expires, either B or C will adopt the route the other one advertises, creating a temporary routing loop.

To avoid routing loops, RIP uses a technique known as *split horizon*. The rule is simple.

> *When sending a RIP update over a particular network interface, never include routing information acquired over that interface.*

One way to look at this rule is from the viewpoint of the routing that occurs within a gateway. If a gateway G learned a route to destination D through the interface for network N, then G's route must specify a next hop that lies on network N. That is, G will route all datagrams headed to D to a gateway on N. Now suppose that G includes its route to destination D when broadcasting a RIP update on network N. If a gateway or host on network N has no current route to D (perhaps because an error has occurred), it will install the advertised route and send all datagrams destined for D to G. If a datagram does arrive at G destined for D, G will forward the datagram to the next hop, which lies on network N. Thus, G will forward datagrams that arrive over network N back out over the same network on which they arrived. Split horizon solves the problem by avoiding advertisements that could cause it.

17.4.4 Poison Reverse

In general, vector-distance protocols like RIP allow routing loops to persist because they do not propagate information about route loss quickly. A heuristic known as *poison reverse* (or *split horizon with poison reverse*) helps solve the problem. It modifies the split horizon technique. Instead of avoiding propagation of routes out over the network from which they arrived, poison reverse uses the updates to carry negative information.

> *When sending a RIP update over a particular network interface, include all routes, but set the metric to infinity for those routes acquired over that interface.*

Poison reverse will break routing loops quickly. If two machines each have a route for destination D that points to the other machine, arranging to have them send an update with the cost set to infinity will break the loop as soon as one machine send its update.

Of course, using split horizon with poison reverse has a disadvantage: it increases the size of update messages (and therefore uses more network bandwidth). For most gateways, however, the increased update message size does not cause problems.

17.4.5 Route Timeout With Poison Reverse

We said that RIP requires gateways to place a timeout on each route and to invalidate the route when the timeout occurs. The most obvious implementation merely removes a route from the routing table when its timer expires. However, when RIP uses poison reverse, it cannot discard routes after they become invalid. Instead, it must keep a record that the route existed and now has cost infinity.

RIP only needs to retain expired routes until outgoing messages propagate the information to neighboring gateways. In principle, RIP only needs to retain an expired route through one update cycle. Because the underlying UDP and IP protocols can drop datagrams, RIP keeps a record of expired routes through four update cycles. After four cycles RIP assumes neighboring gateways have received at least one update that reports the route at cost infinity, so it deletes the route.

17.4.6 Triggered Updates

One additional technique helps make RIP more robust in the presence of large routing loops. The technique, known as *triggered updates*, employs rapid updates to speed the process of convergence after a change.

> *Whenever a gateway changes the metric for a route, it must send an*
> *update message to all its neighbors immediately without waiting for*
> *the usual periodic update cycle.*

Triggered updates help RIP break routing loops that involve more than two gateways because it causes RIP to propagate infinite cost routes without waiting for periodic broadcasts. To understand how triggered updates help, consider a set of n gateways ($n > 2$) which have entered a routing loop. The first gateway advertises its route to the second, which advertises its route to the third, and so on, until the final gateway advertises its route back to the first. In such a situation, the metrics will increase by n after updates pass around the cycle once. Thus, counting to infinity can take an extremely long time, even when infinity is defined to be small. Split horizon alone does not break loops that involve multiple gateways, because for each pair of gateways, the route advertisements only propagate in one direction and never directly back.

Triggered updates improve robustness by propagating routes quickly. In particular, when a gateway G loses its connection to a given destination D, it sends a triggered update to propagate a route for D with cost infinity. Any neighboring gateway that depends on G to reach destination D will receive the update and change its cost for D to infinity. The change in neighbors of G triggers another round of updates sent by those neighbors, and so on. The triggered updates result in a *cascade* of updates. In fact, if the triggered updates occur quickly enough†, they completely prevent routing loops.

17.4.7 Randomization To Prevent Broadcast Storms

The protocol standard specifies that RIP must randomize the transmission of triggered updates. That is:

> *Whenever a gateway changes the metric for a route, it must send an*
> *update messages to all its neighbors after a short random delay, but*
> *without waiting for the usual periodic update.*

To understand how a random delay helps, remember that RIP uses hardware broadcast to deliver update messages, and imagine multiple gateways that share an Ethernet. Think of poison reverse. Whenever one of the gateways sends an update for some destination D, all other gateways on the Ethernet install the change, which triggers updates (including a poison reverse update for the Ethernet over which the information arrived). Thus, all gateways will attempt to broadcast their triggered update simultaneously. A broadcast storm results. In fact, if the site has chosen to purchase all of its gateways from the same vendor, they will all use the same hardware and run the same software, making them generate a triggered response at exactly the same time. To eliminate simultaneous transmission, RIP specifies that a gateway must wait for a small, random delay before sending triggered updates.

---

†*Quickly enough* means that the cascade must complete before any normal updates occur.

17.5 Message Types

RIP provides two basic message types. It allows a client to send a *request* message that asks about specific routes, and it provides a *response* message used either to answer a request or to advertise routes periodically. The protocol standard defines additional message types but they are obsolete.

In general, few clients poll for updates. Instead, most implementations rely on gateways to generate a periodic update message. Technically, the periodic broadcast message is called a *gratuitous response* because it uses the *response* message type even though no *request* message caused it to occur.

17.6 Protocol Characterization

RIP can be characterized by the following:

- Operates at application level
- Uses UDP for all transport
- Limits message size
- Is connectionless
- Achieves reliability with k-out-of-n algorithm
- Specifies fixed timeouts
- Uses a well-known protocol port number
- Uses uniform message format

The next paragraphs discuss each of these.

Level and transport. RIP operates at the application level and uses UDP to carry requests and responses. The chief advantage of using UDP is that it allows clients to send requests to remote gateways (i.e., gateways that do not connect to the same network as the client). The chief disadvantage of using UDP is that RIP must provide its own reliability.

Small message size. RIP limits individual update messages to *512* octets of data. If a gateway needs to propagate more information than will fit in a single message, it sends multiple messages, but does not number or otherwise identify them as a set. Thus, if packet loss occurs, it is possible to receive partial updates without knowing about the loss.

Connectionless communication. RIP maintains no notion of connections, nor does it provide acknowledgements.

K-out-of-N Reliability. RIP achieves reliability using a *k-out-of-n* approach. Each receiver watches for periodic broadcasts and declares routing information to be invalid unless it receives at least *1* out of every *6* updates. A receiver never polls or verifies that a route has expired – it merely waits passively for new updates.

Fixed timeouts. RIP uses fixed values for all timeouts. It broadcasts update messages once every *30* seconds, waits *180* seconds after receiving an update before declaring that a route has become invalid, and retains the route with cost infinity an additional

120 seconds (for poison reverse). These timeouts are independent of the underlying physical networks using RIP or the round-trip time, making it impractical to use RIP on networks that exhibit extremely high delay or high packet loss.

Well-Known Protocol Port. RIP uses protocol port *520* for most communication. Clients always send requests to *520*, and servers always answer from *520*. Furthermore, all periodic update broadcasts originate from *520*; clients can broadcast a request from port *520* to ask all gateways on the local network to generate a response. Only clients ever use a port other than *520*, and they only use such a port when sending a request to a specific gateway; a server sends its response from port *520* to the port from which the request originated.

Uniform message format. RIP uses a single message format for all communication. In requests, the message contains destination addresses for which the client wants routing information, and the metric is not used. In responses, the destination addresses and metrics contain information from the sender's routing table.

17.7 Implementation Of RIP

17.7.1 The Two Styles Of Implementation

Broadly speaking, a designer must choose between two implementation styles. In the first style, RIP keeps its own routing database separate from the routing table that IP uses to forward datagrams. When new information arrives, RIP updates its routing database and then installs changes in the IP routing table. In the second style, RIP uses the same routing table as IP. Because all routes reside in the IP table regardless of their origin, routing table entries may need extra fields that RIP uses.

The advantage of using a separate table lies in separation of functionality. RIP can operate completely independent of IP and only needs to coordinate when it updates the IP routing table. Keeping RIP data separate from the IP routing database also allows the designer to modify RIP data structures, or replace the programs that implement RIP without changing IP.

The chief disadvantage of keeping RIP and IP information separate arises because the separation makes it difficult for RIP to learn about existing routes or install new routes. For example, if the gateway obtains a route through other protocols or if the manager installs a route manually, RIP will not know about the change. Thus, routing updates sent by RIP may not accurately reflect the current routing table. Similarly, RIP may continue to advertise routes after they have been deleted unless the manager also notifies RIP about every change.

Although we have chosen to use the second technique, storing RIP information in the IP routing table has a drawback related to timer management. Because the unified table stores all routing information, it must store the information RIP needs for poison reverse. In particular, it must contain entries for routes that have expired but which are kept for purposes of generating poison reverse updates, even though such routes must not be used when forwarding datagrams. Thus, IP must not use entries in the table that have cost infinity.

17.7.2 Declarations

File *rip.h* contains declarations of the rip message format and constants used throughout the code.

```
/* rip.h */

#define RIPHSIZE        4        /* size of the header in octets          */
#define RIP_VERSION     1        /* RIP version number                    */
#define AF_INET         2        /* Address Family for IP                 */

/* RIP commands codes: */

#define RIP_REQUEST     1        /* message requests routes               */
#define RIP_RESPONSE    2        /* message contains route advertisement  */

/* one RIP route entry */

struct  riprt {
        short   rr_family;       /* 4BSD Address Family                   */
        short   rr_mbz;          /* must be zero                          */
        char    rr_addr[12];     /* the part we use for IP: (0-3)         */
        int     rr_metric;       /* distance (hop count) metric           */
};

#define MAXRIPROUTES    25       /* MAX routes per packet                 */
#define RIP_INFINITY    16       /* dest is unreachable                   */

#define RIPINT          300      /* interval to send (1/10 secs)          */
#define RIPDELTA        50       /* stray RIPINT +/- this (1/10 secs)     */
#define RIPOUTMIN       50       /* min interval between updates (1/10 s) */

#define RIPRTTL         180      /* route ttl (secs)                      */
#define RIPZTIME        120      /* zombie route lifetime (secs)          */

/* RIP packet structure */
struct  rip {
        char    rip_cmd;         /* RIP command                          */
        char    rip_vers;        /* RIP_VERSION, above                   */
        short   rip_mbz;         /* must be zero                         */
        struct  riprt   rip_rts[MAXRIPROUTES];
};

/* RIP process definitions */

extern  int             rip(), ripout();/* processes to implement RIP    */
```

```
#define RIPSTK             5000              /* RIP process stack size      */
#define RIPPRI             50                /* RIP process priority        */
#define RIPNAM             "rip"             /* RIP main process name       */
#define RIPONAM            "ripout"          /* RIP output process name     */
#define RIPARGC            0                 /* Num. args for main RIP proc. */
#define RIPOARGC           0                 /* Num. args for RIP out. proc. */


#define MAXNRIP            5                 /* max # of packets per update */

/* Per-interface RIP send data */
struct   rq {
         Bool                rq_active;      /* TRUE => this data is active */
         IPaddr              rq_ip;          /* destination IP address      */
         unsigned short      rq_port;        /* destination port number     */
/* what we've built already:                */
         struct   ep         *rq_pep[MAXNRIP];     /* packets to send        */
         int                 rq_len[MAXNRIP];      /* length of each         */
/* in-progress packet information            */
         int                 rq_cur;         /* current working packet      */
         int                 rq_nrts;        /* # routes this packet        */
         struct   rip        *rq_prip;       /* current rip data            */
};


extern   int       riplock;                  /* ripin/ripout synchronization */
extern   int       rippid;                   /* PID for ripout() process    */
extern   Bool      dorip;                    /* TRUE => do active RIP        */
```

Structure *rip* defines the RIP message format, while structure *riprt* defines a single route within the message. To maintain compatibility with BSD UNIX systems, the constant that defines the message type has been named *AF_INET*.

17.7.3 Conceptual Organization For Output

Because heuristics like the split horizon and poison reverse require the contents of an update message to vary depending on the interface, RIP cannot generate a single update message and send it on all interfaces. Instead, RIP simultaneously generates a separate copy of the update message for each network interface. When it adds a route to the update message, it applies rules like poison reverse to decide what it should add to each copy.

RIP uses structure *rq* to hold the contents of an individual copy of the update message†. Because not all networks use RIP, the structure contains Boolean field *rq_active* that allows the manager to decide whether RIP should send updates on that interface. The structure seems complicated because RIP may need multiple datagrams to carry the update. It contains an array of pointers to packets (field *rq_pep*), a corresponding array of packet lengths (field *rq_len*), an integer that tells how many packets RIP has added

---

†The output routines organize the individual *rq* structures into array *rqinfo*, which has one entry per network interface.

to the message so far (field *rq_cur*), how many routes RIP has added to the current packet (field *rq_nrts*), and a pointer to the current position in the packet where the next route belongs (field *rq_prip*).

17.8 The Principle RIP Process

Procedure *rip* performs two chores: it initializes the RIP data structures and it handles all incoming RIP packets.

```
/* ripin.c - rip */

#include <conf.h>
#include <kernel.h>
#include <network.h>
#include <proc.h>

/*------------------------------------------------------------------
 * rip  -  do the RIP route exchange protocol
 *------------------------------------------------------------------
 */
PROCESS rip()
{
        struct  xgram   ripbuf;
        struct  rip     *prip;
        int             fd, len;

        fd = open(UDP, ANYFPORT, UP_RIP);
        if (fd == SYSERR)
                panic("rip: cannot open rip port");
        riplock = screate(1);
        if (gateway)
                resume(create(ripout, RIPSTK, RIPPRI, RIPONAM, RIPOARGC));

        while (TRUE) {
                len = read(fd, &ripbuf, sizeof(ripbuf));
                if (len == SYSERR)
                        continue;
                prip = (struct rip *)ripbuf.xg_data;
                if (ripcheck(prip, len) != OK)
                        continue;
                switch (prip->rip_cmd) {
                case RIP_RESPONSE:
                        if (ripbuf.xg_fport == UP_RIP)
                                riprecv(prip, len, ripbuf.xg_fip);
```

```
                               break;
                  case RIP_REQUEST:
                           if (gateway || ripbuf.xg_fport != UP_RIP)
                                   riprepl(prip, len, ripbuf.xg_fip,
                                           ripbuf.xg_fport);
                           break;
                  default:
                           break;
                  }
          }
}


Bool    dorip = FALSE;
int     rippid = BADPID;
int     riplock;
```

    To initialize RIP, procedure *rip* opens UDP port *UP_RIP*, and creates the lock semaphore. It then checks to see if the code executes on a gateway or host, and starts the RIP output process if it finds that it is executing on a gateway.

    After initialization, *rip* enters an infinite loop where it reads the next arriving message into structure *ripbuf* and processes it. According to the standard, RIP must verify that all fields marked *must be zero* contain zeroes. To perform the verification, *Rip* calls function *ripcheck*, and discards incorrect messages.

    After verifying the message, *rip* uses the command type to decide whether the message is a request (*RIP_REQUEST*) or a response (*RIP_RESPONSE*), and calls either *riprepl* or *riprecv* to handle it. Following the protocol standard, it ignores response messages that do not originate at the well-known port (*520*). The standard specifies that gateways must answer all RIP requests, regardless of their originating port, but hosts that run passive RIP must ignore all requests that originate from the well-known port.

17.8.1 Must Be Zero Field Must Be Zero

    Procedure *ripcheck* verifies that fields in the message that the protocol specifies to be zero are indeed zero.

```
/* ripcheck.c - ripcheck */

#include <conf.h>
#include <kernel.h>
#include <network.h>


/*------------------------------------------------------------------------
 *  ripcheck  -  check a RIP packet for proper format
 *------------------------------------------------------------------------
```

```
 */
int ripcheck(prip, len)
struct  rip       *prip;
int               len;
{
        int       i, j, nrts;

        switch (prip->rip_vers) {
        case    0:                      /* never OK              */
                return SYSERR;
        case    1:                      /* more checks below     */
                break;
        default:                        /* >1 always ok          */
                return OK;
        }
        /* check all "must be zero" fields */

        if (prip->rip_mbz)
                return SYSERR;
        nrts = (len - RIPHSIZE)/sizeof(struct riprt);
        for (i=0; i<nrts; ++i) {
                struct  riprt   *prr = &prip->rip_rts[i];

                if (prr->rr_mbz)
                        return SYSERR;
                for (j=IP_ALEN; j<sizeof(prr->rr_addr); ++j)
                        if (prr->rr_addr[j])
                                return SYSERR;
        }
        return OK;      /* this one's ok in my book... */

}
```

According to the standard, *ripcheck* refuses to accept messages with version number *0*. It accepts messages that have version number greater than zero, but only checks zero fields in messages that have version number equal to *1*. When it does check zero fields, *ripcheck* examines the appropriate fields in the message header. It then iterates through all route entries in the message, checking to be sure that address octets not used by IP contain zeroes.

17.8.2 Processing An Incoming Response

Procedure *riprecv* handles incoming response messages. The arguments consist of a pointer to the RIP message, the message length, and the sender's IP address.

```
/* riprecv.c - riprecv */

#include <conf.h>
#include <kernel.h>
#include <network.h>


/*------------------------------------------------------------------------
 *  riprecv  -  process a received RIP advertisement
 *------------------------------------------------------------------------
 */
int riprecv(prip, len, gw)
struct  rip     *prip;
int             len;
IPaddr          gw;
{
        struct  route   *prt;
        IPaddr          mask;
        int             nrts, rn, ifnum;

        nrts = (len - RIPHSIZE)/sizeof(struct riprt);
        prt = rtget(gw, RTF_REMOTE);     /* find the interface number    */
        if (prt == NULL)
                return SYSERR;
        ifnum = prt->rt_ifnum;
        rtfree(prt);
        wait(riplock);                   /* prevent updates until we're done   */
        for (rn=0; rn<nrts; ++rn) {
                struct riprt    *rp = &prip->rip_rts[rn];

                rp->rr_family = net2hs(rp->rr_family);
                rp->rr_metric = net2hl(rp->rr_metric);
                if (!ripok(rp))
                        continue;
                netmask(mask, rp->rr_addr);
                rtadd(rp->rr_addr, mask, gw, rp->rr_metric,
                        ifnum, RIPRTTL);
        }
        signal(riplock);
        return OK;
}
```

After computing the number of entries in the message, *riprecv* calls *rtget* to find the local machine's route to the sending gateway. If the machine has no route to the gateway, it cannot use the update, so it returns *SYSERR*. From the return route, *riprecv* extracts the index of the network interface used to reach the gateway, and places it in variable *ifnum*, which it uses when installing the route.

Riprecv iterates through individual entries in the update message. For each entry, it calls *ripok* to check for malformed or illegal addresses, calls *netmask* to compute the network mask, and calls *rtadd* to add or update the route in the local IP routing table. Note that *rtadd*† applies the RIP update rules: it creates a new route to the destination if no route currently exists, it replaces the metric if a route exists through the sending gateway, and it ignores the route if it already knows a less expensive one. Finally, *rtadd* updates the routing table.

17.8.3 Locking During Update

As we will see, the RIP output process periodically scans the routing table when it forms and sends an update. To insure that the output software does not send triggered updates until all entries in an incoming packet have been processed, *riprecv* waits on semaphore *riplock* before making any changes. It signals the semaphore once changes have been completed.

17.8.4 Verifying An Address

We said that *riprecv* calls procedure *ripok* to verify the format of an address. *Ripok* verifies that the address entry specifies an IP address type, the advertised metric is not more than infinity, the advertised address is not class *D* or *E*, the address does not have a zero octet in the network portion and a nonzero host portion, and the address does not specify the local loopback network (*127*). Other addresses specify valid destinations, and may be used for routing.

See page 94 for a listing of *rtadd.c*.

```
/* ripok.c - ripok */

#include <conf.h>
#include <kernel.h>
#include <network.h>


/*------------------------------------------------------------------------
 *  ripok  -  determine if a received RIP route is ok to install
 *------------------------------------------------------------------------
 */
int ripok(rp)
struct  riprt   *rp;
{
        if (rp->rr_family != AF_INET)
                return FALSE;
        if (rp->rr_metric > RIP_INFINITY)
                return FALSE;
        if (IP_CLASSD(rp->rr_addr) || IP_CLASSE(rp->rr_addr))
                return FALSE;
        if (rp->rr_addr[0] == 0 &&
            !blkequ(rp->rr_addr, ip_anyaddr, IP_ALEN))
                return FALSE;           /* net 0, host non-0        */
        if (rp->rr_addr[0] == 127)
                return FALSE;           /* loopback net             */
        return TRUE;
}
```

17.9 Responding To An Incoming Request

When a request message arrives, *rip* calls procedure *riprepl* to generate a response.

```
/* riprepl.c - riprepl */

#include <conf.h>
#include <kernel.h>
#include <network.h>


/*------------------------------------------------------------------------
 *  riprepl  -  process a received RIP request
 *------------------------------------------------------------------------
 */
int riprepl(pripin, len, gw, port)
struct  rip     *pripin;
int             len;
IPaddr          gw;
```

```
unsigned short   port;
{
        struct   ep        *pep;
        struct   rip       *prip;
        struct   route     *prt, *rtget();
        int                rn, nrts;

        nrts = (len - RIPHSIZE)/sizeof(struct riprc);
        if (nrts == 1 && pripin->rip_rts[0].rr_family == 0 &&
             net2hl(pripin->rip_rts[0].rr_metric) == RIP_INFINITY)
                return ripsend(gw, port);        /* send the full table  */
        pep = (struct ep *)getbuf(Net.netpool);
        /* get to the RIP data... */
        prip = (struct rip *)((struct udp *)
                ((struct ip *)pep->ep_data)->ip_data)->u_data;
        blkcopy(prip, pripin, len);
        for (rn = 0; rn < nrts; ++rn) {
                struct riprt     *rp = &prip->rip_rts[rn];

                if (net2hs(rp->rr_family) != AF_INET)
                        continue;
                prt = rtget(rp->rr_addr, RTF_LOCAL);
                if (prt) {
                        rp->rr_metric = hl2net(prt->rt_metric);
                        rtfree(prt);
                } else
                        rp->rr_metric = hl2net(RIP_INFINITY);
        }
        prip->rip_cmd = RIP_RESPONSE;
        prip->rip_vers = RIP_VERSION;
        prip->rip_mbz = 0;
        udpsend(gw, port, UP_RIP, pep, len, 1);
        return OK;
}
```

RIP allows one special case in requests. The standard specifies that if the request contains exactly one entry that has address family identifier *0* and metric *infinity*, the recipient should generate a full update message as a response. Otherwise, the recipient should respond by supplying its local routes for each address specified in the request.

Riprepl calls procedure *ripsend*, which is also used by the output process, to generate a full update in response to the special case request. For normal requests, *riprepl* allocates a buffer to hold the response. Once it has copied the incoming message into the new buffer, *riprepl* iterates through each entry. It uses *rtget* to look up the local route for the entry, and copies the metric from that route into the response, or assigns *RIP_INFINITY*, if no route exists. Before sending the response, *riprepl* assigns values to the command field in the message header (to make it a response) and the version field (to indicate the appropriate version number). It then calls *udpsend* to transmit the datagram.

17.10 Generating Update Messages

Procedure *ripsend* creates and sends an update.

```
/* ripsend.c - ripsend */

#include <conf.h>
#include <kernel.h>
#include <network.h>


/*------------------------------------------------------------------------
 * ripsend - send a RIP update
 *------------------------------------------------------------------------
 */
int ripsend(gw, port)
IPaddr          gw;                     /* remote gateway (FFFFFFFF => all)    */
unsigned short  port;                   /* remote port                        */
{
        struct  rq      *prq, rqinfo[NIF];      /* here, so reentrant    */
        struct  route   *prt;
        int             i, pn;

        if (ripifset(rqinfo, gw, port) != OK)
                return SYSERR;

        wait(Route.ri_mutex);
        for (i=0; i<RT_TSIZE; ++i)
                for (prt=rttable[i]; prt; prt=prt->rt_next)
                        ripadd(rqinfo, prt);
        if (Route.ri_default)
                ripadd(rqinfo, Route.ri_default);
        signal(Route.ri_mutex);

        for (i=0; i<Net.nif; ++i)
                if (rqinfo[i].rq_active) {
                        prq = &rqinfo[i];
                        for (pn=0; pn<=prq->rq_cur; ++pn)
                                udpsend(prq->rq_ip, prq->rq_port, UP_RIP,
                                        prq->rq_pep[pn], prq->rq_len[pn]);
                }

}
```

Ripsend begins by calling *ripifset* to initialize array *rqinfo*, the array that holds an update message for each of the network interfaces. It then waits on semaphore *Route.ri_mutex* to obtain exclusive use of the routing table, and iterates through all possible routes. For each route, it calls procedure *ripadd*. *Ripadd* implements heuristics like split horizon; it iterates through the set of network interfaces and determines whether to add the route to the copy of the update message associated with each. Finally, after adding all the routes, *ripsend* iterates through the network interfaces and calls *udpsend* to send the appropriate copy of the update message. It does not send an update to the local host because field *rq_active* is *FALSE* in the array element that corresponds to the local host.

17.11 Initializing Copies Of An Update Message

Procedure *ripifset* initializes array *rqinfo*. The second argument either contains the IP address of a client that sent a specific request, or the *all 1s* address, which requests a broadcast to all networks.

```
/* ripifset.c - ripifset */

#include <conf.h>
#include <kernel.h>
#include <network.h>

/*------------------------------------------------------------------------
 * ripifset - set the per-interface data for a RIP update
 *------------------------------------------------------------------------
 */
int ripifset(rqinfo, gw, port)
struct  rq      rqinfo[];
IPaddr          gw;             /* remote gateway (FFFFFFFF => all)     */
unsigned short  port;           /* remote port                         */
{
        struct  route   *prt;
        int             ifn;

        if (!blkequ(gw, ip_maskall, IP_ALEN)) {
                for (ifn=0; ifn<Net.nif; ++ifn)
                        rqinfo[ifn].rq_active = FALSE;
                prt = rtget(gw, RTF_LOCAL);
                if (prt == 0)
                        return SYSERR;
                ifn = prt->rt_ifnum;
```

```
                        rtfree(prt);
                        if (ifn == NI_LOCAL)
                                return SYSERR;
                        blkcopy(rqinfo[ifn].rq_ip, gw, IP_ALEN);
                        rqinfo[ifn].rq_port = port;
                        rqinfo[ifn].rq_active = TRUE;
                        rqinfo[ifn].rq_cur = -1;
                        rqinfo[ifn].rq_nrts = MAXRIPROUTES;
                        return OK;
                }
                /* else, all interfaces */
                for (ifn=0; ifn<Net.nif; ++ifn) {
                        blkcopy(rqinfo[ifn].rq_ip, nif[ifn].ni_brc, IP_ALEN);
                        rqinfo[ifn].rq_port = port;
                        rqinfo[ifn].rq_active = TRUE;
                        rqinfo[ifn].rq_cur = -1;
                        rqinfo[ifn].rq_nrts = MAXRIPROUTES;
                }
                rqinfo[NI_LOCAL].rq_active = FALSE;       /* never do this one    */
                return OK;
        }
```

If the request specifies a particular address, *ripifset* disables RIP processing on all interfaces except the one that leads to the specified address. Otherwise, it enables RIP processing on all interfaces except the pseudo-network interface for the local host. When enabling an interface, *ripifset* initializes the index of routes in the current datagram to *-1*, indicating that there are no datagrams present.

17.11.1 Adding Routes To Copies Of An Update Message

Procedure *ripadd* adds a route to each copy of an update message.

```
/* ripadd.c - ripadd */

#include <conf.h>
#include <kernel.h>
#include <network.h>


/*------------------------------------------------------------------------
 * ripadd  -  add the given route to the RIP packets yet to send
 *------------------------------------------------------------------------
 */
int ripadd(rqinfo, prt)
```

```
struct  rq        rqinfo[];
struct  route     *prt;
{
        IPaddr  net;
        int     i, metric, pn, rn;

        for (i=0; i<Net.nif; ++i) {
                struct  rq        *prq = &rqinfo[i];
                struct  riprt     *rp;

                if (!rqinfo[i].rq_active || nif[i].ni_state != NIS_UP)
                        continue;
                metric = ripmetric(prt, i);
                if (metric == SYSERR)
                        continue;
                if (prq->rq_nrts >= MAXRIPROUTES &&
                    ripstart(prq) != OK)
                        continue;
                pn = prq->rq_cur;
                rn = prq->rq_nrts++;
                rp = &prq->rq_prip->rip_rts[rn];
                rp->rr_family = hs2net(AF_INET);
                rp->rr_mbz = 0;
                netnum(net, prt->rt_net);
                bzero(rp->rr_addr, sizeof(rp->rr_addr));
                if (blkequ(nif[i].ni_net, net, IP_ALEN) ||
                    blkequ(prt->rt_mask, ip_maskall, IP_ALEN)) {
                        blkcopy(rp->rr_addr, prt->rt_net, IP_ALEN);
                } else   /* send the net part only (esp. for subnets)    */
                        blkcopy(rp->rr_addr, net, IP_ALEN);
                rp->rr_metric = hl2net(metric);
                prq->rq_len[pn] += sizeof(struct riprt);
        }
        return OK;
}
```

Given a route as an argument, *ripadd* iterates through the set of network interfaces and examines whether the route should be added to each. If the RIP entry that corresponds to the interface is active and the interface is "up," *ripadd* proceeds to add the route. It calls *ripmetric* to compute a metric. It allocates space in the message being constructed, and calls *ripstart* to allocate another datagram if the current one is full. It fills in the route family and *must be zero* field for the route.

Ripadd compares the destination address of the route to the IP address of the interface over which it will be sent to determine the exact form of address to use. Normally, RIP masks off the subnet and host portions of a destination address and only propagates the network portion. However, it propagates subnet information *within* a subnetted network. Thus, if the interface over which the route should be sent lies on a subnet of the destination address, it propagates the subnet portion of the address along with the network portion. Once *ripadd* computes the correct IP address to advertise and the metric to use, it fills in the next entry in the message and continues iterating through the routes.

17.11.2 Computing A Metric To Advertise

Procedure *ripmetric* computes the metric that will be advertised along with a given route.

```
/* ripmetric.c - ripmetric */

#include <conf.h>
#include <kernel.h>
#include <network.h>

/*------------------------------------------------------------------------
 * ripmetric - compute the RIP metric for a route we advertise
 *------------------------------------------------------------------------
 */
int ripmetric(prt, ifnum)
struct   route   *prt;
int              ifnum;
{
        /* only advertise the net route for our interfaces */

        if (prt->rt_ifnum == NI_LOCAL &&
                        blkequ(prt->rt_mask, ip_maskall, IP_ALEN))
                return SYSERR;

        if (prt->rt_ifnum == ifnum)
                return RIP_INFINITY;    /* poison reverse */
        /* else, add one to our cost */
        return prt->rt_metric + 1;
}
```

Ripmetric implements poison reverse by changing the cost of a route to *infinity* if the route directs datagrams out over the interface on which the route is being advertised. In other cases it translates from the internal metric, which uses cost *0* for direct connections, to the standard RIP metric, which uses cost *1* to direct connections.

17.11.3 Allocating A Datagram For A RIP Message

As we have seen, *ripadd* collects routing advertisements into an update message, making a copy for each network interface. When it finds that it has filled a RIP message completely, *ripadd* calls *ripstart* to allocate a new datagram.

```
/* ripstart.c - ripstart */

#include <conf.h>
#include <kernel.h>
#include <network.h>

/*------------------------------------------------------------------------
 * ripstart - initialize an interface's RIP packet data
 *------------------------------------------------------------------------
 */
int ripstart(prq)
struct  rq      *prq;
{
        struct  ep      *pep;
        struct  ip      *pip;
        struct  udp     *pudp;
        struct  rip     *prip;
        int             pn;

        pn = ++prq->rq_cur;
        if (pn >= MAXNRIP)
                return SYSERR;
        prq->rq_nrts = 0;
        prq->rq_pep[pn] = pep = (struct ep *)getbuf(Net.netpool);
        if (pep == SYSERR)
                return SYSERR;
        pip = (struct ip *)pep->ep_data;
        pudp = (struct udp *)pip->ip_data;
        prip = (struct rip *)pudp->u_data;

        prq->rq_prip = prip;
        prq->rq_len[pn] = RIPHSIZE;
        prip->rip_cmd = RIP_RESPONSE;
```

```
        prip->rip_vers = RIP_VERSION;
        prip->rip_mbz = 0;
        return OK;
}
```

Ripstart takes a single argument that contains a pointer to an entry in the *rqinfo* array. It increments the index of the current datagram in that entry, allocates a buffer for another one, fills fields in the RIP header in the newly allocated buffer, and sets the *must be zero* field in the new datagram to zero.

17.12 Generating Periodic RIP Output

Gateways send RIP responses periodically. To do so, they create a process to execute procedure *ripout*. The output process enters an infinite loop that delays for *30* seconds, and then calls *ripsend* to generate an update on all interfaces. The code is written so that it allows triggered updates using message passing. If a message arrives during the delay, *ripout* aborts the delay and immediately sends the update.

```
/* ripout.c - ripout */

#include <conf.h>
#include <kernel.h>
#include <network.h>


/*------------------------------------------------------------------------
 *  ripout  -  do the RIP route exchange protocol, output side
 *------------------------------------------------------------------------
 */
PROCESS ripout (argc)
{
        int     rnd;

        rippid = getpid();
        dorip = TRUE;
        /* advertise our routes */

        rnd = 0;            /* "randomizer" */
        while (TRUE) {
                sleep10(RIPOUTMIN);       /* minimum time between each    */
                if (++rnd > RIPDELTA)
                        rnd = -RIPDELTA;
                recvtim(RIPINT-RIPOUTMIN+rnd);
```

```
        wait(riplock);
        ripsend(ip_maskall, UP_RIP);
        signal(riplock);
    }
}
```

Although the code seems trivial, it handles three small details. First, to prevent triggered updates from occurring until it has formed and sent one complete update, *ripout* waits on semaphore *riplock* before calling *ripsend*. Second, *ripout* imposes a minimum delay of *RIPOUTMIN* tenths of seconds between updates (even if they are triggered). To insure the minimum delay, it calls *sleep10* directly for *RIPOUTMIN* tenths of seconds before calling *recvitm* for the remaining time.

When computing the remaining time to delay for the call to *recvitm*, *ripout* starts with the standard RIP update period, subtracts the minimum delay that has already occurred, and finally adds a small "random" integer. The small random delay helps RIP avoid broadcast storms caused by triggered updates.

The code simulates random delay by keeping a global integer that it increments by *1* for each call. When the integer becomes larger than *RIPDELTA*, *ripout* sets it to negative *RIPDELTA* and continues.

17.13 Limitations Of RIP

The RIP design limits the environments in which it can be used. First, because RIP uses *16* for infinity, it cannot be used in an internet that has a diameter greater than *15*. Second, because RIP uses fixed values for the update period and timeout, it cannot be used in networks that have high loss. Third, because RIP uses fixed metrics when propagating routes, it cannot be used in internets that use dynamic measures to select routes (i.e., current delay or current load).

17.14 Summary

The Routing Information Protocol, RIP, uses a vector-distance algorithm to propagate routes. To maintain stability, RIP uses heuristics like split horizon, route timeout, and poison reverse.

We examined an implementation in which separate input and output processes handled RIP. The input process accepts a direct query, a response to a direct query, or a periodic response broadcast to all machines on the local network. The output process generates periodic broadcast of updates or triggered updates.

To trigger an update, any program can send a message directly to the output process. To prevent triggered updates from occurring as routes change, the RIP software uses semaphore *riplock*. The output process waits on the semaphore before compiling an update message.

FOR FURTHER STUDY

Hedrick [RFC 1058] defines the protocol and specifies the heuristics discussed in this chapter. It also gives algorithms for handling incoming requests and responses.

EXERCISES

17.1	Procedure *ripsend* allocates array *rqinfo* as an automatic, stack variable. What would happen if it allocated the array as a static, global variable instead?

17.2	Read the code carefully. How does it handle specific requests?

17.3	Consider the interaction between RIP and IP. Describe a design that separates the policy RIP uses to choose routes from the policy that IP uses to forward datagrams.

17.4	Can our RIP software propagate multiple default routes? Explain.

17.5	Suppose a network manager needed to restrict route propagation. How would you modify the code to allow the manager to specify routes that should not be propagated?

18

SNMP: MIB Variables, Representations, And Bindings

18.1 Introduction

The *Simple Network Management Protocol* (*SNMP*) helps network managers locate and correct problems in a TCP/IP internet. Managers invoke an *SNMP client* on their local computer (usually a workstation), and use the client to contact one or more *SNMP servers* that execute on remote machines (usually gateways). SNMP uses a fetch-store paradigm in which each server maintains a set of conceptual variables that include simple statistics, such as a count of packets received, as well as complex variables that correspond to TCP/IP data structures, such as the ARP cache and IP routing tables. SNMP messages either specify that the server should fetch values from variables or store values in variables, and the server translates the requests to equivalent operations on local data structures. Because the protocol does not include other operations, all control must be accomplished through the fetch-store paradigm. In addition to the SNMP protocol, a separate standard for a *Management Information Base* (*MIB*) defines the set of variables that SNMP servers maintain as well as the semantics of each variable. MIB variables record the status of each connected network, traffic statistics, counts of errors encountered, and the current contents of internal data structures such as the machine's IP routing table.

SNMP defines both the syntax and meaning of the messages that clients and servers exchange. It uses *Abstract Syntax Notation One* (*ASN.1*) to specify both the format of messages and MIB variable names†. Thus, unlike most other TCP/IP protocols, SNMP messages do not have fixed fields and cannot be defined with fixed structures.

---

†ASN.1 names are known as *object identifiers*.

This chapter describes the overall organization of SNMP software. It discusses the set of MIB variables and their ASN.1 names, and shows how a server binds ASN.1 names to corresponding internal variables. It considers the operations that SNMP allows, and shows why a server must maintain the lexical ordering among the ASN.1 names it supports. Later chapters consider how a client generates requests and how a server handles them.

18.2 Server Organization And Name Mapping

An SNMP server must accept an incoming request, perform the specified operation, and return a response. Understanding the basics of how servers process messages is important because it helps explain the mapping software shown throughout the remainder of this chapter. Figure 18.1 illustrates the flow of a message through an SNMP server.

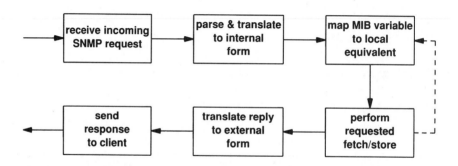

Figure 18.1 The flow of an SNMP message through a server. The server repeats the third and fourth steps for each variable the message specifies.

As Figure 18.1 shows, the server first parses the message and translates to internal form. It then maps the MIB variable specification to the local data item that stores the needed information and performs the fetch or store operation. For fetch operations, it replaces the data area in the SNMP message with the value that it fetches. If the message specifies multiple variables, the server iterates through the third and fourth steps for each one. Finally, once all operations have been performed, the server translates the reply from internal form to external form, and returns it to the server.

The next sections describe MIB variables and concentrate on the details of name mapping. Later chapters show the remaining server software.

18.3 MIB Variables

The MIB defines variables that an SNMP server must maintain. To be more precise, the MIB defines a set of *conceptual* variables that an SNMP server must be able to access. In many cases, it is possible to use conventional variables to store the items the MIB requires. However, in other cases, the internal data structures used by TCP/IP protocols may not exactly match the variables required by the MIB. In such cases, SNMP must be able to compute the necessary MIB values from available data structures. As an example of using computation in place of a variable, consider how a gateway might store the time a system has been operational. Many systems simply record the time at which the system started, and compute the time the system has been operating by subtracting the startup time from the current time. Thus, SNMP software can simulate a MIB "variable" that contains the time since last startup. It performs the computation whenever a request arrives to read a value from the MIB variable. To summarize:

> *The MIB defines conceptual variables that do not always correspond directly to the data structures a gateway uses. SNMP software may perform computation to simulate some of the conceptual variables, but the remote site will remain unaware of the computation.*

Broadly speaking, variables in the MIB can be partitioned into two classes: *simple variables* and *tables*. Simple variables include types such as signed or unsigned integers and character strings. They also include data aggregates that correspond to *structures* in programming languages like C or *records* in languages like Pascal. In general, a gateway maintains one instance of each simple variable (e.g., a single integer that counts the total number of datagrams that IP receives). Tables correspond to one-dimensional arrays; a single table can contain multiple instances of a variable. For example, the MIB defines a table that corresponds to the set of network interfaces connected to a machine; the table has one entry for each network interface. The MIB defines other conceptual tables that correspond to the IP routing table on the server's machine, the ARP cache, and the set of TCP connections.

While the size of simple variables is known a priori, the size of a table can change as time proceeds. For example, the size of the table that corresponds to the ARP cache varies from one moment to the next as old entries time out or as new entries are added. At any time, the MIB address translation table has one entry for each binding in the ARP cache. If the time-to-live expires on an ARP binding, the cache management software removes it. The corresponding MIB table will contain one less entry.

18.3.1 Fields Within Tables

Each entry in a MIB table can have multiple fields, which may themselves be simple variables or tables. Thus, it is possible to define an elementary data aggregate such as an array of integers, or a more complicated one such as an array of pairs of address bindings.

18.4 MIB Variable Names

The MIB uses ASN.1 to name all variables. ASN.1 defines a hierarchical namespace, so the name of each variable reflects its position in the hierarchy. The point of the ASN.1 hierarchy is to carefully distribute *authority* to assign names to many organizations. The scheme guarantees that although many organizations assign names concurrently, the resulting names are guaranteed to be *unique* and *absolute*. For example, the hierarchy leading to MIB names starts with the *International Organization for Standardization (ISO)*. It follows through the *organization* subhierarchy, the United States *Department of Defense* subhierarchy, the *Internet* subhierarchy, the *management* subhierarchy, and the *MIB* subhierarchy. Each part of the hierarchy has been assigned a label, and a name is written as a sequence of labels that denote subhierarchies, with periods separating the labels. The label for the most significant hierarchy appears on the left. Thus, the MIB variable in the *ip* subhierarchy that counts incoming IP datagrams, *ipInReceives*, is named

$$iso.org.dod.internet.mgmt.mib.ip.ipInReceives$$

As the example shows, MIB names can be quite long. Of course, names for items in tables will be even longer than names for simple variables because they contain additional labels that encode the index of the table entry and the field desired in that entry.

18.4.1 Numeric Representation Of Names

When sending and receiving messages, SNMP does not store variable names as text strings. Instead, it uses a numeric form of ASN.1 to represent each name. Because the numeric representation is more compact than a textual representation, it saves space in packets.

The numeric form of ASN.1 assigns a unique (usually small) integer to each label in a name, and represents the name as a sequence of integers. For example, the sequence of numeric labels for the name of variable *ipInReceives* is

$$1.3.6.1.2.1.4.3$$

When they appear in an SNMP message, the numeric representation of simple variable names has a zero appended to specify that the name represents the only instance of that variable in the MIB, so the exact form becomes

$$1.3.6.1.2.1.4.3.0$$

18.5 Lexicographic Ordering Among Names

ASN.1 defines a *lexicographic ordering* among names that provides a fundamental part of the SNMP functionality. The lexical ordering allows clients to ask a server for the set of currently available variables, and to search a table without knowing its size.

The lexical ordering among names is similar to the ordering of words in a dictionary, and is defined using their numeric representations. If the numeric representations are identical, we say that the names are lexically equal. Otherwise, the ordering is determined by comparing the labels. If one of the two names is an exact prefix of the other, we say that the shorter one is lexically less than the longer one. If neither is a prefix of the other, and they are not identical, there must be at least one label that differs. Let n_1, n_2, n_3,... denote the numeric labels in name n and let m_1, m_2, m_3,... denote the numeric labels of m. Find the first label, i, for which n_i differs from m_i. If n_i is less than m_i, we say that n is lexically less than m. Otherwise, we say that m is lexically greater than n. To summarize:

> *Lexicographic ordering among names of MIB variables is defined using the numeric representation of ASN.1 object identifiers. Two names are lexically equal if they have identical representations. A name is lexically less than another if it is a prefix, or if it has a numerically lower value in the first label that differs.*

18.6 Prefix Removal

Because SNMP software only needs to handle MIB variables, and because all MIB variable names begin with the same prefix, the software can eliminate needless computation and save space by representing names internally with the common prefix removed. In particular, each name in a packet must begin with the sequence for MIB variables:

$$iso \, . \, org \, . \, dod \, . \, internet \, . \, mgmt \, . \, mib$$

or, numerically:

$$1 \, . \, 3 \, . \, 6 \, . \, 1 \, . \, 2 \, . \, 1$$

Once an SNMP server examines the prefix to insure that the name does indeed refer to a MIB variable, it can ignore the prefix and use only the remainder of the name internally. As we will see, doing so saves time and keeps internal representations smaller. Similarly, a client can save space by adding the common prefix when it is ready to send a message. We can summarize:

> *SNMP software improves performance by storing and manipulating*
> *suffixes of MIB names. It adds the common prefix before sending a*
> *name in a message to another machine, and removes the common pre-*
> *fix (after verifying it) when a message arrives.*

18.7 Operations Applied To MIB Variables

Before examining the data structures SNMP software uses to store information, it is important to consider how the server will use those data structures. A client can issue three basic commands to a server. Two of the commands are obvious and require a straightforward mapping. The client sends a *set-request* to assign a value to a variable. It sends a *get-request* to fetch the value currently stored in a variable. Before it can perform the request, the server must map the numerically encoded ASN.1 names found in the incoming request into the appropriate internal variables that store values for those names.

Clients can also issue a *get-next-request* command. Unlike *set-request* or *get-request* commands, a *get-next-request* does not specify the name of an item to retrieve. Instead, it specifies a name, and asks the server to respond with the name and value of the variable that occurs *next* in the lexical sequence. The server finds the next variable with a name lexically greater than the specified name, and performs a *get-request* operation on that variable to obtain the value.

The *get-next-request* command is especially useful for accessing values in a table of unknown size. A client can continually issue *get-next-request* commands and have the server move through values in the table automatically. Each request specifies the name of the variable returned in the previous response, allowing the server to specify the name of the next item in its response. The process of stepping through entries one at a time is called *walking the table*.

18.8 Names For Tables

To facilitate use of the *get-next-request* command, some MIB names correspond to entire tables instead of individual items. These names do not have individual values, and clients cannot use them directly in *get-request* commands. However, the client can specify the name of a table in a *get-next-request* command to retrieve the first item in the table. For example, the MIB defines the name

$$iso.org.dod.internet.mgmt.mib.ip.ipAddrTable$$

to refer to a conceptual table of IP addresses by which the server's machine† is known. The numeric equivalent is

$$1.3.6.1.2.1.4.20$$

---

†The standard uses the term *entity agent* to refer to the machine on which a server executes.

A *get-request* command that uses a table name will fail because the name does not correspond to an individual item. However, the name is important because it allows clients to find the first item in a table without knowing the name of the previous MIB variable. The client issues a *get-next-request* using the table name to extract the first item in the table. It uses the name returned in the response, and then issues *get-next-request* commands to step through items in the table one at a time.

One final rule complicates the implementation of data structures that support *get-next-request* commands: a *get-next-request* always skips to the next simple variable in the lexicographic ordering. More important, the current contents of variables available at a given server determine the set of names that the server skips. In particular, a *get-next-request* command always skips an empty table. So, if a server's ARP cache happens to be empty when the client sends a *get-next-request* for it, the server will skip to the lexicographically next, possibly unrelated, variable. To summarize:

> *Servers only return the values of simple variables in response to a* get-next-request *command; they must skip empty tables when the request arrives.*

As a consequence, the server cannot simply use a lexically ordered list of MIB variables to determine which variable satisfies a *get-next-request* command. Instead, it must contain code that examines items in the lexical ordering, skips any that are empty, and finds the first simple variable in the next nonempty item.

18.9 Conceptual Threading Of The Name Hierarchy

If MIB variables are arranged in a hierarchy according to their ASN.1 names, they define a tree. The definition of *lexically next* can be thought of as a set of threads in the tree as Figure 18.2 illustrates.

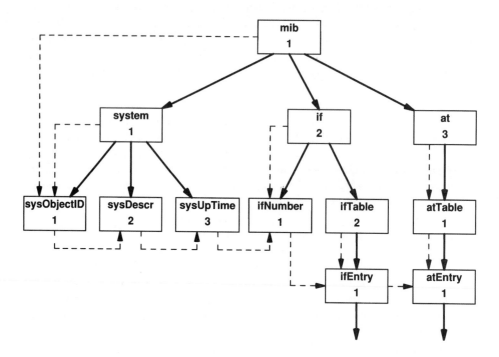

Figure 18.2 Part of the conceptual naming tree for MIB variables. Dashed lines show the set of threads in the tree that define the lexically next item. The lexical ordering skips nodes that correspond to tables.

18.10 Data Structure For MIB Variables

SNMP must keep information about each conceptual MIB variable. The implementation uses an array to store the information, where each item in the array corresponds to a single MIB variable. Structure *mib_info*, found in file *mib.h*, defines the contents of each item.

```
/* mib.h */

/* mib information structure: 1 per mib entry;  Initialized in snmib.c  */
struct mib_info {
        char    *mi_name;       /* name of mib variable in English    */
        char    *mi_prefix;     /* prefix in English (e.g., "tcp.")   */
        struct  oid mi_objid;   /* object identifier                  */
        int     mi_vartype;     /* type: integer, aggregate, octet str */
```

```
        Bool    mi_writable;    /* is this variable writable?            */
        Bool    mi_varleaf;     /* is this a leaf with a single value    */
        int     (*mi_func)();   /* function to implement get/set/getnext*/
        int     mi_param;       /* parameter used with function          */
        struct  mib_info *mi_next; /* pointer to next var. in lexi-order*/
};

extern  struct mib_info mib[];  /* array with one entry per MIB variable*/
extern  int mib_entries;        /* number of entries in mib array        */

/* Information about MIB tables.  Contains functions to implement        */
/* operations upon variables in the tables.                             */
struct tab_info {
        int     (*ti_get)();    /* get operation                         */
        int     (*ti_getf)();   /* get first operation                   */
        int     (*ti_getn)();   /* getnext operation                     */
        int     (*ti_set)();    /* set operation                         */
        int     (*ti_match)();  /* match operation: is a given oid       */
                                /*    found in the current table?        */
        struct  mib_info *ti_mip; /* pointer to mib information record   */
};

extern  struct tab_info tabtab[]; /* table of MIB table information      */

#define LEAF            1       /* This MIB variable is a leaf.          */
#define NLEAF           0       /* This MIB variable is not a leaf.      */

#define T_TCPTABLE      0x0     /* var is the TCP conn. table            */
#define T_RTTABLE       0x1     /* var is the routing table              */
#define T_AETABLE       0x2     /* var is the address entry tbl          */
#define T_ATTABLE       0x3     /* var is the addr translat tbl          */
#define T_IFTABLE       0x4     /* var is the interface table            */
/*#define T_EGPTABLE     0x5*/   /* var is the egp table                  */
#define T_AGGREGATE     0x6     /* var is an aggregate                   */

/* this type specifies in mib.c that the object is a table.  The value is
   different than any of the ASN.1 types that SNMP uses. */
#define T_TABLE                 01
```

Each item in the array contains sufficient information to identify a variable, including its ASN.1 name (object identifier), its type, and whether it is writable.

18.10.1 Using Separate Functions To Perform Operations

Most of the SNMP server data structures focus on providing efficient name mapping. When an ASN.1 name arrives in a request, the server must be able to recognize it, and call a procedure that will honor the request. Instead of trying to encode all information about how to satisfy a request, the implementation invokes a function. It passes the function three arguments: the request, a parameter (usually a memory address), and a pointer to the *mib* entry for the name. Field *mi_func* in structure *mib_info* contains the address of the function to call for a given variable.

Many of the functions needed to access variables are quite straightforward: they merely translate from the internal data representation to the ASN.1 format used in SNMP messages. For such cases, it is possible to encode the type of conversion and the address of the variable in the *mib* entry, and arrange to have a single procedure handle the conversion. However, if the server does not have an explicit representation available for a given MIB variable, requests to fetch or store a value from that variable may require more computation than merely converting representations. Certainly, requests to access items in conceptual MIB tables require computation to translate from the MIB name to the local data structures used to store the information. Finally, SNMP must provide a way to compute which item satisfies a *get-next-request* command. To keep the implementation uniform while providing sufficient generality to accommodate all requests, the implementation always uses a function to handle requests. We can summarize:

> *The amount of computation required to apply a given request to a given MIB variable depends on the variable and the request. Using a separate function to handle access requests keeps the implementation uniform, and allows the server to use a single mechanism to handle all requests.*

18.11 A Data Structure For Fast Lookup

As we will see later, array *mib* contains the bindings between ASN.1 names (object identifiers) and internal variables. If sequential search were used, finding an entry could be time consuming. To make name binding efficient, the software uses an auxiliary hash table as Figure 18.3 illustrates.

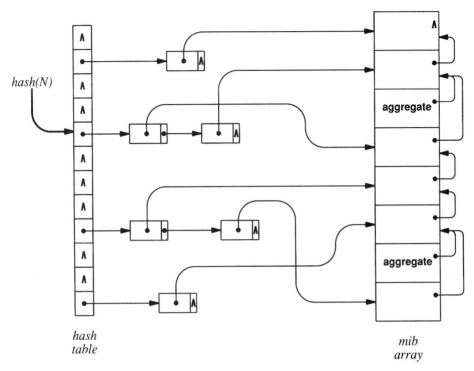

Figure 18.3 The *mib* array and hash table *snhtab* that speeds MIB variable
lookup. Arrows on the right hand side show lexical links used
for *get-next-requests*; the lexical order skips nonleaf items.

The technique used is known as *bucket hashing*. The hash table itself consists of
an array of pointers. Each pointer gives the address of a linked list of nodes that
represent the MIB variables that hash to that address. To find the information for a
MIB variable, the software computes the hash function using the numeric representation
of the variable name, selects a linked list from the hash table, and searches the list.
Each entry on the list contains a pointer to the MIB variable it represents as well as a
pointer to the next item on the list.

In practice, a simple hashing scheme works well. Of the 89† variables defined in
the MIB, hashing into an array of *101* positions produces lists with an average length
slightly greater than *1*. Thus, most lookups can be found immediately and do not require the software to search a linked list.

---

†Our example code specifies only *82* items because it does not include EGP variables.

18.12 Implementation Of The Hash Table

File *snhash.h* contains declarations of the hash table and nodes on the linked lists.

```
/* snhash.h */

struct snhnode {                        /* hash table node structure   */
        struct mib_info *sh_mip;        /* points to a mib record       */
        struct snhnode *sh_next;        /* next node in this hash bucket*/
};

#define S_HTABSIZ       101             /* hash table size - a prime #  */
#define S_HTRADIX       21              /* hash table radix             */

#define S_NUMTABS       5               /* number of table objects      */

extern  struct  snhnode *snhtab[];      /* the hash table               */
```

Structure *snhnode* defines the contents of a node on one of the linked lists. Each node only contains a pointer to an entry in the *mib* array and a pointer to the next node on the list.

18.13 Specification Of MIB Bindings

File *snmib.c* contains code that initializes the *mib* array to contain one entry per MIB variable. The entry contains all information about the MIB object, including the numerical representation of its ASN.1 name, the address of an internal variable that contains the value associated with the MIB variable, and the address of a function that can be called to perform SNMP operations on the variable. Note that the pointer to the next item in the lexicographically ordered list of variables is set to zero in each of these static declarations. Although the lexical pointers are not initialized in the declaration, all MIB objects must be specified in reverse lexicographic order. SNMP software will initialize the lexical pointers at system startup.

```
/* snmib.c */

#include <conf.h>
#include <kernel.h>
#include <network.h>
#include <snmp.h>
#include <mib.h>
```

```
#include <asn1.h>
#include <snmpvars.h>

extern int sntable(), snleaf();
extern struct oid SysObjectID;

/* All table and leaf variables that are found in the MIB */
struct mib_info mib[] = {
        { "system", "", { {1}, 1}, T_AGGREGATE,
            FALSE, NLEAF, 0, 0, 0},
        { "sysDescr", "system.", { {1, 1, 0}, 3}, ASN1_OCTSTR,
            FALSE, LEAF, snleaf, (int) &SysDescr, 0},
        { "sysObjectID", "system.", { {1, 2, 0}, 3}, ASN1_OBJID,
            FALSE, LEAF, snleaf, (int) &SysObjectID, 0},
        { "sysUpTime", "system.", { {1, 3, 0}, 3}, ASN1_TIMETICKS,
            FALSE, LEAF, snleaf, (int) &SysUpTime, 0},
        { "if", "", { {2}, 1}, T_AGGREGATE,
            FALSE, NLEAF, 0, 0, 0},
        { "ifNumber", "if.", { {2, 1, 0}, 3}, ASN1_INT,
            FALSE, LEAF, snleaf, (int) &IfNumber, 0},
        { "ifTable", "if.", { {2, 2}, 2}, T_AGGREGATE,
            TRUE, NLEAF, 0, 0, 0},
        { "ifEntry", "if.ifTable.", { {2, 2, 1}, 3}, T_TABLE,
            TRUE, NLEAF, sntable, (int) &tabtab[T_IFTABLE], 0},
        { "at", "", { {3}, 1}, T_AGGREGATE,
            TRUE, NLEAF, 0, 0, 0},
        { "atTable", "at.", { {3, 1}, 2}, T_AGGREGATE,
            TRUE, NLEAF, 0, 0, 0},
        { "atEntry", "at.atTable.", { {3, 1, 1}, 3}, T_TABLE,
            TRUE, NLEAF, sntable, (int) &tabtab[T_ATTABLE], 0},
        { "ip", "", { {4}, 1}, T_AGGREGATE,
            TRUE, NLEAF, 0, 0, 0},
        { "ipForwarding", "ip.", { {4, 1, 0}, 3}, ASN1_INT,
            FALSE, LEAF, snleaf, (int) &IpForwarding, 0},
        { "ipDefaultTTL", "ip.", { {4, 2, 0}, 3}, ASN1_INT,
            TRUE, LEAF, snleaf, (int) &IpDefaultTTL, 0},
        { "ipInReceives", "ip.", { {4, 3, 0}, 3}, ASN1_COUNTER,
            FALSE, LEAF, snleaf, (int) &IpInReceives, 0},
        { "ipInHdrErrors", "ip.", { {4, 4, 0}, 3}, ASN1_COUNTER,
            FALSE, LEAF, snleaf, (int) &IpInHdrErrors, 0},
        { "ipInAddrErrors", "ip.", { {4, 5, 0}, 3}, ASN1_COUNTER,
            FALSE, LEAF, snleaf, (int) &IpInAddrErrors, 0},
        { "ipForwDatagrams", "ip.", { {4, 6, 0}, 3}, ASN1_COUNTER,
```

```
        FALSE, LEAF, snleaf, (int) &IpForwDatagrams, 0},
{ "ipInUnknownProtos", "ip.", { {4, 7, 0}, 3}, ASN1_COUNTER,
        FALSE, LEAF, snleaf, (int) &IpInUnknownProtos, 0},
{ "ipInDiscards", "ip.", { {4, 8, 0}, 3}, ASN1_COUNTER,
        FALSE, LEAF, snleaf, (int) &IpInDiscards, 0},
{ "ipInDelivers", "ip.", { {4, 9, 0}, 3}, ASN1_COUNTER,
        FALSE, LEAF, snleaf, (int) &IpInDelivers, 0},
{ "ipOutRequests", "ip.", { {4, 10, 0}, 3}, ASN1_COUNTER,
        FALSE, LEAF, snleaf, (int) &IpOutRequests, 0},
{ "ipOutDiscards", "ip.", { {4, 11, 0}, 3}, ASN1_COUNTER,
        FALSE, LEAF, snleaf, (int) &IpOutDiscards, 0},
{ "ipOutNoRoutes", "ip.", { {4, 12, 0}, 3}, ASN1_COUNTER,
        FALSE, LEAF, snleaf, (int) &IpOutNoRoutes, 0},
{ "ipReasmTimeout", "ip.", { {4, 13, 0}, 3}, ASN1_INT,
        FALSE, LEAF, snleaf, (int) &IpReasmTimeout, 0},
{ "ipReasmReqds", "ip.", { {4, 14, 0}, 3}, ASN1_COUNTER,
        FALSE, LEAF, snleaf, (int) &IpReasmReqds, 0},
{ "ipReasmOKs", "ip.", { {4, 15, 0}, 3}, ASN1_COUNTER,
        FALSE, LEAF, snleaf, (int) &IpReasmOKs, 0},
{ "ipReasmFails", "ip.", { {4, 16, 0}, 3}, ASN1_COUNTER,
        FALSE, LEAF, snleaf, (int) &IpReasmFails, 0},
{ "ipFragOKs", "ip.", { {4, 17, 0}, 3}, ASN1_COUNTER,
        FALSE, LEAF, snleaf, (int) &IpFragOKs, 0},
{ "ipFragFails", "ip.", { {4, 18, 0}, 3}, ASN1_COUNTER,
        FALSE, LEAF, snleaf, (int) &IpFragFails, 0},
{ "ipFragCreates", "ip.", { {4, 19, 0}, 3}, ASN1_COUNTER,
        FALSE, LEAF, snleaf, (int) &IpFragCreates, 0},
{ "ipAddrTable", "ip.", { {4, 20}, 2}, T_AGGREGATE,
        FALSE, NLEAF, 0, 0, 0},
{ "ipAddrEntry", "ip.ipAddrTable.", { {4, 20, 1}, 3}, T_TABLE,
        FALSE, NLEAF, sntable, (int) &tabtab[T_AETABLE], 0},
{ "ipRoutingTable", "ip.", { {4, 21}, 2}, T_AGGREGATE,
        TRUE, NLEAF, 0, 0, 0},
{ "ipRouteEntry", "ip.ipRoutingTable.", { {4, 21, 1}, 3}, T_TABLE,
        TRUE, NLEAF, sntable, (int) &tabtab[T_RTTABLE], 0},
{ "icmp", "", { {5}, 1}, T_AGGREGATE,
        FALSE, NLEAF, 0, 0, 0},
{ "icmpInMsgs", "icmp.", { {5, 1, 0}, 3}, ASN1_COUNTER,
        FALSE, LEAF, snleaf, (int) &IcmpInMsgs, 0},
{ "icmpInErrors", "icmp.", { {5, 2, 0}, 3}, ASN1_COUNTER,
        FALSE, LEAF, snleaf, (int) &IcmpInErrors, 0},
{ "icmpInDestUnreachs", "icmp.", { {5, 3, 0}, 3}, ASN1_COUNTER,
        FALSE, LEAF, snleaf, (int) &IcmpInDestUnreachs, 0},
```

```
{ "icmpInTimeExcds", "icmp.", { {5, 4, 0}, 3}, ASN1_COUNTER,
      FALSE, LEAF, snleaf, (int) &IcmpInTimeExcds, 0},
{ "icmpInParmProbs", "icmp.", { {5, 5, 0}, 3}, ASN1_COUNTER,
      FALSE, LEAF, snleaf, (int) &IcmpInParmProbs, 0},
{ "icmpInSrcQuenchs", "icmp.", { {5, 6, 0}, 3}, ASN1_COUNTER,
      FALSE, LEAF, snleaf, (int) &IcmpInSrcQuenchs, 0},
{ "icmpInRedirects", "icmp.", { {5, 7, 0}, 3}, ASN1_COUNTER,
      FALSE, LEAF, snleaf, (int) &IcmpInRedirects, 0},
{ "icmpInEchos", "icmp.", { {5, 8, 0}, 3}, ASN1_COUNTER,
      FALSE, LEAF, snleaf, (int) &IcmpInEchos, 0},
{ "icmpInEchoReps", "icmp.", { {5, 9, 0}, 3}, ASN1_COUNTER,
      FALSE, LEAF, snleaf, (int) &IcmpInEchoReps, 0},
{ "icmpInTimestamps", "icmp.", { {5, 10, 0}, 3}, ASN1_COUNTER,
      FALSE, LEAF, snleaf, (int) &IcmpInTimestamps, 0},
{ "icmpInTimestampReps", "icmp.", { {5, 11, 0}, 3}, ASN1_COUNTER,
      FALSE, LEAF, snleaf, (int) &IcmpInTimestampReps, 0},
{ "icmpInAddrMasks", "icmp.", { {5, 12, 0}, 3}, ASN1_COUNTER,
      FALSE, LEAF, snleaf, (int) &IcmpInAddrMasks, 0},
{ "icmpInAddrMaskReps", "icmp.", { {5, 13, 0}, 3}, ASN1_COUNTER,
      FALSE, LEAF, snleaf, (int) &IcmpInAddrMaskReps, 0},
{ "icmpOutMsgs", "icmp.", { {5, 14, 0}, 3}, ASN1_COUNTER,
      FALSE, LEAF, snleaf, (int) &IcmpOutMsgs, 0},
{ "icmpOutErrors", "icmp.", { {5, 15, 0}, 3}, ASN1_COUNTER,
      FALSE, LEAF, snleaf, (int) &IcmpOutErrors, 0},
{ "icmpOutDestUnreachs", "icmp.", { {5, 16, 0}, 3}, ASN1_COUNTER,
      FALSE, LEAF, snleaf, (int) &IcmpOutDestUnreachs, 0},
{ "icmpOutTimeExcds", "icmp.", { {5, 17, 0}, 3}, ASN1_COUNTER,
      FALSE, LEAF, snleaf, (int) &IcmpOutTimeExcds, 0},
{ "icmpOutParmProbs", "icmp.", { {5, 18, 0}, 3}, ASN1_COUNTER,
      FALSE, LEAF, snleaf, (int) &IcmpOutParmProbs, 0},
{ "icmpOutSrcQuenchs", "icmp.", { {5, 19, 0}, 3}, ASN1_COUNTER,
      FALSE, LEAF, snleaf, (int) &IcmpOutSrcQuenchs, 0},
{ "icmpOutRedirects", "icmp.", { {5, 20, 0}, 3}, ASN1_COUNTER,
      FALSE, LEAF, snleaf, (int) &IcmpOutRedirects, 0},
{ "icmpOutEchos", "icmp.", { {5, 21, 0}, 3}, ASN1_COUNTER,
      FALSE, LEAF, snleaf, (int) &IcmpOutEchos, 0},
{ "icmpOutEchoReps", "icmp.", { {5, 22, 0}, 3}, ASN1_COUNTER,
      FALSE, LEAF, snleaf, (int) &IcmpOutEchoReps, 0},
{ "icmpOutTimestamps", "icmp.", { {5, 23, 0}, 3}, ASN1_COUNTER,
      FALSE, LEAF, snleaf, (int) &IcmpOutTimestamps, 0},
{ "icmpOutTimestampReps","icmp.", { {5, 24, 0}, 3}, ASN1_COUNTER,
      FALSE, LEAF, snleaf, (int) &IcmpOutTimestampReps, 0},
{ "icmpOutAddrMasks", "icmp.", { {5, 25, 0}, 3}, ASN1_COUNTER,
```

```
                FALSE, LEAF, snleaf, (int) &IcmpOutAddrMasks, 0},
        { "icmpOutAddrMaskReps", "icmp.", { {5, 26, 0}, 3}, ASN1_COUNTER,
                FALSE, LEAF, snleaf, (int) &IcmpOutAddrMaskReps, 0},
        { "tcp", "", { {6}, 1}, T_AGGREGATE,
                FALSE, NLEAF, 0, 0, 0},
        { "tcpRtoAlgorithm", "tcp.", { {6, 1, 0}, 3}, ASN1_INT,
                FALSE, LEAF, snleaf, (int) &TcpRtoAlgorithm, 0},
        { "tcpRtoMin", "tcp.", { {6, 2, 0}, 3}, ASN1_INT,
                FALSE, LEAF, snleaf, (int) &TcpRtoMin, 0},
        { "tcpRtoMax", "tcp.", { {6, 3, 0}, 3}, ASN1_INT,
                FALSE, LEAF, snleaf, (int) &TcpRtoMax, 0},
        { "tcpMaxConn", "tcp.", { {6, 4, 0}, 3}, ASN1_INT,
                FALSE, LEAF, snleaf, (int) &TcpMaxConn, 0},
        { "tcpActiveOpens", "tcp.", { {6, 5, 0}, 3}, ASN1_COUNTER,
                FALSE, LEAF, snleaf, (int) &TcpActiveOpens, 0},
        { "tcpPassiveOpens", "tcp.", { {6, 6, 0}, 3}, ASN1_COUNTER,
                FALSE, LEAF, snleaf, (int) &TcpPassiveOpens, 0},
        { "tcpAttemptFails", "tcp.", { {6, 7, 0}, 3}, ASN1_COUNTER,
                FALSE, LEAF, snleaf, (int) &TcpAttemptFails, 0},
        { "tcpEstabResets", "tcp.", { {6, 8, 0}, 3}, ASN1_COUNTER,
                FALSE, LEAF, snleaf, (int) &TcpEstabResets, 0},
        { "tcpCurrEstab", "tcp.", { {6, 9, 0}, 3}, ASN1_COUNTER,
                FALSE, LEAF, snleaf, (int) &TcpCurrEstab, 0},
        { "tcpInSegs", "tcp.", { {6, 10, 0}, 3}, ASN1_COUNTER,
                FALSE, LEAF, snleaf, (int) &TcpInSegs, 0},
        { "tcpOutSegs", "tcp.", { {6, 11, 0}, 3}, ASN1_COUNTER,
                FALSE, LEAF, snleaf, (int) &TcpOutSegs, 0},
        { "tcpRetransSegs", "tcp.", { {6, 12, 0}, 3}, ASN1_COUNTER,
                FALSE, LEAF, snleaf, (int) &TcpRetransSegs, 0},
        { "tcpConnTable", "tcp.", { {6, 13}, 2}, T_AGGREGATE,
                FALSE, NLEAF, 0, 0, 0},
        { "tcpConnEntry", "tcp.tcpConnTable.", { {6, 13, 1}, 3}, T_TABLE,
                FALSE, NLEAF, sntable, (int) &tabtab[T_TCPTABLE], 0},
        { "udp", "", { {7}, 1}, T_AGGREGATE,
                FALSE, NLEAF, 0, 0, 0},
        { "udpInDatagrams", "udp.", { {7, 1, 0}, 3}, ASN1_COUNTER,
                FALSE, LEAF, snleaf, (int) &UdpInDatagrams, 0},
        { "udpNoPorts", "udp.", { {7, 2, 0}, 3}, ASN1_COUNTER,
                FALSE, LEAF, snleaf, (int) &UdpNoPorts, 0},
        { "udpInErrors", "udp.", { {7, 3, 0}, 3}, ASN1_COUNTER,
                FALSE, LEAF, snleaf, (int) &UdpInErrors, 0},
        { "udpOutDatagrams", "udp.", { {7, 4, 0}, 3}, ASN1_COUNTER,
                FALSE, LEAF, snleaf, (int) &UdpOutDatagrams, 0}
```

```
};

int mib_entries = sizeof(mib) / sizeof(struct mib_info);

/* Funcs that implement get,getfirst,getnext,set, and match for tables  */
extern int
        stc_get(),      stc_getf(),     stc_getn(),     stc_set(),
        stc_match(),    srt_get(),      srt_getf(),     srt_getn(),
        srt_set(),      srt_match(),    sae_get(),      sae_getf(),
        sae_getn(),     sae_set(),      sae_match(),    sat_get(),
        sat_getf(),     sat_getn(),     sat_set(),      sat_match(),
        sif_get(),      sif_getf(),     sif_getn(),     sif_set(),
        sif_match();

struct tab_info tabtab[] = {
        { stc_get, stc_getf, stc_getn, stc_set, stc_match, 0, },
        { srt_get, srt_getf, srt_getn, srt_set, srt_match, 0, },
        { sae_get, sae_getf, sae_getn, sae_set, sae_match, 0, },
        { sat_get, sat_getf, sat_getn, sat_set, sat_match, 0, },
        { sif_get, sif_getf, sif_getn, sif_set, sif_match, 0 }
};
```

18.14 Internal Variables Used In Bindings

File *snmpvars.h* declares the types of internal variables used in MIB bindings.

```
/* snmpvars.h */


/* System & Interface MIB */


extern char      *SysDescr;
extern unsigned
        SysUpTime, IfNumber;


/* IP MIB */
extern unsigned
        IpForwarding, IpDefaultTTL, IpInReceives, IpInHdrErrors,
        IpInAddrErrors, IpForwDatagrams, IpInUnknownProtos, IpInDiscards,
        IpInDelivers, IpOutRequests, IpOutDiscards, IpOutNoRoutes,
        IpReasmTimeout, IpReasmReqds, IpReasmOKs, IpReasmFails, IpFragOKs,
        IpFragFails, IpFragCreates;


/* ICMP MIB */
extern unsigned
        IcmpInMsgs, IcmpInErrors, IcmpInDestUnreachs, IcmpInTimeExcds,
        IcmpInParmProbs, IcmpInSrcQuenchs, IcmpInRedirects, IcmpInEchos,
        IcmpInEchoReps, IcmpInTimestamps, IcmpInTimestampReps,
        IcmpInAddrMasks, IcmpInAddrMaskReps, IcmpOutMsgs, IcmpOutErrors,
        IcmpOutDestUnreachs, IcmpOutTimeExcds, IcmpOutParmProbs,
        IcmpOutSrcQuenchs, IcmpOutRedirects, IcmpOutEchos,
        IcmpOutEchoReps, IcmpOutTimestamps, IcmpOutTimestampReps,
        IcmpOutAddrMasks, IcmpOutAddrMaskReps;


/* UDP MIB */
extern unsigned
        UdpInDatagrams, UdpNoPorts, UdpInErrors, UdpOutDatagrams;


/* TCP MIB */
extern unsigned
        TcpRtoAlgorithm, TcpRtoMin, TcpRtoMax, TcpMaxConn, TcpActiveOpens,
        TcpPassiveOpens, TcpAttemptFails, TcpEstabResets, TcpCurrEstab,
        TcpInSegs, TcpOutSegs, TcpRetransSegs;
```

18.15 Hash Table Lookup

Function *getmib* uses the hash table to find the MIB entry that corresponds to a given name (object identifier). It calls function *hashoid* to compute the hash of the name. To form an integer value that represents the object id, *hashoid* treats the identifier as a sequence of digits in radix *S_HTRADIX*. It iterates through the object identifier, multiplying by the radix and adding a new "digit" at each step.

The source code for both *getmib* and *hashoid* can be found in file *snhash.c*, which also contains the hash table initialization procedure *hashinit*.

```c
/* snhash.c - getmib, hashoid, hashinit */

#include <conf.h>
#include <kernel.h>
#include <network.h>
#include <snmp.h>
#include <mib.h>
#include <snhash.h>

struct   snhnode *snhtab[S_HTABSIZ];

extern struct tab_info  tabtab[];

/*------------------------------------------------------------------------
 * getmib - find mib record for the given object id
 *------------------------------------------------------------------------
 */
struct mib_info *getmib(oip)
struct oid        *oip;
{
        struct snhnode  *hp;
        int             loc, i;

        loc = hashoid(oip);      /* try the regular hash table */
        for (hp = snhtab[loc]; hp; hp = hp->sh_next)
                if (oidequ(oip, &hp->sh_mip->mi_objid))
                        return hp->sh_mip;
        for (i = 0; i < S_NUMTABS; ++i)            /* try the table table */
                if (blkequ(tabtab[i].ti_mip->mi_objid.id, oip->id,
                    tabtab[i].ti_mip->mi_objid.len * 2))
                        return tabtab[i].ti_mip;
        return 0;
}

/*------------------------------------------------------------------------
 * hashoid - hash the object id
 *------------------------------------------------------------------------
 */
int hashoid(oip)
struct oid        *oip;
{
```

```
        register unsigned tot;
        register int     i;

        for (tot = 0, i = oip->len - 1; i >= 0; i--)
                tot = tot * S_HTRADIX + oip->id[i];
        return tot % S_HTABSIZ;
}


/*------------------------------------------------------------------
 * hashinit - initialize the hash table
 *------------------------------------------------------------------
 */
hashinit()
{
        int i;
        register struct snhnode **ht;
        register struct mib_info *mp;
        struct mib_info        *lastnodep;
        struct snhnode         *hp;
        int loc, tabtabct;

        /* clear the hash table */
        ht = snhtab;
        for (i = 0; i < S_HTABSIZ; i++)
                *ht++ = 0;
        lastnodep = 0;

        tabtabct = 0;
        for (i=0, mp = &mib[mib_entries - 1]; i<mib_entries; i++, mp--) {
                loc = hashoid(&mp->mi_objid);
                hp = (struct snhnode *) getmem(sizeof(struct snhnode));
                hp->sh_mip = mp;
                hp->sh_next = snhtab[loc];
                snhtab[loc] = hp;
                mp->mi_next = lastnodep;
                /* (node == table) ==> insert into array of tables */

                if (mp->mi_vartype == T_TABLE)
                        tabtab[tabtabct++].ti_mip = mp;
                if (mp->mi_varleaf || mp->mi_vartype == T_TABLE)
                        lastnodep = mp;
        }
}
```

18.16 SNMP Structures And Constants

File *snmp.h* contains the definitions of data structures and symbolic constants used throughout the code.

```
/* snmp.h - strequ, oidequ */


#define SNMPD            snmpd         /* SNMP server code          */
extern  int              SNMPD();      /* SNMP server daemon        */
#define SNMPSTK          8000          /* SNMP server stack size    */
#define SNMPPRI          20            /* SNMP server priority      */
#define SNMPDNAM         "snmpd"       /* SNMP server daemon name    */


#define SMAXOBJID        32            /* max # of sub object ids   */
#define OBJSUBIDTYPE     unsigned short /* type of sub object ids   */


/* strequ - return TRUE if strings x and y are the same            */
#define strequ(x,y)      (strcmp((x), (y)) == 0)


#define u_char           unsigned char


struct oid {                          /* object identifier         */
        OBJSUBIDTYPE     id[SMAXOBJID]; /* array of sub-identifiers  */
        int              len;         /* length of this object id   */
};


/*
 * oidequ - check if the lengths of the oid's are the same, then check
 *          the contents of the oid's
 */
#define oidequ(x,y)      ((x)->len == (y)->len && \
                         blkequ((x)->id, (y)->id, (y)->len * 2))

/* Structure that contains the value of an SNMP variable.          */
struct snval {
        unsigned char    sv_type;     /* variable type             */
        union {                       /* value of var is one of these */
                int      sv_int;      /* variable is one of: integer, */
                                      /* counter, gauge, timeticks  */
                struct {              /* variable is a (octet) string */
                        char *sv_str; /* string's contents         */
                        int sv_len;   /* string's length           */
                } sv_str;
```

```
            struct  oid sv_oid;        /* variable is an object id    */
            IPaddr  sv_ipaddr;         /* variable is an IP address   */
    } sv_val;
};


/* Functions to access parts of the above snval structure            */
#define SVTYPE(bl)        ((bl)->sb_val.sv_type)
#define SVINT(bl)         ((bl)->sb_val.sv_val.sv_int)
#define SVSTR(bl)         ((bl)->sb_val.sv_val.sv_str.sv_str)
#define SVSTRLEN(bl)      ((bl)->sb_val.sv_val.sv_str.sv_len)
#define SVOID(bl)         ((bl)->sb_val.sv_val.sv_oid.id)
#define SVOIDLEN(bl)      ((bl)->sb_val.sv_val.sv_oid.len)
#define SVIPADDR(bl)      ((bl)->sb_val.sv_val.sv_ipaddr)


/*
 * Each snblist node contains an SNMP binding in one of 2 forms: ASN.1
 * encoded form or internal form.  The bindings list is doubly-linked
 */
struct snbentry {
        struct  oid sb_oid;        /* object id in internal form   */
        struct  snval sb_val;      /* value of the object          */
        u_char  *sb_alstr;         /* ASN.1 string containing the  */
                                   /* object id and its value      */
        int     sb_alslen;         /* length of the ASN.1 string   */
        struct  snbentry *sb_next; /* next node in the bind list   */
        struct  snbentry *sb_prev; /* previous node in the list    */
};


/* Structure that holds a complete description of an SNMP request     */
struct req_desc {
        u_char  reqtype;           /* request type                  */
        u_char  reqid[10];         /* request identifier            */
        int     reqidlen;          /* length of the identifier      */
        u_char  err_stat;          /* error status                  */
        u_char  err_idx;           /* error index                   */
        int     err_stat_pos;      /* position of error status in   */
                                   /* the ASN.1 encoding            */
        int     err_idx_pos;       /* position of error index       */
        int     pdutype_pos;       /* position of pdu type          */
        struct  snbentry *bindlf;  /* front of bindings list        */
        struct  snbentry *bindle;  /* end of bindings list          */
};


#define SNMPMAXSZ      U_MAXLEN     /* max SNMP request size         */
```

```
#define SNMPPORT         161                /* SNMP server UDP port          */

/* SNMP error types                                                         */
#define SNMP_OK          0                  /* no error                      */
#define SERR_TOO_BIG     1                  /* reply would be too long       */
#define SERR_NO_SUCH     2                  /* no such object id exists       */
#define SERR_BAD_VALUE   3                  /* bad value in a set operation  */

#define SVERS_LEN        1                  /* SNMP version is 1 byte long   */
#define SVERSION         0                  /* current SNMP version          */

#define SCOMM_STR        "public"           /* SNMP community string         */

/* operations to be applied to an SNMP object                               */
#define SOP_GET          1                  /* get operation                 */
#define SOP_GETN         2                  /* getnext operation             */
#define SOP_GETF         3                  /* get first operation           */
#define SOP_SET          4                  /* set operation                 */

/* standard version and community string -- backwards */
static char SNVCBACK[] = {
        'c', 'i', 'l', 'b', 'u', 'p', 0x06, 0x04 /* ASN1_OCTSTR */,
        SVERSION, SVERS_LEN, 0x02 /* ASN1_INT */
};
#define SNVCLEN          sizeof(SNVCBACK) /* length of SNVCBACK              */

/* SNMP client return codes                                                 */
#define SCL_OK           0                  /* good response -- no errors    */
#define SCL_OPENF        1                  /* open fails                    */
#define SCL_WRITEF       2                  /* write fails                   */
#define SCL_NORESP       3                  /* no response from server       */
#define SCL_READF        4                  /* read fails                    */
#define SCL_BADRESP      5                  /* bad response                  */
#define SCL_BADREQ       6                  /* bad request                   */

/* Table specific constants                                                 */
#define SNUMF_AETAB      4                  /* 4 fields in an Addr Entry     */
#define SNUMF_ATTAB      3                  /* 3 fields in an Addr Transl. Entry */
#define SNUMF_IFTAB      21                 /* 21 fields in an Interface Entry */
#define SNUMF_RTTAB      10                 /* 10 fields in a Route Table Entry */
#define SNUMF_TCTAB      5                  /* 5 fields in a TCP Connection Entry */

#define SAE_OIDLEN       3                  /* all sae variables start with 4.20.1 */
#define SAT_OIDLEN       3                  /* all sat variables start with 3.1.1 */
```

```
#define SIF_OIDLEN        3        /* all sif variables start with 2.2.1    */
#define SRT_OIDLEN        3        /* all srt variables start with 4.21.1   */
#define STC_OIDLEN        3        /* all stc variables start with 6.13.1   */
```

ASN.1 defines the exact representation for all objects sent in an SNMP message, including variable names (object identifiers), integers, sequences, IP addresses, and SNMP commands. Usually, ASN.1 represents each object with a *type*, *length*, and *value*. The *type*, which specifies what kind of object follows, distinguishes between integers, commands, and counters. The *length* specifies the number of octets in the representation, and the *value* consists of the octets that comprise the object.

18.17 ASN.1 Representation Manipulation

File *asn1.h* contains definitions of symbolic constants used to specify ASN.1 types. Most are self-explanatory. The *sequence* type is used to denote a repetition of items (e.g., sequence of integers), and can be thought of as corresponding to an array in a programming language. The *NULL* type is used when no value is needed.

```
/* asn1.h - A1_SIGNED */

/* constants for parsing an SNMP packet, according to ASN.1               */

/* ASN.1 object types */
#define ASN1_SEQ               0x30     /* sequence object            */
#define ASN1_INT               0x02     /* integer                    */
#define ASN1_OCTSTR            0x04     /* octet string               */
#define ASN1_NULL              0x05     /* null                       */
#define ASN1_OBJID             0x06     /* object identifier          */
#define ASN1_IPADDR            0x40     /* ip address                 */
#define ASN1_COUNTER           0x41     /* counter                    */
#define ASN1_GAUGE             0x42     /* gauge                      */
#define ASN1_TIMETICKS         0x43     /* time ticks                 */

/* Protocol Data Unit types -- SNMP specific                              */
#define PDU_GET                0xA0     /* get request                */
#define PDU_GETN               0xA1     /* get-next request           */
#define PDU_RESP               0xA2     /* response                   */
#define PDU_SET                0xA3     /* set request                */
#define PDU_TRAP               0xA4     /* trap message               */

/* Constants used for conversion of objects to/from ASN.1 notation        */
#define CHAR_BITS        8                    /* number of bits per char   */
```

```
#define CHAR_HIBIT        0x80            /* octet with the high bit set  */
#define BYTE2_HIBIT       0x8000          /* 2 bytes with high bit set    */
#define BYTE3_HIBIT       0x800000        /* 3 bytes with high bit set    */
#define BYTE4_HIBIT       0x80000000      /* 4 bytes with high bit set    */

#define A1_SIGNED(x)      ((x) == ASN1_INT)

/* the standard MIB prefix - 1.3.6.1.2.1                                  */
extern char MIB_PREFIX[];

/* the standard MIB prefix is encoded by ASN.1 into 5 octets              */
#define MIB_PREF_SZ       5
```

18.17.1 Representation Of Length

ASN.1 uses two representations for the length field in an object specification as Figure 18.4 illustrates. If the object requires fewer than *128* octets, ASN.1 uses a short form in which a single octet encodes the object length. Because the 8-bit binary representations of values less than *128* have the high-order bit set to zero, programs use the high-order bit to check for the short form.

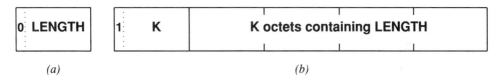

(a)   *(b)*

Figure 18.4 The ASN.1 encoding of object lengths. The short form in (a) is used to represent lengths less than *128*, while the long-form in (b) is used to represent longer lengths. The high-order bit of the first byte distinguishes the two forms.

In the long form, ASN.1 uses a multiple-octet integer to encode a length. The first octet has the high-order bit set (to specify long form), and contains an integer K in the low-order *7* bits ($K>1$). The next K octets contain a binary integer that specifies the length of the object that follows. Thus, to extract a long-form length, a program first reads the single-octet, finds K, and then reads a K-octet binary number. Function *alreadlen* performs the operation. Function *alwritelen*, found in the same file, creates the ASN.1 encoding of a length. It handles the short form by storing the length directly, and it handles the long form for integers that require either one or two octets (i.e., it only handles integers less than *65536*). Restricting an SNMP object to a length of less than *64K* is reasonable because a larger object could not fit into an IP datagram.

```c
/* alrwlen.c - alreadlen, alwritelen */

#include <conf.h>
#include <kernel.h>
#include <network.h>
#include <snmp.h>
#include <asn1.h>

/*------------------------------------------------------------------------
 * alreadlen - read and return the length of an ASN.1 encoded object
 *------------------------------------------------------------------------
 */
int alreadlen(pack, lenlen)
unsigned char   *pack;
int             *lenlen;        /* length of length specification */
{
        int     totlen;
        int     i;

        /* if the high bit is NOT set, then len is in short form */
        if (!((*pack) & CHAR_HIBIT)) {
                *lenlen = 1;
                return (*pack) & ~CHAR_HIBIT;   /* use only low bits */
        }
        /*
         * else, using long form where bit 7 = 1, and bits 6 - 0 encode
         * the number of subsequent octets that specify the length
         */
        *lenlen = (*pack++ & ~CHAR_HIBIT) + 1;

        for (i = 0, totlen = 0; i < (*lenlen) - 1; i++)
                totlen = (totlen << CHAR_BITS) | (int) *pack++;
        return totlen;
}


/*------------------------------------------------------------------------
 * alwritelen - write the length of an object in ASN.1 encoded form
 *------------------------------------------------------------------------
 */
int alwritelen(pp, len)                 /* return number of bytes required */
u_char  *pp;
int     len;
{
        /* if len < 128 then use short form */
        if (len < CHAR_HIBIT) {
```

```
            *pp = len;
            return 1;
    }
    /* use long form, where bit 7 = 1, and bits 6 - 0 encode the
            number of subsequent octets that specify the length */
    if (len <= 255) {
            *pp++ = CHAR_HIBIT | 1;
            *pp = len & 0xff;
            return 2;
    }
    /* else, assume len <= 65535 (2^16 - 1) */
    *pp++ = CHAR_HIBIT | 2;
    *pp++ = len >> CHAR_BITS;
    *pp = len & 0xff;
    return 3;
}
```

18.17.2 Converting Integers To ASN.1 Form

ASN.1 represents all values as variable-length fields. To encode an integer, one must find the number of significant (nonzero) bytes in it, and then copy that many bytes into the encoding. Functions *alreadint* and *alwriteint* perform the translation.

```c
/* a1rwint.c - a1readint, a1writeint */

#include <conf.h>
#include <kernel.h>
#include <network.h>
#include <snmp.h>
#include <asn1.h>

#define h2asn    blkcopy

/*------------------------------------------------------------------------
 * a1readint - convert an ASN.1 encoded integer into a machine integer
 *------------------------------------------------------------------------
 */
int a1readint(pack, len)
u_char  *pack;
int     len;
{
        register int    tot;
        u_char          neg;
        int             tlen;

        if ((tlen = len) > sizeof(int))
                return 0;
        tot = *pack & ~CHAR_HIBIT;
        neg = *pack & CHAR_HIBIT;
        for (tlen--, pack++ ; tlen > 0 ; tlen--, pack++)
                tot = (tot << CHAR_BITS) | (int) *pack;
        if (neg)
                tot -= (1 << ((len * CHAR_BITS) - 1));
        return tot;
}

/*------------------------------------------------------------------------
 * a1writeint - convert an integer into its ASN.1 encoded form
 *------------------------------------------------------------------------
 */
int a1writeint(val, buffp, a1type)
int     val;
u_char  *buffp;
int     a1type;
{
        unsigned        tmp, numbytes;
        register u_char *bp;
```

```
bp = buffp;
tmp = val;
if (A1_SIGNED(altype) && val < 0)
        tmp = -val;
if (tmp < (unsigned) CHAR_HIBIT)
        *bp++ = numbytes = (u_char) 1;
else if (tmp < (unsigned) BYTE2_HIBIT)
        *bp++ = numbytes = (u_char) 2;
else if (tmp < (unsigned) BYTE3_HIBIT)
        *bp++ = numbytes = (u_char) 3;
else if (tmp < (unsigned) BYTE4_HIBIT)
        *bp++ = numbytes = (u_char) 4;
else {  /* 5 bytes for unsigned with high bit set */
        *bp++ = (u_char) 5;      /* length */
        *bp++ = (u_char) 0;
        numbytes = 4;
}
h2asn(bp, ((char *) &val) + (sizeof(int) - numbytes), numbytes);
bp += numbytes;
return bp - buffp;
}
```

18.17.3 Converting Object Ids to ASN.1 Form

Internally, the software uses structure *oid* (defined in file *snmp.h*) to store an ASN.1 object id. Procedures *alreadoid* and *alwriteoid* convert from standard ASN.1 to the internal representation and vice versa.

```c
/* alrwoid.c - alreadoid, alwriteoid */

#include <conf.h>
#include <kernel.h>
#include <network.h>
#include <snmp.h>
#include <asn1.h>

char MIB_PREFIX[] = { 0x2b, 0x6, 0x1, 0x2, 0x1 };     /* 1.3.6.1.2.1 */

/*------------------------------------------------------------------------
 * alreadoid - convert an ASN.1 encoded object id into internal form
 *------------------------------------------------------------------------
 */
int alreadoid(pack, objidlen, objid)
unsigned char   *pack;
int             objidlen;
struct oid      *objid;
{
        int     val;
        u_char  *pp;

        objid->len = 0;
        pp = pack;

        /* verify the required 1.3.6.1.2.1 prefix */
        if (! blkequ(MIB_PREFIX, pp, MIB_PREF_SZ))
                return SYSERR;
        pp += MIB_PREF_SZ;

        for (; pp < pack + objidlen; objid->len++) {
                if (! (*pp & CHAR_HIBIT)) {
                        objid->id[objid->len] = *pp++;
                        continue;
                }
                /*
                 * using long form, where bits 6 - 0 of each
                 * octet are used; (bit 7 == 0) ==> last octet
                 */
                val = 0;
                do
                        val = (val << 7) | (int) (*pp & ~CHAR_HIBIT);
                while (*pp++ & CHAR_HIBIT);     /* high bit set */
                objid->id[objid->len] = val;
        }
        return OK;
}
```

```
/*-------------------------------------------------------------------------
 * alwriteoid - convert an object id into ASN.1 encoded form
 *-------------------------------------------------------------------------
 */
int alwriteoid(packp, oidp)
unsigned char   *packp;
struct oid      *oidp;
{
        register u_char *pp;
        int             i;
        u_char          *objidp, *lenp;

        pp = packp;
        lenp = pp++;    /* save location of objid len */
        objidp = pp;
        /* prepend the standard MIB prefix. */
        blkcopy(pp, MIB_PREFIX, MIB_PREF_SZ);
        pp += MIB_PREF_SZ;

        for (i=0; i < oidp->len; i++)
                if (oidp->id[i] < CHAR_HIBIT)    /* short form */
                        *pp++ = oidp->id[i];
                else {                               /* long form */
                        if (oidp->id[i] >= (u_short) (BYTE2_HIBIT >> 1))
                                *pp++ = (u_char) (oidp->id[i] >> 14) |
                                        CHAR_HIBIT;
                        *pp++ = (u_char) (oidp->id[i] >> 7) | CHAR_HIBIT;
                        *pp++ = (u_char) (oidp->id[i] & ~CHAR_HIBIT);
                }
        *lenp = pp - objidp;    /* assign the length of the objid */
        return pp - packp;
}
```

Because all object ids that the client and server manipulate begin with the same prefix, the software can improve efficiency by removing the prefix on input and adding the prefix on output. The ASN.1 representation makes prefix recognition difficult because it encodes the first two numeric labels of an object identifier in a single octet. Thus, the prefix:

$$1.3.6.1.2.1$$

is encoded into a 5-octet string that begins with *43*† (hexadecimal *0x2b*) followed by octets that contain *6*, *1*, *2*, and *1*.

---

†ASN.1 combines the first two subidentifiers, *a* and *b*, using the expression *a*40+b*.

If any label in the object id is greater than *127*†, ASN.1 uses an extended representation to store the value. Only *7* bits in each octet contain data; ASN.1 uses the high-order bit to mark the end of subidentifiers. Figure 18.5 illustrates the encoding.

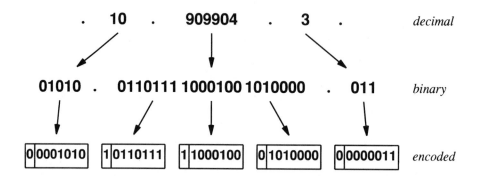

Figure 18.5 Part of an ASN.1 object identifier, shown in decimal, binary, and encoded form. The ASN.1 encoding uses multiple octets to encode integers greater than *127*. A zero in the high-order bit of an octet marks the end of a subidentifier.

18.17.4 A Generic Routine For Converting Values

Now that we have reviewed low-level routines that convert values between the internal representation and the ASN.1 representation used in SNMP messages, we can understand how they are used. Function *alreadval* takes an argument that specifies an ASN.1 object type as well as a pointer to a value. It uses the type to decide which conversion routine to use to translate the item from ASN.1 to internal form. A related routine, *alwriteval* performs the translation for output. Both routines use the functions described earlier in this chapter to perform the conversion.

```
/* alrwval.c - alreadval, alwriteval */

#include <conf.h>
#include <kernel.h>
#include <network.h>
#include <snmp.h>
#include <asn1.h>


/*-------------------------------------------------------------------
 * alreadval - convert object in ASN.1 encoded form into internal form
 *-------------------------------------------------------------------
 */
```

---

†None of the ASN.1 names permanently assigned to MIB variables currently has a numeric label greater than *127*. However, object identifiers for some tables do sometimes contain larger values.

```
int a1readval(val, type, vallen, pack)
struct snval    *val;
int             type;
int             vallen;
unsigned char   *pack;
{
        val->sv_type = type;

        switch (type) {
        case ASN1_INT:
        case ASN1_COUNTER:
        case ASN1_GAUGE:
        case ASN1_TIMETICKS:
                val->sv_val.sv_int = a1readint(pack, vallen);
                return OK;
        case ASN1_OCTSTR:
                val->sv_val.sv_str.sv_len = vallen;
                val->sv_val.sv_str.sv_str = (char *) pack;
                return OK;
        case ASN1_NULL:
                return OK;
        case ASN1_OBJID:
                return a1readoid(pack, vallen, &(val->sv_val.sv_oid));
        case ASN1_IPADDR:
                blkcopy(val->sv_val.sv_ipaddr, pack, vallen);
                return OK;
        default:
                return SYSERR;
        }
}


/*------------------------------------------------------------------------
 * a1writeval - convert the value of a variable into ASN.1 equivalent.
 *------------------------------------------------------------------------
 */
int a1writeval(bl, bp)                  /* Return number of bytes required. */
struct snbentry *bl;
u_char          *bp;
{
        u_char *origbp;

        origbp = bp;
        *bp++ = SVTYPE(bl);
```

```
        switch(SVTYPE(bl)) {
        case ASN1_INT:
        case ASN1_COUNTER:
        case ASN1_GAUGE:
        case ASN1_TIMETICKS:
                bp += alwriteint(SVINT(bl), bp, SVTYPE(bl));
                break;
        case ASN1_NULL:
                *bp++ = (u_char) 0;
                break;
        case ASN1_OCTSTR:
                bp += alwritelen(bp, SVSTRLEN(bl));
                blkcopy(bp, SVSTR(bl), SVSTRLEN(bl));
                bp += SVSTRLEN(bl);
                freemem(SVSTR(bl), SVSTRLEN(bl));
                break;
        case ASN1_IPADDR:
                *bp++ = IP_ALEN;
                blkcopy(bp, SVIPADDR(bl), IP_ALEN);
                bp += IP_ALEN;
                break;
        case ASN1_OBJID:
                bp += alwriteoid(bp, &bl->sb_val.sv_val.sv_oid);
                break;
        default:
                break;
        }

        return bp - origbp;
}
```

18.18 Summary

SNMP allows managers to interrogate or control gateways. A manager invokes client software that contacts one or more SNMP servers that operate on remote gateways. SNMP uses a fetch/store paradigm in which the server maintains a conceptual set of variables that map onto TCP/IP data structures in the gateway.

The Management Information Base (MIB) specifies a set of variables that gateways must maintain. SNMP uses ASN.1 syntax to represent messages, and ASN.1 object identifiers to name MIB variables. When a server receives a message, it must map the numeric representation of the ASN.1 variable names into local variables that store the corresponding values. Our implementation keeps an array of MIB variables, but uses a hash table to speed lookup. In addition, it uses pointers to maintain the lexical ordering among names needed for *get-next-request* operations.

We examined functions that convert values from the ASN.1 representation used in SNMP messages to the internal form used by the gateway. Although ASN.1 syntax is tedious, it is not difficult.

FOR FURTHER STUDY

Case, Fedor, Schoffstall, and Davin [RFC 1157] contains the standard for SNMP. ISO [May 87a] and [May 87b] contain the standard for ASN.1 and specify the encoding. McCloghrie and Rose [RFC 1156] specifies the MIB, while McCloghrie and Rose [RFC 1155] contains the SMI rules for naming MIB variables. Rose [RFC 1158] proposes a MIB-II for use with SNMP.

EXERCISES

18.1   Suppose the current set of MIB variables were numbered sequentially from *1* through *89* instead of assigned ASN.1 object identifiers. How much code could be eliminated?

18.2   Compare the ASN.1 hierarchical naming scheme to the numbering scheme suggested in the previous exercise. What are the advantages and disadvantages of each scheme?

18.3   What are the advantages and disadvantages of assigning pointers for the lexicographic ordering among MIB variables in the declarations in file *snmib.c*?

18.4   Consider macro *oidequ* defined in file *snmp.h*. Why does it check the object lengths explicitly?

18.5   Read the protocol specification to find out what the *community* field represents. Why does the server send and expect the value *public* in this field?

18.6   Read the standard to find out how the first two labels of an ASN.1 object identifier are encoded into a single octet. Why does ASN.1 specify such an encoding?

18.7   Explain why procedures like *alreadint* are inherently machine dependent. How might *alreadint* change for a different architecture?

19

SNMP: Client And Server

19.1 Introduction

The previous chapter described SNMP software, and showed data structures used to look up and bind ASN.1 names for MIB variables to variables on the local gateway. This chapter describes the implementation of an SNMP server, and shows how it parses messages. In addition, it examines an SNMP client that shares many of the utility procedures used by the server. The next chapter continues the discussion by concentrating on procedures that implement fetch and store operations for specific tables.

19.2 Data Representation In The Server

In principle, an SNMP server is simple. It consists of a single process that repeatedly waits for an incoming message, performs the specified operations, and returns the result. The most important part of the message consists of a sequence of *get, set*, and *get-next* requests†, along with the ASN.1 object identifier to which each should be applied. The server looks up each identifier in the sequence, and applies the specified operation to it.

In practice, many small details complicate the code. The message itself uses ASN.1 representation for all fields, so the server cannot use a fixed structure to describe the message format. Instead, it must step through the message, parsing each field as it goes. Furthermore, because each value is represented in ASN.1 format, the server must translate them to the appropriate internal form.

To simplify the procedures that implement individual fetch or store operations, our server uses the local machine's native encoding for values like integers. It parses each incoming message, and translates the fields from ASN.1 representation to an internal

---

†Throughout the remainder of the text, we will abbreviate *get-request*, *set-request*, and *get-next-request* to *get, set*, and *get-next*.

403

data structure. The server manipulates the internal form, and translates it back to the required ASN.1 representation before sending a reply. We can summarize:

> *To optimize performance, the SNMP server translates incoming mes-
> sages from ASN.1 representation to an internal, fixed-field form that
> stores most values using the native hardware representation. It per-
> forms operations using the internal representation, and translates
> back to the ASN.1 representation before sending a reply.*

19.3 Server Implementation

Procedure *snmpd* implements the main SNMP server algorithm. File *snmp.h*† contains declarations for the data structures it uses.

```
/* snmpd.c - snmpd */

#include <conf.h>
#include <kernel.h>
#include <network.h>
#include <snmp.h>
#include <asn1.h>


/*-------------------------------------------------------------------------
 * snmpd - open the SNMP port and handle incoming queries
 *-------------------------------------------------------------------------
 */
int snmpd()
{
        int             snmpdev, len;
        struct xgram    *query;
        struct req_desc rqd;

        sninit();
        query = (struct xgram *) getmem(sizeof (struct xgram));
        /* open the SNMP server port */
        if ((snmpdev = open(UDP, ANYFPORT, SNMPPORT)) == SYSERR)
                return SYSERR;
        while (TRUE) {
                /*
                 * In this mode, give read the size of xgram, it returns
                 * number of bytes of *data* in xgram.
                 */
                len = read(snmpdev, query, sizeof(struct xgram));
```

---

†See page 387 for a listing of *snmp.h*.

```
                    /* parse the packet into the request desc. structure */
                    if (snparse(&rqd, query->xg_data, len) == SYSERR) {
                            snfreebl(rqd.bindlf);
                            continue;
                    }
                    /* convert ASN.1 representations to internal forms */
                    if (sna2b(&rqd) == SYSERR) {
                            snfreebl(rqd.bindlf);
                            continue;
                    }
                    if (snrslv(&rqd) == SYSERR) {
                            query->xg_data[rqd.pdutype_pos] = PDU_RESP;
                            query->xg_data[rqd.err_stat_pos] = rqd.err_stat;
                            query->xg_data[rqd.err_idx_pos] = rqd.err_idx;
                            if (write(snmpdev, query, len) == SYSERR)
                                    return SYSERR;
                            snfreebl(rqd.bindlf);
                            continue;
                    }
                    len = mksnmp(&rqd, query->xg_data, PDU_RESP);
                    if (len == SYSERR) {
                            query->xg_data[rqd.pdutype_pos] = PDU_RESP;
                            query->xg_data[rqd.err_stat_pos] = rqd.err_stat;
                            query->xg_data[rqd.err_idx_pos] = rqd.err_idx;
                            if (write(snmpdev, query, len) == SYSERR)
                                    return SYSERR;
                            snfreebl(rqd.bindlf);
                            continue;
                    }
                    if (write(snmpdev, query, len) == SYSERR)
                            return SYSERR;
                    snfreebl(rqd.bindlf);
            }
    }
```

Snmpd begins by opening the UDP port SNMP uses (constant *SNMPPORT* in the code). It then enters an infinite loop in which it calls *read* to wait for the next incoming message. When a message arrives, *snmpd* calls *snparse* to parse and convert the message to its internal form, and store it in the request data structure (*req_desc*). In addition to extracting fields in the header, *snmpd* calls function *sna2b* to extract the sequence of object identifiers from the message and convert them into a linked list. Nodes on the list each correspond to one binding; they are defined by structure *snbentry* in file *snmp.h*. During the conversion, *sna2b* translates each ASN.1 object identifier to an internal representation.

Once it has converted the message and list of names to internal form, *snmpd* calls *snrslv* to resolve the query. Resolution consists of performing the specified *get*, *set*, or *get-next* operation for each identifier in the list. After completing the resolution, *snmpd* calls *mksnmp* to form a reply message, and *write* to send the reply to the client.

If an error prevents successful resolution, the server creates an error reply by storing an *error type code* and an *error index* in the message. The error type code gives the reason for the error, and the error index specifies the name in the query that caused the error.

Once the server finishes sending a reply, it calls *snfreebl* to free the linked list of names, and returns to the beginning of the main loop to await the next incoming message.

19.4 Parsing An SNMP Message

Function *snparse* decodes an SNMP message by extracting its fields. Because the ASN.1 representation allows each field to have a variable size, the task is tedious. The parser must move a pointer through all fields in the message, finding the field length and extracting the value.

```
/* snparse.c - snparse */

#include <conf.h>
#include <kernel.h>
#include <network.h>
#include <snmp.h>
#include <asn1.h>
/*------------------------------------------------------------------
 * snparse - convert the ASN.1-encoded SNMP packet into internal form
 *------------------------------------------------------------------
 */
int snparse(rqdp, snmppack, len)
struct req_desc *rqdp;
u_char          *snmppack;
int             len;
{
        struct snbentry *bl, *lastbl;
        register u_char *packp;
        int             totpacklen, commlen, pdulen, totbindlen, lenlen;
        int             varbindlen;
        u_char          *packendp;

        packp = snmppack;
        packendp = snmppack + len;
```

```
/* sequence operator and total packet length */
if (*packp++ != ASN1_SEQ ||
    (totpacklen = alreadlen(packp, &lenlen)) < 0)
        return SYSERR;
packp += lenlen;

/* verify total length, version, community */
if (packendp != packp + totpacklen ||
    *packp++ != ASN1_INT ||
    *packp++ != SVERS_LEN ||
    *packp++ != SVERSION ||
    *packp++ != ASN1_OCTSTR ||
    (commlen = alreadlen(packp, &lenlen)) < 0)
        return SYSERR;
packp += lenlen;
if (strncmp(packp, SCOMM_STR, commlen) != 0)
        return SYSERR;
packp += commlen;

/* PDU type and length */
if (*packp == PDU_TRAP)
        return SYSERR;
rqdp->pdutype_pos = packp - snmppack;
rqdp->reqtype = *packp++;
if ((pdulen = alreadlen(packp, &lenlen)) < 0)
        return SYSERR;
packp += lenlen;

/* verify PDU length */
if (packendp != packp + pdulen)
        return SYSERR;
/* request id */
if (*packp++ != ASN1_INT ||
    (rqdp->reqidlen = alreadlen(packp, .&lenlen)) < 0)
        return SYSERR;
packp += lenlen;
blkcopy(rqdp->reqid, packp, rqdp->reqidlen);
packp += rqdp->reqidlen;

/* error status */
if (*packp++ != ASN1_INT || *packp++ != 1)
        return SYSERR;
rqdp->err_stat = *packp;
```

```
        rqdp->err_stat_pos = packp++ - snmppack;


        /* error index */
        if (*packp++ != ASN1_INT || *packp++ != 1)
                return SYSERR;
        rqdp->err_idx = *packp;
        rqdp->err_idx_pos = packp++ - snmppack;


        /* sequence of variable bindings */
        if (*packp++ != ASN1_SEQ ||
            (totbindlen = a1readlen(packp, &lenlen)) < 0)
                return SYSERR;
        packp += lenlen;


        /* verify variable bindings length */
        if (packendp != packp + totbindlen)
                return SYSERR;
        /* build doubly-linked bindings list; fill in only sb_a1str's   */
        rqdp->bindlf = rqdp->bindle = (struct snbentry *) NULL;
        do {
                bl = (struct snbentry *) getmem(sizeof(struct snbentry));
                bl->sb_next = 0;
                bl->sb_prev = 0;
                if (rqdp->bindlf) {
                        lastbl->sb_next = bl;
                        bl->sb_prev = lastbl;
                        lastbl = bl;
                } else
                        lastbl = rqdp->bindlf = bl;
                bl->sb_a1str = packp;
                if (*packp++ != ASN1_SEQ ||
                    (varbindlen = a1readlen(packp, &lenlen)) < 0)
                        return SYSERR;
                packp += lenlen;
                bl->sb_a1slen = varbindlen;
                packp += varbindlen;
        } while (packp < packendp);
        /* check that the entire packet has now been parsed */
        if (packp != packendp)
                return SYSERR;
        rqdp->bindle = lastbl;
        return OK;
}
```

An SNMP message begins with a *sequence* operator and a total message length. If the length does not agree with the length of the datagram, *snparse* returns an error code. *Snparse* then verifies that the second field is an integer that contains the correct SNMP version number. The third field is known as a *community* field, and is used for authentication. Our implementation honors the community string *public*, which is the standard value for servers that do not require clients to authenticate themselves.

Snparse verifies that the fourth field does not specify a *trap* operation (i.e., that it is a *get*, *set*, or a *get-next* request). Servers, not clients, generate *trap* messages.

Snparse checks the fifth field to make sure it correctly specifies the length of the remaining message, and then extracts the request identification from the sixth field. It also verifies that the error status and error index in the seventh and eighth fields have not been set.

After checking the error status and index fields, *snparse* reaches a sequence of bindings. In both requests and responses, each binding consists of a pair. In a *get* request or *get-next* request, each binding specifies a variable name (ASN.1 object identifier) and the associated value *NULL*. In a response, the server replaces *NULL* values with the values requested by the client. In a *set* request, the bindings specify nonnull values for each name; the server assigns these values to the specified variables.

Snparse iterates through the sequence of bindings and allocates an *snbentry* node for each binding. Each node contains a pointer to the ASN.1 representation of the object identifier in the original message. The node is linked into the list that has a head and tail pointer in the message's *req_desc* structure as Figure 19.1 illustrates.

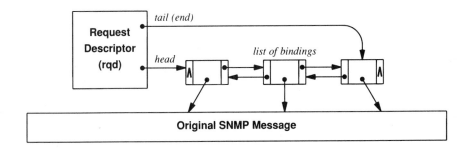

Figure 19.1 The data structure created by *snparse*. Each node on the binding
list corresponds to a MIB variable. The node points to an
ASN.1 object identifier found in the original message.

Once *snparse* finishes extracting the expected fields from the message, it verifies that no additional octets remain.

19.5 Converting ASN.1 Names In The Binding List

After *snparse* finishes extracting fields from an incoming message, structure *req_desc* contains the contents. To make the object names easier to access, the server calls function *sna2b* to convert object identifiers and values from the message into fixed-length internal representations. *Sna2b* iterates through the linked list of bindings, and parses the ASN.1 syntax for each. It calls *a1readoid* to extract the suffix of the object id and store it in field *sb_oid* of the node. It also extracts the associated value from the original message and stores it in field *sb_val*.

```
/* sna2b.c - sna2b */

#include <conf.h>
#include <kernel.h>
#include <network.h>
#include <snmp.h>
#include <asn1.h>


/*------------------------------------------------------------------------
 * sna2b - convert an ASN.1 encoded binding into internal form
 *------------------------------------------------------------------------
 */
int sna2b(rqdp)
struct req_desc *rqdp;
{
        register u_char *sp;
        struct snbentry *bl;
        int             lenlen, objidlen, vallen;
        u_char          type;

        for (bl = rqdp->bindlf; bl; bl = bl->sb_next) {
                sp = bl->sb_a1str;
                /* match the sequence operator and length of bindings */
                if (*sp++ != ASN1_SEQ || a1readlen(sp, &lenlen) < 0)
                        return SYSERR;
                sp += lenlen;
                /* object identifier type, length, objid */
                if (*sp++ != ASN1_OBJID ||
                    (objidlen = a1readlen(sp, &lenlen)) < 0)
                        return SYSERR;
                sp += lenlen;
                if (a1readoid(sp, objidlen, &bl->sb_oid) == SYSERR)
                        return SYSERR;
                sp += objidlen;
```

```
                    /* object's value */
                    type = *sp++;
                    if ((vallen = a1readlen(sp, &lenlen)) < 0)
                            return SYSERR;
                    sp += lenlen;
                    if (a1readval(&bl->sb_val, type, vallen, sp) == SYSERR)
                            return SYSERR;
                    sp += vallen;
                    bl->sb_a1slen = 0;
        }
        return OK;
}
```

19.6 Resolving A Query

Once an incoming message has been converted to internal form, the server calls
snrslv to resolve it.

```
/* snrslv.c - snrslv */

#include <conf.h>
#include <kernel.h>
#include <network.h>
#include <snmp.h>
#include <mib.h>
#include <asn1.h>

/* Set the error status and error index in a request descriptor. */
#define seterr(errval)          rqdp->err_stat = errval;        \
                                rqdp->err_idx = i;

/*-------------------------------------------------------------------
 * snrslv - resolve the list of specified variable bindings
 *-------------------------------------------------------------------
 */
snrslv(rqdp)
struct req_desc *rqdp;
{
        struct  snbentry *bl;
        struct  mib_info *np, *getmib();
        int     i, op, err;

        for (bl = rqdp->bindlf, i = 1; bl; bl = bl->sb_next, i++) {
```

```
        /* use getmib to look up object id */
        if ((np = getmib(&bl->sb_oid)) == 0) {
                seterr(SERR_NO_SUCH);
                return SYSERR;
        }
        /* call function to apply specified operation          */
        if (np->mi_func == 0) { /* objid is an aggregate        */
                /* only getnext allows nonexistent names        */
                if (rqdp->reqtype != PDU_GETN) {
                        seterr(SERR_NO_SUCH);
                        return SYSERR;
                }
                /* use getfirst for getnext on an aggregate */
                if (err = ((*np->mi_next->mi_func)
                        (bl, np->mi_next, SOP_GETF))) {
                        seterr(err);
                        return SYSERR;
                }
        } else { /* function in table ==> single item or table  */
                switch (rqdp->reqtype) {
                case PDU_GET:   op = SOP_GET;   break;
                case PDU_GETN:  op = SOP_GETN;  break;
                case PDU_SET:   op = SOP_SET;   break;
                }
                /* use getfirst for getnext on table entry        */
                if (oidequ(&bl->sb_oid, &np->mi_objid) &&
                    np->mi_vartype == T_TABLE) {
                        if (op == SOP_GETN)
                                op = SOP_GETF;
                }
                if (err = ((*np->mi_func)(bl, np, op))) {
                        seterr(err);
                        return SYSERR;
                }
        }
    }
    return OK;
}
```

Resolution consists of applying the operation specified in the request to each variable on the binding list. Thus, *snrslv* iterates through the binding list. It calls *getmib* to look up each object identifier in the *mib* array. If no match can be found, *snrslv* returns an error.

Once it has found an entry for the object, *snrslv* examines field *mi_func* in the entry. If the field contains *NULL*, the entry corresponds to an aggregate instead of a variable. Because aggregate names can only be used in *get-next* requests, *snrslv* returns an error unless the requested operation is *get-next*. If field *mi_func* does not contain *NULL*, it contains the address of a function that interprets operations for the variable.

19.7 Interpreting The Get-Next Operation

In the case of a *get-next* request, *snrslv* changes the operation to *get-first*, and applies it to the lexically next item in the MIB. *Get-first* is part of the implementation, and not part of the SNMP protocol. To understand why *get-first* arises, consider the semantics of *get-next* carefully. When *get-next* specifies an object identifier, the server must apply the request to the MIB variable that lexically follows the specified name. If the server follows the lexical pointer in the MIB table to find the next name, and then attempts to apply *get-next* to the new item, an infinite iteration results. On the other hand, if the server looks up the identifier, follows the lexical pointer to the next item, and applies the *get* operation, the operation will fail if the lexically next item corresponds to an empty table instead of a simple variable. Thus, the server must follow lexical pointers until it finds a simple variable. The example code uses the *get-first* operation to do exactly that. When applied to a simple variable, *get-first* is the same as *get*. When applied to an aggregate, however, *get-first* is the same as *get-next*. To summarize:

> *The* get-first *operation accommodates* get-next *requests for an arbitrary lexical ordering of MIB items by finding the next variable in the lexical order to which the* get *operation applies. It then applies the* get *request to that item.*

To understand how *snrslv* uses *get-first*, study the code again. If the specified name corresponds to an aggregate, *snrslv* finds field *mi_func* empty, so it applies *get-first* to the lexically next item on the list. If it finds a table (*mi_vartype* contains *T_TABLE*), *snrslv* changes a *get-next* operation into a *get-first* before calling the function that implements operations.

19.8 Indirect Application Of Operations

We have seen that *snrslv* consults the *mib* array to determine which function to call to apply an operation to a given variable. It passes an operation code, a pointer to the node on the binding list, and a pointer to the *mib* entry that corresponds to the variable. The purpose of using indirection is to avoid the duplication that results from building separate functions for each MIB variable. Instead, a few functions contain all the code needed for error checking and common operations. For example, function *snleaf* handles operations on simple variables.

```
/* snleaf.c - snleaf */

#include <conf.h>
#include <kernel.h>
#include <network.h>
#include <snmp.h>
#include <mib.h>
#include <asn1.h>


/*------------------------------------------------------------------------
 * snleaf - perform the requested operation on the leaf SNMP variable
 *------------------------------------------------------------------------
 */
int snleaf(bindl, mip, op)
struct snbentry *bindl;
struct mib_info *mip;
int             op;
{
        int             len;
        char            *strp;
        struct oid      *oip;

        if (op == SOP_GETN) {
                if (mip->mi_next)
                        return((*mip->mi_next->mi_func)
                                (bindl, mip->mi_next, SOP_GETF));
                return SERR_NO_SUCH;
        }
        if (op == SOP_SET) {
                if (! mip->mi_writable)
                        return SERR_NO_SUCH;
                switch(mip->mi_vartype) {
                case ASN1_INT:
                        if (SVTYPE(bindl) != ASN1_INT)
                                return SERR_BAD_VALUE;
                        if (mip->mi_param == 0)
                                return SERR_NO_SUCH;
                        *((int *) mip->mi_param) = SVINT(bindl);
                        break;
                case ASN1_OCTSTR:
                        if (SVTYPE(bindl) != ASN1_OCTSTR)
                                return SERR_BAD_VALUE;
                        blkcopy(strp, SVSTR(bindl), SVSTRLEN(bindl));
                        *(strp + SVSTRLEN(bindl)) = '\0';
                        break;
```

```
                case ASN1_OBJID:
                        if (SVTYPE(bindl) != ASN1_OBJID)
                                return SERR_BAD_VALUE;
                        oip->len = SVSTRLEN(bindl);
                        blkcopy(oip->id, SVSTR(bindl), oip->len * 2);
                        break;
                }
                return SNMP_OK;
        }
        if (op == SOP_GETF) {
                /* put the correct objid into the binding list. */
                bindl->sb_oid.len = mip->mi_objid.len;
                blkcopy(bindl->sb_oid.id, mip->mi_objid.id,
                        mip->mi_objid.len * 2);
        }
        SVTYPE(bindl) = mip->mi_vartype;

        switch(mip->mi_vartype) {
        case ASN1_INT:
        case ASN1_TIMETICKS:
        case ASN1_GAUGE:
        case ASN1_COUNTER:
                SVINT(bindl) = *((int *) mip->mi_param);
                break;
        case ASN1_OCTSTR:
                strp = *(char **) mip->mi_param;
                if (strp == NULL) {
                        SVSTRLEN(bindl) = 0;
                        SVSTR(bindl) = NULL;
                        break;
                }
                len = SVSTRLEN(bindl) = strlen(strp);
                SVSTR(bindl) = (char *) getmem(len);
                blkcopy(SVSTR(bindl), strp, len);
                break;
        case ASN1_OBJID:
                oip = (struct oid *) mip->mi_param;
                SVOIDLEN(bindl) = oip->len;
                blkcopy(SVOID(bindl), oip->id, oip->len * 2);
                break;
        }
        return SNMP_OK;
}
```

Snleaf tests the operation argument to choose an action. It handles *get-next* operations by invoking *get-first* on the succeeding item in the lexical order. It handles *set* operations by storing the value from the binding list node in the appropriate variable in memory (field *mi_param* in the *mib* table specifies the memory address). It handles *get* (and *get-first*) requests by copying the value from the appropriate variable in memory into the binding list node.

19.9 Indirection For Tables

In the *mib* array, entries that correspond to tables use field *mi_param* to store a pointer to the table's *tabtab* entry. The *tabtab* entry for a given table contains pointers to functions that implement each of the SNMP operations on that table. Thus, procedure *sntable* uses the *tabtab* entry and the specified operation to choose and invoke a function that implements that operation on a specific table.

```
/* sntable.c - sntable */

#include <conf.h>
#include <kernel.h>
#include <network.h>
#include <snmp.h>
#include <mib.h>


/*------------------------------------------------------------------------
 * sntable - call function to operate on a table-embedded variable
 *------------------------------------------------------------------------
 */
int sntable(bindl, mip, op)
struct snbentry *bindl;
struct mib_info *mip;
int             op;
{
        int     numifaces = Net.nif - 1;

        /*
         * mip->mi_param holds a pointer to an entry in tabtab that
         * contains the pointers to functions for each table
         */
        switch (op) {
        case SOP_GET:
                return (*mip->mi_param->ti_get)(bindl, numifaces);
        case SOP_GETF:
                return (*mip->mi_param->ti_getf)(bindl, mip, numifaces);
```

```
      case SOP_SET:
              return (*mip->mi_param->ti_set)(bindl, mip, numifaces);
      case SOP_GETN:
              return (*mip->mi_param->ti_getn)(bindl, mip, numifaces);
      }
      return SYSERR;
}
```

19.10 Generating A Reply Message Backward

Once the server has resolved the entries in a request, it creates a reply and sends the reply back to the client. Reply messages have the same format as request messages, with each field using an ASN.1 representation. The representation requires the header to contain the message length, which cannot be known until the representation of each field has been computed. Furthermore, because the size of the message length field itself depends on the size of the remainder of the message, it is impossible to know how much space to skip for the length field when constructing the message.

To simplify message construction, our code avoids the problem of unknown lengths by building the message backward. It generates fields in reverse order, and within fields, it generates octets in reverse order. Thus, once the entire message has been generated, it is simply reversed for transmission. To summarize:

> *The ASN.1 representation makes message generation difficult because all fields, including message length fields, use a variable-size format. To simplify construction, the message is generated backward and reversed before transmission.*

Procedure *mksnmp* handles creation of both request messages and response messages, and both the client and server invoke it.

```
/* mksnmp.c - mksnmp */

#include <conf.h>
#include <kernel.h>
#include <sleep.h>
#include <network.h>
#include <snmp.h>
#include <asn1.h>


#define SNMAXHLEN         32        /* length of a "maximum" SNMP header    */

u_char  snmpbuff[SNMPMAXSZ];        /* global scratch buffer                */

/*------------------------------------------------------------------------
 * mksnmp - make an snmp packet and return its length
 *------------------------------------------------------------------------
 */
int mksnmp(rqdp, snmppack, pdutype)
struct req_desc *rqdp;
u_char          *snmppack;
u_char           pdutype;
{
        register u_char      *pp, *cp;
        struct   snbentry    *bl;
        u_char               tmpbuff[40];
        int                  len, mtu, estlen;

        pp = snmpbuff;
        if (rqdp->reqidlen == 0) {  /* if id len == 0, get new reqid    */
                blkcopy(rqdp->reqid, (char *) &clktime, sizeof(clktime));
                rqdp->reqidlen = sizeof(clktime);
        }
        snb2a(rqdp);     /* convert bindings to ASN.1 notation           */

        /* check total length of the packet to be created               */
        mtu = IP_MAXLEN;

        /* add up total length of ASN.1 representations of variables     */
        for (estlen=0, bl=rqdp->bindlf; estlen<mtu && bl; bl=bl->sb_next)
                estlen += bl->sb_a1slen;
        /*
         * if too long, or if adding the header makes it too long,
         * set error status to tooBig and return
         */
```

```
        if (bl || (estlen + SNMAXHLEN >= mtu)) {
                rqdp->err_stat = SERR_TOO_BIG;
                rqdp->err_idx = 0;
                return SYSERR;
        }
        /* go backwards through snbentry, writing out the bindings    */
        for (bl=rqdp->bindle; bl; bl=bl->sb_prev) {
                cp = &bl->sb_alstr[bl->sb_alslen-1];
                while (cp >= bl->sb_alstr)
                        *pp++ = *cp--;
        }
        /* write the length of the bindings and an ASN1_SEQ type      */
        len = alwritelen(tmpbuff, pp - snmpbuff);
        for (cp = &tmpbuff[len-1]; cp >= tmpbuff; )
                *pp++ = *cp--;
        *pp++ = ASN1_SEQ;

        /* write the error index and error status -- 1 byte integers */
        *pp++ = (u_char) rqdp->err_idx;
        *pp++ = (u_char) 1;
        *pp++ = ASN1_INT;
        *pp++ = (u_char) rqdp->err_stat;
        *pp++ = (u_char) 1;
        *pp++ = ASN1_INT;

        /* write the request id, its length, and its type */
        for (cp = &rqdp->reqid[rqdp->reqidlen-1]; cp >= rqdp->reqid; )
                *pp++ = *cp--;
        *pp++ = rqdp->reqidlen;
        *pp++ = ASN1_INT;

        /* write the packet length and pdutype */
        len = alwritelen(tmpbuff, pp - snmpbuff);
        for (cp = &tmpbuff[len-1]; cp >= tmpbuff; )
                *pp++ = *cp--;
        *pp++ = pdutype;

        /* write the community and the version */
        blkcopy(pp, SNVCBACK, SNVCLEN);
        pp += SNVCLEN;

        /* write the total packet length */
        len = alwritelen(tmpbuff, pp - snmpbuff);
        for (cp = &tmpbuff[len-1]; cp >= tmpbuff; )
```

```
              *pp++ = *cp--;
         *pp++ = ASN1_SEQ;

         /* reverse the entire finished packet */
         for (--pp, cp = snmppack; pp >= snmpbuff; )
                 *cp++ = *pp--;
         return cp - snmppack;
}
```

Mksnmp begins by checking the *request id* field (*reqid*). In a response, the id will contain whatever value the client sent in the request. For a request generated by a client, the id field will be zero, so *mksnmp* uses the current time of day as a unique id.

After checking the request id, *mksnmp* calls *snb2a* to convert all object identifiers in the binding list to ASN.1 form. It then adds the resulting lengths and an estimate of the message header size to obtain an estimate of the total message length. If the estimate exceeds the maximum UDP datagram buffer size, *mksnmp* returns an error.

The formation of an outbound message parallels the recognition of an incoming message. *Mksnmp* takes fixed fields from structure *req_desc*, and converts each to its ASN.1 representation. Finally, it reverses the message.

19.11 Converting From Internal Form to ASN.1

Procedure *snb2a* provides the inverse of *sna2b*; it converts an object identifier from internal form to its ASN.1 representation.

```
/* snb2a.c - snb2a */

#include <conf.h>
#include <kernel.h>
#include <network.h>
#include <snmp.h>
#include <asn1.h>

extern u_char snmpbuff[];

/*------------------------------------------------------------------------
 * snb2a - convert the list of bindings from internal form into ASN.1
 *------------------------------------------------------------------------
 */
int snb2a(rqdp)
struct req_desc *rqdp;
```

```
{
        register u_char *bp;
        int              len;
        struct snbentry *bl;
        u_char           *ap;

        for (bl = rqdp->bindlf; bl; bl = bl->sb_next) {
                bp = snmpbuff;   /* used for temporary working space */
                *bp++ = ASN1_OBJID;
                bp += alwriteoid(bp, &bl->sb_oid);
                bp += alwriteval(bl, bp);
                /*
                 * We need to allocate bytes in sb_alstr but can't do it
                 * until we know how many bytes it takes to write the
                 * length of the binding,  so we write that length into
                 * snmpbuff at the end of the binding. Then we can alloc
                 * space, and transfer the data.
                 */
                len = alwritelen(bp, bp - snmpbuff);
                bl->sb_alslen = bp - snmpbuff + len + 1;
                ap = bl->sb_alstr = (u_char *) getmem(bl->sb_alslen);
                *ap++ = ASN1_SEQ;
                blkcopy(ap, bp, len);   /* write in the length spec.     */
                ap += len;
                blkcopy(ap, snmpbuff, bp - snmpbuff);
        }
}
```

19.12 Utility Functions Used By The Server

The server invokes utility procedure *snfreebl* to free the linked list of bindings after it sends a reply back to the client that issued a request.

```
/* snfreebl.c - snfreebl */

#include <conf.h>
#include <kernel.h>
#include <network.h>
#include <snmp.h>


/*------------------------------------------------------------------------
 * snfreebl - free memory used for ASN.1 strings and snbentry nodes
 *------------------------------------------------------------------------
 */
snfreebl(bl)
struct snbentry *bl;
{
        register struct snbentry        *pbl;

        if (bl == 0)
                return;
        for (pbl = bl, bl = bl->sb_next; bl; pbl = bl, bl = bl->sb_next) {
                freemem(pbl->sb_a1str, pbl->sb_a1slen);
                freemem(pbl, sizeof(struct snbentry));
        }
        freemem(pbl->sb_a1str, pbl->sb_a1slen);
        freemem(pbl, sizeof(struct snbentry));
}
```

Given a pointer to the binding list, *snfreebl* moves along it and deallocates both the memory used to hold the ASN.1 form of the binding and the node itself.

19.13 Implementation Of An SNMP Client

An SNMP client must generate and send a request to a server, wait for a response, and verify that the response matches the request. Procedure *snclient* performs the client function. It accepts as an argument the address of a request descriptor that contains the information in the message, including the desired operation and a list of bindings to which the operation should be applied. It calls *mksnmp* to generate a message in ASN.1 representation, *open* to open a descriptor that can be used to send datagrams, and *write* to send the message.

```
/* snclient.c - snclient */

#include <conf.h>
#include <kernel.h>
#include <network.h>
#include <snmp.h>

/*------------------------------------------------------------------------
 * snclient - send an SNMP request and wait for the response
 *------------------------------------------------------------------------
 */
int snclient(rqdp, fport, stdout)
struct req_desc *rqdp;
char            *fport;
int             stdout;
{
        struct snbentry *bindl;
        u_char          buff[SNMPMAXSZ], reqidsave[10], reqidsavelen;
        int             snmpdev, len;

        rqdp->reqidlen = 0;
        rqdp->err_stat = 0;
        rqdp->err_idx = 0;

        if ((len = mksnmp(rqdp, buff, rqdp->reqtype)) == SYSERR)
            return SCL_BADREQ;
        blkcopy(reqidsave, rqdp->reqid, rqdp->reqidlen);
        reqidsavelen = rqdp->reqidlen;

        /* open the SNMP port and put into data mode */
        if ((snmpdev = open(UDP, fport, ANYLPORT)) == SYSERR ||
            control(snmpdev, DG_SETMODE, DG_DMODE | DG_TMODE) == SYSERR) {
                close(snmpdev);
                return SCL_OPENF;
        }
        if (write(snmpdev, buff, len) == SYSERR) {
                close(snmpdev);
                return SCL_WRITEF;
        }
        /* retry once, on timeout */
        if ((len = read(snmpdev, buff, SNMPMAXSZ)) == TIMEOUT)
                len = read(snmpdev, buff, SNMPMAXSZ);
        if (len == TIMEOUT) {
                close(snmpdev);
```

```
                    return SCL_NORESP;
            } else if (len == SYSERR) {
                    close(snmpdev);
                    return SCL_READF;
            }
            if (snparse(rqdp, buff, len) == SYSERR) {
                    close(snmpdev);
                    return SCL_BADRESP;
            }
            if (reqidsavelen != rqdp->reqidlen ||
                ! blkequ(reqidsave, rqdp->reqid, reqidsavelen)) {
                    close(snmpdev);
                    return SCL_BADRESP;
            }
            /* convert the sb_alstr's to objid's and their values */
            if (sna2b(rqdp) == SYSERR) {
                    close(snmpdev);
                    return SCL_BADRESP;
            }
            close(snmpdev);
            return SCL_OK;
    }
```

Because UDP is unreliable, an SNMP client must implement its own strategy for timeout and retransmission. Our example client implements timeout, but only one retransmission. To do so, *snclient* calls *control* to place the UDP descriptor in timed mode (*DG_TMODE*). In timed mode, *read* operations either return a datagram or the special value *TIMEOUT* if the timer expires before any datagram arrives. If *snclient* does not receive a response within two timeout periods, it closes the descriptor and returns an error code.

If *snclient* does receive a response, it calls *snparse* to convert the response into internal form. It then compares the id field of the response to the id field of the request to verify that the message is a response to the request that was sent. If so, *snclient* calls *sna2b* to translate the ASN.1 representation of each object identifier to its internal form.

19.14 Initialization Of Variables

Procedure *sninit* initializes all simple counters and variables used by SNMP that are not initialized as part of the normal system startup. *Sninit* also calls *hashinit* to initialize the hash table used to optimize MIB name lookup. Of course, MIB variables that correspond to tables (e.g., the routing table) are initialized by the TCP/IP software.

```
/* sninit.c - sninit */

#include <conf.h>
#include <kernel.h>
#include <network.h>
#include <ctype.h>
#include <snmp.h>
#include <mib.h>
#include <snmpvars.h>


extern char vers[];

char    *SysDescr;
struct oid SysObjectID = { {0}, 1};

/* System & Interface MIB */
unsigned SysUpTime, IfNumber;

/* IP MIB */
unsigned IpForwarding, IpDefaultTTL, IpInReceives, IpInHdrErrors,
        IpInAddrErrors, IpForwDatagrams, IpInUnknownProtos, IpInDiscards,
        IpInDelivers, IpOutRequests, IpOutDiscards, IpOutNoRoutes,
        IpReasmTimeout, IpReasmReqds, IpReasmOKs, IpReasmFails, IpFragOKs,
        IpFragFails, IpFragCreates;

/* ICMP MIB */
unsigned IcmpInMsgs, IcmpInErrors, IcmpInDestUnreachs, IcmpInTimeExcds,
        IcmpInParmProbs, IcmpInSrcQuenchs, IcmpInRedirects, IcmpInEchos,
        IcmpInEchoReps, IcmpInTimestamps, IcmpInTimestampReps,
        IcmpInAddrMasks, IcmpInAddrMaskReps, IcmpOutMsgs, IcmpOutErrors,
        IcmpOutDestUnreachs, IcmpOutTimeExcds, IcmpOutParmProbs,
        IcmpOutSrcQuenchs, IcmpOutRedirects, IcmpOutEchos,
        IcmpOutEchoReps, IcmpOutTimestamps, IcmpOutTimestampReps,
        IcmpOutAddrMasks, IcmpOutAddrMaskReps;

/* UDP MIB */
unsigned UdpInDatagrams, UdpNoPorts, UdpInErrors, UdpOutDatagrams;

/* TCP MIB */
unsigned TcpRtoAlgorithm, TcpRtoMin, TcpRtoMax, TcpMaxConn,
        TcpActiveOpens, TcpPassiveOpens, TcpAttemptFails, TcpEstabResets,
        TcpCurrEstab, TcpInSegs, TcpOutSegs, TcpRetransSegs;

int snmpinitialized = FALSE;
```

```
/*-------------------------------------------------------------------------
 * sninit - initialize the data structures for the SNMP server and client
 *-------------------------------------------------------------------------
 */
sninit()
{
        int     i;

        if (snmpinitialized)
                return; /* if SNMP data structures already initialized */
        snmpinitialized = TRUE;
        hashinit();

        /* initialize most SNMP variables */
        SysUpTime = 0;
        SysDescr = vers;

        IfNumber = Net.nif - 1;

        IpDefaultTTL = IP_TTL;          IpInReceives = 0;
        IpInHdrErrors = 0;              IpInAddrErrors = 0;
        IpForwDatagrams = 0;            IpInUnknownProtos = 0;
        IpInDiscards = 0;               IpInDelivers = 0;
        IpOutRequests = 0;              IpOutDiscards = 0;
        IpOutNoRoutes = 0;              IpReasmTimeout = IP_FTTL;
        IpReasmReqds = 0;               IpReasmOKs = 0;
        IpReasmFails = 0;               IpFragOKs = 0;
        IpFragFails = 0;                IpFragCreates = 0;
        IcmpInMsgs = 0;                 IcmpInErrors = 0;
        IcmpInDestUnreachs = 0;         IcmpInTimeExcds = 0;
        IcmpInParmProbs = 0;            IcmpInSrcQuenchs = 0;
        IcmpInRedirects = 0;            IcmpInEchos = 0;
        IcmpInEchoReps = 0;             IcmpInTimestamps = 0;
        IcmpInTimestampReps = 0;        IcmpInAddrMasks = 0;
        IcmpInAddrMaskReps = 0;         IcmpOutMsgs = 0;
        IcmpOutErrors = 0;              IcmpOutDestUnreachs = 0;
        IcmpOutTimeExcds = 0;           IcmpOutParmProbs = 0;
        IcmpOutSrcQuenchs = 0;          IcmpOutRedirects = 0;
        IcmpOutEchos = 0;               IcmpOutEchoReps = 0;
        IcmpOutTimestamps = 0;          IcmpOutTimestampReps = 0;
        IcmpOutAddrMasks = 0;           IcmpOutAddrMaskReps = 0;
        TcpRtoAlgorithm = 4;            TcpRtoMin = TCP_MINRXT*10;
        TcpRtoMax = TCP_MAXRXT*10;      TcpMaxConn = Ntcp;
```

```
TcpActiveOpens = 0;          TcpPassiveOpens = 0;
TcpAttemptFails = 0;         TcpEstabResets = 0;
TcpCurrEstab = 0;            TcpInSegs = 0;
TcpOutSegs = 0;              TcpRetransSegs= 0;
UdpInDatagrams = 0;          UdpNoPorts = 0;
UdpInErrors = 0;             UdpOutDatagrams = 0;


for (i=0; i<Net.nif; ++i)
        nif[i].ni_lastchange = 0;
}
```

19.15 Summary

An SNMP server accepts incoming requests, performs the operation specified, and returns the result to the client. Although conceptually simple, the server code is dominated by conversions between the ASN.1 representation used in SNMP messages and the internal representation of values. The server parses an incoming message and converts it into a structure that uses fixed-format fields. It then uses the *mib* array to map from an object identifier and operation to a function that performs the specified operation. The server uses a separate data structure that specifies the functions for each table. By using indirection, the server can avoid having a separate function for each variable.

Client software shares most of the procedures used by the server. The client forms a message, sends it, and waits for a response. It must implement timeout, and if needed, retransmission. When a response arrives, the client parses the message and converts fields from the ASN.1 representation to an internal, fixed-field format. The client also compares the id field in a response to that in the request to insure they match.

FOR FURTHER STUDY

Case, Fedor, Schoffstall, and Davin [RFC 1157] describes the operation of a client and server.

EXERCISES

19.1   Procedure *snparse* encodes the SNMP message format in a sequence of statements that parse it. Can you devise a scheme that encodes the format in a data structure instead? (Hint: think of a conventional compiler.)

19.2   The *snmib* data structure provides only one pointer for a function that implements *get*, *set*, and *get-next* operations. Compare this design to an alternative in which the structure contains a separate pointer for each operation similar to an entry in array *tabtab*. What are the advantages of each implementation?

19.3   Estimate the percentage of the code devoted to parsing and converting messages between ASN.1 and the internal representation. What percentage of the total SNMP code does it represent? Do the same for IP. What conclusions can you draw?

19.4   When the client specifies a *get-next* operation and gives the name of a data aggregate, *snrslv* follows the lexical pointer and invokes the function on the next item (using expression **np->mi_next->mi_func*). Explain why *snrslv* does not need to check whether field *mi_func* is empty.

19.5   Design a user interface for the client that allows a manager to use SNMP without knowing what variables are available in the MIB.

19.6   How long should a client wait for a response to an SNMP request? How many times should a client retransmit?

19.7   The set of bindings in an SNMP *get* request specify pairs consisting of object identifiers and the value *NULL*. Why does the protocol include *NULL* values when they are unnecessary?

19.8   Read the SNMP protocol specification. Does it specify the range of values for individual variables like *IpForwarding*? If it does, give examples of variables and possible values. Does the server shown here check for values out of range in an SNMP *set* request? Explain.

20

SNMP: Table Access
Functions

20.1 Introduction

The previous chapter examined an SNMP server, and showed how it used the function pointer in a *mib* entry to invoke an operation indirectly. When a message arrives, the server converts it to internal form, and stores it in the request descriptor structure. The request structure contains a pointer to a linked list of object names to which the specified operation must be applied. For simple MIB variables like integers, access is straightforward. Underlying access functions merely copy a value between an internal data structure used by the TCP/IP software and the binding list node. Once the server has performed the specified operation, it translates the request descriptor, along with items in the binding list, back into external form, and sends a reply.

This chapter concentrates on the underlying functions that handle *get*, *set*, and *get-next* requests for tables. It shows how the software maps from conceptual MIB tables into the data structures used by TCP/IP, and how underlying access functions implement operations on the tables. Finally, it examines additional data structures needed by SNMP that implement the entries in conceptual tables that do not correspond to existing data structures.

20.2 Table Access

Unlike simple variables that map to a location in memory, tables require additional software that maps the conceptual SNMP table into the corresponding internal data structure. For MIB tables, the server provides a mechanism that allows each table to have three functions that implement *get*, *set*, and *get-next* operations. As Chapter 19 shows, server software uses indirection to choose the correct access function by following a pointer in the *tabtab* array†; the array contains a separate pointer for each operation.

20.3 Object Identifiers For Tables

The five entries in array *tabtab* that correspond to tables do not contain full object identifiers. Instead, they only contain a prefix of the object identifier for the table. The reason is simple: the complete object identifier for an item in a table includes a prefix that identifies the table itself, as well as a suffix that identifies a particular entry in the table and a specific field within that entry. When checking an identifier, *getmib*‡ first checks to see if it matches a simple variable by looking it up in the hash table. Hash table lookups use exact match comparison. If no exact match can be found, *getmib* compares the identifier to the set of prefixes that correspond to MIB tables.

Once a prefix match has been found, the server invokes an underlying access function indirectly. The access function parses the suffix of the object identifier, and uses it to select an entry in the table as well as a field within that entry. For many tables, the MIB uses an IP address to select an entry. The IP address is encoded in the object identifier by including its dotted decimal representation. The next section provides an example.

20.4 Address Entry Table Functions

The MIB defines a conceptual *address entry table* that corresponds to the set of IP addresses for the interfaces on a machine. Each item in the table has four fields: an IP address (*ipAdEntAddr*), a network interface index (*ipAdEntIfIndex*), a subnet mask (*ipAdEntMask*), and a broadcast address (*ipAdEntBcastAddr*). Although the TCP/IP software does not have a data structure defined exactly this way, the network interface array, *nif*, contains the needed information.

To identify an item in the conceptual *address entry table*, client software creates an ASN.1 object identifier with a prefix that specifies the table, and a suffix that specifies an individual field within a specific table entry. For example, the object identifier

$$1.3.6.1.2.1.4.20.1.1.128.10.2.3$$

specifies the standard MIB prefix (*1.3.6.1.2.1*), the *ip* subhierarchy (*4*), the *ipAddrTable*

---

†Page 378 contains the listing of file *snmib.c* in which *tabtab* is defined.
‡Page 385 contains the listing of file *snhash.c* in which *getmib* appears.

(20), an *ipAddrEntry* (1), a field within that entry (1), and an IP address used as the index for the entry (*128.10.2.3*). Thus, we can think of the object identifier as representing:

standard-MIB-prefix . ip . ipAddrTable . ipAddrEntry . field . IPaddress

The access software for each table includes a matching function that tests whether a given object exists in the table. As we have seen, when a query arrives that specifies a variable in a table, the server uses a prefix of the object identifier to select the appropriate table, and then calls the table's matching function to decide whether the specified item exists. For example, function *sae_match* performs the test for the address entry table.

```
/* sae_match.c - sae_match */

#include <conf.h>
#include <kernel.h>
#include <network.h>
#include <snmp.h>
#include <mib.h>
#include <asn1.h>
#include <snhash.h>

/*------------------------------------------------------------------
 * sae_match - check if a variable exists in the IP Address Entry Table
 *------------------------------------------------------------------
 */
int sae_match(bindl, iface, field, numifaces)
struct snbentry *bindl;
int             *iface;
int             *field;
int             numifaces;
{
        int     oidi;

        oidi = SAE_OIDLEN;         /* skip over fixed part of objid */

        if ((*field = bindl->sb_oid.id[oidi++]) > SNUMF_AETAB)
                return SYSERR;
        for (*iface = 1; *iface <= numifaces; (*iface)++)
                if (soipequ(&bindl->sb_oid.id[oidi],
                                nif[*iface].ni_ip, IP_ALEN))
                        break;
        if (*iface > numifaces)
```

```
                return SYSERR;
        oidi += IP_ALEN;
        if (oidi != bindl->sb_oid.len)   /* verify oidi at end of objid  */
                return SYSERR;
        return OK;
}
```

The code is straightforward. *Sae_match* skips the part of the object identifier that identifies the address entry table and the address entry structure. It then extracts the integer that specifies which field of the table entry is desired, and stores the value at the location given by argument *field*. If the value specified is out of the valid range, *sae_match* returns an error code to indicate that the object identifier does not correspond to a valid table entry.

Once it has found a valid field specification, *sae_match* iterates through all network interfaces, comparing the remaining four values of the object identifier to the IP address of each interface. If it finds a match, *sae_match* stores the interface number in the address given by argument *iface*, and returns a code that specifies it found a match. If no match can be found, *sae_match* returns an error code that specifies the object identifier does not correspond to a valid entry.

20.4.1 Get Operation For The Address Entry Table

Procedure *sae_get* implements the *get* operation for an item in the address entry table.

```
/* sae_get.c - sae_get */

#include <conf.h>
#include <kernel.h>
#include <network.h>
#include <snmp.h>
#include <mib.h>
#include <asn1.h>


/*------------------------------------------------------------------------
 * sae_get - perform a get on a variable in the IP Address Entry Table
 *------------------------------------------------------------------------
 */
int sae_get(bindl, numifaces)
struct snbentry *bindl;
int             numifaces;
{
        int     iface, field;
```

```
    if (sae_match(bindl, &iface, &field, numifaces) == SYSERR)
            return SERR_NO_SUCH;
    switch (field) {
    case 1:             /* ipAdEntAddr */
            SVTYPE(bindl) = ASN1_IPADDR;
            blkcopy(SVIPADDR(bindl), nif[iface].ni_ip, IP_ALEN);
            return SNMP_OK;
    case 2:             /* ipAdEntIfIndex */
            SVTYPE(bindl) = ASN1_INT;
            SVINT(bindl) = iface;
            return SNMP_OK;
    case 3:             /* ipAdEntNetMask */
            SVTYPE(bindl) = ASN1_IPADDR;
            blkcopy(SVIPADDR(bindl), nif[iface].ni_mask, IP_ALEN);
            return SNMP_OK;
    case 4:             /* ipAdEntBcastAddr */
            SVTYPE(bindl) = ASN1_INT;
            SVINT(bindl) = (nif[iface].ni_brc[IP_ALEN - 1] & 0x01);
            return SNMP_OK;
    default:
            break;
    }
    return SERR_NO_SUCH;
}
```

Sae_get uses *sae_match* to find the interface that matches the object identifier. If the identifier does not correspond to a valid entry, it returns an error. If it finds a match, *sae_get* proceeds to access the desired information.

The *switch* statement chooses one of the fields in the conceptual table entry, using the *field* code set by *sae_match*. The code that implements a given field stores both a type and a value in the binding list node, and returns to the caller.

20.4.2 Get-First Operation For The Address Entry Table

Function *sae_getf* implements the *get-first* operation for items in the address entry table.

```
/* sae_getf.c - sae_getf */

#include <conf.h>
#include <kernel.h>
#include <network.h>
#include <snmp.h>
#include <mib.h>
#include <asn1.h>


/*-------------------------------------------------------------------
 * sae_getf - perform a getfirst on a variable in the IPAddr Entry Table
 *-------------------------------------------------------------------
 */
sae_getf(bindl, mip, numifaces)
struct snbentry *bindl;
struct mib_info *mip;
int             numifaces;
{
        int     iface, oidi;

        iface = sae_findnext(-1, numifaces);

        /* write the objid into the bindings list and call get func */
        blkcopy(bindl->sb_oid.id, mip->mi_objid.id, mip->mi_objid.len*2);
        oidi = mip->mi_objid.len;

        bindl->sb_oid.id[oidi++] = (u_short) 1; /* field */
        sip2ocpy(&bindl->sb_oid.id[oidi], nif[iface].ni_ip);
        bindl->sb_oid.len = oidi + IP_ALEN;

        return sae_get(bindl, numifaces);
}
```

To find the lexically first entry in the table, *sae_getf* calls function *sae_findnext*, passing it *-1* as a starting interface. *Sae_findnext* finds the first interface and returns its index. Once it knows the interface number, *sae_getf* computes the correct object identifier for the interface, and uses it to replace the identifier in the binding list node. To construct the identifier, *sae_getf* inserts *1* into the field value (to identify the first field), and calls procedure *sip2ocpy* to copy the IP address of the entry into the object identifier. Finally, *sae_getf* invokes *sae_get* to obtain the requested information.

20.4.3 Get-Next Operation For The Address Entry Table

Function *sae_getn* implements the *get-next* operation for items in the address entry table.

```
/* sae_getn.c - sae_getn */

#include <conf.h>
#include <kernel.h>
#include <network.h>
#include <snmp.h>
#include <mib.h>
#include <asn1.h>


/*------------------------------------------------------------------------
 * sae_getn - perform a getnext on a variable in the IPAddr Entry Table
 *------------------------------------------------------------------------
 */
int sae_getn(bindl, mip, numifaces)
struct snbentry *bindl;
struct mib_info *mip;
int             numifaces;
{
        int     field, iface, oidi;

        if (sae_match(bindl, &iface, &field, numifaces) == SYSERR)
                return SERR_NO_SUCH;
        if ((iface = sae_findnext(iface, numifaces)) == -1) {
                iface = sae_findnext(-1, numifaces);
                if (++field > SNUMF_AETAB)
                        return (*mip->mi_next->mi_func)
                                (bindl, mip->mi_next, SOP_GETF);
        }
        /* The fixed part of the objid is correct. Update the rest    */
        oidi = SAE_OIDLEN;

        bindl->sb_oid.id[oidi++] = (u_short) field;
        sip2ocpy(&bindl->sb_oid.id[oidi], nif[iface].ni_ip);
        bindl->sb_oid.len = oidi + IP_ALEN;

        return sae_get(bindl, numifaces);
}
```

Implementation of the *get-next* operation requires three steps. First, *sae_getn* uses *sae_match* to find the entry in the table specified by the object identifier in the binding list node. Second, it follows the lexical order defined for the table to locate the "next" item. Third, it applies the *get* operation.

To find the lexically next item in the table, *sae_getn* calls function *sae_findnext*, passing it as an argument the interface at which to start. If *sae_findnext* returns a valid interface, no further searching is required. However, it *sae_findnext* returns the value *-1*, it means that no more entries exist in the table beyond the one specified by the object id.

When *sae_getn* reaches the end of the table, it must increment the field value and move back to the lexically first item in the table. Ultimately, when it increments past the final field in the last table entry, *sae_getn* invokes the *get-first* function on the lexically next item in the MIB. For the case where incrementing the field results in a valid value, *sae_getn* must find the lexically first entry in the table. To find the lexically first item, it calls *sae_findnext*, passing it *-1* as the starting interface.

20.4.4 Incremental Search In The Address Entry Table

Procedure *sae_findnext* searches the address entry table to find the item that follows a given item in the lexical order.

```
/* sae_findn.c - sae_findnext */

#include <conf.h>
#include <kernel.h>
#include <network.h>


/*------------------------------------------------------------------------
 * sae_findnext - find the next interface in the lexical ordering
 *------------------------------------------------------------------------
 */
int sae_findnext(iface, numifaces)
int     iface;
int     numifaces;
{
        int     i, nextif;

        for (nextif = -1, i = 1; i <= numifaces; ++i) {
                if (iface >= 0 &&
                    blkcmp(nif[i].ni_ip,nif[iface].ni_ip,IP_ALEN) <= 0)
                        continue;
                if (nextif < 0 ||
                    blkcmp(nif[i].ni_ip,nif[nextif].ni_ip,IP_ALEN) < 0)
                        nextif = i;
```

```
        }
        return nextif;
}
```

We think of argument *iface* as a starting interface. When *iface* contains *-1*, *sae_findnext* starts from the beginning, and locates the table item that has the lexicographically smallest object identifier (i.e., the "first" item in the table in lexicographic order). When argument *iface* contains a positive value, *sae_findnext* starts with that interface and locates the entry that follows it in the lexicographic order (i.e., the "next" item in the table after *iface*).

If *sae_findnext* locates the desired item in the table, it returns its index. Otherwise, it returns *-1* to indicate that the starting interface is last in the lexicographic ordering.

20.4.5 Set Operation For The Address Entry Table

Because the address entry table does not permit managers to change entries, the implementation of *set* is trivial. Function *sae_set* merely returns an error if called.

```
/* sae_set.c - sae_set */

#include <conf.h>
#include <kernel.h>
#include <network.h>
#include <snmp.h>

/*------------------------------------------------------------------------
 * sae_set - return error: the IP Address Entry Table is read-only
 *------------------------------------------------------------------------
 */
sae_set()
{
        return SERR_NO_SUCH;
}
```

20.5 Address Translation Table Functions

The MIB defines a conceptual address translation table that corresponds to the ARP cache. Each entry in the table has three fields: the index of the network interface from which the entry was obtained (*atIfIndex*), the physical address in the entry (*atPhysAddress*), and the IP address in the entry (*atNetAddress*). The ASN.1 name for an item in the table encodes the IP address field of the entry.

The general form of an object identifier for an address translation table entry is

standard-MIB-prefix . at . atTable . atEntry . field . iface . 1 . IPaddress

A prefix identifies the table and address table structure, while the remaining octets specify the *field* in an entry, the interface for an entry, a type (*1*), and an IP address.

When an object identifier specifies an item in the address translation table, the SNMP server checks only a prefix of the identifier that identifies the table. It then calls table-specific functions that must parse the remainder of the object identifier and verify that it corresponds to a valid table entry. Function *sat_match* compares the object identifier suffix with entries in the table to see if any entry matches the specified name.

```
/* sat_match.c - sat_match */

#include <conf.h>
#include <kernel.h>
#include <network.h>
#include <snmp.h>
#include <mib.h>


/*------------------------------------------------------------------
 * sat_match - check if a variable exists in the Addr Translation Table
 *------------------------------------------------------------------
 */
int sat_match(bindl, iface, entry, field, numifaces)
struct snbentry *bindl;
int             *iface;
int             *entry;
int             *field;
int             numifaces;
{
        int     oidi;
        struct  arpentry *pae;

        oidi = SAT_OIDLEN;
        if ((*field = bindl->sb_oid.id[oidi++]) > SNUMF_ATTAB)
                return SYSERR;
        if ((*iface = bindl->sb_oid.id[oidi++]) > numifaces)
                return SYSERR;
        oidi++;         /* skip over the 1 */
        /*
         * oidi now points to IPaddr.  Read it and match it against
         * the correct arp cache entry to get entry number
         */
```

```
for (*entry = 0; *entry < ARP_TSIZE; (*entry)++) {
        pae = &arptable[*entry];
        if (pae->ae_state != AS_FREE &&
            pae->ae_pni == &nif[*iface] &&
            soipequ(&bindl->sb_oid.id[oidi],pae->ae_pra,IP_ALEN))
                break;
}
if (*entry >= ARP_TSIZE)
        return SYSERR;
if (oidi + IP_ALEN != bindl->sb_oid.len)
        return SYSERR;   /*  oidi is not at end of objid */
return OK;
}
```

After extracting the field and interface specifications, *sat_match* compares the four-octet IP address to the IP address stored in each entry in the ARP cache. It returns *OK* if a match is found, and *SYSERR* otherwise.

20.5.1 Get Operation For The Address Translation Table

Function *sat_get* implements the *get* operation for the address translation table. After calling *sat_match* to find the correct ARP entry, it uses a switch statement to select the requested field, and copies the information into the request descriptor.

```
/* sat_get.c - sat_get */

#include <conf.h>
#include <kernel.h>
#include <network.h>
#include <snmp.h>
#include <mib.h>
#include <asn1.h>


/*-------------------------------------------------------------------------
 * sat_get - do a get on a variable in the Address Translation Table
 *-------------------------------------------------------------------------
 */
int sat_get(bindl, numifaces)
struct snbentry *bindl;
int             numifaces;
{
        int     iface, entry, field;

        if (sat_match(bindl, &iface, &entry, &field, numifaces) == SYSERR)
                return SERR_NO_SUCH;
        switch(field) {
        case 1:              /* atIfIndex */
                SVTYPE(bindl) = ASN1_INT;
                SVINT(bindl) = iface;
                return SNMP_OK;
        case 2:              /* atPhysAddress */
                SVTYPE(bindl) = ASN1_OCTSTR;
                SVSTR(bindl) = (char *) getmem(EP_ALEN);
                blkcopy(SVSTR(bindl), arptable[entry].ae_hwa,
                        EP_ALEN);
                SVSTRLEN(bindl) = EP_ALEN;
                return SNMP_OK;
        case 3:              /* atNetAddress */
                SVTYPE(bindl) = ASN1_IPADDR;
                blkcopy(SVIPADDR(bindl), arptable[entry].ae_pra,
                        IP_ALEN);
                return SNMP_OK;
        default:
                break;
        }
        return SERR_NO_SUCH;
}
```

20.5.2 Get-First Operation For The Address Translation Table

Function *sat_getf* implements the *get-first* operation for the address translation table.

```
/* sat_getf.c - sat_getf */

#include <conf.h>
#include <kernel.h>
#include <network.h>
#include <snmp.h>
#include <mib.h>
#include <asn1.h>
#include <snhash.h>

/*------------------------------------------------------------------------
 * sat_getf - do a getfirst on a variable in the Address Translation Table
 *------------------------------------------------------------------------
 */
int sat_getf(bindl, mip, numifaces)
struct snbentry *bindl;
struct mib_info *mip;
int             numifaces;
{
        int     iface, entry, oidi;

        for (iface=1; iface <= numifaces; ++iface)
                if ((entry = sat_findnext(-1, iface)) >= 0)
                        break;
        if (iface > numifaces) {  /* no active interface found */
                if (mip->mi_next)
                        return (*mip->mi_next->mi_func)
                                (bindl, mip->mi_next, SOP_GETF);
                return SERR_NO_SUCH;            /* no next node */
        }
        blkcopy(bindl->sb_oid.id, mip->mi_objid.id, mip->mi_objid.len*2);
        oidi = mip->mi_objid.len;

        bindl->sb_oid.id[oidi++] = (u_short) 1;         /* field      */
        bindl->sb_oid.id[oidi++] = (u_short) iface;
        bindl->sb_oid.id[oidi++] = (u_short) 1;
        sip2ocpy(&bindl->sb_oid.id[oidi], arptable[entry].ae_pra);
        bindl->sb_oid.len = oidi + IP_ALEN;

        return sat_get(bindl, numifaces);
}
```

The conceptual address translation table partitions entries into sets that correspond to individual interfaces, and places all entries from a given interface adjacent in the lexicographic ordering. Thus, to find the lexically first entry, *sat_getf* must iterate through each possible interface, one at a time. On each iteration, it calls *sat_findnext* to see if the cache contains any entries for the given interface. As soon as *sat_findnext* reports that it has found a valid entry, *sat_getf* stops the search. However, if the ARP cache is completely empty, the iteration will continue until all interfaces have been examined. In such cases, *sat_getf* applies the *get-first* operation to the lexically next item in the MIB (provided one exists).

If it finds a nonempty entry in the ARP cache, *sat_getf* constructs an object identifier that corresponds to the entry, and calls *sat_get* to extract the value. When constructing the object identifier, it uses field 1 because the object identifier for the first field will be lexically least.

20.5.3 Get-Next Operation For The Address Translation Table

Function *sat_getn* provides the *get-next* operation for the address translation table.

```
/* sat_getn.c - sat_getn */

#include <conf.h>
#include <kernel.h>
#include <network.h>
#include <snmp.h>
#include <mib.h>
#include <asn1.h>


/*------------------------------------------------------------------------
 * sat_getn - do a getnext on a variable in the Address Translation Table
 *------------------------------------------------------------------------
 */
int sat_getn(bindl, mip, numifaces)
struct snbentry *bindl;
struct mib_info *mip;
int             numifaces;
{
        int     entry, iface, field, oidi, i;

        if (sat_match(bindl, &iface, &entry, &field, numifaces) == SYSERR)
                return SERR_NO_SUCH;
        for (i=1; field <= SNUMF_ATTAB && i<=numifaces; ++i) {
                if ((entry = sat_findnext(entry, iface)) >= 0)
                        break;
                if (++iface > numifaces) {
```

```
                        iface = 1;
                        ++field;
                }
        }
        if (entry < 0)
                return (*mip->mi_next->mi_func)
                                (bindl, mip->mi_next, SOP_GETF);
        oidi = SAT_OIDLEN;        /* 3.1.1 */

        bindl->sb_oid.id[oidi++] = (u_short) field;
        bindl->sb_oid.id[oidi++] = (u_short) iface;
        bindl->sb_oid.id[oidi++] = (u_short) 1;
        sip2ocpy(&bindl->sb_oid.id[oidi], arptable[entry].ae_pra);
        bindl->sb_oid.len = oidi + IP_ALEN;

        return sat_get(bindl, numifaces);
}
```

Sat_getn uses *sat_match* to find the table entry that matches the specified object identifier. It then calls function *sat_findnext* to search the ARP cache for the next valid entry for that same interface. If no such entry exists in the ARP cache, it tries finding an entry for the next interface. If it exhausts all possible interfaces, *sat_getn* increments the field number, and begins searching the table again. The iteration terminates either because *sat_findnext* has found a valid entry that follows the starting entry, or because no such entry exists. If *sat_getn* has exhausted all possible interfaces without finding an entry, it applies the *get-first* operation to the object that follows the address translation table in the lexical ordering. Otherwise, *sat_getn* constructs an object identifier for the new entry, and calls *sat_get* to extract the value.

20.5.4 Incremental Search In The Address Entry Table

Function *sat_findnext* searches for an entry in the ARP cache according to the lexical order imposed by the MIB.

```
/* sat_findn.c - sat_findnext, satcmp */

#include <conf.h>
#include <kernel.h>
#include <network.h>

/*------------------------------------------------------------------------
 * sat_findnext - for given iface, find next resolved arp entry
 *------------------------------------------------------------------------
 */
int sat_findnext(entry, iface)
int     entry;
int     iface;
{
        int     i, next;

        next = -1;
        for (i = 0; i < ARP_TSIZE; ++i) {
                struct arpentry *pae = &arptable[i];

                if (pae->ae_state == AS_FREE ||
                    pae->ae_pni != &nif[iface] ||
                    (entry >= 0 && satcmp(pae, &arptable[entry]) <= 0))
                        continue;
                if (next < 0 || satcmp(pae, &arptable[next]) < 0)
                        next = i;
        }
        return next;
}


/*------------------------------------------------------------------------
 * satcmp - compare two ARP table entries in SNMP lexicographic order
 *------------------------------------------------------------------------
 */
int satcmp(pae1, pae2)
struct  arpentry        *pae1, *pae2;
{
        int     rv;

        if (rv = (pae1->ae_prlen - pae2->ae_prlen))
                return rv;
        return blkcmp(pae1->ae_pra, pae2->ae_pra, pae1->ae_prlen);
}
```

Sat_findnext uses argument *entry* as an index that specifies a starting point, and argument *iface* to select entries for a single interface. It searches the ARP cache, looking only at valid entries that correspond to interface *iface*. If argument *entry* contains *-1*, *sat_findnext* remembers the first entry that matches *iface*. Once it has a candidate entry, *sat_findnext* only replaces that value if it finds another entry greater than the initial entry and less than the candidate.

20.5.5 Order From Chaos

The MIB address translation table illustrates an interesting idea: that it is possible to define structure and order for any system data structure. Although our implementation of ARP stores all entries for all network interfaces in a single cache, the MIB defines the conceptual table to be indexed by interface, as if ARP caches existed for each interface. The address table access functions make it appear that separate tables exist by imposing an order on how items can be searched. Thus, when accessing the address translation table, an SNMP client remains completely unaware of the underlying implementation.

20.5.6 Set Operation For The Address Translation Table

Unlike the address entry table shown above, the address translation table allows managers to assign values to variables as well as fetch them. Function *sat_set* provides the *set* operation.

```
/* sat_set.c - sat_set */

#include <conf.h>
#include <kernel.h>
#include <network.h>
#include <snmp.h>
#include <mib.h>
#include <asn1.h>


/*-------------------------------------------------------------------
 * sat_set - do a set on a variable in the Address Translation Table
 *-------------------------------------------------------------------
 */
int sat_set(bindl, mip, numifaces)
struct snbentry *bindl;
struct mib_info *mip;
int             numifaces;
{
        int     iface, entry, field;

        if (sat_match(bindl, &iface, &entry, &field, numifaces) == SYSERR)
                return SERR_NO_SUCH;
        switch (field) {
        case 1:          /* atIfIndex */
                if (SVTYPE(bindl) != ASN1_INT)
                        return SERR_BAD_VALUE;
                if (SVINT(bindl) <= 0)
                        return SERR_BAD_VALUE;
                if (SVINT(bindl) > numifaces)
                        return SERR_BAD_VALUE;
                arptable[entry].ae_pni = &nif[SVINT(bindl)];
                return SNMP_OK;
        case 2:          /* atPhysAddress */
                if (SVTYPE(bindl) != ASN1_OCTSTR)
                        return SERR_BAD_VALUE;
                if (SVSTRLEN(bindl) != EP_ALEN)
                        return SERR_BAD_VALUE;
                blkcopy(arptable[entry].ae_hwa, SVSTR(bindl), EP_ALEN);
                return SNMP_OK;
        case 3:          /* atNetAddress */
                if (SVTYPE(bindl) != ASN1_IPADDR)
                        return SERR_BAD_VALUE;
                blkcopy(arptable[entry].ae_pra, SVIPADDR(bindl), IP_ALEN);
                return SNMP_OK;
```

```
default:
        break;
}
return SERR_NO_SUCH;
}
```

Sat_set checks the value type to verify that it matches the object type to which it must be assigned. In most cases, *sat_set* also checks to see that the value is in the legal range before making the assignment.

20.6 Network Interface Table Functions

The MIB defines a conceptual *network interface table* that holds information about each network interface. The server uses entries in array *nif†* to store the information needed for the conceptual MIB table.

20.6.1 Interface Table ID Matching

ASN.1 object identifiers for items in the network interface table are constructed like identifiers for the tables examined previously. A prefix of the name specifies the table, while the suffix specifies a field within the table and the network interface. The general form is

standard-MIB-prefix . interfaces . ifTable . ifTableEntry . field . iface

Function *sif_match* decodes the suffix and verifies that the values are valid.

---

†See page 28 for a listing of file *netif.h* that contains the declaration of *nif*.

```
/* sif_match.c - sif_match */

#include <conf.h>
#include <kernel.h>
#include <network.h>
#include <snmp.h>
#include <mib.h>

/*------------------------------------------------------------------
 * sif_match - check if a variable exists in the Interfaces Table.
 *------------------------------------------------------------------
 */
int sif_match(bindl, iface, field, numifaces)
struct snbentry *bindl;
int             *iface;
int             *field;
int             numifaces;
{
        int     oidi;

        oidi = SIF_OIDLEN;
        if ((*field = bindl->sb_oid.id[oidi++]) > SNUMF_IFTAB)
                return SYSERR;
        if ((*iface = bindl->sb_oid.id[oidi++]) > numifaces)
                return SYSERR;
        if (oidi != bindl->sb_oid.len)
                return SYSERR;   /* oidi is not at end of objid */
        return OK;
}
```

20.6.2 Get Operation For The Network Interface Table

Because the MIB interface table defines *21* fields per entry, operations like *get* and *set* require more code than the tables examined earlier. For example, function *sif_get* provides the *get* operation.

```
/* sif_get.c - sif_get */

#include <conf.h>
#include <kernel.h>
#include <network.h>
#include <snmp.h>
#include <mib.h>
```

```
#include <asn1.h>

/*-------------------------------------------------------------------
 * sif_get - perform a get on a variable in the Interfaces Table
 *-------------------------------------------------------------------
 */
int sif_get(bindl, numifaces)
struct snbentry *bindl;
int             numifaces;
{
        int     iface, field, sl;

        if (sif_match(bindl, &iface, &field, numifaces) == SYSERR)
                return SERR_NO_SUCH;
        switch (field) {
        case 1:             /* ifIndex */
                SVTYPE(bindl) = ASN1_INT;
                SVINT(bindl) = iface;
                return SNMP_OK;
        case 2:             /* ifDescr */
                SVTYPE(bindl) = ASN1_OCTSTR;
                SVSTRLEN(bindl) = sl = strlen(nif[iface].ni_descr);
                SVSTR(bindl) = (char *) getmem(sl);
                blkcopy(SVSTR(bindl), nif[iface].ni_descr, sl);
                return SNMP_OK;
        case 3:             /* ifType */
                SVTYPE(bindl) = ASN1_INT;
                SVINT(bindl) = nif[iface].ni_mtype;
                return SNMP_OK;
        case 4:             /* ifMtu */
                SVTYPE(bindl) = ASN1_INT;
                SVINT(bindl) = nif[iface].ni_mtu;
                return SNMP_OK;
        case 5:             /* ifSpeed */
                SVTYPE(bindl) = ASN1_GAUGE;
                SVINT(bindl) = nif[iface].ni_speed;
                return SNMP_OK;
        case 6:             /* ifPhysAddress */
                SVTYPE(bindl) = ASN1_OCTSTR;
                SVSTR(bindl) = (char *) getmem(nif[iface].ni_hwa.ha_len);
                blkcopy(SVSTR(bindl), nif[iface].ni_hwa.ha_addr,
                        SVSTRLEN(bindl) = nif[iface].ni_hwa.ha_len);
                return SNMP_OK;
        case 7:             /* ifAdminStatus */
```

```
                    SVTYPE(bindl) = ASN1_INT;
                    SVINT(bindl) = nif[iface].ni_admstate;
                    return SNMP_OK;
        case 8:                /* ifOperStatus */
                    SVTYPE(bindl) = ASN1_INT;
                    SVINT(bindl) = nif[iface].ni_state;
                    return SNMP_OK;
        case 9:                /* ifLastChange */
                    SVTYPE(bindl) = ASN1_TIMETICKS;
                    SVINT(bindl) = nif[iface].ni_lastchange;
                    return SNMP_OK;
        case 10:               /* ifInOctets */
                    SVTYPE(bindl) = ASN1_COUNTER;
                    SVINT(bindl) = nif[iface].ni_ioctets;
                    return SNMP_OK;
        case 11:               /* ifInUcastPkts */
                    SVTYPE(bindl) = ASN1_COUNTER;
                    SVINT(bindl) = nif[iface].ni_iucast;
                    return SNMP_OK;
        case 12:               /* ifInNUcastPkts */
                    SVTYPE(bindl) = ASN1_COUNTER;
                    SVINT(bindl) = nif[iface].ni_inucast;
                    return SNMP_OK;
        case 13:               /* ifInDiscards */
                    SVTYPE(bindl) = ASN1_COUNTER;
                    SVINT(bindl) = nif[iface].ni_idiscard;
                    return SNMP_OK;
        case 14:               /* ifInErrors */
                    SVTYPE(bindl) = ASN1_COUNTER;
                    SVINT(bindl) = nif[iface].ni_ierrors;
                    return SNMP_OK;
        case 15:               /* ifInUnknownProtos */
                    SVTYPE(bindl) = ASN1_COUNTER;
                    SVINT(bindl) = nif[iface].ni_iunkproto;
                    return SNMP_OK;
        case 16:               /* ifOutOctets */
                    SVTYPE(bindl) = ASN1_COUNTER;
                    SVINT(bindl) = nif[iface].ni_ooctets;
                    return SNMP_OK;
        case 17:               /* ifOutUcastPkts */
                    SVTYPE(bindl) = ASN1_COUNTER;
                    SVINT(bindl) = nif[iface].ni_oucast;
                    return SNMP_OK;
        case 18:               /* ifOutNUcastPkts */
```

```
                SVTYPE(bindl) = ASN1_COUNTER;
                SVINT(bindl) = nif[iface].ni_onucast;
                return SNMP_OK;
        case 19:         /* ifOutDiscards */
                SVTYPE(bindl) = ASN1_COUNTER;
                SVINT(bindl) = nif[iface].ni_odiscard;
                return SNMP_OK;
        case 20:         /* ifOutErrors */
                SVTYPE(bindl) = ASN1_COUNTER;
                SVINT(bindl) = nif[iface].ni_oerrors;
                return SNMP_OK;
        case 21:         /* ifOutQLen */
                SVTYPE(bindl) = ASN1_GAUGE;
                SVINT(bindl) = lenq(nif[iface].ni_outq);
                return SNMP_OK;
        default:
                break;
        }
        return SERR_NO_SUCH;
}
```

As the code shows, the interface table has conceptual fields for the hardware type, the maximum transfer unit, the physical address, and for counters such as the number of input and output errors that have occurred. The code translates each conceptual field into a corresponding field of the array that the local software uses to store interface information.

20.6.3 Get-First Operation For The Network Interface Table

Function *sif_getf* defines the *get-first* operation for the network interface table.

```
/* sif_getf.c - sif_getf */

#include <conf.h>
#include <kernel.h>
#include <network.h>
#include <snmp.h>
#include <mib.h>
#include <asn1.h>


/*------------------------------------------------------------------
 * sif_getf - perform a getfirst on a variable in the Interfaces Table
 *------------------------------------------------------------------
 */
int sif_getf(bindl, mip, numifaces)
struct snbentry *bindl;
struct mib_info *mip;
int             numifaces;
{
        int     oidi;

        blkcopy(bindl->sb_oid.id, mip->mi_objid.id, mip->mi_objid.len*2);
        oidi = mip->mi_objid.len;

        bindl->sb_oid.id[oidi++] = (u_short) 1;        /* field        */
        bindl->sb_oid.id[oidi++] = (u_short) 1;        /* interface    */
        bindl->sb_oid.len = oidi;

        return sif_get(bindl, numifaces);
}
```

Unlike tables discussed earlier, the network interface table does not use data values as an index. Instead, we think of the interface table as a one-dimensional array indexed by an integer between *1* and the maximum number of interfaces. For such a table, the implementation of the *get-first* operation is extremely simple. *Sif_getf* constructs an object identifier that specifies field *1* of interface *1* in the network interface table. It then calls the *get* operation to extract the value.

20.6.4 Get-Next Operation For The Network Interface Table

Function *sif_getn* provides the *get-next* operation for the network interface table.

```
/* sif_getn.c - sif_getn */

#include <conf.h>
#include <kernel.h>
#include <network.h>
#include <snmp.h>
#include <mib.h>

/*------------------------------------------------------------------------
 * sif_getn - perform a getnext on a variable in the Interfaces Table.
 *------------------------------------------------------------------------
 */
sif_getn(bindl, mip, numifaces)
struct snbentry *bindl;
struct mib_info *mip;
int             numifaces;
{
        int     oidi, field, iface;

        if (sif_match(bindl, &iface, &field, numifaces) == SYSERR)
                return SERR_NO_SUCH;
        if (++iface > numifaces) {
                iface = 1;
                if (++field > SNUMF_IFTAB)
                        return (*mip->mi_next->mi_func)
                                (bindl, mip->mi_next, SOP_GETF);
        }
        oidi = SIF_OIDLEN;      /* 2.2.1 */

        bindl->sb_oid.id[oidi++] = (u_short) field;
        bindl->sb_oid.id[oidi++] = (u_short) iface;
        bindl->sb_oid.len = oidi;

        return sif_get(bindl, numifaces);
}
```

Because object identifiers for table entries can be constructed without knowing the table contents, *sif_getn* does not need to search. It first increments the interface number. If the value exceeds the maximum number of interfaces, *sif_getn* sets the interface number to *1* and increments the field number. If the field number exceeds the maximum number of fields, no additional entries exist, so *sif_getn* applies the *get-first* operation to the next variable in the MIB lexical ordering.

As with other tables, the *get-next* operation requires an application of the *get* operation after the next object has been found. Thus, if *sif_getn* finds a valid successor, it constructs an object identifier for the new item, and then calls *sif_get* to extract the value.

20.6.5 Set Operation For The Network Interface Table

The network interface table allows managers to set the administrative status field; other fields only allow read access. As a result, the implementation returns an error code for all other fields. Function *sif_set.c* contains the code.

```
/* sif_set.c - sif_set */

#include <conf.h>
#include <kernel.h>
#include <network.h>
#include <snmp.h>
#include <mib.h>
#include <asn1.h>


/*------------------------------------------------------------------------
 * sif_set - perform a set on a variable in the Interfaces Table
 *------------------------------------------------------------------------
 */
int sif_set(bindl, mip, numifaces)
struct snbentry *bindl;
struct mib_info *mip;
int             numifaces;
{
        int iface, field;

        if (sif_match(bindl, &iface, &field, numifaces) == SYSERR)
                return SERR_NO_SUCH;
        /* the only settable object here is ifAdminStatus (ifEntry 7) */
        if (field != 7)
                return SERR_NO_SUCH;
        if (SVTYPE(bindl) != ASN1_INT)
                return SERR_BAD_VALUE;
        if (SVINT(bindl) < 0 || SVINT(bindl) > 1)
                return SERR_BAD_VALUE;
        /* value is OK, so install it */
        nif[iface].ni_admstate = SVINT(bindl);
        return SNMP_OK;
}
```

After verifying that the request specifies field *ifAdminStatus*, *sif_set* checks the value to insure it is a positive integer, and checks the interface specification to insure it specifies a valid interface. If the value is valid, *sif_set* makes the assignment.

20.7 Routing Table Functions

The MIB defines a conceptual table that corresponds to a gateway's IP routing table. Like object identifiers for items in the address entry table, an object id for the routing table encodes both a field designator and an IP address that SNMP uses as an index into the table. The object identifiers have the following general form:

standard-MIB-prefix . ip . ipRoutingTable . ipRouteEntry . field *. IPdestaddr*

The *IPdestaddr* portion of the identifier gives a 4-octet IP address used to identify the route.

Matching function *srt_match* extracts the field specification, and matches the suffix of the object id against the IP address of a routing table entry.

```
/* srt_match.c - srt_match */

#include <conf.h>
#include <kernel.h>
#include <network.h>
#include <snmp.h>
#include <mib.h>


/*------------------------------------------------------------------------
 * srt_match - check if a variable exists in the current Routing Table
 *------------------------------------------------------------------------
 */
int srt_match(bindl, rtp, rtl, field)
struct snbentry *bindl;
struct route    **rtp;
int             *rtl;
int             *field;
{
        int     oidi, i;
        Bool    found;

        oidi = SRT_OIDLEN;
        if ((*field = bindl->sb_oid.id[oidi++]) > SNUMF_RTTAB)
                return SYSERR;
        /* oidi points to IP address to match in the routing table. */
```

```
        for (found = FALSE, i = 0; !found && i < RT_TSIZE; i++)
            for (*rtp = rttable[i]; *rtp; *rtp = (*rtp)->rt_next)
                if (found = soipequ(&bindl->sb_oid.id[oidi],
                                    (*rtp)->rt_net, IP_ALEN))
                    break;
        if (!found ||                           /* not there         */
            oidi + IP_ALEN != bindl->sb_oid.len) /* not end of object id*/
                return SYSERR;
        *rtl = i - 1;
        return OK;
}
```

Srt_match assigns argument *field* the field identifier from the object id, and searches the IP routing table for an entry that matches the IP address given in the object id. The search iterates through all locations of the routing table, and follows the linked list of routes that extends from each. *Srt_match* returns *OK* if it finds an exact match, and returns *SYSERR* otherwise.

20.7.1 Get Operation For The Routing Table

The MIB routing table variable contains ten fields. The obvious fields correspond to the destination IP address (*ipRouteDest*), the address of the next-hop for that destination (*ipRouteNextHop*), and the index of the interface over which traffic will be sent to the next hop (*ipRouteIfIndex*). The table also contains fields that specify the protocol that installed the route (*ipRouteProto*), the type of route (*ipRouteType*), and the time-to-live value for the route (*ipRouteAge*). Function *srt_get* implements the *get* operation for the routing table. It calls *srt_match* to find a route that matches the specified object identifier, and then uses the specified field to select the correct piece of code to satisfy the request.

```
/* srt_get.c - srt_get */

#include <conf.h>
#include <kernel.h>
#include <network.h>
#include <snmp.h>
#include <mib.h>
#include <asn1.h>


/*------------------------------------------------------------------------
 * srt_get - perform a get on a variable in the Routing Table
 *------------------------------------------------------------------------
 */
```

```
int srt_get(bindl, numifaces)
struct snbentry *bindl;
int             numifaces;
{
        struct  route *rtp;
        int     rtl, field;

        if (srt_match(bindl, &rtp, &rtl, &field) == SYSERR)
                return SERR_NO_SUCH;
        switch(field) {
        case 1:         /* ipRouteDest */
                SVTYPE(bindl) = ASN1_IPADDR;
                blkcopy(SVIPADDR(bindl), rtp->rt_net, IP_ALEN);
                return SNMP_OK;
        case 2:         /* ipRouteIfIndex */
                SVTYPE(bindl) = ASN1_INT;
                SVINT(bindl) = rtp->rt_ifnum;
                return SNMP_OK;
        case 3:         /* ipRouteMetric1 */
                SVTYPE(bindl) = ASN1_INT;
                SVINT(bindl) = rtp->rt_metric;
                return SNMP_OK;
        case 4:         /* ipRouteMetric2 */
        case 5:         /* ipRouteMetric3 */
        case 6:         /* ipRouteMetric4 */
                SVTYPE(bindl) = ASN1_INT;
                SVINT(bindl) = -1;
                return SNMP_OK;
        case 7:         /* ipRouteNextHop */
                SVTYPE(bindl) = ASN1_IPADDR;
                blkcopy(SVIPADDR(bindl), rtp->rt_gw, IP_ALEN);
                return SNMP_OK;
        case 8:         /* ipRouteType */
                SVTYPE(bindl) = ASN1_INT;
                if (rtp->rt_metric)
                    SVINT(bindl) = 4;   /* remote */
                else
                    SVINT(bindl) = 3;   /* direct */
                return SNMP_OK;
        case 9:         /* ipRouteProto */
                SVTYPE(bindl) = ASN1_INT;
                SVINT(bindl) = 1;                       /* other */
                return SNMP_OK;
        case 10:                /* ipRouteAge */
```

```
                SVTYPE(bindl) = ASN1_INT;
                SVINT(bindl) = rtp->rt_ttl;
                return SNMP_OK;
        default:
                break;
        }
        return SERR_NO_SUCH;
}
```

Srt_get handles most requests as expected, by accessing the appropriate field of the IP routing structure. Because the local routing table does not include multiple metrics, *srt_get* returns *-1* for requests that correspond to routing metrics *2* through *4*. *Srt_get* always returns the code for *other* (*1*) when a client requests field *ipRouteProto*. Although some routes may have been installed by the local system, by RIP, or by ICMP, *srt_get* has no way of knowing because the local routing table does not distinguish among them. This is an example where the conceptual MIB table includes variables that not only do not exist, but also cannot be computed without making significant changes in the underlying system.

20.7.2 Get-First Operation For The Routing Table

Function *srt_getf* implements the *get-first* operation for the routing table.

```
/* srt_getf.c - srt_getf */

#include <conf.h>
#include <kernel.h>
#include <network.h>
#include <snmp.h>
#include <mib.h>
#include <asn1.h>


/*------------------------------------------------------------------
 * srt_getf - perform a getfirst on a variable in the Routing Table
 *------------------------------------------------------------------
 */
int srt_getf(bindl, mip, numifaces)
struct snbentry *bindl;
struct mib_info *mip;
int             numifaces;
{
        int             rtl, oidi;
        struct route    *rtp, *srt_findnext();
```

```
rtl = -1;          /* use first field, first route */
if ((rtp = srt_findnext(rtp, &rtl)) == 0) {
        if (mip->mi_next)
                return (*mip->mi_next->mi_func)
                        (bindl, mip->mi_next, SOP_GETF);
        return SERR_NO_SUCH;    /* no next node */
}
blkcopy(bindl->sb_oid.id, mip->mi_objid.id, mip->mi_objid.len*2);
oidi = mip->mi_objid.len;

bindl->sb_oid.id[oidi++] = (u_short) 1;          /* field */
sip2ocpy(&bindl->sb_oid.id[oidi], rtp->rt_net);
bindl->sb_oid.len = oidi + IP_ALEN;

return srt_get(bindl, numifaces);
}
```

When searching for a route, *srt_getf* must be sure to select one that has the lexically smallest object identifier. It calls function *srt_findnext* to scan the table and extract such a route. If the table is empty, *srt_findnext* returns *-1*, and *srt_getf* invokes the *get-first* operation on the next item in the MIB lexical order. If it finds an item, *srt_getf* creates the correct object id, and invokes the *get* operation on that item.

20.7.3 Get-Next Operation For The Routing Table

The *get-next* operation for the routing table differs from the *get-next* operation for previous tables in one significant way: the IP routing table may contain multiple routes for a given destination. The reason is simple: although the MIB defines a destination address as the key for table lookup, the routing table can contain multiple routes for a single key. In particular, the routing table can contain a host-specific route, a subnet-specific route, and a network-specific route for each destination. Consider what happens if the table contains all three for some destination *D*. A *get-next* for *D* finds the host-specific route, and then uses the "next" route in the table. Unfortunately, the next route happens to be the subnet-specific route, which has the same destination IP address. If *get-next* constructs an object identifier for the response, it will be identical to the object identifier used in the request. Thus, a subsequent *get-next* will match the first route entry again, and the client will be unable to move through the table.

To handle the problem of ambiguous destination addresses, our implementation of *get-next* ignores routing table entries that have a destination address equal to that in the object identifier supplied. We can summarize:

Using only the destination IP address as a key for the MIB routing table prevents complete table access because an IP routing table may have multiple routes for a given destination address. When performing the get-next *operation, our implementation skips multiple routing table entries that have the same destination address as the request.*

Function *srt_getn* implements the *get-next* operation for the routing table. It calls function *srt_findnext* to handle the problem of address ambiguity.

```
/* srt_getn.c - srt_getn */

#include <conf.h>
#include <kernel.h>
#include <network.h>
#include <snmp.h>
#include <mib.h>
#include <asn1.h>


/*------------------------------------------------------------------------
 * srt_getn - perform a getnext on a variable in the Routing Table
 *------------------------------------------------------------------------
 */
int srt_getn(bindl, mip, numifaces)
struct snbentry *bindl;
struct mib_info *mip;
int             numifaces;
{
        struct  route   *rtp, *srt_findnext();
        int             rtl, field, oidi;

        if (srt_match(bindl, &rtp, &rtl, &field) == SYSERR)
                return SERR_NO_SUCH;
        if ((rtp = srt_findnext(rtp, &rtl)) == 0) {
                rtp = (struct route *) NULL;
                rtl = 0;                /* set route hash table list to 0 */
                rtp = srt_findnext(rtp, &rtl);
                if (++field > SNUMF_RTTAB)
                        return (*mip->mi_next->mi_func)
                                (bindl, mip->mi_next, SOP_GETF);
        }
        oidi = SRT_OIDLEN;      /* 4.21.1 */

        bindl->sb_oid.id[oidi++] = field;
```

```
          sip2ocpy(&bindl->sb_oid.id[oidi], rtp->rt_net, IP_ALEN);
          bindl->sb_oid.len = oidi + IP_ALEN;

          return srt_get(bindl, numifaces);
}
```

20.7.4 Incremental Search In The Routing Table

Srt_findnext searches the routing table for the "next" entry in lexicographic order.

```
/* srt_findn.c - srt_findnext */

#include <conf.h>
#include <kernel.h>
#include <network.h>

/*-----------------------------------------------------------------------
 * srt_findnext - find next route in the lexicographic ordering
 *-----------------------------------------------------------------------
 */
struct route *srt_findnext(rtp, rtl)
struct route    *rtp;
int             *rtl;
{
        struct route    *nextrtp, *trtp;
        int             i, nextrtl;

        for (i = 0, nextrtl = -1; i < RT_TSIZE; i++)
                for (trtp = rttable[i]; trtp; trtp = trtp->rt_next) {
                        if (rtl >= 0 &&
                            blkcmp(trtp->rt_net,rtp->rt_net,IP_ALEN)<=0)
                                continue;
                        if (nextrtl < 0 || blkcmp(trtp->rt_net,
                                        nextrtp->rt_net, IP_ALEN) < 0) {
                                nextrtp = trtp;
                                nextrtl = i;
                        }
                }
        if (nextrtl == -1)      /* no next route found */
                return 0;
        *rtl = nextrtl;
        return nextrtp;
}
```

When called with argument *rtp* equal to *-1*, *srt_findnext* locates the lexically least entry; when called with a specific route, it finds the route that follows it, skipping multiple routes that have the same destination address.

20.7.5 Set Operation For The Routing Table

Function *srt_set* implements the *set* operation for the routing table.

```
/* srt_set.c - srt_set */

#include <conf.h>
#include <kernel.h>
#include <network.h>
#include <snmp.h>
#include <mib.h>
#include <asn1.h>

/*-----------------------------------------------------------------------
 * srt_set - perform a set operation on a variable in the Routing Table
 *-----------------------------------------------------------------------
 */
int srt_set(bindl, mip, numifaces)
struct snbentry *bindl;
struct mib_info *mip;
int             numifaces;
{
        struct  route   *rtp;
        int             rtl, field;

        if (srt_match(bindl, &rtp, &rtl, &field) == SYSERR)
                return SERR_NO_SUCH;
        switch (field) {
        case 1:             /* ipRouteDest */
                if (SVTYPE(bindl) != ASN1_IPADDR)
                    return SERR_BAD_VALUE;
                blkcopy(rtp->rt_net, SVIPADDR(bindl), IP_ALEN);
                return SNMP_OK;
        case 2:             /* ipRouteIfIndex */
                if (SVTYPE(bindl) != ASN1_INT ||
                    SVINT(bindl) <= 0 || SVINT(bindl) > numifaces)
                        return SERR_BAD_VALUE;
                rtp->rt_ifnum = SVINT(bindl);
                break;
        case 3:             /* ipRouteMetric1 */
```

```
                if (SVTYPE(bindl) != ASN1_INT || SVINT(bindl) < 0)
                        return SERR_BAD_VALUE;
                rtp->rt_metric = SVINT(bindl);
                break;
        case 4:             /* ipRouteMetric2 */
        case 5:             /* ipRouteMetric3 */
        case 6:             /* ipRouteMetric4 */
                break;
        case 7:             /* ipRouteNextHop */
                if (SVTYPE(bindl) != ASN1_IPADDR)
                        return SERR_BAD_VALUE;
                blkcopy(rtp->rt_gw, SVIPADDR(bindl), IP_ALEN);
                break;
        case 8:             /* ipRouteType */
                /* route type is invalid (2) ==> should remove route
                   from routing table */
                if (SVTYPE(bindl) != ASN1_INT ||
                    SVINT(bindl) < 1 || SVINT(bindl) > 4)
                        return SERR_BAD_VALUE;
                if (SVINT(bindl) == 2)   /* route invalid */
                        (void) rtdel(rtp->rt_net, rtp->rt_mask);
                break;
        case 9:             /* ipRouteProto */
                break;
        case 10:                 /* ipRouteAge */
                if (SVTYPE(bindl) != ASN1_INT ||
                    SVINT(bindl) < 0)
                        return SERR_BAD_VALUE;
                rtp->rt_ttl = SVINT(bindl);
                break;
        default:
                return SERR_NO_SUCH;
        }
        return SNMP_OK;
}
```

For most fields of the routing table, *srt_set* translates assignment requests into appropriate assignments to fields in the routing table. Assignments to fields that the local software does not provide (e.g., multiple routing metrics) have no effect. *Srt_set* checks most values to insure that they are valid before assigning them.

Srt_set contains one interesting special case. The protocol standard specifies that assigning *invalid* to field *ipRouteType* means that the route should be removed from the table. If the request assigns *invalid* (2) to the *ipRouteType* field, *srt_set* calls *rtdel* to remove the route.

20.8 TCP Connection Table Functions

The MIB defines a table that contains all active TCP connections. Object identifiers for the TCP connection table have the following general form:

standard-MIB-prefix . tcp . tcpConnTable . tcpConnEntry . remainder

where *remainder* consists of five fields:

field . localIP . localport . remoteIP . remoteport

As expected, the object identifier contains the standard MIB prefix, specifies that the item lies in the TCP subhierarchy, and then specifies the connection table as well as the connection table entry. The *localIP*, *localport*, *remoteIP*, and *remoteport* portions of the identifier give the IP addresses and protocol port numbers of the connection endpoints, while the *field* selects among the fields in a table entry. As with other tables, a matching function verifies that an identifier correctly matches the connection table, and extracts the value of the field selector. Procedure *stc_match* performs the matching.

```
/* stc_match.c - stc_match */

#include <conf.h>
#include <kernel.h>
#include <network.h>
#include <snmp.h>
#include <mib.h>
#include <asn1.h>


/*------------------------------------------------------------------
 * stc_match - check if a variable exists in the TCP connections table
 *------------------------------------------------------------------
 */
int stc_match(bindl, field, tcbn)
struct snbentry *bindl;
int             *field, *tcbn;
{
        int     oidi = STC_OIDLEN;
        IPaddr  lip, rip;
        int     lport, rport;

        if ((*field = bindl->sb_oid.id[oidi++]) > SNUMF_TCTAB)
                return SYSERR;
        so2ipcpy(lip, &bindl->sb_oid.id[oidi]);
        oidi += IP_ALEN;
```

```
        lport = bindl->sb_oid.id[oidi++];
        so2ipcpy(rip, &bindl->sb_oid.id[oidi]);
        oidi += IP_ALEN;
        rport = bindl->sb_oid.id[oidi++];

        for (*tcbn = 0; *tcbn < Ntcp; ++(*tcbn)) {
                if (tcbtab[*tcbn].tcb_state == TCPS_FREE)
                        continue;
                if (lport == tcbtab[*tcbn].tcb_lport &&
                    rport == tcbtab[*tcbn].tcb_rport &&
                    blkequ(rip, tcbtab[*tcbn].tcb_rip, IP_ALEN) &&
                    blkequ(lip, tcbtab[*tcbn].tcb_lip, IP_ALEN))
                        break;
        }
        if (*tcbn >= Ntcp || oidi != bindl->sb_oid.len)
                return SYSERR;
        return OK;
}
```

After extracting the *field* selector, *stc_match* searches the TCB table to find a valid entry that matches the connection endpoints specified in the object identifier. It compares both the local and remote address and port pairs because TCP uses both endpoints to identify a connection. If *stc_match* finds a connection that matches the object identifier, it assigns argument *tcbn* the index in array *tcbtab* at which information about the connection can be found, and returns *OK*. Otherwise, it returns the error code *SYSERR*.

20.8.1 Get Operation For The TCP Connection Table

Each entry in the conceptual MIB connection table has five fields that correspond to the connection state, the local IP address, the local TCP port number, the remote IP address, and the remote TCP port number. Procedure *stc_get* implements the *get* operation for the connection table by using the field selector to choose among the five items.

```
/* stc_get.c - stc_get */

#include <conf.h>
#include <kernel.h>
#include <network.h>
#include <snmp.h>
#include <mib.h>
#include <asn1.h>

/*------------------------------------------------------------------------
 * stc_get - perform a get on a variable in the TCP connections table
 *------------------------------------------------------------------------
 */
int stc_get(bindl)
struct snbentry *bindl;
{
        int     field, tcbn;

        if (stc_match(bindl, &field, &tcbn) == SYSERR)
                return SERR_NO_SUCH;
        switch (field) {
        case 1:          /* tcpConnState */
                SVTYPE(bindl) = ASN1_INT;
                SVINT(bindl) = tcbtab[tcbn].tcb_state;
                break;
        case 2:          /* tcpConnLocalAddress */
                SVTYPE(bindl) = ASN1_IPADDR;
                blkcopy(SVIPADDR(bindl), tcbtab[tcbn].tcb_lip, IP_ALEN);
                break;
        case 3:          /* tcpConnLocalPort */
                SVTYPE(bindl) = ASN1_INT;
                SVINT(bindl) = tcbtab[tcbn].tcb_lport;
                break;
        case 4:          /* tcpConnRemAddress */
                SVTYPE(bindl) = ASN1_IPADDR;
                blkcopy(SVIPADDR(bindl), tcbtab[tcbn].tcb_rip, IP_ALEN);
                break;
        case 5:          /* tcpConnRemPort */
                SVTYPE(bindl) = ASN1_INT;
                SVINT(bindl) = tcbtab[tcbn].tcb_rport;
                break;
        default:
                return SERR_NO_SUCH;
        }
        return SNMP_OK;
}
```

20.8.2 Get-First Operation For The TCP Connection Table

Procedure *stc_getf* provides the *get-first* operation for the TCP connection table. *Stc_getf* calls *stc_findnext* to search array *tcbtab* until it finds the allocated TCB that has the lexically least identifier. If no TCB has been allocated, the MIB connection table is defined to be empty, so *stc_getf* applies the *get-first* operation to the next variable in the lexical order, and returns the result. If it finds a valid connection, *stc_getf* constructs an object identifier for the connection, applies the *get* operation to it, and returns the result.

```
/* stc_getf.c - stc_getf */

#include <conf.h>
#include <kernel.h>
#include <network.h>
#include <snmp.h>
#include <mib.h>
#include <asn1.h>

/*------------------------------------------------------------------------
 * stc_getf - do a getfirst on a variable in the TCP connection table
 *------------------------------------------------------------------------
 */
int stc_getf(bindl, mip, numifaces)
struct snbentry *bindl;
struct mib_info *mip;
int             numifaces;
{
        int     oidi, tcbn;

        /* find first connection, if any */
        tcbn = stc_findnext(-1);
        if (tcbn < 0) {
                if (mip->mi_next)
                        return((*mip->mi_next->mi_func)
                                (bindl, mip->mi_next, SOP_GETF));
                return SERR_NO_SUCH;
        }
        blkcopy(bindl->sb_oid.id, mip->mi_objid.id, mip->mi_objid.len*2);
        oidi = mip->mi_objid.len;

        bindl->sb_oid.id[oidi++] = (u_short) 1; /* field */
        sip2ocpy(&bindl->sb_oid.id[oidi], tcbtab[tcbn].tcb_lip);
        oidi += IP_ALEN;
        bindl->sb_oid.id[oidi++] = (u_short) tcbtab[tcbn].tcb_lport;
```

```
        sip2ocpy(&bindl->sb_oid.id[oidi], tcbtab[tcbn].tcb_rip);
        oidi += IP_ALEN;
        bindl->sb_oid.id[oidi++] = (u_short) tcbtab[tcbn].tcb_rport;
        bindl->sb_oid.len = oidi;

        return stc_get(bindl);
}
```

20.8.3 Get-Next Operation For The TCP Connection Table

Procedure *stc_getn* implements the *get-next* operation for the connection table.

```
/* stc_getn.c - stc_getn */

#include <conf.h>
#include <kernel.h>
#include <network.h>
#include <snmp.h>
#include <mib.h>
#include <asn1.h>

/*------------------------------------------------------------------
 * stc_getn - do a getnext on a variable in the TCP connection table
 *------------------------------------------------------------------
 */
stc_getn(bindl, mip)
struct snbentry *bindl;
struct mib_info *mip;
{
        int     oidi, field, tcbn, ttcbn;

        if (stc_match(bindl,&field,&tcbn) == SYSERR)
                return SERR_NO_SUCH;
        /* search for next connection */
        if ((tcbn = stc_findnext(tcbn)) < 0) {
                tcbn = stc_findnext(-1);
                if (++field > SNUMF_TCTAB)
                        return((*mip->mi_next->mi_func)
                                (bindl, mip->mi_next, SOP_GETF));
        }
        oidi = STC_OIDLEN;      /* 6.13.1 */

        bindl->sb_oid.id[oidi++] = (u_short) field;
```

```
        sip2ocpy(&bindl->sb_oid.id[oidi], tcbtab[tcbn].tcb_lip);
        oidi += IP_ALEN;
        bindl->sb_oid.id[oidi++] = (u_short) tcbtab[tcbn].tcb_lport;
        sip2ocpy(&bindl->sb_oid.id[oidi], tcbtab[tcbn].tcb_rip);
        oidi += IP_ALEN;
        bindl->sb_oid.id[oidi++] = (u_short) tcbtab[tcbn].tcb_rport;
        bindl->sb_oid.len = oidi;

        return stc_get(bindl);
}
```

Stc_getn uses *stc_match* to find the TCB that matches the specified identifier. It then calls procedure *stc_findnext* to search for the next valid connection. Once *stc_findnext* finds a valid entry in *tcbtab*, it returns the index. If it finds a valid connection, *stc_getn* constructs an object identifier for the entry, applies the *get* operation, and returns the result.

If no more valid entries exist, *stc_getn* increments the field specification, moves back to the start of array *tcbtab*, and continues the search. Finally, after exhausting all fields of all valid connections, *stc_getn* applies the *get-first* operation to the lexically next MIB variable, and returns the result.

20.8.4 Incremental Search In The TCP Connection Table

Procedure *stc_findnext* searches the table of TCBs for the TCB that lexically follows the one specified by argument *tcbn*.

```c
/* stc_findn.c - stc_findnext, sntcpcmp */

#include <conf.h>
#include <kernel.h>
#include <network.h>

/*------------------------------------------------------------------------
 * stc_findnext - search the TCP connection table for the next valid entry
 *------------------------------------------------------------------------
 */
int stc_findnext(tcbn)
int     tcbn;
{
        int     i, next;

        for (i = 0, next = -1; i < Ntcp; ++i) {
                if (tcbtab[i].tcb_state == TCPS_FREE ||
                    (tcbn >= 0 && sntcpcmp(i, tcbn) <= 0))
                        continue;
                if (next < 0 || sntcpcmp(i, next) < 0)
                        next = i;
        }
        return next;
}


/*------------------------------------------------------------------------
 * sntcpcmp - compare two TCP connections in SNMP lexical ordering
 *------------------------------------------------------------------------
 */
int sntcpcmp(tcb1, tcb2)
int     tcb1, tcb2;
{
        int     rv;

        if (rv=blkcmp(tcbtab[tcb1].tcb_lip,tcbtab[tcb2].tcb_lip,IP_ALEN))
                return rv;
        if (rv = (tcbtab[tcb1].tcb_lport - tcbtab[tcb2].tcb_lport))
                return rv;
        if (rv=blkcmp(tcbtab[tcb1].tcb_rip,tcbtab[tcb2].tcb_rip,IP_ALEN))
                return rv;
        if (rv = (tcbtab[tcb1].tcb_rport - tcbtab[tcb2].tcb_rport))
                return rv;
        return 0;
}
```

To find the lexical order imposed by the MIB for a pair of connections, the software must evaluate all four components of the connection endpoints. The local IP address is the most significant field, the local protocol port is the next significant field, the remote IP address is the next significant field, and the remote protocol port number is the least significant field. Function *sntcpcmp* compares two endpoints according to the lexicographic order. It returns zero if they are equal, a value less than zero if the first is lexically less than the second, and a value greater than zero if the first is lexically greater than the second.

20.8.5 Set Operation For The TCP Connection Table

The MIB defines all values in the TCP connection table to be read-only, so a server must return an error in response to a *set* request. Procedure *stc_set* returns the appropriate error value.

```
/* stc_set.c - stc_set */

#include <conf.h>
#include <kernel.h>
#include <network.h>
#include <snmp.h>
#include <mib.h>
#include <asn1.h>

/*-------------------------------------------------------------------
 * stc_set - return error: the TCP Connections Table is read-only
 *-------------------------------------------------------------------
 */
stc_set(bindl, mip)
struct snbentry *bindl;
struct mib_info *mip;
{
        return SERR_NO_SUCH;
}
```

20.9 Summary

Table access functions differ from access functions for simple variables because the server must interpret part of the object identifier as an index to a specific table entry. *Get* and *set* operations require the client to supply the full name of the table entry. The *get-next* operation allows the client to walk tables without knowing the exact names for all items.

We reviewed the implementation of the MIB address entry table, network interface table, address translation table, IP routing table, and TCP connection table. Each table requires routines that provide *get*, *get-next*, and *set* operations. In addition, our implementation includes a *match* function for each table that matches object identifiers against available table entries, a *findnext* function that finds the next entry in the lexicographic order, and a *get-first* function that handles a *get-next* request for empty tables.

FOR FURTHER STUDY

More details on the names of MIB variables can be found in McCloghrie and Rose [RFC 1156] and [RFC 1155]. The MIB-II documented in Rose [RFC 1158] proposes several changes to the tables described here.

EXERCISES

20.1   Should a manager be allowed to *set* the hardware address in an address translation table entry? Why or why not?

20.2   What is the exact form of an ASN.1 object identifier for the *ipRouteNextHop* field in an *ipRoutingTable* entry for IP address 128.10.2.3?

20.3   Can SNMP access all fields in all IP routing table entries? Why or why not?

20.4   What will the server return if a client issues an SNMP *get-next* request with an object identifier that specifies the last entry in the address translation table?

20.5   Can SNMP be used to create a new entry in any of the tables shown here? Explain.

20.6   The implementation shown does not provide a table of EGP information. Read the MIB specification, and make a list of all fields required for the EGP table.

21

Implementation In Retrospect

21.1 Introduction

This brief chapter takes a retrospective look at the implementation presented in previous chapters. It analyzes the code, points to strengths and weaknesses in the protocols from an implementation perspective, and draws conclusions about the design of protocol software.

21.2 Statistical Analysis Of The Code

Analyzing a system as large as the one covered in this text is difficult because no single measure provides an accurate assessment. Furthermore, it is impossible to measure "difficulty" or "effort" because the man-months of effort depend on the skill and background of the programmers involved. Thus, we have chosen to avoid such evaluations, and look instead at objective measures of the resulting code.

Two measurements of the software verify our intuitive assessments, and provide sufficient data to support a few conclusions. The first measurement counts the number of functions or procedures used to implement a given protocol; the second counts the number of lines of code. While we understand that the division of software into procedures depends on the programmer, and the number of lines of code depends on the coding style, these measures say much about the relative complexity of implementing the major protocols.

21.3 Lines Of Code For Each Protocol

The first measure to evaluate the software considers the lines of code required to implement each protocol. The code evaluated includes all pieces of the software discussed in the text, as well as several machine-dependent support procedures not shown. It has been divided into nine groups†: *TCP*, *SNMP*, *NET* (the network device driver and network interface routines), *IP* (including all routines that handle routing, fragmentation and reassembly, and broadcast), *OTHER*, *ARP*, *UDP*, *RIP*, and *ICMP*. The *OTHER* group, includes utilities, such as the checksum procedures and initialization routines. The evaluation did not include other operating system functions or the code for other protocols (e.g., the code for *rwho* was omitted from consideration).

The code considered includes approximately 15,000 lines. Figure 21.1 shows the lines of code in each group as a percentage of the total code considered. As the figure shows, TCP requires the most code. Of course, TCP provides the most functionality of all protocols considered, and handles the most types of errors. By contrast, IP requires fewer than half as many lines of code because it does not need sophisticated retransmission or acknowledgement. Even IP, ICMP, and UDP together do not account for as much code as TCP.

The size of the network interface code may seem excessive, but readers should recall that it includes the device driver code as well as the interface between IP and the device. Device drivers are inherently hardware-dependent. They usually require many lines of code to handle the details of DMA memory, hardware interfaces, and hardware interrupt processing. Thus, the code needed for the interface is not unusual.

The amount of code required for SNMP provides the only real surprise. SNMP accounts for nearly as much code as TCP even though it provides only a simple service. The reason is simple: unlike TCP, SNMP tries to be as general as possible. It uses variable-length encodings for every field (including the field lengths themselves!). Thus, extracting even a simple integer field from an SNMP message requires much computation, even though current computers cannot handle more then *32*-bit integers. In fact, the SNMP code contains an ad hoc parser for a cumbersome and tedious language. To summarize:

> *Analysis reveals that the variable-length field encoding used by SNMP makes the code much larger (and slower) than the other TCP/IP protocols.*

---

†The groups are listed here in decreasing order by size.

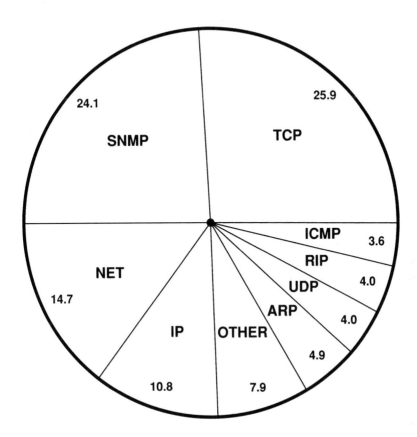

Figure 21.1 Lines of code used to implement each major protocol as a percentage of the total. Category *OTHER* includes miscellaneous utility functions, such as the one used to compute checksums, as well as initialization code.

21.4 Functions And Procedures For Each Protocol

Figure 21.2 shows another measure of the code. It reports the number of procedures and functions used to implement each protocol as a percentage of the approximately 300 routines used for the entire system. The counts exclude operating system procedures and general-purpose library routines that are not part of the TCP/IP software.

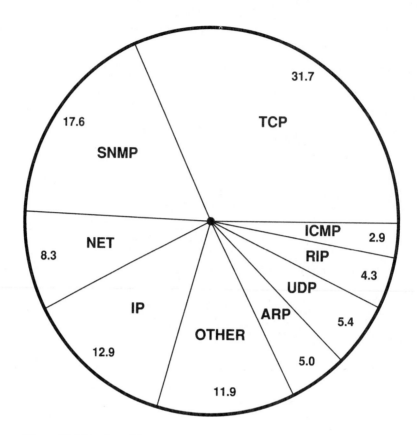

Figure 21.2 Number of functions and procedures used to implement each protocol as a percentage of the total. The chart follows the order Figure 21.1 uses.

Of course, individual coding style can influence the number of procedures used. Although several programmers have contributed to the code considered here, they all started by studying the Xinu system and adopting its style. One person wrote most of the code, and all code has been reviewed to make it conform to the desired style. Thus, it seems reasonable to assume that the coding style is relatively uniform, and that variations among individual programming talents do not account for significant differences.

Assuming relative uniformity among the modules is important because it allows us to use the division into functions as a measure of difficulty. In particular:

> *If uniform coding style is used throughout a piece of software, the number of functions used to implement a given part gives a rough measure of its complexity.*

Using this idea allows us to understand more about the protocols. As Figure 21.2 shows, TCP is by far the most complex. Again, intuition dictates that TCP is the most complex of the protocols considered because it provides the most functionality. However, it is interesting to compare how TCP ranks in lines of code (Figure 21.1) to how it ranks in functions used (Figure 21.2). The conclusion we can draw is that the rich functionality in TCP arises because it provides many services, not because any one service is complicated.

By contrast to its rank when protocols are ordered by number of lines (Figure 21.1), IP moves to third position when ranked by number of functions (Figure 21.2). The explanation is again simple: like TCP, IP has many facets that together provide its functionality.

SNMP provides another surprise in Figure 21.2. When ranked by the number of functions used in the implementation instead of the number of lines used, the percentage of the total devoted to SNMP shrinks considerably. To understand why, consider procedures like *snparse*. Although the procedure is long, it does not perform a complex task. Like much of the SNMP code, it trudges through the task of parsing an ASN.1 encoding and converting it to an internal fixed-field format. Thus, the SNMP implementation takes much space (and time), but does not require especially clever coding.

21.5 Summary

An analysis of the code provides few surprises. As expected, TCP requires the most code because it provides the most services and handles the most problems. In fact, TCP accounts for slightly more code than IP, ICMP, UDP, and ARP combined. The network interface accounts for a large portion of the code because it includes device drivers.

Assuming a uniform coding style, the division into functions provides a measure of complexity. According to this measure, both TCP and IP are relatively complex. Compared to TCP, the SNMP code has fewer procedures, but the average size of each procedure is larger. Thus, it is not as complex as TCP, even though it accounts for much of the total code volume. Many of the SNMP procedures concentrate on translating from the unwieldy variable-length encoding to a fixed-field internal form.

EXERCISES

21.1   The analysis reported here came from a version of the code available in late 1990. Obtain a machine-readable copy of the software and compare values reported here to those for later versions of the software.

21.2   Should ASN.1 procedures be included when counting SNMP code? Explain.

21.3   The example code provides gateway functions. What percentage of the code can be eliminated if it runs on a host that has only one network connection?

21.4   Obtain a machine-readable copy of the software described in the text. What percentage of *OTHER* code accounts for domain name system software?

21.5   Estimate the total amount of space used by each protocol by estimating the size of the data structures each uses.

21.6   Verify that the coding style does not differ among protocols. To do so, obtain a machine-readable copy of the software, build a program that removes comments and unnecessary white space from the code, and apply the program to all procedures. Does the ratio of sizes of compressed code to uncompressed code differ for different protocols?

21.7   Compare our implementation of TCP/IP to another one (e.g., the one distributed with BSD UNIX). Are there significant differences in lines of code or number of functions and procedures?

Appendix 1

Cross Reference Of Procedure Calls

Introduction

Because any software system as large as TCP consists of hundreds of procedures stored in hundreds of files, studying the code can be difficult. Reading code from a large system is especially frustrating simply because the reader cannot easily find procedures and variables. In particular, it is most difficult to find references to a given procedure, because they can appear anywhere.

Computer scientists formalize the relationship among procedure calls into a *call graph*. The call graph for a set of procedures is a directed graph in which each node corresponds to a single procedure, and an edge from node *A* to node *B* means procedure *A* calls procedure *B*. For simple programs, a pictorial representation of the call graph suffices. For large systems, however, a pictorial representation becomes too large and complex to make it useful; textual representations become necessary.

This appendix provides a textual representation of the call graph for all procedures used in the text. It expresses the relationship *is called by* as well as the usual *calls* relationship. The information is organized into an alphabetical list of all procedures and in-line macros used in the example TCP code†. Each entry in the alphabetical list gives the name of a procedure or macro, the name of the file in which the definition appears, the page number in the text on which the file appears (if it does), the names of all files that contain references, and the names of all procedures referenced in the defining file.

---

†To make names easier to find, they have been sorted with uppercase and lowercase letters treated identically, and with underscores ignored. Thus, one finds *TCP_HLEN* immediately before *tcphowmuch*.

a1readint in a1rwint.c, *pg. 394*
called in: a1rwval.c
calls: a1writeint

a1readlen in a1rwlen.c, *pg. 392*
called in: sna2b.c snparse.c
calls: a1writelen

a1readoid in a1rwoid.c, *pg. 396*
called in: a1rwval.c sna2b.c
calls: a1writeoid

a1readval in a1rwval.c, *pg. 398*
called in: sna2b.c
calls: a1readint a1readoid a1writeint
a1writelen a1writeoid a1writeval

A1_SIGNED macro in asn1.h, *pg. 390*

called in: a1rwint.c

a1writeint in a1rwint.c, *pg. 394*
called in: a1rwval.c
calls: a1readint

a1writelen in a1rwlen.c, *pg. 392*
called in: a1rwval.c mksnmp.c
snb2a.c
calls: a1readlen

a1writeoid in a1rwoid.c, *pg. 396*
called in: a1rwval.c snb2a.c
calls: a1readoid

a1writeval in a1rwval.c, *pg. 398*
called in: snb2a.c
calls: a1readint a1readoid a1readval
a1writeint a1writelen a1writeoid

addarg in addarg.c
called in: shell.c
calls: isbadpid

addflag macro in x_net.c

arpadd in arpadd.c, *pg. 47*
called in: arp_in.c
calls: arpalloc

arpalloc in arpalloc.c, *pg. 52*
called in: arpadd.c netwrite.c
calls: arpdq

arpdq in arpdq.c, *pg. 55*
called in: arpalloc.c arptimer.c
calls: icmp

arpfind in arpfind.c, *pg. 42*
called in: arp_in.c netwrite.c

arp_in in arp_in.c, *pg. 49*
called in: ni_in.c
calls: arpadd arpfind arpqsend hs2net
net2hs

arpinit in arpinit.c, *pg. 56*
called in: netstart.c

arpprint in arpprint.c
called in: x_arp.c
calls: printone

arpqsend in arpqsend.c, *pg. 48*
called in: arp_in.c
calls: netwrite

arpsend in arpsend.c, *pg. 44*
called in: arptimer.c netwrite.c
calls: hs2net

arptimer in arptimer.c, *pg. 54*
called in: slowtimer.c
calls: arpdq arpsend

ascdate in ascdate.c
called in: x_date.c x_who.c
calls: isleap

BTOP macro in dma.h

BYTE macro in network.h
called in: fclient.c x_dumper.c
  x_finger.c x_ns.c

cksum in cksum.c, *pg. 70*
called in: icmp.c icmp_in.c ipfsend.c
  ipproc.c ipputp.c

DELAY macro in slu.h

dn_cat macro in domain.h
called in: ip2name.c name2ip.c

dnparse in dnparse.c
called in: tcpbind.c
calls: isdigit

dot2ip in dot2ip.c
called in: name2ip.c x_conf.c
  x_route.c x_snmp.c

dot2oid in x_snmp.c
calls: dot2ip echoch erase1 eraseall
  eraseword find_completions
  getnewbl getword initgetword ip2dot
  isalpha isdigit name2ip objd2oid
  parseoid parseoidlist parseset
  parsevalue print_completion
  sendquery snclient snerr snfreebl
  sninit snmpprint snusage strequ
  strnequ

dsdirec macro in disk.h

dssync macro in disk.h

dump in x_dumper.c
calls: name2ip summary

echoch in x_snmp.c
calls: dot2ip dot2oid erase1 eraseall
  eraseword find_completions
  getnewbl getword initgetword ip2dot
  isalpha isdigit name2ip objd2oid
  parseoid parseoidlist parseset
  parsevalue print_completion
  sendquery snclient snerr snfreebl
  sninit snmpprint snusage strequ
  strnequ

echod in echod.c
calls: echop

ECHOMAX macro in icsetdata.c,
  pg. 139

echop in echod.c
calls: echod

efaceinit in initgate.c
called in: inithost.c
calls: initgate netnum ofaceinit rtadd
  setmask

egp in egp.c

erase1 in x_snmp.c
calls: dot2ip dot2oid echoch eraseall
  eraseword find_completions
  getnewbl getword initgetword ip2dot
  isalpha isdigit name2ip objd2oid
  parseoid parseoidlist parseset
  parsevalue print_completion
  sendquery snclient snerr snfreebl
  sninit snmpprint snusage strequ
  strnequ

eraseall in x_snmp.c
calls: dot2ip dot2oid echoch erase1
eraseword find_completions
getnewbl getword initgetword ip2dot
isalpha isdigit name2ip objd2oid
parseoid parseoidlist parseset
parsevalue print_completion
sendquery snclient snerr snfreebl
sninit snmpprint snusage strequ
strnequ

eraseword in x_snmp.c
calls: dot2ip dot2oid echoch erase1
eraseall find_completions getnewbl
getword initgetword ip2dot isalpha
isdigit name2ip objd2oid parseoid
parseoidlist parseset parsevalue
print_completion sendquery snclient
snerr snfreebl sninit snmpprint
snusage strequ strnequ

ethcntl in ethcntl.c
calls: ethstrt set_bit

ethdemux in ethdemux.c
called in: ethinter.c
calls: net2hs ni_in

ethinit in ethinit.c
calls: ethstrt hi8 low16 printcsr0

ethinter in ethinter.c
calls: ethdemux ethwstrt printcsr0

ethstrt in ethstrt.c
called in: ethcntl.c ethinit.c
calls: hi8 low16 printcsr0

ethwrite in ethwrite.c
calls: ethwstrt hs2net

ethwstrt in ethwstrt.c
called in: ethinter.c ethwrite.c
othwrite.c

EVENT macro in tcpfsm.h, *pg. 176*
called in: tcpout.c tqdump.c

fd_to_dd macro in io.h

fgetc macro in io.h

find_completions in x_snmp.c
calls: dot2ip dot2oid echoch erase1
eraseall eraseword getnewbl getword
initgetword ip2dot isalpha isdigit
name2ip objd2oid parseoid
parseoidlist parseset parsevalue
print_completion sendquery snclient
snerr snfreebl sninit snmpprint
snusage strequ strnequ

findfd macro in io.h

FindName in x_conf.c
calls: dot2ip ip2name

finger in fclient.c, *pg. 312*
calls: name2ip

fingerd in fserver.c, *pg. 314*

firstid macro in q.h

firstkey macro in q.h

fopen macro in name.h

fputc macro in io.h

freestk macro in mem.h

getaddr in getaddr.c
calls: getiaddr rarpsend

get_bit in ethcntl.c
calls: ethcntl ethstrt set_bit

getchar macro in io.h

get_hashbit in ethcntl.c
calls: ethcntl ethstrt set_bit

getiaddr in getaddr.c
called in: getname.c getnet.c
netstart.c
calls: getaddr rarpsend

getiname in getname.c
called in: netstart.c
calls: getiaddr getname ip2name

getinet in getnet.c
calls: getiaddr getnet

getmib in snhash.c, *pg. 385*
called in: snprint.c snrslv.c
calls: hashinit hashoid oidequ

getname in getname.c
called in: login.c name2ip.c rwhod.c
shell.c x_uptime.c x_who.c
calls: getiaddr getiname ip2name

getnet in getnet.c
calls: getiaddr getinet

getnewbl in x_snmp.c
calls: dot2ip dot2oid echoch erase1
eraseall eraseword find_completions
getword initgetword ip2dot isalpha
isdigit name2ip objd2oid parseoid
parseoidlist parseset parsevalue
print_completion sendquery snclient
snerr snfreebl sninit snmpprint
snusage strequ strnequ

GETPHYS macro in dma.h

getsim in inithost.c
calls: efaceinit inithost ofaceinit

getutim in getutim.c
called in: login.c netstart.c rwhod.c
shell.c
calls: net2hl net2xt

getword in x_snmp.c
calls: dot2ip dot2oid echoch erase1
eraseall eraseword find_completions
getnewbl initgetword ip2dot isalpha
isdigit name2ip objd2oid parseoid
parseoidlist parseset parsevalue
print_completion sendquery snclient
snerr snfreebl sninit snmpprint
snusage strequ strnequ

gname in name2ip.c
calls: dn_cat dot2ip getname hs2net
name2ip net2hs resolve

h2vax macro in network.h

hashinit in snhash.c, *pg. 385*
called in: sninit.c
calls: getmib hashoid oidequ

hashoid in snhash.c, *pg. 385*
calls: getmib hashinit oidequ

hi8 macro in network.h
called in: ethinit.c ethstrt.c

hl2net macro in network.h
called in: ripadd.c riprepl.c rwhod.c
tcph2net.c

hs2net macro in network.h
called in: arpsend.c arp_in.c
ethwrite.c ip2name.c iph2net.c
name2ip.c rarpsend.c ripadd.c
tcph2net.c tcprmss.c udph2net.c

iarg in x_net.c
calls: addflag ip2dot noarg parg
tcpfnames

ibdisp macro in iblock.h

ibtodb macro in iblock.h

icerrok in icerrok.c, *pg. 136*
called in: icmp.c
calls: isbrc

icmp in icmp.c, *pg. 133*
called in: arpdq.c icmp_in.c
ipftimer.c ipproc.c ipputp.c
ipredirect.c local_out.c netstart.c
udp_in.c x_ping.c
calls: cksum icerrok icsetbuf
icsetdata icsetsrc ipsend

icmp_in in icmp_in.c, *pg. 126*
called in: local_out.c
calls: cksum icmp icredirect icsetsrc
ipsend netmask setmask

icredirect in icredirect.c, *pg. 128*
called in: icmp_in.c
calls: netmask rtadd rtdel rtfree rtget

icsetbuf in icsetbuf.c, *pg. 137*
called in: icmp.c

icsetdata in icsetdata.c, *pg. 139*
called in: icmp.c
calls: isodd

icsetsrc in icsetsrc.c, *pg. 132*
called in: icmp.c icmp_in.c
calls: netmatch

initgate in initgate.c
called in: netstart.c
calls: efaceinit netnum ofaceinit
rtadd setmask

initgetword in x_snmp.c
calls: dot2ip dot2oid echoch erase1
eraseall eraseword find_completions
getnewbl getword ip2dot isalpha
isdigit name2ip objd2oid parseoid
parseoidlist parseset parsevalue
print_completion sendquery snclient
snerr snfreebl sninit snmpprint
snusage strequ strnequ

inithost in inithost.c
called in: netstart.c
calls: efaceinit getsim ofaceinit

ip2dot in ip2dot.c
called in: ip2name.c x_net.c
x_routes.c x_snmp.c

ip2name in ip2name.c
called in: getname.c x_conf.c
x_routes.c
calls: dn_cat hs2net ip2dot net2hs

IP_CLASSA macro in ip.h, *pg. 68*
called in: netmask.c netnum.c
rthash.c

IP_CLASSB macro in ip.h, *pg. 68*
called in: netmask.c netnum.c
rthash.c

IP_CLASSC macro in ip.h, *pg. 68*
called in: netmask.c netnum.c
rthash.c

IP_CLASSD macro in ip.h, *pg. 68*
called in: ipproc.c netmask.c
netnum.c ripok.c rthash.c

IP_CLASSE macro in ip.h, *pg. 68*
called in: ipproc.c netmask.c
netnum.c ripok.c rthash.c

isbaddev macro in io.h
called in: x_mount.c

isbadpid macro in proc.h
called in: addarg.c rarp_in.c udp_in.c

isbadport macro in ports.h

isbadsem macro in sem.h

isbrc in isbrc.c, *pg. 72*
called in: icerrok.c ipdbc.c netmatch.c
netwrite.c

iscntrl macro in ctype.h

isdigit macro in ctype.h
called in: dnparse.c x_snmp.c

isempty macro in q.h

isleap macro in date.h
called in: ascdate.c

islower macro in ctype.h

isodd macro in kernel.h
called in: icsetdata.c

isprint macro in ctype.h
called in: snprint.c

isprshort macro in ctype.h

ispunct macro in ctype.h

isspace macro in ctype.h

ISUOPT macro in tcpuopt.c, *pg. 336*

isupper macro in ctype.h

ISVALID macro in dma.h

isxdigit macro in ctype.h

lastkey macro in q.h

level macro in io.h

lexan in lexan.c
called in: shell.c

lfing in lfing.c
called in: x_finger.c

local_out in local_out.c
called in: netwrite.c
calls: icmp icmp_in ipdstopts ipreass

login in login.c
calls: getname getutim

low16 macro in network.h
called in: ethinit.c ethstrt.c

ltim2ut macro in date.h

major macro in systypes.h

makedev macro in systypes.h

marked macro in mark.h
called in: rwhod.c x_who.c

max macro in kernel.h
called in: tcprwindow.c

min macro in kernel.h
called in: tcppersist.c tcprexmt.c
tcpsmss.c tcpsndlen.c tcpwinit.c
tcpxmit.c

minor macro in systypes.h

mkarp in rarpsend.c
calls: hs2net rarpsend rtadd

MKEVENT macro in tcpfsm.h,
pg. 176
called in: tcpkick.c tcpkilltimers.c
tcppersist.c tcprexmt.c tcprtt.c
tcpswindow.c tcpwait.c tcpxmit.c

mksnmp in mksnmp.c, *pg. 418*
called in: snclient.c snmpd.c
calls: a1writelen snb2a

MOVC macro in dma.h

MOVL macro in dma.h

MOVSB macro in dma.h

MOVSL macro in dma.h

MOVSW macro in dma.h

mprint in x_mount.c
calls: isbaddev

name2ip in name2ip.c
called in: fclient.c x_dumper.c
x_finger.c x_ns.c x_ping.c x_snmp.c
calls: dn_cat dot2ip getname gname
hs2net net2hs resolve

N_BADMAG macro in a.out.h

N_BSSADDR macro in a.out.h

N_DATADDR macro in a.out.h

net2hl macro in network.h
called in: getutim.c riprecv.c riprepl.c
rwhoind.c tcpnet2h.c tcpsmss.c

net2hs macro in network.h
called in: arp_in.c ethdemux.c
ip2name.c ipnet2h.c ipputp.c
name2ip.c rarp_in.c riprecv.c
riprepl.c tcpnet2h.c tcpsmss.c
udpnet2h.c

net2xt macro in date.h
called in: getutim.c

netdump in netdump.c

netmask in netmask.c, *pg. 88*
called in: icmp_in.c icredirect.c
ipredirect.c rarp_in.c riprecv.c
setmask.c
calls: netnum

netmatch in netmatch.c, *pg. 87*
called in: icsetsrc.c rtget.c
calls: isbrc

netnum in netnum.c, *pg. 86*
called in: initgate.c netmask.c
rarp_in.c ripadd.c

netstart in netstart.c
calls: arpinit getiaddr getiname
getutim icmp initgate inithost
ipfinit rtadd rwho udpecho

netwrite in netwrite.c, *pg. 45*
called in: arpqsend.c ipfsend.c
ipputp.c
calls: arpalloc arpfind arpsend isbrc
local_out

NIGET macro in netif.h, *pg. 28*
called in: ipgetp.c

ni_in in ni_in.c, *pg. 35*
called in: ethdemux.c
calls: rarp_in

noarg in x_net.c
calls: addflag iarg ip2dot parg
tcpfnames

nonempty macro in q.h

N_PAGSIZ macro in a.out.h

N_SEGSIZ macro in a.out.h

N_STROFF macro in a.out.h

N_SYMOFF macro in a.out.h

N_TXTADDR macro in a.out.h

N_TXTOFF macro in a.out.h

objd2oid in x_snmp.c
calls: dot2ip dot2oid echoch erase1
eraseall eraseword find_completions
getnewbl getword initgetword ip2dot
isalpha isdigit name2ip parseoid
parseoidlist parseset parsevalue
print_completion sendquery snclient
snerr snfreebl sninit snmpprint
snusage strequ strnequ

ofaceinit in initgate.c
called in: inithost.c
calls: efaceinit initgate netnum rtadd
setmask

oidequ macro in snmp.h, *pg. 387*
called in: snhash.c snrslv.c

othinit in othinit.c

othwrite in othwrite.c
calls: ethwstrt

parg in x_net.c
calls: addflag iarg ip2dot noarg
tcpfnames

parseoid in x_snmp.c
calls: dot2ip dot2oid echoch erase1
eraseall eraseword find_completions
getnewbl getword initgetword ip2dot
isalpha isdigit name2ip objd2oid
parseoidlist parseset parsevalue
print_completion sendquery snclient
snerr snfreebl sninit snmpprint
snusage strequ strnequ

parseoidlist in x_snmp.c
calls: dot2ip dot2oid echoch erase1
eraseall eraseword find_completions
getnewbl getword initgetword ip2dot
isalpha isdigit name2ip objd2oid
parseoid parseset parsevalue
print_completion sendquery snclient
snerr snfreebl sninit snmpprint
snusage strequ strnequ

parseset in x_snmp.c
calls: dot2ip dot2oid echoch erase1
eraseall eraseword find_completions
getnewbl getword initgetword ip2dot
isalpha isdigit name2ip objd2oid
parseoid parseoidlist parsevalue
print_completion sendquery snclient
snerr snfreebl sninit snmpprint
snusage strequ strnequ

parsevalue in x_snmp.c
calls: dot2ip dot2oid echoch erase1
eraseall eraseword find_completions
getnewbl getword initgetword ip2dot
isalpha isdigit name2ip objd2oid
parseoid parseoidlist parseset
print_completion sendquery snclient
snerr snfreebl sninit snmpprint
snusage strequ strnequ

print_completion in x_snmp.c
calls: dot2ip dot2oid echoch erase1
eraseall eraseword find_completions
getnewbl getword initgetword ip2dot
isalpha isdigit name2ip objd2oid
parseoid parseoidlist parseset
parsevalue sendquery snclient snerr
snfreebl sninit snmpprint snusage
strequ strnequ

printcsr0 in ethinit.c
called in: ethinter.c ethstrt.c
calls: ethinit ethstrt hi8 low16

printone in arpprint.c
calls: arpprint

PTOB macro in dma.h

putchar macro in io.h

rarp_in in rarp_in.c
called in: ni_in.c
calls: isbadpid net2hs netmask
netnum setmask

rarpsend in rarpsend.c
called in: getaddr.c
calls: hs2net mkarp rtadd

resolve in name2ip.c
calls: dn_cat dot2ip getname gname
hs2net name2ip net2hs

rfing in x_finger.c
calls: lfing name2ip

rip in ripin.c, *pg. 351*
calls: ripcheck riprecv riprepl

ripadd in ripadd.c, *pg. 360*
called in: ripsend.c
calls: hl2net hs2net netnum ripmetric
ripstart

ripcheck in ripcheck.c, *pg. 352*
called in: ripin.c

ripifset in ripifset.c, *pg. 359*
called in: ripsend.c
calls: rtfree rtget

ripmetric in ripmetric.c, *pg. 362*
called in: ripadd.c

ripok in ripok.c, *pg. 356*
called in: riprecv.c

ripout in ripout.c, *pg. 364*
calls: ripsend

riprecv in riprecv.c, *pg. 354*
called in: ripin.c
calls: net2hl net2hs netmask ripok
rtadd rtfree rtget

riprepl in riprepl.c, *pg. 356*
called in: ripin.c
calls: hl2net net2hl net2hs ripsend
rtfree rtget udpsend

ripsend in ripsend.c, *pg. 358*
called in: ripout.c riprepl.c
calls: ripadd ripifset udpsend

ripstart in ripstart.c, *pg. 363*
called in: ripadd.c

roundew macro in mem.h

roundmb macro in mem.h

rtadd in rtadd.c, *pg. 94*
called in: icredirect.c initgate.c
netstart.c rarpsend.c riprecv.c
setmask.c x_route.c
calls: rthash rtinit rtnew

rtdel in rtdel.c, *pg. 98*
called in: icredirect.c setmask.c
srt_set.c x_route.c
calls: rthash

rtdump in rtdump.c
calls: rtinit

RTFREE macro in route.h, *pg. 83*
called in: rtadd.c rtdel.c rtfree.c
rttimer.c

rtfree in rtfree.c, *pg. 99*
called in: icredirect.c ipdbc.c ipproc.c
ipredirect.c ripifset.c riprecv.c
riprepl.c tcpbind.c tcpcon.c
tcpwinit.c udpsend.c x_route.c

rtget in rtget.c, *pg. 90*
called in: icredirect.c ipdbc.c ipproc.c
ipredirect.c ripifset.c riprecv.c
riprepl.c tcpbind.c tcpcon.c
tcpwinit.c udpsend.c x_route.c
calls: netmatch rthash rtinit

rthash in rthash.c, *pg. 89*
called in: rtadd.c rtdel.c rtget.c

rtinit in rtinit.c, *pg. 92*
called in: rtadd.c rtdump.c rtget.c

rtnew in rtnew.c, *pg. 97*
called in: rtadd.c

rttimer in rttimer.c, *pg. 92*
called in: slowtimer.c

RUDK macro in tcb.h, *pg. 166*
called in: tcprurg.c

RUHK macro in tcb.h, *pg. 166*
called in: tcpaddhole.c tcpgetdata.c

rwcomp in x_uptime.c
calls: getname

rwho in rwho.c
called in: netstart.c

rwhod in rwhod.c
calls: getname getutim hl2net
marked udpsend

rwhoind in rwhoind.c
calls: net2hl

sae_findnext in sae_findn.c, *pg. 436*
called in: sae_getf.c sae_getn.c

sae_get in sae_get.c, *pg. 432*
called in: sae_getf.c sae_getn.c
snmib.c
calls: sae_match

sae_getf in sae_getf.c, *pg. 434*
called in: snmib.c
calls: sae_findnext sae_get sip2ocpy

sae_getn in sae_getn.c, *pg. 435*
called in: snmib.c
calls: sae_findnext sae_get sae_match
sip2ocpy

sae_match in sae_match.c, *pg. 431*
called in: sae_get.c sae_getn.c
snmib.c
calls: soipequ

sae_set in sae_set.c, *pg. 437*
called in: snmib.c

satcmp in sat_findn.c, *pg. 444*
calls: sat_findnext

sat_findnext in sat_findn.c, *pg. 444*
called in: sat_getf.c sat_getn.c
calls: satcmp

sizeof in snmib.c, *pg. 378*
calls: sae_get sae_getf sae_getn
sae_match sae_set sif_get sif_getf
sif_getn sif_match sif_set snleaf
sntable srt_get srt_getf srt_getn
srt_match srt_set stc_get stc_getf
stc_getn stc_match stc_set

slowtimer in slowtimer.c, *pg. 78*
calls: arptimer ipftimer rttimer

sna2b in sna2b.c, *pg. 410*
called in: snclient.c snerr.c snmpd.c
calls: a1readlen a1readoid a1readval

snb2a in snb2a.c, *pg. 420*
called in: mksnmp.c
calls: a1writelen a1writeoid
a1writeval

snclient in snclient.c, *pg. 423*
called in: x_snmp.c
calls: mksnmp sna2b snparse

snerr in snerr.c
called in: x_snmp.c
calls: sna2b snmpprint_objid

snfreebl in snfreebl.c, *pg. 422*
called in: snmpd.c x_snmp.c

sninit in sninit.c, *pg. 425*
called in: snmpd.c x_snmp.c
calls: hashinit

snleaf in snleaf.c, *pg. 414*
called in: snmib.c

snmpd in snmpd.c, *pg. 404*
calls: mksnmp sna2b snfreebl sninit
snparse snrslv

snmpprint in snprint.c
called in: x_snmp.c
calls: getmib isprint snmpprint_objid
snmpprint_objname snmpprint_val

snmpprint_objid in snprint.c
called in: snerr.c
calls: getmib isprint snmpprint
snmpprint_objname snmpprint_val

snmpprint_objname in snprint.c
calls: getmib isprint snmpprint
snmpprint_objid snmpprint_val

snmpprint_val in snprint.c
calls: getmib isprint snmpprint
snmpprint_objid snmpprint_objname

snparse in snparse.c, *pg. 406*
called in: snclient.c snmpd.c
calls: a1readlen

snrslv in snrslv.c, *pg. 411*
called in: snmpd.c
calls: getmib oidequ seterr

sntable in sntable.c, *pg. 416*
called in: snmib.c

sntcpcmp in stc_findn.c, *pg. 470*
calls: stc_findnext

snusage in x_snmp.c
calls: dot2ip dot2oid echoch erase1
eraseall eraseword find_completions
getnewbl getword initgetword ip2dot
isalpha isdigit name2ip objd2oid
parseoid parseoidlist parseset
parsevalue print_completion
sendquery snclient snerr snfreebl
sninit snmpprint strequ strnequ

so2ipcpy in snoip.c
called in: stc_match.c
calls: sip2ocpy soipequ

soipequ in snoip.c
called in: sae_match.c sat_match.c
srt_match.c
calls: sip2ocpy so2ipcpy

SPA macro in arp.h, *pg. 40*
called in: arpadd.c arpsend.c arp_in.c
rarpsend.c

srt_findnext in srt_findn.c, *pg. 461*
called in: srt_getf.c srt_getn.c

srt_get in srt_get.c, *pg. 456*
called in: snmib.c srt_getf.c srt_getn.c
calls: srt_match

srt_getf in srt_getf.c, *pg. 458*
called in: snmib.c
calls: sip2ocpy srt_findnext srt_get

srt_getn in srt_getn.c, *pg. 460*
called in: snmib.c
calls: sip2ocpy srt_findnext srt_get
srt_match

srt_match in srt_match.c, *pg. 455*
called in: snmib.c srt_get.c srt_getn.c
srt_set.c
calls: soipequ

srt_set in srt_set.c, *pg. 462*
called in: snmib.c
calls: rtdel srt_match

stc_findnext in stc_findn.c, *pg. 470*
called in: stc_getf.c stc_getn.c
calls: sntcpcmp

stc_get in stc_get.c, *pg. 466*
called in: snmib.c stc_getf.c
stc_getn.c
calls: stc_match

stc_getf in stc_getf.c, *pg. 467*
called in: snmib.c
calls: sip2ocpy stc_findnext stc_get

stc_getn in stc_getn.c, *pg. 468*
called in: snmib.c
calls: sip2ocpy stc_findnext stc_get
stc_match

stc_match in stc_match.c, *pg. 464*
called in: snmib.c stc_get.c stc_getn.c
calls: so2ipcpy

stc_set in stc_set.c, *pg. 471*
called in: snmib.c

strequ macro in snmp.h, *pg. 387*
called in: x_snmp.c

strnequ in x_snmp.c
calls: dot2ip dot2oid echoch erase1
eraseall eraseword find_completions
getnewbl getword initgetword ip2dot
isalpha isdigit name2ip objd2oid
parseoid parseoidlist parseset
parsevalue print_completion
sendquery snclient snerr snfreebl
sninit snmpprint snusage strequ

SUDK macro in tcb.h, *pg. 166*
called in: tcpsndlen.c tcpwurg.c

SUHK macro in tcb.h, *pg. 166*
called in: tcpshskip.c tcpsndlen.c

summary in x_dumper.c
calls: dump name2ip

SVINT macro in snmp.h, *pg. 387*
called in: a1rwval.c sae_get.c
sat_get.c sat_set.c sif_get.c sif_set.c
snleaf.c srt_get.c srt_set.c stc_get.c
x_snmp.c

SVIPADDR macro in snmp.h, *pg. 387*
called in: a1rwval.c sae_get.c
sat_get.c sat_set.c srt_get.c srt_set.c
stc_get.c x_snmp.c

SVOID macro in snmp.h, *pg. 387*
called in: snleaf.c x_snmp.c

SVOIDLEN macro in snmp.h, *pg. 387*

called in: snleaf.c x_snmp.c

SVSTR macro in snmp.h, *pg. 387*
called in: a1rwval.c sat_get.c
sat_set.c sif_get.c snleaf.c x_snmp.c

SVSTRLEN macro in snmp.h, *pg. 387*

called in: a1rwval.c sat_get.c
sat_set.c sif_get.c snleaf.c x_snmp.c

SVTYPE macro in snmp.h, *pg. 387*
called in: a1rwval.c sae_get.c
sat_get.c sat_set.c sif_get.c sif_set.c
snleaf.c srt_get.c srt_set.c stc_get.c
x_snmp.c

TCB macro in tcpfsm.h, *pg. 176*
called in: tcpout.c tqdump.c

tcballoc in tcballoc.c, *pg. 178*
called in: tcplisten.c tcpmopen.c

tcbdealloc in tcbdealloc.c, *pg. 179*
called in: tcpclose.c tcpclosing.c
tcpcon.c tcpout.c tcpsynrcvd.c
tcptimewait.c
calls: tcpkilltimers

tcpabort in tcpabort.c, *pg. 212*
called in: tcpclosewait.c
tcpestablished.c tcpfin1.c tcpfin2.c
tcplastack.c tcprexmt.c tcpsynrcvd.c
calls: tcpkilltimers tcpwakeup

tcpacked in tcpacked.c, *pg. 279*
called in: tcpclosewait.c tcpclosing.c
tcpestablished.c tcpfin1.c tcpfin2.c
tcplastack.c tcpsynrcvd.c tcpsynsent.c
tcptimewait.c
calls: tcpackit tcpostate tcpreset
tcprtt

tcpackit in tcpackit.c, *pg. 281*
called in: tcpacked.c tcpinp.c
calls: ipsend tcpcksum tcprwindow

tcpaddhole in tcpaddhole.c, *pg. 297*
called in: tcprurg.c
calls: uqfree

tcpbind in tcpbind.c, *pg. 318*
called in: tcpmopen.c
calls: dnparse rtfree rtget tcpnxtp

tcpcksum in tcpcksum.c, *pg. 184*
called in: tcpackit.c tcpinp.c
tcpreset.c tcpsend.c

tcpclose in tcpclose.c, *pg. 329*
calls: tcbdealloc tcpkick

tcpclosed in tcpclosed.c, *pg. 194*
called in: tcpswitch.c
calls: tcpreset

tcpclosewait in tcpclosewait.c, *pg. 202*
called in: tcpswitch.c
calls: tcpabort tcpacked tcpreset
tcpswindow

tcpkick in tcpkick.c, *pg. 258*
called in: tcpclose.c tcpcon.c
   tcpdata.c tcpgetdata.c tcpostate.c
   tcpswindow.c tcpwr.c
calls: tmleft tmset

tcpkilltimers in tcpkilltimers.c,
   pg. 254
called in: tcbdealloc.c tcpabort.c
   tcpsynsent.c tcpwait.c
calls: tmclear

tcplastack in tcplastack.c, *pg. 203*
called in: tcpswitch.c
calls: tcpabort tcpacked tcpreset

tcplisten in tcplisten.c, *pg. 218*
called in: tcpswitch.c
calls: tcballoc tcpdata tcpreset
   tcpsync tcpwinit

tcplq in tcplq.c, *pg. 332*
called in: tcpcntl.c

tcpmcntl in tcpmcntl.c, *pg. 322*

tcpmopen in tcpmopen.c, *pg. 316*
calls: tcballoc tcpbind tcpcon
   tcpserver tcpsync

tcpnet2h in tcpnet2h.c, *pg. 184*
called in: tcpinp.c
calls: net2hl net2hs

tcpnxtp in tcpnxtp.c, *pg. 320*
called in: tcpbind.c

tcpok in tcpok.c, *pg. 188*
called in: tcpinp.c
calls: tcprcvurg

tcpopts in tcpopts.c, *pg. 271*
called in: tcpinp.c
calls: tcpsmss

tcpostate in tcpostate.c
called in: tcpacked.c
calls: tcpkick

tcpout in tcpout.c, *pg. 226*
calls: tcbdealloc

tcppersist in tcppersist.c, *pg. 228*
called in: tcpswitch.c
calls: min tcpsend tmset

tcpputc in tcpputc.c, *pg. 327*
calls: tcpwr

tcprcvurg in tcprcvurg.c, *pg. 290*
called in: tcpok.c
calls: uqalloc uqfree

tcpread in tcpread.c, *pg. 324*
called in: tcpgetc.c
calls: tcpgetdata tcprurg tcpwakeup

tcpreset in tcpreset.c, *pg. 238*
called in: tcpacked.c tcpclosed.c
   tcpclosewait.c tcpclosing.c
   tcpestablished.c tcpfin1.c tcpfin2.c
   tcpinp.c tcplastack.c tcplisten.c
   tcpsynrcvd.c tcpsynsent.c
   tcptimewait.c
calls: ipsend tcpcksum tcph2net

tcprexmt in tcprexmt.c, *pg. 264*
called in: tcpswitch.c tcpxmit.c
calls: min tcpabort tcpsend tmset

tcprhskip in tcprhskip.c, *pg. 298*
called in: tcpgetdata.c
calls: uqfree

tcprmss in tcprmss.c, *pg. 272*
called in: tcpsend.c
calls: hs2net

tcpwr in tcpwr.c, *pg. 328*
called in: tcpcntl.c tcpputc.c
tcpwrite.c
calls: tcpgetspace tcpkick tcpwakeup
tcpwurg

tcpwrite in tcpwrite.c, *pg. 327*
calls: tcpwr

tcpwurg in tcpwurg.c, *pg. 302*
called in: tcpwr.c
calls: uqalloc uqfree

tcpxmit in tcpxmit.c, *pg. 230*
called in: tcpidle.c tcpswitch.c
calls: min tcphowmuch tcprexmt
tcpsend tcpsndurg tmclear tmleft
tmset

tfcoalesce in tfcoalesce.c, *pg. 210*
called in: tcpdodat.c

tfinsert in tfinsert.c, *pg. 208*
called in: tcpdodat.c

THA macro in arp.h, *pg. 40*
called in: arpsend.c arp_in.c
rarpsend.c rarp_in.c

tmclear in tmclear.c, *pg. 252*
called in: tcpkilltimers.c tcprtt.c
tcpswindow.c tcpxmit.c tmset.c

tmleft in tmleft.c, *pg. 254*
called in: tcpkick.c tcpxmit.c

tmset in tmset.c, *pg. 256*
called in: tcpkick.c tcppersist.c
tcprexmt.c tcpwait.c tcpxmit.c
calls: tmclear

toascii macro in ctype.h

tolower macro in ctype.h

toupper macro in ctype.h

TPA macro in arp.h, *pg. 40*
called in: arpsend.c arp_in.c
rarpsend.c rarp_in.c

tqdump in tqdump.c
calls: tqwrite

tqwrite in tqdump.c
called in: x_timerq.c
calls: tqdump

truncew macro in mem.h

truncmb macro in mem.h

udpcksum in udpcksum.c, *pg. 158*
called in: udpsend.c udp_in.c

udpecho in udpecho.c
called in: netstart.c

udph2net in udph2net.c, *pg. 156*
called in: udpsend.c
calls: hs2net

udp_in in udp_in.c, *pg. 156*
called in: local_out.c
calls: icmp isbadpid udpcksum
udpnet2h

udpnet2h in udpnet2h.c, *pg. 155*
called in: udp_in.c
calls: net2hs

udpnxtp in udpnxtp.c, *pg. 160*

udpsend in udpsend.c, *pg. 161*
called in: riprepl.c ripsend.c rwhod.c
calls: ipsend rtfree rtget udpcksum
udph2net

unmarked macro in mark.h
called in: tcpinit.c

upalloc in upalloc.c, *pg. 154*

uqalloc in uqalloc.c, *pg. 292*
called in: tcprcvurg.c tcpsndlen.c
tcpwurg.c
calls: uqinit

uqfree in uqfree.c, *pg. 294*
called in: tcpaddhole.c tcpgetdata.c
tcprcvurg.c tcprhskip.c tcprurg.c
tcpshskip.c tcpsndlen.c tcpwurg.c

uqinit in uqinit.c, *pg. 294*
called in: uqalloc.c

uqprint in uqprint.c

ut2ltim macro in date.h
called in: x_who.c

vax2h macro in network.h
called in: x_rls.c

x_arp in x_arp.c
calls: arpprint xarpusage

xarpusage in x_arp.c
calls: arpprint

x_bpool in x_bpool.c

x_cat in x_cat.c

x_close in x_close.c

x_conf in x_conf.c
calls: dot2ip ip2name

x_cp in x_cp.c

x_creat in x_create.c

x_date in x_date.c
calls: ascdate

x_devs in x_devs.c

x_dg in x_dg.c

x_dumper in x_dumper.c
calls: dump name2ip summary

x_echo in x_echo.c

x_exit in x_exit.c

x_finger in x_finger.c
calls: lfing name2ip rfing

x_help in x_help.c

x_ifstat in x_ifstat.c

x_kill in x_kill.c

x_mem in x_mem.c

x_mount in x_mount.c
calls: isbaddev mprint

x_mv in x_mv.c

x_net in x_net.c
calls: addflag iarg ip2dot noarg parg
tcpfnames

x_ns in x_ns.c
calls: name2ip

x_ping in x_ping.c
calls: icmp name2ip

x_ps in x_ps.c

x_reboot in x_reboot.c

x_rf in x_rf.c

x_rls in x_rls.c
calls: vax2h

x_rm in x_rm.c

x_route in x_route.c
 calls: dot2ip rtadd rtdel rtfree rtget
  xrtusage

x_routes in x_routes.c
 calls: ip2dot ip2name

xrtusage in x_route.c
 calls: dot2ip rtadd rtdel rtfree rtget

x_sleep in x_sleep.c

x_snap in x_snap.c

x_snmp in x_snmp.c
 calls: dot2ip dot2oid echoch erase1
  eraseall eraseword find_completions
  getnewbl getword initgetword ip2dot
  isalpha isdigit name2ip objd2oid
  parseoid parseoidlist parseset
  parsevalue print_completion
  sendquery snclient snerr snfreebl
  sninit snmpprint snusage strequ
  strnequ

xt2net macro in date.h

x_timerq in x_timerq.c
 calls: tqwrite

x_unmou in x_unmou.c

x_uptime in x_uptime.c
 calls: getname rwcomp

x_who in x_who.c
 calls: ascdate getname marked
  ut2ltim

ZSTimeConst macro in zsreg.h

Appendix 2

Xinu Procedures And Functions Used In The Code

Introduction

The code throughout this text uses procedures and functions provided by the Xinu operating system. Many of the functions correspond to Xinu *system calls*, while others correspond to library functions. Although it is possible to understand the TCP/IP protocol software without knowing the internal details of how these Xinu procedures operate, understanding the service each function provides is essential to a detailed understanding of how TCP/IP operates.

This chapter provides a brief description of all procedures and functions that are not shown in the text. It explains their purpose and the arguments they use.

In general, Xinu system calls and library routines are "functions" in the sense that they always return a value. However, few system calls are functions in the mathematical sense because almost all have side-effects. Errors usually result in a return value of *SYSERR* (or, in some cases, specific error codes); procedures that operate without error return *OK*.

Alphabetical Listing

The following pages contain a listing, in alphabetical order, of names and arguments for all procedures and functions used by the code that are not otherwise shown in the text. Because the exact details of how these routines operate is unimportant, no distinction is drawn between library procedures and Xinu system calls. The brief explanations are intended to help readers understand the protocol software in the text, and do not describe possible problems or exceptions. Thus, programmers should obtain more information about the arguments and calling conventions before attempting to write programs that call these routines.

atoi (string)

Extract an integer in ASCII format from *string* and return it as the function value.

blkcmp (ptr1, ptr2, nbytes)

Compare the *nbytes* bytes starting at address *ptr1* to the *nbytes* bytes starting at address *ptr2*, returning zero if the bytes are identical. If the blocks are not equal, find the first byte that differs, and return a negative integer if that byte is less in the first block than the corresponding byte in the second block, and a positive integer otherwise.

blkcopy (toptr, fromptr, nbytes)

Copy *nbytes* bytes from address *fromptr* to address *toptr*.

blkequ (ptr1, ptr2, nbytes)

Compare *nbytes* bytes starting at locations *ptr1* and *ptr2*, returning *TRUE* if they are equal, and *FALSE* otherwise.

chprio (pid, newprio)

Change CPU scheduling priority of process *pid* to *newprio*, and return the old priority as the function value.

close (dev)

Close device *dev* (for TCP, this deletes the connection).

control (dev, func, arg1, arg2)

Control device *dev*, applying function *func* with arguments *arg1* and *arg2*. Control operations are device-dependent.

create (caddr, ssize, prio, pn, nargs, arg...)

Create a process to execute code at address *caddr*, with initial stack size *ssize*, CPU priority *prio*, process name *pn*, *nargs* arguments, and argument value(s) starting with *arg*.

deq (indx)

Remove first item from list with index *indx*, and return it.

disable (ps)

Save processor status word in *ps*, and disable CPU interrupts.

enq (item, indx, key)

Insert *item* on the ordered list with index *indx*, using integer *key* to choose a position for the item.

fprintf (dev, fmt, value...)

Format *value(s)* according to format *fmt*, and send results to device *dev*.

freebuf (bufptr)

Free buffer at address *bufptr*, and return to buffer pool.

freemem (memptr, nbytes)

Free *nbytes* bytes of memory at address *memptr*.

freeq (indx)

Delete the list with index *indx*, returning all memory to the free list.

getbuf (poolid)

Get a buffer from buffer pool *poolid*.

getc (dev)

Read one character from device *dev*; block until one arrives.

getdmem (nbytes)

Allocate *nbytes* bytes of memory that can be used for DMA I/O.

getidprom (buf, size)

Get up to *size* bytes from the hardware ID prom, and store in buffer *buf*.

getmem (nbytes)

Allocate *nbytes* bytes of memory from the free list, and return a pointer to it.

getpid ()

Return the process id of the currently executing process.

getprio ()

Return the CPU priority of the currently executing process.

gettime (tptr)

Obtain the local time, expressed in seconds past the epoch date (January 1, 1970), and place in the long integer with address *tptr*.

index (str, ch)

Return the index of the first occurrence of character *ch* in string *str*, or zero if *ch* does not occur in *str*.

initq ()

Initialize the general-purpose list mechanism at system startup (must precede *newq*).

kill (pid)

Destroy the process with id *pid*.

kprintf (fmt, value...)

Convert *value(s)* to an ascii string according to format *fmt* and print on the console like *printf*, but bypass the interrupt system so it can be used to debug the operating system kernel.

mark (ptr)

Causes the kernel to remember that location *ptr* has been "initialized" and can be tested with function *unmarked*.

mkpool (bufsiz, numbufs)

Create a buffer pool containing *numbufs* buffers, each of which is *bufsiz* bytes long, and return the pool identifier.

mount (prefix, dev, replace)

Add new name *prefix* to the file namespace, and associate it with device *dev* and replacement string *replace*.

nammap (name, newname)

Map a *name* through the namespace, write the new name in *newname*, and return the device identifier as the function value.

newq (size, type)

Allocate a new list that can hold up to *size* nodes, use *type* to determine whether mutual exclusion for the list is controlled with a semaphore or by disabling interrupts, and return the list index.

open (dev, name, mode)

Open file or object with *name* using device *dev* and access mode *mode*, returning the device descriptor of the new device used to access the object.

panic (message)

Write string *message* on the console, and halt (abort) the operating system as well as all applications immediately.

pcount (portid)

Return the number of messages currently waiting at port *portid*, or negative *n* if *n* processes are blocked waiting for messages to arrive.

pcreate (count)

Create a new port with space for up to *count* messages, and return its identifier.

pdelete (portid, dispose)

Delete port with identifier *portid*, calling procedure *dispose* to dispose of each message that is waiting.

preceive (portid)

Extract the next message from port *portid*, blocking until one arrives if the port is empty.

printf (fmt, value...)

Convert *value(s)* to an ASCII string according to format *fmt*, and write on the console device.

psend (portid, message)

Deposit integer *message* on port with id *portid*, blocking until space becomes available in the port.

putc (dev, ch)

Write the single character (byte) *ch* to device *dev*.

qsort (darray, n, isize, cmp)

Quicksort *n* values, each of *isize* bytes, in array *darray*, using function *cmp* to make comparisons between items.

read (dev, buf, len)

Read up to *len* bytes of data from device *dev* and place in buffer *buf*, returning the number of bytes read. The exact semantics of *read* depend on the device, but most devices block the caller until data arrives.

receive ()

Block the calling process until a message arrives for that process, and then return the message.

recvclr ()

Without blocking, return a message if one has arrived for the calling process, or *OK* otherwise.

recvtim (maxdelay)

Block the calling process until a message arrives or *maxdelay* tenths of seconds elapse, returning the message or *TIMEOUT*.

remove (fname, key)

Remove file with name *fname*, using *key* as protection key.

rename (file1, file2)

Change the name of file *file1* to *file2*.

restore (ps)

Restore CPU interrupts to the status saved in *ps* by *disable*.

resume (pid)

Resume a previously suspended process with id *pid*.

rindex (str, ch)

Return index of last occurrence of character *ch* in string *str*, or zero if *ch* does not appear in *str*.

scount (sid)

Return the current count of semaphore with id *sid*; counts of negative *n* mean *n* processes are blocked on the semaphore.

screate (icount)

Create a new semaphore with initial count *icount*, and return its id.

sdelete (sid)

Delete the semaphore with id *sid*, and unblock any processes that may be blocked on it.

seek (dev, pos)

Seek to position *pos* on device *dev*; the exact semantics are device dependent.

seeq (indx)

Search through list with index *indx* one item at a time, without removing the items; the list only remembers one search position at any instant.

send (pid, msg)

Send message *msg* to process with identifier *pid*, but discard the message if the process already has an unread message waiting.

sendf (pid, msg)

Send message *msg* to process with identifier *pid*, overwriting any previously unread message.

set_evec (vec, func)

Assign hardware exception vector *vec* a pointer to exception handling function *func*.

setdev (pid, idev, odev)
Set the standard input and output devices for process with id *pid* to *idev* and *odev*, respectively.

setnok (nok, pid)
Set the "next-of-kin" for process with id *pid* to *nok*, allowing *nok* to be notified if process *pid* terminates.

signal (sid)
Signal semaphore with id *sid*, allowing a process to continue if any are blocked on the semaphore.

sleep (sdelay)
Delay the calling process *sdelay* seconds before returning.

sleep10 (tsdelay)
Delay the calling process *tsdelay* tenths of seconds before returning.

sprintf (str, fmt, value...)
Convert *value(s)* to an ASCII string according to format *fmt*, and place results in string *str*.

strcat (tostr, fromstr)
Concatenate a copy of null-terminated string *fromstr* to the end of null-terminated string *tostr*.

strcmp (str1, str2)
Compare null-terminated strings *str1* and *str2*, and return an integer less than zero, equal to zero, or greater than zero, to indicate that *str1* is lexically less than, equal to, or greater than *str2*.

strcpy (tostr, fromstr)
Copy the contents of null-terminated string *fromstr* to null-terminated string *tostr*.

strlen (str)
Return the length of null-terminated string *str* measured in bytes, not including the null terminating character.

strncat (tostr, fromstr, maxlen)
Concatenate a copy of null-terminated string *fromstr* to the end of null-terminated string *tostr*, but do not exceed maximum length *maxlen* bytes.

strncmp (str1, str2, maxlen)
Compare up to *maxlen* bytes from null-terminated strings *str1* and *str2*, and return an integer less than zero, equal to zero, or greater than zero, to indicate that *str1* is lexically less than, equal to, or greater than *str2*.

strncpy (tostr, fromstr, maxlen)

Copy null-terminated string *fromstr* to null-terminated string *tostr*, but do not exceed maximum length *maxlen* bytes.

suspend (pid)

Suspend (block) the process with id *pid*.

unmount (prefix)

Remove the namespace mapping that has a name prefix equal to *prefix*.

wait (sid)

Decrement the count of semaphore with id *sid*, and block the calling process on that semaphore if the resulting count is negative; a process blocked on a semaphore can only continue after another process calls *signal* for the semaphore.

write (dev, buf, len)

Write *len* bytes from buffer *buf* to device *dev*. The exact semantics of *write* depend on the device, but most devices block the caller until all bytes can be written.

Bibliography

ABRAMSON, N. [1970], The ALOHA System – Another Alternative for Computer Communications, *Proceedings of the Fall Joint Computer Conference.*

ABRAMSON, N. and F. KUO (EDS.) [1973], *Computer Communication Networks,* Prentice Hall, Englewood Cliffs, New Jersey.

ANDREWS, D. W., and G. D. SHULTZ [1982], A Token-Ring Architecture for Local Area Networks: An Update, *Proceedings of Fall 82 COMPCON,* IEEE.

BALL, J. E., E. J. BURKE, I. GERTNER, K. A. LANTZ, and R. F. RASHID [1979], Perspectives on Message-Based Distributed Computing, *IEEE Computing Networking Symposium,* 46-51.

BBN [1981], A History of the ARPANET: The First Decade, *Technical Report* Bolt, Beranek, and Newman, Inc.

BBN [December 1981], Specification for the Interconnection of a Host and an IMP (revised), *Technical Report 1822,* Bolt, Beranek, and Newman, Inc.

BERTSEKAS D. and R. GALLAGER [1987], *Data Networks,* Prentice-Hall, Englewood Cliffs, New Jersey.

BIRRELL, A., and B. NELSON [February 1984], Implementing Remote Procedure Calls, *ACM Transactions on Computer Systems,* 2(1), 39-59.

BOGGS, D., J. SHOCH, E. TAFT, and R. METCALFE [April 1980], Pup: An Internetwork Architecture, *IEEE Transactions on Communications.*

BORMAN, D., [April 1989], Implementing TCP/IP on a Cray Computer, *Computer Communication Review,* 19(2), 11-15.

BROWN, M., N. KOLLING, and E. TAFT [November 1985], The Alpine File System, *Transactions on Computer Systems,* 3(4), 261-293.

BROWNBRIDGE, D., L. MARSHALL, and B. RANDELL [December 1982], The Newcastle Connections or UNIXes of the World Unite!, *Software – Practice and Experience,* 12(12), 1147-1162.

CERF, V., and E. CAIN [October 1983], The DOD Internet Architecture Model, *Computer Networks.*

CERF, V., and R. KAHN [May 1974], A Protocol for Packet Network Interconnection, *IEEE Transactions of Communications,* Com-22(5).

CERF, V. [October 1989], A History of the ARPANET, *ConneXions, The Interoperability Report,* 480 San Antonio Rd, Suite 100, Mountain View, California.

CHERITON, D. R. [1983], Local Networking and Internetworking in the V-System, *Proceedings of the Eighth Data Communications Symposium.*

CHERITON, D. R. [April 1984], The V Kernel: A Software Base for Distributed Systems, *IEEE Software,* 1(2), 19-42.

CHERITON, D. [August 1986], VMTP: A Transport Protocol for the Next Generation of Communication Systems, *Proceedings of ACM SIGCOMM '86,* 406-415.

CHERITON, D., and T. MANN [May 1984], Uniform Access to Distributed Name Interpretation in the V-System, *Proceedings IEEE Fourth International Conference on Distributed Computing Systems,* 290-297.

CHESSON, G. [June 1987], Protocol Engine Design, *Proceedings of the 1987 Summer USENIX Conference,* Phoenix, AZ.

CLARK, D. [December 1985], The structure of Systems Using Upcalls, *Proceedings of the Tenth ACM Symposium on Operating Systems Principles,* 171-180.

CLARK, D., M. LAMBERT, and L. ZHANG [August 1987], NETBLT: A High Throughput Transport Protocol, *Proceedings of ACM SIGCOMM '87.*

COHEN, D., [1981], On Holy Wars and a Plea for Peace, *IEEE Computer,* 48-54.

COMER, D. E. and J. T. KORB [1983], CSNET Protocol Software: The IP-to-X25 Interface, *Computer Communications Review,* 13(2).

COMER, D. E. [1984], *Operating System Design – The XINU Approach,* Prentice-Hall, Englewood Cliffs, New Jersey.

COMER, D. E. [1987], *Operating System Design Vol II. – Internetworking With XINU,* Prentice-Hall, Englewood Cliffs, New Jersey.

COMER, D. E., T. NARTEN, and R. YAVATKAR [April 1987], The Cypress Network: A Low-Cost Internet Connection Technology, *Technical Report TR-653,* Purdue University, West Lafayette, IN.

COMER, D. E., T. NARTEN, and R. YAVATKAR [1987], The Cypress Coaxial Packet Switch, *Computer Networks and ISDN Systems,* vol. 14:2-5, 383-388.

COTTON, I. [1979], Technologies for Local Area Computer Networks, *Proceedings of the Local Area Communications Network Symposium.*

CROWLEY, T., H, FORSDICK, M. LANDAU, and V. TRAVERS [June 1987], The Diamond Multimedia Editor, *Proceedings of the 1987 Summer USENIX Conference, Phoenix, AZ.*

DALAL Y. K., and R. S. PRINTIS [1981], 48-Bit Absolute Internet and Ethernet Host Numbers, Proceedings of the Seventh Data Communications Symposium.

DEERING S. E., and D. R. CHERITON [May 1990], Multicast Routing in Datagram Internetworks and Extended LANs, ACM Transactions on Computer Systems, 8(2), 85-110.

DENNING P. J., [September-October 1989], The Science of Computing: Worldnet, in American Scientist, 432-434.

DENNING P. J., [November-December 1989], *The Science of Computing: The ARPANET After Twenty Years*, in American Scientist, 530-534.

DIGITAL EQUIPMENT CORPORATION., INTEL CORPORATION, and XEROX CORPORATION [September 1980], *The Ethernet: A Local Area Network Data Link Layer and Physical Layer Specification.*

DION, J. [Oct. 1980], The Cambridge File Server, *Operating Systems Review,* 14(4), 26-35.

DRIVER, H., H. HOPEWELL, and J. IAQUINTO [September 1979], How the Gateway Regulates Information Control, *Data Communications.*

EDGE, S. W. [1979], Comparison of the Hop-by-Hop and Endpoint Approaches to Network Interconnection, in *Flow Control in Computer Networks,* J-L. GRANGE and M. GIEN (EDS.), North-Holland, Amsterdam, 359-373.

EDGE, S. [1983], An Adaptive Timeout Algorithm for Retransmission Across a Packet Switching Network, *Proceedings of ACM SIGCOMM '83.*

ENSLOW, P. [January 1978], What is a 'Distributed' Data Processing System? *Computer,* 13-21.

FALK, G. [1983], The Structure and Function of Network Protocols, in *Computer Communications, Volume I: Principles,* CHOU, W. (ED.), Prentice-Hall, Englewood Cliffs, New Jersey.

FARMER, W. D., and E. E. NEWHALL [1969], An Experimental Distributed Switching System to Handle Bursty Computer Traffic, *Proceedings of the ACM Symposium on Probabilistic Optimization of Data Communication Systems,* 1-33.

FCCSET [November 1987], A Research and Development Strategy for High Performance Computing, *Report from the Executive Office of the President and Office of Science and Technology Policy.*

FEDOR, M. [June 1988], GATED: A Multi-Routing Protocol Daemon for UNIX, *Proceedings of the 1988 Summer USENIX conference,* San Francisco, California.

FEINLER, J., O. J. JACOBSEN, and M. STAHL [December 1985], *DDN Protocol Handbook Volume Two, DARPA Internet Protocols,* DDN Network Information Center, SRI International, 333 Ravenswood Avenue, Room EJ291, Menlo Park, California.

FRANK, H., and W. CHOU [1971], Routing in Computer Networks, *Networks,* 1(1), 99-112.

FRANK, H., and J. FRISCH [1971], *Communication, Transmission, and Transportation Networks,* Addison-Wesley, Reading, Massachusetts.

FRANTA, W. R., and I. CHLAMTAC [1981], *Local Networks,* Lexington Books, Lexington, Massachusetts.

FRICC [May 1989], *Program Plan for the National Research and Education Network,* Federal Research Internet Coordinating Committee, US Department of Energy, Office of Scientific Computing report ER-7.

FRIDRICH, M., and W. OLDER [December 1981], The Felix File Server, *Proceedings of the Eighth Symposium on Operating Systems Principles,* 37-46.

FULTZ, G. L., and L. KLEINROCK, [June 14-16, 1971], Adaptive Routing Techniques for Store-and-Forward Computer Communication Networks, presented at *IEEE International Conference on Communications,* Montreal, Canada.

GERLA, M., and L. KLEINROCK [April 1980], Flow Control: A Comparative Survey, *IEEE Transactions on Communications.*

GOSIP [April 1989], U.S. Government Open Systems Interconnection Profile (GOSIP) version 2.0, GOSIP Advanced Requirements Group, National Institute of Standards and Technology (NIST).

GRANGE, J-L., and M. GIEN (EDS.) [1979], *Flow Control in Computer Networks,* North-Holland, Amsterdam.

GREEN, P. E. (ED.) [1982], *Computer Network Architectures and Protocols,* Plenum Press, New York.

HINDEN, R., J. HAVERTY, and A. SHELTZER [September 1983], The DARPA Internet: Interconnecting Heterogeneous Computer Networks with Gateways, *Computer.*

INTERNATIONAL ORGANIZATION FOR STANDARDIZATION [June 1986a], Information processing systems — Open Systems Interconnection — *Transport Service Definition,* International Standard number 8072, ISO, Switzerland.

INTERNATIONAL ORGANIZATION FOR STANDARDIZATION [July 1986b], Information processing systems — Open Systems Interconnection — *Connection Oriented Transport Protocol Specification,* International Standard number 8073, ISO, Switzerland.

INTERNATIONAL ORGANIZATION FOR STANDARDIZATION [May 1987a], Information processing systems — Open Systems Interconnection — *Specification of Basic Specification of Abstract Syntax Notation One (ASN.1),* International Standard number 8824, ISO, Switzerland.

INTERNATIONAL ORGANIZATION FOR STANDARDIZATION [May 1987b], Information processing systems — Open Systems Interconnection — *Specification of Basic Encoding Rules for Abstract Syntax Notation One (ASN.1),* International Standard number 8825, ISO, Switzerland.

INTERNATIONAL ORGANIZATION FOR STANDARDIZATION [May 1988a], Information processing systems — Open Systems Interconnection — *Management Information Service Definition, Part 2: Common Management Information Service,* Draft International Standard number 9595-2, ISO, Switzerland.

INTERNATIONAL ORGANIZATION FOR STANDARDIZATION [May 1988a], Information processing systems — Open Systems Interconnection — *Management Information Protocol Definition, Part 2: Common Management Information Protocol,* Draft International Standard number 9596-2.

JACOBSON, V. [August 1988], Congestion Avoidance and Control, *Proceedings ACM Sigcomm '88.*

JAIN, R. [January 1985], On Caching Out-of-Order Packets in Window Flow Controlled Networks, *Technical Report,* DEC-TR-342, Digital Equipment Corporation.

JAIN, R. [March 1986], Divergence of Timeout Algorithms for Packet Retransmissions, *Proceedings Fifth Annual International Phoenix Conference on Computers and Communications,* Scottsdale, AZ.

JAIN, R. [October 1986], A Timeout-Based Congestion Control Scheme for Window Flow-Controlled Networks, *IEEE Journal on Selected Areas in Communications,* Vol. SAC-4, no. 7.

JAIN, R., K. RAMAKRISHNAN, and D-M. CHIU [August 1987], Congestion Avoidance in Computer Networks With a Connectionless Network Layer. *Technical Report*, DEC-TR-506, Digital Equipment Corporation.

JENNINGS, D. M., L. H. LANDWEBER, and I. H. FUCHS [February 28, 1986], Computer Networking for Scientists and Engineers, *Science* vol 231, 941-950.

JUBIN, J. and J. TORNOW [January 1987], The DARPA Packet Radio Network Protocols, *IEEE Proceedings*.

KAHN, R. [November 1972], Resource-Sharing Computer Communications Networks, *Proceedings of the IEEE*, 60(11), 1397-1407.

KARN, P., H. PRICE, and R. DIERSING [May 1985], Packet Radio in the Amateur Service, *IEEE Journal on Selected Areas in Communications*,

KARN, P., and C. PARTRIDGE [August 1987], Improving Round-Trip Time Estimates in Reliable Transport Protocols, *Proceedings of ACM SIGCOMM '87*.

KENT, C., and J. MOGUL [August 1987], Fragmentation Considered Harmful, *Proceedings of ACM SIGCOMM '87*.

KLINE, C. [August 1987], Supercomputers on the Internet: A Case Study, *Proceedings of ACM SIGCOMM '87*.

KOCHAN, S. G., and P. H. WOODS [1989], *UNIX Networking*, Hayden Books, Indianapolis, IN.

LABARRE, L. (ED.) [December 1989], OSI Internet Management: Management Information Base, *Internet Draft <IETF.DRAFTS>DRAFT-IETF-SNMP-MIB2-01.TXT*, DDN Network Information Center, SRI International, Ravenswood, CA.

LAMPSON, B. W., M. PAUL, and H. J. SIEGERT (EDS.) [1981], *Distributed Systems - Architecture and Implementation (An Advanced Course)*, Springer-Verlag, Berlin.

LANZILLO, A. L., and C. PARTRIDGE [January 1989], Implementation of Dial-up IP for UNIX Systems, *Proceedings 1989 Winter USENIX Technical Conference*, San Diego, CA.

LAQUEY, T. L., [July 1989], *User's Directory of Computer Networks*, Digital Press, Bedford, MA.

LAZAR, A. [November 1983], Optimal Flow Control of a Class of Queuing Networks in Equilibrium. *IEEE Transactions on Automatic Control*, Vol. AC-28:11.

LEFFLER, S., M. McKUSICK, M. KARELS, and J. QUARTERMAN [1989], *The Design and Implementation of the 4.3BSD UNIX Operating System*, Addison Wesley, 1989.

LYNCH, D. C., and O. J. JACOBSEN (PUBLISHER and EDITOR) [1987-], ConneXions, the Interoperability Report, *Interop Incorporated*, 480 San Antonio Rd, Suite 100, Mountain View, California.

LYNCH, D. C., (PRESIDENT) [1987-], The Annual Interop Conference *Interop Incorporated*, 480 San Antonio Rd, Suite 100, Mountain View, California.

MCNAMARA, J. [1982], *Technical Aspects of Data Communications*, Digital Press, Digital Equipment Corporation, Bedford, Massachusetts.

MCQUILLAN, J. M., I. RICHER, and E. ROSEN [May 1980], The New Routing Algorithm for the ARPANET, *IEEE Transactions on Communications*, (COM-28), 711-719.

MERIT [November 1987], Management and Operation of the NSFNET Backbone Network: A Proposal Funded by the National Science Foundation and the State of Michigan, *MERIT Incorporated*, Ann Arbor, Michigan.

METCALFE, R. M., and D. R. BOGGS [July 1976], Ethernet: Distributed Packet Switching for Local Computer Networks, *Communications of the ACM,* 19(7), 395-404.

MILLER, C. K., and D. M. THOMPSON [March 1982], Making a Case for Token Passing in Local Networks, *Data Communications.*

MILLS, D., and H-W. BRAUN [August 1987], The NSFNET Backbone Network, *Proceedings of ACM SIGCOMM '87.*

MITCHELL, J., and J. DION [April 1982], A Comparison of Two Network-Based File Servers, *Communications of the ACM,* 25(4), 233-245.

MORRIS, R. [1979], Fixing Timeout Intervals for Lost Packet Detection in Computer Communication Networks, *Proceedings AFIPS National Computer Conference*, AFIPS Press, Montvale, New Jersey.

NAGLE, J. [April 1987], On Packet Switches With Infinite Storage, *IEEE Transactions on Communications*, Vol. COM-35:4.

NARTEN, T. [Sept. 1989], Internet Routing, *Proceedings ACM SIGCOMM '89.*

NEEDHAM, R. M. [1979], System Aspects of the Cambridge Ring, *Proceedings of the ACM Seventh Symposium on Operating System Principles,* 82-85.

NELSON, J. [September 1983], 802: A Progress Report, *Datamation.*

OPPEN, D., and Y. DALAL [October 1981], The Clearinghouse: A Decentralized Agent for Locating Named Objects, Office Products Division, XEROX Corporation.

PARTRIDGE, C. [June 1986], Mail Routing Using Domain Names: An Informal Tour, *Proceedings of the 1986 Summer USENIX Conference*, Atlanta, GA.

PARTRIDGE, C. [June 1987], Implementing the Reliable Data Protocol (RDP), *Proceedings of the 1987 Summer USENIX Conference*, Phoenix, Arizona.

PETERSON, L. [1985], *Defining and Naming the Fundamental Objects in a Distributed Message System,* Ph.D. Dissertation, Purdue University, West Lafayette, Indiana.

PIERCE, J. R. [1972], Networks for Block Switching of Data, *Bell System Technical Journal,* 51.

POSTEL, J. B. [April 1980], Internetwork Protocol Approaches, *IEEE Transactions on Communications*, COM-28, 604-611.

POSTEL, J. B., C. A. SUNSHINE, and D. CHEN [1981], The ARPA Internet Protocol, *Computer Networks.*

QUARTERMAN, J. S. [1990], *The Matrix: Computer Networks and Conferencing Systems Worldwide*, Digital Press, Digital Equipment Corporation, Maynard, MA.

QUARTERMAN, J. S., and J. C. HOSKINS [October 1986], Notable Computer Networks, *Communications of the ACM,* 29(10).

REYNOLDS, J., J. POSTEL, A. R. KATZ, G. G. FINN, and A. L. DESCHON [October 1985], The DARPA Experimental Multimedia Mail System, *IEEE Computer.*

RITCHIE, D. M., and K. THOMPSON [July 1974], The UNIX Time-Sharing System, *Communications of the ACM*, 17(7), 365-375; revised and reprinted in *Bell System Technical Journal*, 57(6), [July-August 1978], 1905-1929.

ROSE, M. (ED.) [October 1989], Management Information Base for Network Management of TCP/IP-based Internets, *Internet Draft <IETF.DRAFTS>DRAFT-IETF-OIM-MIB2-00.TXT*, DDN Network Information Center, SRI International, Ravenswood, CA.

ROSENTHAL, R. (ED.) [November 1982], *The Selection of Local Area Computer Networks*, National Bureau of Standards Special Publication 500-96.

SALTZER, J. [1978], Naming and Binding of Objects, *Operating Systems, An Advanced Course*, Springer-Verlag, 99-208.

SALTZER, J. [April 1982], Naming and Binding of Network Destinations, *International Symposium on Local Computer Networks*, IFIP/T.C.6, 311-317.

SALTZER, J., D. REED, and D. CLARK [November 1984], End-to-End Arguments in System Design, *ACM Transactions on Computer Systems*, 2(4), 277-288.

SCHWARTZ, M., and T. STERN [April 1980], *IEEE Transactions on Communications*, COM-28(4), 539-552.

SHOCH, J. F. [1978], Internetwork Naming, Addressing, and Routing, *Proceedings of COMPCON*.

SHOCH, J. F., Y. DALAL, and D. REDELL [August 1982], Evolution of the Ethernet Local Computer Network, *Computer*.

SNA [1975], *IBM System Network Architecture – General Information*, IBM System Development Division, Publications Center, Department E01, P.O. Box 12195, Research Triangle Park, North Carolina, 27709.

SOLOMON, M., L. LANDWEBER, and D. NEUHEGEN [1982], The CSNET Name Server, *Computer Networks* (6), 161-172.

STALLINGS, W. [1984], *Local Networks: An Introduction*, Macmillan Publishing Company, New York.

STALLINGS, W. [1985], *Data and Computer Communications*, Macmillan Publishing Company, New York.

STEVENS, W. R. [1990], *UNIX Network Programming*, Prentice-Hall, Englewood Cliffs, New Jersey.

SWINEHART, D., G. MCDANIEL, and D. R. BOGGS [December 1979], WFS: A Simple Shared File System for a Distributed Environment, *Proceedings of the Seventh Symposium on Operating System Principles*, 9-17.

TANENBAUM, A. [1981], *Computer Networks: Toward Distributed Processing Systems*, Prentice-Hall, Englewood Cliffs, New Jersey.

TICHY, W., and Z. RUAN [June 1984], Towards a Distributed File System, *Proceedings of Summer 84 USENIX Conference*, Salt Lake City, Utah, 87-97.

TOMLINSON. R. S. [1975], Selecting Sequence Numbers, *Proceedings ACM SIGOPS/SIGCOMM Interprocess Communication Workshop*, 11-23, 1975.

WARD, A. A. [1980], TRIX: A Network-Oriented Operating System, *Proceedings of COMPCON,* 344-349.

WATSON, R. [1981], Timer-Based Mechanisms in Reliable Transport Protocol Connection Management, *Computer Networks,* North-Holland Publishing Company.

WEINBERGER, P. J. [1985], The UNIX Eighth Edition Network File System, *Proceedings 1985 ACM Computer Science Conference,* 299-301.

WELCH, B., and J. OSTERHAUT [May 1986], Prefix Tables: A Simple Mechanism for Locating Files in a Distributed System, *Proceedings IEEE Sixth International Conference on Distributed Computing Systems,* 1845-189.

WILKES, M. V., and D. J. WHEELER [May 1979], The Cambridge Digital Communication Ring, *Proceedings Local Area Computer Network Symposium.*

XEROX [1981], Internet Transport Protocols, *Report XSIS 028112,* Xerox Corporation, Office Products Division, Network Systems Administration Office, 3333 Coyote Hill Road, Palo Alto, California.

ZHANG, L. [August 1986], Why TCP Timers Don't Work Well, *Proceedings of ACM SIGCOMM '86.*

Index

Notes

Notes

Notes

Notes

Notes

Notes

Notes

Notes